Peripheries of Nineteenth-Century French Studies

Peripheries of Nineteenth-Century French Studies

Views from the Edge

Edited by Timothy Raser

DELAWARE

Newark: University of Delaware Press
London: Associated University Presses

Associated University Presses
440 Forsgate Drive
Cranbury, NJ 08512

Associated University Presses
16 Barter Street
London WC1A 2AH, England

Associated University Presses
P.O. Box 338, Port Credit
Mississauga, Ontario
Canada L5G 4L8

The paper used in this publication meets the requirements of the American National Standard for Permanence of Paper for Printed Library Materials Z39.48-1984

Library of Congress Cataloging-in-Publication Data

Peripheries of nineteenth-century French studies : view from the edge / edited by Timothy Raser.
p. cm.
Includes bibliographical references and index.
ISBN 0-87413-765-9 (alk. paper)
1. French literature—19th century—History and criticism. I. Title: Peripheries of 19th-century French studies. II. Raser, Timothy Bell.

PQ281 .P48 2002
840.9′007—dc21 2001057006

PRINTED IN THE UNITED STATES OF AMERICA

Contents

Illustrations

Acknowledgements

TO THOSE WHO CONTRIBUTED PAPERS FOR THIS VOLUME, I WOULD like to express my deep gratitude, whether those papers are found here or not: all were of such quality that choosing those to appear was more a question of arrangement than of judgment. I would like also to thank Doris Kadish for her help in organizing the colloquium from which these papers were taken, and her guidance in the publishing process. Thanks go to Mary Donaldson-Evans of the University of Delaware for her generous help in reading the manuscripts, and her advice on the many changes that were made. Finally, special thanks go to Christine Retz of Associated University Presses for her invaluable assistance in the final publication process.

I would like to thank the following publishers for their kind permission to reprint sections of their works: Éditions Gallimard, for permission to use passages from the critical apparatus of the *Œuvres completes* of Villiers de l'Isle-Adam (©Gallimard, 1986) and *La Comédie humaine* by Honoré de Balzac (©Gallimard, 1976–80); Routledge, for use of Richard Ekins's *Male Femaling: A Grounded Theory Approach to Cross-Dressing and Sex-Changing* (©1997, Routledge); Elsevier Science, for Kathryn Ayers's "The only good woman isn't a woman at all: *The Crying Game* and the Politics of Misogyny," reprinted from *Women's Studies International Forum, 1997*, p. 334, (1997 with permission of Elsevier Science; Éditions du Seuil, for permission to use passages from Antoine Compagnon's *La Troisième République des lettres: De Flaubert à Proust* (©1983 Éditions du Seuil) and from Pierre Birnbaum's *"La France aux français": Histoire des haines nationalistes* (©1993, Éditions du Seuil); Manchester University Press for permission to reprint from John MacKenzie's *Orientalism: History, Theory and the Arts* (©1995, Manchester University Press); Georges Borchardt, Inc., for permission to quote from *Discipline and Punish: The Birth of the Prison* by Michel Foucault (New York: Pantheon, 1977), originally published in French as *Surveiller et Punir: Naissance de la prison* (©1975,

Les Éditions Gallimard, reprinted by permission of Georges Borchardt, Inc.; the Trustees of Boston University for permission to use passages of Gabriel Moyal's "Making the Revolution Private: Balzac's *Les Chouans* and *Un Épisode sous la Terreur*," *Studies in Romanticism* 28, no. 4 (1989) (© Boston University, 1989); Éditions Flammarion, for permission to use passages from Alain Daguerre's *L'ABCDaire de Delacroix et de l'Orient* (©1994 Éditions Flammarion), from Edgar Pisani's *Delacroix: Le Voyage au Maroc* (©1994 Éditions Flammarion); Continuum, for permission to quote Mark Simpson's *Male Impersonators: Men Performing Masculinity* (©1994 Cassell plc); to Charles C. Thomas Publisher, Ltd., for permission to reprint passages form Maurice Tinterow's *Foundations of Hypnosis: From Mesmer to Freud* (©1970 Charles C. Thomas Publisher, Ltd.); to Desclée de Brouwer, SA, for permission to use long extracts of Bruno Viard's, *À la source perdue du socialisme français* (©1997 Desclée de Brouwer, SA); Johns Hopkins University Press, for permission to quote Yoram Carmeli's "Text, Traces, and the Reification of Totality," in *New Literary History* 25, no. 1 (1995) (©1995, Johns Hopkins University Press); Universitiy of Press of Virginia for permission to reprint from Richard Maxwell's *The Mysteries of Paris and London* (©1992 University Press of Virginia) and permission to reprint from Assia Djebar's *Women of Algiers in Their Apartment* (©1992, University Press of Virginia); the British Film Institute for permission to quote from Jane Giles's *The Crying Game* (©1995 BFI Publishing); Éditions Christian Pirot for permission to quote their edition of Jean Lorrain, *Une Femme par jour* (©1983, Éditions Christian Pirot); Librarie Plon, for permission to quote Hugues Le Roux, *Les Jeux du cirque et de la vie foraine* (©1899, Librairie Plon); Duke University Press, for permission to quote from Amy Zilliax, "The Scorpion and the Frog: Agency and Identity in Neil Jordan's *The Crying Game*" in *Camera Obscura* 12, no. 35 (©1995 Camera Obscura); Thames and Hudson, Ltd., for permission to use Abigail Solomon-Godeau's *Male Trouble: A Crisis in Representation* (©1997, Thames and Hudson); Cambridge University Press for permission to reprint from Alan Gauld's *A History of Hypnotism* (©1992, Cambridge University Press) and permission to reprint from Eric Hobsbawm's *Nations and Nationality since 1780: Programme, Myth, Reality* (©1990, Cambridge University Press); to Gunter Narr Verlag for permission to reprint from Hugues Hotiers's "La Transgression au cirque" and Peta Tait's "Danger Delights," both found in *Kodikas Code Ars Se-*

meiotica (©1984 and (1996, respectively); the University of Pennsylvania Press, for permission to quote from Vern Bullough and Bonnie Bullough *Cross-Dressing, Sex, and Gender* (©1993, University of Pennsylvania Press); the Modern Language Association, for permission to reprint from Sandy Petrey's " Castration, Speech Acts, and the Realist Difference: *S/Z* vs. *Sarrasine*" (©1990, PMLA); Blackwell Publishers for permission to quote extensively from the Roland Barthes' *S/Z* (©1996 Blackwell Publishers); *New Theatre Quarterly*, for permission to quote from Peta Tait's "Danger Delights: Texts of Gender and Race in Aerial Performance" (©1992, New Theatre Quarterly); *Comparative Drama* for permission to quote from Yvonne Noble's "Castrati, Balzac, and BartheS/Z" *Comparative Drama* 31 (©1997, Comparative Drama); the Estate of Craig Owens for permission to quote from Craig Owens, *Beyond Recognition: Representation, Power, and* Culture (©1992, University of California Press); Routledge, Inc, part of The Taylor & Francis Group for permission to reprint from Marjorie Garber's *Vested Interests: Cross-Dressing and Cultural Anxiety* (©1992) and to reprint from Judith Butler's *Gender Trouble: Feminism and the Subversion of Identity* (©1990) and to reprint from Roberta Pearson's and William Uricchio's *The Many Lives of Batman: Critical Approaches to a Superhero and His Media* (©1991) and to reprint from Diane Fuss's *Inside/Out: Lesbian Theories, Gay Theories* (©1991): these texts are reproduced by permission of Routledge, Inc., a part of The Taylor & Francis Group; Éditions Albin Michel for permission to quote from their edition of Guy de Maupassant's *Contes et nouvelles* (©1959 Éditions Albin Michel); New Directions Paperbacks, for permission to quote from a text by Ezra Pound, taken from *Guide to Kulchur*, copyright (1970 by Ezra Pound, reprinted by permission of New Directions Publishing Corp.; Oxford University Press for permission to quote from Emile Zola's *The Ladies'* Paradise (©1995, by permission of Oxford University Press), and Éditions Balzac-Le Griot for permission for extensive use of Marc Angenot's *1889* (©1989, Le Préambule).

I thank also Yale University Art Gallery for permission to reproduce Charles Meryon's *Le Stryge*, the gift of "A Lover of Prints, in grateful recognition of the Founder of the Etching Collection," and SARL *Le Monde* for permission to use Hocine's photograph of two Algerian women distraught over the massacre of 23 September, 1997 (©1997, Le Monde).

Peripheries of Nineteenth-Century French Studies

Nineteenth-Century French Studies: Views from the Edge

TIMOTHY RASER

"MUST LITERARY HISTORY MAKE ANTIQUARIANS OF ALL OF US? OR does *1889* in reality not perform the more Nietzschean function of letting us forget the nineteenth century once and for all?" The question closed Fredric Jameson's plenary session at the Nineteenth-Century French Studies Colloquium held in Athens, Georgia, in 1997, where the influential critic had analyzed, extensively, Marc Angenot's *1889: Un état du discours social*, an enormous, underrecognized work about the state of printed discourse in France in 1889. Noting the characteristic themes of the age (decline, media-consciousness, the subordination of all discourse to narrative form), as well as its obsessions (e.g., the pervasiveness of medical metaphors), Jameson asked whether the feeling of closure produced by the very success of Angenot's project indicates anything other than the limits of "the horizon of our sight, which has been so oppressively limited to this year and this age, this nineteenth century." When history supplies an adequate context, will the particularities of a period's works—their beauty, their originality, their interest—become nothing more than a tissue of banalities shared with most other works of that period?

Certainly, Jameson and Angenot with him, are acutely conscious that the very sense of closure inspired by the triumph of bourgeois culture is largely responsible for the fascist reaction that was to follow, and whose initiator, Maurice Barrès, just happened to have been born in this year, 1889. Barrès's works would repeat all of the historical assumptions so prevalent in that year, save one: that of decline, which he strove to forget, "cynically and joyously." The oppressiveness of historical closure, our belated awareness that things could have gone differently, is what strikes Jameson most forcefully in this work he admires so much, and it is thus fortuitous that the colloquium itself took as its theme the "peripheries" of the nineteenth century, as if the very closure of those studies in France, in the nineteenth century, and in literature were at the heart of the question.

It would be consoling, Jameson writes, to think that literature, or poetry in particular, could stand apart from "social discourse," whose very presence in great works is so troubling; consoling to think that in some cases, "social discourse" is not our absolute horizon. But no, this certainly is not the case: there is no discourse outside of historical discourse; it is all we have. The result is woeful, to say the least: "we find ourselves back in the universal stupidity of Flaubert, the ineluctable dizziness at human imbecility, the inevitable nausea of the social world and the world of speech itself." And thus the question arises: "Is it possible that if we knew as much about their archive and their context as Angenot knows about 1889, the texts of Proust or Musil would also be observed to disintegrate into a tissue of stupidities and commonplaces; those of Joyce into masses of the most obvious intentions?" The question cannot be of greater import for students of literature, for with its answer stands or falls the very reason for such study. If literature, no matter how great, ultimately only echoes its historical context, there is no genius to find in it, no originality, no "literarity." Like other writings, it is condemned to repeat, perhaps more densely, perhaps more intensely, the banalities of its day. And conversely, only if something can be found outside of this "horizon" can the study of literature even start.

The proceedings of the colloquium focus on peripheries of nineteenth-century French studies, and we choose thus to present essays discussing such peripheries: generic, geographical, and chronological. The question overarching this volume is that of closure: is the study of literature or art reducible to that of its context, its horizon? Or does such study open onto something else: the artist in all of her idiosyncrasies, the work in its particularity, or the precise moment, with its hints of the future?

This volume thus opposes essays that underline closure, to others that suggest openings. In the first set, the implicit thesis is that context determines meaning: that the historical moment, social structures, and geographical horizons allow only certain things to be said, permit only certain "creations." In the second, the authors seek something beyond that horizon: in some cases, our twentieth century, our culture, our concerns, but in others, efforts simply to go beyond the limits of the printed page in nineteenth-century France. Inevitably, of course—Jennifer Forrest's essay comes to mind—arguments trace closure the better to underline efforts to escape, and others—I think of Rosemary Lloyd—an argument for novelty indicates just how predictable the surrounding discourse was. In a third chapter I place a group of essays all dealing with works by Balzac, showing in their sequence and variety how a single author could embody both the closure of social discourse and an effort to escape from it.

Melanie Hawthorne's essay on Tola Dorian is perhaps the most similar, thematically and conceptually, to Fredric Jameson's. Hawthorne takes the same historical moment, the same preoccupation with mediocrity, and the same menace of fascism on the horizon as her topics. Here, the subject is the Russian immigrant, Tola Dorian, better known as the editor of *La Revue d'Aujourd'hui* than as the poet she also was. Further marginalizing Dorian is the fact that her career extends into the twentieth century, making of her something of a pariah to scholars of both centuries. Indeed her *Revue d'Aujourd'hui* attempted, during its short existence, to define its historical moment—1890—by recounting gossip, *faits divers,* and by presenting personalities, as well as providing a forum wherein to display literary efforts. And among those the review presents is the marquis de Morès, a key if flamboyant figure in the development of fascism in France, and it appears that the writer of the article presenting Morès might well have been Dorian herself. Other articles tend in the same directions: the anti-Semitism in Paul Adam's "L'Or des juifs," for example, echoes that of Tola Dorian's play *Domitien.*

What is troubling about this trend, Hawthorne writes, is that "while *La Revue d'Aujourd'hui* may seem peripheral, ex-centric, today, it may not have seemed so to its contemporaries, to whom it appeared to be merely popular journalism." It exemplifies, if need be, the social discourse that led to such explosions of violence, later, as the one from Barrès that Jameson indicated. And what is neglected by relegating *La Revue d'Aujourd'hui* to the "mediocre" is the awareness that new movements start somewhere, and major currents—in the present case, twentieth-century fascism—always start as minor phenomena. Indeed, the danger of centering, canonizing, or consecrating literary studies is that they will certainly neglect apparently peripheral works which will, in another historical moment, reveal themselves to be central.

Bruno Viard's essay on Pierre Leroux examines closure from a different angle: geographical closure. An essayist, journalist, and early socialist, Leroux's predominantly political writings are little-known outside of France. But his role as friend, supporter, and promoter of Victor Hugo is emblematic of the significance such fringe characters can achieve. While presenting Leroux as prescient, an advocate of multiculturalism a century and a half before it came into fashion, Viard indirectly shows the closure of the French cultural establishment of the late eighteenth and early nineteenth centuries. Awareness of the Orient was eclipsed by that of the Middle East, and much that France owed to Persia, India, and China was paid instead to Athens and Jerusalem. Viard argues that Leroux was the most vocal advocate of expanding French horizons: he tried to bring knowledge of the Orient to the attention of French readers, to show how Socratic philosophy found a model in Buddhist practice, and how Western ethics and the "golden rule" owe a debt to the teachings of Confucius. Both Mosaic and Christian history prove to have been influenced by, if not copied from, Eastern mythology. And even democracy, that most French of institutions, sprang not from French soil, but from the East: neither Socratic nor Christian politics were genuinely democratic.

A comparable concern with parochialism is visible in Grant Crichfield's article on Charles Nodier's pictorial documentation of the Prince d'Orléans's expedition to Algeria in 1839. This expedition, whose purpose was to prepare northeastern Algeria for permanent occupation by the French, implies even greater ideological blindness than does the resistance to oriental culture against which Leroux fought. The *Journal* of the expedition, ostensibly a souvenir for its participants, exemplifies a representational practice which functions ultimately to legitimize a regime and its conduct. Of particular interest to Crichfield are the woodcuts or *grands-bois* which illustrate the handsome volume, for here is a nonverbal, apparently innocent, element serving an ideological purpose. And of course, image and text interact to convey explicitly messages only implied by the text: the beneficence of the French presence, indicated by gestures of gratitude on the part of Arabs receiving food from the soldiers; the superiority of the French to the Arabs as indicated by higher positioning in a woodcut, and so forth.

Other images, however, represent the French from the Arabs' point of view: invaders in a hostile land; hunted rather than hunters; objects of curiosity for a people content with their own institutions. These images provide a counterpoint to the doctrinal message of the text, and illustrate a different side of the expedition: the undercurrent of danger and violence that upholds colonialism. Here, Crichfield argues, is a voice not often heard in discussions of the expedition; this voice, which is heard, paradoxically, through its images rather than its words, makes the *Journal* polyphonic, and implies that different media have such different agendas that one might usefully complement another, expanding the latter's horizons.

But one can hardly say that the visual arts are less permeated by their context than is writing. Sarah Davies Cordova opposes two artists, a male painter of the nineteenth century, and a contemporary female writer, and shows both the constraints of historical closure, and how such closure endures. The two artists in question are Eugène Delacroix and Assia Djebar, both of whom undertook to represent women in Algeria. Starting from a photograph of a woman ostensibly responding to the recent massacre in Benthala, Cordova asks what role pictorial representation plays in relations between colonized and colonizer. The fact that the picture was only distributed in the West, and was mislabeled when distributed, suggests that these pictures speak very specific languages. In the present case, the choice of a *pietà*-like image appeals to Western sensibilities, and arouses compassion among westerners that images disseminated in the Algerian press could not.

But what has happened has falsified both the image and the perception of the event: a text—Michel Guerrin's description of the photo, or our received ideas concerning feminine sorrow—supplants the voice of women, and implies a supremacy of images over words. This, in fact, is the concern of Assia Djebar's "Femmes d'Alger dans leur appartement," a volume of stories published in 1980, proof, if any were needed, that the colonist's discourse echoes for decades after his departure. More to the point still, the title of the volume is taken from Delacroix's famous paintings, done shortly after the first French incursion into what is now known as Algeria. Ripples of deeds and representations from the French nineteenth century are still expanding, still producing effects and discourse far away and long afterwards, enclosing and informing words and images generations later. As expected, even the first representations of the colonized were stereotypical: Delacroix's paintings were done years after his visit to Algeria, the fruits of memory, not observation. For instance, the painter saw Algeria as a modern Greece, not as a country in its own right.

A political agenda was strongest in the case of literature, where the educational apparatus defined what was French and what was not during a long debate at the end of the century. This agenda undertook to make literature—as defined by the canon—nothing less than the expression of ideology. Far from being a discourse different from, or at least distinguished from other discourses, the assimilation of literature and nationalist ideology is the subject of Martin Guiney's essay on "*L'Education nationale* and Salvation through Literature." With national education already firmly established, Guiney argues, debate in France in the 1880s turned to what would be taught to future citizens of France. This debate, and its results, are apparent in manuals written during the last decades of the last century, as the Third Republic tried to impose a program of learning on its children. Guiney's essay thus examines how "literature" is redefined to advance the concerns of the moment in several pamphlets from this period addressing the question of literature's uses. One telling problem discussed therein is the "Latin question," where the French asked whether Latin (or Greek) should be made a compulsory part of preparation for the *baccalauréat*. The question has many dimensions, ranging from the role of Latin in literary studies, to the appropriateness of teaching the language of the Church in state schools. From *La Question du latin*, wherein the problem of state support of any discipline is brought forward, Guiney goes on to Roehrich's translation of *La Chanson de Roland*, which was made to integrate (or even convert) children into French citizenship through "knowledge" of France's history. Such history was presented as a *credo*, complete with a confession and articles of faith. Here the closure of "social discourse" coincides with the closure of ideology.

The second part of the volume includes essays that analyze works from the opposite perspective: as artifacts that cannot be accounted for entirely in terms of the social discourse of their moment and whose meaning lies beyond their historical context. Here are messages coded in a variety of ways, and these practices may retain their interest even when their circumstances have been exhaustively analyzed: consider the example of the circus, as presented by Jennifer Forrest in her discussion of female acrobats. Forrest shows how women were subject to stereotyping in the area of the circus identical to those characterizing the more familiar world of letters: preconceptions that women simply did not have the strength necessary for the feats demanded of them, disbelief when these feats were accomplished, appreciation of them as objects of desire rather than as competent performers. This was so true that, while performing identical stunts to those performed by men, female acrobats signified gender, while men signified "strength," "agility," or some other quality. And yet, even within the constraints of such prejudice and preconception, writers acknowledged a free space for female acrobats, one where they were no longer seen as women, but as performers: "gender disappears completely in flight." Thus, a preference, in the works of several writers, for lady acrobats.

What was really at play of course were contradictions implicit in the construction of gender: how certain costumes, poses, and actions define one as male or female, even in the field of acrobatics, where gender's real consequences are slight. But these concerns come back with a regularity and oppressiveness entirely akin to that felt by Jameson as he contemplates the repetitions of banalities constituting written discourse in 1889, and extending into the literary field. Here, Forrest designates a peripheral field which exhibits the same characteristics as literary exoticism, and which reveals the same intentions: a desire to produce an alternate reality is behind both the circus and exotic literature, and both might indeed do so. But whether they do so or not, what is sure is that they indicate a resistance to the enveloping social discourse of the moment.

Take also the example of Rosemary Lloyd's essay on Zola's *Au bonheur des dames*. For Lloyd, the department store, especially the new department store depicted in the novel, represents a frontier: the gateway to the consumer society nascent in the latter half of the nineteenth century. But because this store caters to women, it also represents a frontier between the sexes, where commercialism, devised by men, addresses women as consumers, whose desires must be manipulated. As the store's name suggests, however, "Au Bonheur des dames" suggests a much greater reward for dutiful consumption. Strangely too, this novel, Lloyd claims, has a strong link to the visual arts, particularly still-lifes, where Zola's interest in rhopography—the representation of the everyday—anticipates our own decade.

Because the store's owner, Mouret, falls in love with the heroine, Denise, the novel articulates a complicated intersection of desires: the merchant wishes to stimulate sales through his window displays, but is unable to satisfy his own lust for one of his clients. The dialectic of merchant and client is thus balanced with a dialectic of the sexes, and the conflict of classes is paired with the promise of evolution inherent in all narratives. It is certainly true that the novel represents the social discourse of its period, a discourse where marketing converges with literary forms, but it is equally true that both advertising and narrative produce a by-product—desire—that is not strictly assimilable to that discourse. Further, that desire is not strictly limited to the characters depicted, but is also characteristic of the narrative, which longs for accomplishment in a future moment, our own consumption-society.

If we look at John Anzalone's "Artful Shenanigans," though, a homologous lesson comes forth: Anzalone takes as his subject a film of Jean Renoir's, *La Chienne*. There is no future in this dark drama and, one could say, no nineteenth century either. But Jean Renoir was of course the son of Pierre-Auguste Renoir, and the subject of this film, beyond any depiction of deception, complicity, and fraud, is of course, painting itself: ostensibly the paintings of a certain Maurice Legrand, who, as the lover of Lulu, more-or-less knowingly supplies paintings to her to sign with her name and sell as hers. Questions of ownership come out here with force: when Legrand's paintings become successful, is it because of Lulu, because of her pimp, Dédé, or because of the art critics whose reviews brought attention to the paintings? Prostitution is written into all of the relationships portrayed in the film, and, Anzalone argues, is intimately related to painting in particular.

But why should we be concerned with the implications of a film from 1932? For if the first four decades of the twentieth century are indeed "peripheral" to the nineteenth century, what would not be considered a periphery? Certainly, a son is "peripheral" to a father, and film is "peripheral" to painting, and if painting was to the nineteenth century, as we have every reason to believe it was, as film is to the twentieth, Jean Renoir's consideration of painting is of great importance: speaking from the point of view of film, he is able to describe the relation of art to its market far more explicitly than his father ever did, and his description is very disabused indeed. What was true of painting is now true of film, so much so that one could say that Renoir is allegorizing the metamorphosis of painting into film, showing us, as he does, how a genre overtakes its own context.

This lesson is most flagrantly, and, perhaps, most outrageously argued by Illinca Zarifopol-Johnston in her essay on

Notre-Dame de Paris and *Batman*. Zarifopol-Johnston indicates uncanny instances where that gothic masterpiece of the '80s, *Batman*, appeals to Hugo's novel as an intertext. From the architecture of Tim Burton's film to Batman's cloak, through the twisted love Batman feels for Vicki Vail, Zarifopol-Johnston points out similarities between the two works, and underlines what once was obvious, but what has become less so: in its time, the novel was, like the film, a work of popular culture. But between the two works, something has happened: the pessimism, even the fatalism of Hugo's novel has given way, in Burton's film, to an apocalyptic vision of the present. Where Claude Frollo broods over the future of decorative architecture in a world where the printed page has triumphed, Batman (and Joker) live in a world where the image has replaced its concrete referent.

Viewed from the perspective of a contemporary pop-culture icon, *Notre-Dame de Paris* appears to prophesy concerns about urban decline, cultural satiety, and violence, but this historical observation quickly recedes as one realizes that the apocalypse alluded to in the novel never fails to arrive. Beyond indicating a literary "source" for a contemporary film, the *Notre-Dame de Paris/Batman* intertext suggests that the popular peripheries of high literature state more explicitly themes that are only implicit in novels, poems, or plays: here, *Batman* brings out the apocalyptic thrust of *Notre-Dame de Paris*, which once stated, can no longer recede into the background. Revolutions, both political and artistic, the baleful decline of civilization from a high point long ago, the missed opportunities in human relations, all the currents drawn out by *Batman*, make *Notre-Dame de Paris* a fitting prologue to a cartoonish depiction of our own anxieties.

The tension between the certainty of the closure of the historical moment and the desire to escape from it is exemplified nowhere better than in the works of Balzac, who, of course, is the exemplar of the historical novelist. It is thus not surprising that in a collection centered on the predicament of historical closure, Balzac's novels and stories should come so frequently to the fore, and thus, to exemplify these tensions, five essays on Balzac constitute the third part. Perhaps obviously, Balzac's *Les Chouans*, about the Breton reaction to the extension of the French Revolution, comes to mind in several essays. First among them is Marie-Pierre Le Hir's analysis of the concept of national identity in the novel, specifically, how *Les Chouans*, nominally about Brittany, addresses instead the question of how to determine national identity. Here, the word "race" comes to the fore: Le Hir points out that the use of myth and stereotype in Balzac's novel posits the Chouans as a race distinct from, and more primitive than, the French. Locked in an archaic world, Balzac's Bretons are unaffected by history, remaining Celtic beneath their Breton exterior.

More troubling is Balzac's consistent description of the Bretons as non-Catholic, or bad Catholics: why does he, that great user of stereotypes, go against the type that considers Brittany as reactionary and religious. Le Hir argues that Balzac's effort to distinguish Catholics and Bretons amounts to an attempt to deny the latter French identity, and, correlatively, to define French identity as essentially Catholic.

But why should he claim that France is essentially Catholic? Le Hir argues that Balzac's Catholicism is nostalgic, part of a political conservatism, but also an intellectual response to the rationalism of the Enlightenment: his Catholicism is just one instance of a more general repudiation of reason and preference for sentiment. Thus, Balzac uses the Breton periphery to define the French center, even when evidence for his characterization lacks. This effort to establish, at any cost, a Breton identity and hence, a French identity, betrays a fundamental anxiety about the latter, the real subject of this meditation on the Breton "race."

Les Chouans is also analyzed by Mary Jane Cowles, but from the point of view of reading. If the revolution represents the ideal of rationality and enlightenment, then resistance must imply the irrational: a world of darkness, superstition, and confusion, principles that endanger the revolution that seeks to dispel them. This play is taken up by the symbol of the compass used on consular directives, the emblem of reason and man's domination of nature, but also a sign of reading itself, uncertain and demanding interpretation. Bonaparte's intentions, meanings, and decisions, for the soldiers embattled in Brittany, are always obscure, and Power, centrally located in Paris, is difficult to read from the peripheries. The spy Marie, however, is more centrally positioned: does her reading of power prove more accurate? No: for her, the trees obscure the forest, and only the "genius" of the minister perceives the true meaning of the war. Cowles suggests then that behind the text of history lies another discourse, consisting of intentions, agendas, and so on, accessible only by reading, reading of the most rigorous sort. And though this discourse is contemporary with it, because it is encrypted for later decoding, it cannot be part of the social discourse.

One example of such later decoding is done by Michael Tilby, who examines how the forest, a traditional symbol of loss of control and the irrational, is figured in Balzac's novels. Abandoning the conventional representations of the forest found in his early novels, Balzac used the theme to new purpose in *Le Curé de village*, where it suggests crime, violence, sexuality, and desire. In *Les Paysans*, descriptions of the forest go further, serving as a code, transmitting a narrative of desire and transgression. As such, it becomes a signifier, not a referent, and Balzac's realism acquires allegorical significance. Further, descriptions of the forest escape censuring mechanisms that control other elements of the text, and transmit meanings only implied by the narrative. Following Tilby's argument, the forest, and with it, peripheries more generally, are double: on one hand, such topoi repeat the concerns of their era (in the present case, the romantic interest in untamed nature), but on the other, they also say things that cannot be said elsewhere, and like the unconscious (Freud's formulation of which in *The Interpretation of Dreams* dates from the very end of this nineteenth century), formulate a new series of questions.

In the case of Dorothy Kelly's essay on Balzac, the literary text opens onto a concept of linguistic power. What must be noted here is that while Balzac's fantastic narratives might be assimilated to magic, in others this is impossible, and consequently their ideological dimension must be taken more seriously. Kelly studies *La Peau de chagrin*, *Sarrasine*, and *Le Chef d'œuvre inconnu* for evidence of a link—according to Balzac—between two distinct worlds. Mesmer's experiments fascinated Balzac; he saw in hypnotism a genuine mental power, and attributed this power to several of his characters, interpreting hypnotism as the victory of one will over another. Further, Kelly argues that the dominance of one person's will, so often to be found in Balzac's works, is not simply a symbol of manipulation, but also a physical ability of the mind to act on others and the material world, which it does through language.

Language, indeed, is essential to human activity: as Chabert recognizes in *Le Colonel Chabert*, the masses of documents attesting to his death are every bit as difficult to remove as the bodies under which he was buried at Eylau, and just changing the words on those documents will take an even greater effort. Now, if language defines us, establishes our identities, controls our actions, and if mind can change language, cannot mind change identity? Such is the question Kelly analyzes: many of Balzac's characters' identities depend on acts of language, performatives implicit or explicit in the speech recorded in the novels: la Zambinella from *Sarrasine*, for example, is a woman or a man depending on the nouns and pronouns used to designate her/him.

But can mind actually create something? Frenhofer of *Le Chef d'œuvre inconnu* could certainly be dismissed as mad, unable to abandon a delusion visible to everyone else. Or, indeed, he could actually believe he has created something, a representation, perhaps, or more significantly, a real woman: this dangerous conceit is far more frequent in Balzac's works than it would first appear, and its significance needs to be assessed. But in any case, Kelly shows here an attribute of language that far exceeds that of social discourse.

The last analysis of Balzac's works is by Owen Heathcote, who, like Illinca Zarifopol-Johnston, detects links between nineteenth-century narrative and twentieth-century film, between words and images, between the past and its future. Like Dorothy Kelly, Owen Heathcote returns to Balzac's *Sarrasine*, which since Barthes's *S/Z* has elicited continuing commentary, to use it as the unexpected intertext of Neil Jordan's film *The Crying Game*. Keeping to the surface to start (and in any discussion of *Sarrasine* and *The Crying Game*, discussion of surfaces is required), Heathcote notes the theme of cross-dressing shared by the two works, and its correlate of this theme, the theme of castration. From this observation, he considers the two works' depictions of violence: the violence of castration, to be sure, but the implicit violence lying beneath cross-dressing: homophobia and the disguises it requires. What Heathcote remarks is that neither *Sarrasine* nor *The Crying Game* unambiguously renounces homosexuality, critical readings to the contrary, and that the theme of cross-dressing operates in these works to subvert facile distinctions of gender and its associated roles. With that claim, the apparently superficial and marginal theme of cross-dressing is revealed to be at the core of the works, not a periphery but a center.

With respect to the nineteenth century more generally, a late-twentieth-century reprise (and in the cinema, to boot) of a theme used one hundred and fifty years earlier can only appear peripheral. At the core, however, of both works is repression of sexuality, a repression shared by our society and Balzac's. What

Neil Jordan's contribution to mass culture suggests then is that, after a century and a half, Balzac's work can be read for the first time, free of the ideology whose effects it laments, and which, finally, it has succeeded in undoing. With this hope we have perhaps gone beyond the social discourse and the closure Jameson laments.

The essay by Françoise Gaillard on Gérard de Nerval's *Aurélia* functions as an epilogue. A canonical work of literature, and one from the middle of the century at that, *Aurélia* would appear easily assimilable to the social discourse of its day. But since its publication in 1865, this text has never failed to exercise a fascination on its readers. The hallucinations described in *Aurélia*, Gaillard writes, both recall the Revolution and announce the twentieth century, by way of a critique of the Enlightenment. As *Aurélia*'s narrator wanders in Paris, he approaches the Place de la Concorde, where he wonders how man will survive the death of God. This question, Gaillard argues, was inherited from the Enlightenment, whose atheism displaced the concept of God, and whose political agenda caused the king to be executed on that very site. Such a question announces Nietzsche's critique of religion, but also offers reflections on the possibility of doing without God. Nerval's response is madness, for he does not believe that reason is adequate to the task: the death of God made the hubris of the enlightenment visible to all. Not everything could be explained with the laws of reason; there existed obscure areas unreceptive to rational approach. Thus, *Aurélia* opens onto the twentieth century, where madness and the unconscious undergo reassessment, and the space left by the absence of God is filled with the new science of psychoanalysis. Nerval's text is thus at the peripheries of nineteenth-century literature from many points of view: it appeals to the previous century, while announcing the next one; but also, it ceases to be a literary reflection to become an essay in religion, philosophy, and psychology, an indication that social discourse can never fully account for its many facets.

Certainly, it should be possible to distinguish literary works from those that are not, even if such a distinction depends only on a judgment of literary quality. But just as certainly, literature tends to spread, taking over works that, when published, were read for qualities other than their literarity. The essays of this volume thus all discuss literature *about* peripheries: economic, psychological, and social. What becomes increasingly apparent as one reads them though is that discussions *of* frontiers tend to become invitations or exhortations to cross frontiers in a transgressive act that is perhaps at the core of this topic. An observation is necessary here: considerations of the peripheries of literature tend to bring up discussions of fate, as though some overwhelming force lurked at literature's edges. When Lloyd notes that Zola's department store cannot fail but points to a society of mass consumerism, or when Kelly and Forrest write that Balzac's fantasies of creation, for the former, or the Goncourts' descriptions of the circus, for the latter, lead unavoidably to all-too-familiar constructions of gender, or when Guiney argues that the discourse of education defines literature according to the interests of the state, or when Hawthorne states that it is precisely in "the trash heap of history" that evidence of nascent fascism is to be found, in all these cases history itself takes on a definite form. As one looks beyond the confines of genre, the similarities between what is inside that field and what is outside of it become increasingly apparent. The terrible certainty of *what is* at a given moment, and the concurrent certainty that there is nothing else, bring these writers to conclude in a social determinism arching over wide areas of literature's peripheries.

"Center everywhere, circumference nowhere." Pascal's aphorism appears twice in this collection, and summarizes aptly the dialectical tension inscribed in all of these essays. Everywhere in this volume, the nineteenth century witnesses the dissolution of centers: political, conceptual, geographical. Correspondingly, peripheries take on importance, but they seem to recede before one's eyes: is the true frontier of France the forest, Brittany, Algeria, or India? Is the frontier of literature journalism, the visual arts, or cinema? Is the nineteenth century, which saw the ascension of the bourgeoisie, over? Or is it still with us? If these questions are still with us, we cannot, even if we wish to, close the book on the nineteenth century once and for all.

The Story of a Year: Continuities and Discontinuities in Marc Angenot's *1889*

FREDRIC JAMESON

AS I WANTED TO SAY SOMETHING HERE ABOUT AN UNUSUAL nineteenth-century literary history—a uniquely idiosyncratic literary and cultural history of the nineteenth century—I found myself wishing that I could also say something a little more general about literary histories and also about the nineteenth century. I have been interested in literary history as a form or genre for some time, without being able to observe the crystallization of a theory, or to discern the outlines of a model. I found myself reflecting on a number of key texts—Marx's *18th Brumaire*, Barthes's *Writing Zero Degree*, Adorno's *Philosophy of Modern Music*—which I wanted to call dialectical histories or historiographies, without it being clear (to me) how the concept of the dialectical was meant to function here: was it to be a methodological signal, about a certain procedure such histories always needed to perform on the preexisting stereotypes of history that they came into the world to correct, reverse, overcome, or undermine in one way or another? But then in that case these were to be thought of as exemplary texts, which could be imitated by other historians and replicated for other historical periods and other kinds of historical content. Leaving aside the question of whether the dialectic should really be thought of in that way as a method at all, I also wondered whether we needed copies of these unique narratives exactly, even if it should prove possible to reproduce them at all. For what tends to make all theoretical or philosophical questions of genre boring and intolerably old-fashioned is the persistence in them of the schema of the universal and the particular, or the general and the individual—worse yet, the genus and the species. But ours is an age peculiarly allergic to universals—whether for all that it is a nominalist age exactly is another question—at any rate, problems, which like this generic one invite us to rehearse the old formulas of the universal and the particular without challenging it in any way, tend to be discarded en route, like so much excess baggage. Was the nineteenth century more inclined to give universals the benefit of the doubt than we are? It is a question that might well go to the heart of the matter, and which will perhaps be addressed later.

At any rate, the solution to the question of literary history will only come at the price of disposing of this issue of generic universals in one way or another; and I have always appreciated Claudio Guillen's idea that the genres form unique historical conjunctures, and that texts are not to be classified in individual generic categories like items dropped in a box, but rather that each unique text is to be grasped as an individuality presided over by a generic constellation like so many stars in the sky.[1] The genre is here not a classification scheme but an idea: the text comes into a world in which that idea also has a certain prestige and needs to be reckoned with: thus, the individual text is "about" the generic idea, just as it is also "about" a certain number of other things. But how you negotiate this "about" is another problem altogether.

I would like to short-circuit the model of the universal and the particular in a different way; or rather I want to suggest that these unique historiographic performances that interest me are characterized by just such a capacity and that they somehow all do exactly that: they neutralize the concept of universals by problematizing the practice of historiography as such, without abandoning it altogether. For this last—getting rid of the generic practice—is the one kind of solution to our problem that will do us no good, namely, a principled repudiation of historical narrative altogether, on the grounds that we cannot think of any way of justifying it philosophically. My view is rather that what distinguishes these literary histories formally is that they call into question, absolutely and by their own practice, the very notion of doing literary history at all: but they do so by way of a literary historiography which does not provide a model and cannot be repeated. There is a rhetorical term for this, I believe: the hapax legomenon, which designates a category for which there exists only a single item or specimen; a universal for which there is only one particular. Such literary histories give you history, then, they acknowledge the problem as such—that of historiography, that of universal genres; but they do away with it by historicizing it, and by offering one final historical narrative which explains why the problem can never be solved, that is to say why no model of literary history can be given, why you can't imitate this one, which however *is* a kind of literary history; and in short, how you can have it both ways, find the very notion of literary history problematized as the age always thought it should be, and yet have a historical paradigm in the process.

If this way of doing literary history (and of not doing it) makes any sense at all, then we probably need to add on another generic question. For the lowest level of all literary history is the manual, which, sewn together with a few threadbare concepts about influences and the evolution of forms, essentially furnished names, titles, and dates: even in an age which has problematized the name (death of the author) and the title (textualization of the older "work of art"),—what it has done with the date may well be the topic of my argument in this essay. Even under such conditions, we probably still need to look things up from time to time: will these lofty new self-destructing metahistories do that for us, and can they be put to basely practical uses of that kind? I think so, at least selectively, and I imagine that the "facts" they furnish along these lines also have something to do with the problem of the canon, or at least that they furnish countercanons, alternate canons, alternate lists and dates, which problematize the categories of all those things as well and foreground the historical construction of such literary and cultural "facts" in the first place.

So much for literary history, at least for the moment; now we need to see if we can say something about the nineteenth century, which may in fact be the topic—since it is itself the very century of history, the historicist century par excellence. What else can be more distinctive about this particular age, obsessed with narrative historical and other, and upon which—the first age not to have produced an organic style in its own right—all the monuments and archives of the past begin to sink.

It is true that twentieth-century history—even twentieth-century literary history—has tended to eat away at this idea of a nineteenth-century one, until there seems to be very little left of the latter. When you enlarge the notion of modernity, for example, you end up drawing a whole collection of formerly nineteenth-century phenomena into it, which now come to be seen as incomplete or emergent precursors or ancestors of their full twentieth-century forms: in the same way, industrialization—so nineteenth-century a thing once upon a time—comes to be seen as a preparatory stage for Fordism, if not post-Fordism altogether; while the emergence of the nineteenth-century press now comes to seem but a pallid foreshadowing of our own "media," Napoleon III a feeble anticipation of the great modern twentieth-century dictators, the various arts of the last century little more than a trial run for the triumphant moderns of the beginning of our own avant-gardes.

It was not always so: here is Ezra Pound on *Ulysses*: "the end, the summary, of a period, that period is branded by La Tour du Pin in his phrase 'age of usury'. . . . The catharsis of *Ulysses*, the joyous satisfaction . . . was to feel that here was the JOB DONE and finished, the diagnosis and cure was here. The sticky, molasses-covered filth of current print, all the fuggs, all the foeters, the whole boil of the European mind, had been lanced."[2] I believe that Kenner somewhere marvels at this characterization of *Ulysses*, and we might want to as well; but it is rather the disgust with the nineteenth century I want to dwell on for a moment longer, grasped as being at one with the "European mind." It is as though this European nineteenth century, which begins with Balzac, at once reveals itself to be an immense junk shop, full of dusty or broken objects, mildewed textiles, antiquated furniture, that has to be thrown out: insalubrious dank passageways that have to be torn down to let the sun in; eccentric people and publishing houses full of cranky and eccentric books and ideas, for which a satire very different from the joyous and social seventeenth- and eighteenth-century kind was needed: this century, then, seems to end with Céline's *Mort à crédit*; while most French characterizations of it will project the nineteenth century as the century of that object of disgust par excellence, the *bourgeoisie* and its mode of values and way of life.

Alongside this, I would like to set a rather different exhibit, Roland Barthes's well-documented taste for the nineteenth century and its leisurely "realistic novels," a nostalgia for this extraordinary bourgeois century and its secular furnishings and occupations which reminds us that in France the nineteenth century may be thought to have outlasted formal chronology very long indeed, perhaps all the way to the onset of the Fifth Republic . . .[3]. I am unable to say which camp Walter Benjamin belongs in, who certainly gave a whole decade of his last years to a virtual immersion in this nineteenth century, from which, however, he also claimed he longed to awake: "this imminent awakening stands like the wooden horse of the Greeks within a Troy of dreams."[4] One has the same question to pose to the Surrealists, whose *marché aux puces* is itself one immense nineteenth century in which the Balzacian talisman is perhaps to be found, and then lost again. But does anyone still need to awaken from the nineteenth century? And do we still need to lance the boil of its sickening, nauseous bourgeois culture? I do think that this remains the best way to live with the nineteenth century: this impossibility of indifference, this obligation to feel either nostalgia or disgust, if not both alternately and in rhythms that somehow define the present for you as well.

At any rate, the book I want to talk about here very much keeps faith with this unavoidable alternation: it is the *1889* of Marc Angenot, a cube of some twelve hundred pages printed in Montreal in the centenary year of the title, and therefore perhaps not so well-known as it ought to be, nor so readily available in American libraries.[5] But it is already, I believe, a classic if anything ever was, and an intervention which, if it does not exactly "blast open the continuum of history" in Benjamin's revolutionary spirit, then at least makes it impossible for us to go on living with this late nineteenth century in the traditional way (if there ever was a traditional way).

As for the form of this literary history, however, it belongs to an identifiable if uncommon subgenre that we may call "the story of a year." Of its various exemplars, I only want to mention here James Chandler's recent *England in 1819*, which has the formal interest for us of a reflexive history: he argues indeed that the very idea of a dated situation, the concept of a "year" as a category in its own right and a specific marker of cultural history as such, dates from precisely this "year" which is his subject. We will eventually want to ask ourselves whether anything of this reflexivity, this autodesignation, characterizes Angenot's own work. On one level the question merely has to do with the year itself: is 1889 a decisive year, as the year of Peterloo certainly was, or is it merely representative, and might we not have dipped into the stream of time a thousand days earlier or later? It is certain that many interesting things happen in this year: the centenary of the French Revolution, for example, and the Universal Exposition, the opening of the Eiffel Tower and the flight and suicide of General Boulanger; across the Channel the mystery of Jack the Ripper, and closer to home the first publications of two unknown writers, Henri Bergson, with *Les Données immédiates de la conscience*, and Maurice Barrès, with *Un Homme libre*; the love-death double suicide at Meyerling of the Archduke Rudolph of Habsburg and his lover, and the appearance of one of the climactic novels of Zola's Rougon-Macquart series, *La Bête humaine*. Enough to fill up any year, you will say, particularly if as is customary we add that it is the year of birth of Charlie Chaplin, Adolf Hitler, Martin Heidegger, and Jean Cocteau; but precisely, something similar could be said about any year, I'm afraid; every year is crammed full of just such astonishing and forgotten, yet unforgettable, *actualité* (a concept to which we will return). So we must presumably be careful not to reify the date in question, not to allow our arbitrarily chosen methodological frame to turn into this or that watershed, turning point, beginning, or ending of something.

We must also distinguish Angenot's year from other such stories by an implacable methodological decision. *1889*, subtitled *un état du discours social* (A State of Social Discourse), concludes a scholarly project which involved reading every text published in France during that period, including a systematic review of journals and periodicals, including the parliamentary debates, the Belgian press as well, a sampling of cookbooks, and so forth (I forgot to say that 1889 was also the year that saw the first "bande dessinée" ["comic strip"]). Angenot's decision, however, analogous to Barthes's in *Système de la mode*, excludes everything that is not written or printed: thus, the concept of "discours social" is distinguished from "cultural studies" generally by its omission of cultural practices and nonlinguistic "texts" of all kinds (although the words that go with the music allow Angenot a first significant probe of the "café concert"). I think that this methodological choice also ties him closely to the surface of "la chose imprimée" ("printed things"): attitudes, conscious and unconscious, are certainly revealed throughout these analyses, but "objective spirit" (or what Sartre liked, precisely for this nineteenth century, to call "objective neurosis") is never allowed to organize itself into an autonomous and free-floating social object of some kind, even though the terminology of ideology, *doxa*, hegemony, and the like is certainly pressed into service (and we will want to examine that shortly as well).

At any rate, a project of this magnitude would certainly seem to qualify Angenot for the medal of a "hero of social discourse," if one existed. The Italians call an *uomo coraggioso* a heroic trencherman, who is able, like Herr Jakob Schmidt or the climbers of Mount Everest, to put away anything in front of him, simply because it is there. The Chinese meanwhile respect and envy the strong stomach, the infinite reading capacity, and experience of the Mandarin: a commitment perhaps more ambiguous in the West, where it can also be an occasion for disgust and nausea, as Angenot's opening invocation of *Bouvard et Pécuchet* suggests. But as I recall, Bouvard and Pécuchet, while occasionally exhausted, astonished, or in despair, never themselves feel nausea at their task: a reaction reserved for author and reader, as it is, perhaps, in the case of *1889*, which lances the boil of nineteenth-century ideology as comprehensively as Pound thought *Ulysses* did, yet another *coupe synchronique* which takes on a somewhat different interest in this context.

For this is perhaps the modernist, rather than the postmodern, strategy: to let history define itself as a totality of the cross-section, an immense yet ultimately limited inventory of "everything that is the case." Postmodern cultural historiography tends rather to be fancifully diachronic, I would think, and by the choice of an outlandish theme—Virilio's take on velocity, let's say—to pick out a chronological trajectory as bizarre as any García Márquez family tree. These trajectories are antirepresentational with a vengeance, and I'm tempted to say that their very power depends on the arbitrariness of their theme or starting point; to them also applies Angenot's denomination of the artifact, the construction or modeled entity, a characterization which for him holds for any partial or limited corpus:

> Tout travail historique qui isole un champ culturel, un genre, un complex discursif—fût-ce en réinscrivant à l'arrière-plan l'esquisse d'une culture globale—produit un artefact dont l'apparente cohésion résulte d'un aveuglement aux flux interdiscursifs qui circulent et aux règles topographiques qui établissent, sous diverses contraintes, une coexistence générale des scriptibles. (1083)
>
> (Any historical work that isolates a cultural field, a genre, a discursive complex—even by reinscribing the sketch of a global culture in the background—produces an artifact whose apparent cohesion results from its blindness to the interdiscursive flows that circulate and to the topographical rules that establish, under various constraints, a general coexistence of writings.)

On the other hand, we may also wonder whether the synchronic method does not equally determine false perspectives of its own, most notably the baleful Foucauldian totality, in which the positing of the airtight system projects a well-nigh nightmarish closure.

But let's first outline Angenot's account of the preoccupations of this particular year, which begin, unsurprisingly, with French chauvinism and xenophobia, with the concept of the national language and all the legitimations and illegitimations that entails—accents and foreigners, illiteracy and cultural distinction, the narcissisms of class and the universalizing fetishisms of the "grande nation" (as those significantly range from revolutionary republicanism to older and newer forms of reaction), along with fear of Germany, contempt for "perfide Albion," malaise in the face of Americanization (a word already in use in that period, apparently), along with the whole iconology of imperialism—higher and lower races, the "mission civilisatrice," and so forth (Angenot instructively reminds us that the first opposition to Jules Ferry's imperialism comes from the right rather than the left). This sink of unwholesome representations inspires some mixed feelings on which I want to dwell for a moment. First of all, I would have liked to have all this identified from the outset as bourgeois culture par excellence, at the first truly secular moment of the first truly bourgeois state (leaving Holland aside): surely all the French literature of interest to us (at least since the Revolution) has always held precisely this bourgeois culture in scorn and loathing—even Flaubert, who found so much of it within himself, was able to repudiate it by way of self-loathing. But I think that Angenot's position (like the more global Foucauldian one I alluded to) forbids him to acknowledge any negativity or critique or distance which would somehow fall outside the system. To be sure, he cannot take a diachronic nor even a sociological view of this mass of textual data, and must therefore omit the interpretive identification I have offered between a certain culture and a certain social class. But more than that—and the example of Flaubert could certainly be pressed into service for this alternative view—the possibility of negating the system is either programmed into the system itself and thereby remains part and parcel of it, or it is a retrospective illusion, obvious enough for us today but not available to the contemporaries.

Meanwhile, what of that retrospective viewpoint which is necessarily ours, and for which most of this constellation of attitudes—lumped together no doubt as "nationalism"—will be caricatural and scarcely invite sympathy or comprehension? Republicanism itself—the Jacobin tradition—has not had a very good press in recent times; I'll come back to it in a moment. As for the left attitudes or even what Americans call liberal ones, Angenot has an unpleasant surprise in store for us in his companion volume, *L'Utopie collectiviste*, which patiently elaborates the analogous interrelated stupidities of the Second

International in this same period. To be sure, the United States is not exactly a nation-state like the European ones: whatever corresponds to nationalism in this country is not likely either to have the same kind of class determination and class style; and we might be more likely to describe it as a "Eurocentrism" (an odd word to use, to be sure) or as a complex form of racism and white superiority. Or perhaps we think we are beyond all this, and that another century has at least been good for something. But in that case, the fable no longer tells us about ourselves, and it is not clear what we should do with this dead social and cultural history.

I want to add something else, however, which is that this first anatomy of French cultural "identity" (as we might say nowadays) is for Angenot not merely a set of ideologies among others, it is the very subject-position of all the enunciations that make up the "social discourse" of *1889*. And it occurs to me that literary or cultural histories rarely begin in this fashion, with an account of the collective or hegemonic subject-position: we're generally given some facts of social history, some of the ideas "in the air," a few of the great debates and the great cultural issues or problems; but the collective space from which such judgments and acts and works flow remains empty and indeterminate, unless we decide to objectify and externalize it, and identify it with a ruling class we can again see from the outside. Meanwhile, a deep and inveterate, dare I say patriotic, populism has generally prevented American intellectuals from painting so absolute a picture as this one of universal *Bêtise*.

Now I want to go on to sketch in the three basic directions in which this immense historiographic tour de force develops: they are a general sense of twilight and decline, in this fin de siècle; a perplexed awareness of the increasing saturation of social space with media information (in this period of the newspapers and what Angenot calls "publicistique" ["publicistics"]); and finally an omnipresent and dominant form of thinking and writing which he calls "le romanesque général" ("the general novelistic"), and which narrativizes information and reality in some well-nigh universal fashion and which is novelistic, not because it comes from novels, but rather, the other way round, because the very rich novelistic production of the period feeds on it as its raw material and transforms it ceaselessly into its own cultural commodities.

The decline of the West, and more significantly and urgently, the decline of France itself and the innumerable threats to

French civilization and culture: this is for Angenot (and, long before, Spengler) the predominant obsession of 1889, a kind of collective cultural hypochondria (we will see shortly why the medical figure is not a gratuitous one here). We may of course want to observe that things are no different today; and to hazard the guess that some such collective national self-doubts were endemic in France ever since the loss of the race with England. Angenot's characterization of the causes for this collective anxiety, of the situation to which it is a response—and it should be understood that strictly speaking, according to the premises of the analysis of "social discourse," he cannot posit a cause, but merely reconstruct the situation on the basis of so many symptomatic discourses—is a loosely Deleuzian one: if I am more hesitant about his use of the word "deterritorialization," it is on the one hand because of the more joyous and liberatory feeling the word seems to have among Deleuzians, and on the other because it is not clear to me whether it means much more than secularization, Weberian *Entzauberung*, or whatever other sociological cliché one wishes to summon up for the malaise that is inspired by developing capitalism and commodification. Nor does it have to mean any more than that, since the word is simply meant to designate the inaccessible and itself enigmatic or mysterious source of a generalized anxiety which, as an effect, is more palpable in these texts than any supposed cause. Or rather, the litany of supposed and hypothesized causes makes up the very substance and fabric of this social text, for which Angenot coins the word "anxiogène" ("anxiogenic"). The inventory is rich and savorous, the etiologies range from racial degeneracy to neurasthenia, from "symbolism" to syphilis, from the press and political venality to various "modern" technological developments (such as cremation, a hot topic in this period): the anti-Semitisms have a field day, laying the groundwork for the Dreyfus case, only a few short years down the road; but anticlericalism is also highly developed, along with the predictable emergence of a secessionist Roman Catholic culture, even more intensely aware of "decadence" than the secular culture all around it. Here we may make a link with the conception of the novelistic or the narrative: for the conception of decline offers the interpretive framework in which all kinds of facts and events, scandals, new cultural movements, fashions, ideas, and pronouncements, can be read and understood. Reality—but as we shall see in a moment, it would be more accurate to say, "actuality"—is scrutinized for the signs of decay, and it is only in terms of this rewriting, this larger historical dramatization and narrativization, that things find their most satisfying meanings. This emergence of the category of the "signs of the times"; this obsessive symptomatology of current events and social developments—this is, I think, one of the phenomena Angenot has in mind when he invokes "le romanesque général" ("the general novelistic").

At the same time, the omnipresent feeling of decadence offers an instructive context for new kinds of literary or cultural interpretation. Think, for example, of the list of figural synonyms which proliferate in order to translate all the shades of this feeling: "gâchis" ("waste"), "crise" ("crisis"), "nuit, crépuscule" ("night, twilight"), "chute, abîme" ("fall, abyss"), "effrondrement" ("collapse"), "dissolution" ("dissolution"), "chaos" ("chaos"), "catastrophe" ("catastrophe"), etc. (374–75). If one considers "high literature" to be working over this primal raw material of ideology which Bakhtin described as social language itself, a transformation of that raw material into a tangible object (as Althusser suggested)—not merely an object of what used to be called "æsthetic value," but also an object on which a critical position can be taken and which can offer itself for analysis—then perhaps new perspectives become available for a rethinking of this period. Mallarmé's great shipwreck, for example, the immense "naufrage" of his poetic hero, can in that case be taken less as a questionable and melodramatic symbol of some kind, part of the poetic *bric-à-brac* of the "fin de siècle," and something closer to a working over of just this ideology of the shipwreck and the catastrophe so deeply inscribed in the language and collective ideology of this anxious period: yet something a little more than a mere remedy against anxiety, no doubt, and perhaps a little less than a full-blown ideological analysis or self-awareness. Meanwhile, on an even more massive scale, no one can doubt the kinship with the pattern of baleful heredity which gives Zola's Rougon-Macquart cycle its organizational pretext: whether any critical distance can also be attributed to this fundamental ideologeme of decline and fall is a question we must also return to later on.

Heredity, symptomatology; so many symptoms of the fin de siècle Weltanschauung we are tempted to say, without asking ourselves whether the word "symptom" is not itself profoundly symptomatic. And indeed the other omnipresent feature of the ideology of decline lies in the prestige of medical discourse as a privileged mode of interpretation throughout this whole period.

The balefulness of the medical is something we have long since learned, from Foucault and so many others: that it rests on apprehensions about the body and sexuality has also become obvious, so that it may be less popular to observe that such apprehensions are no longer quite so important in our culture: "le dispositif de *médicalisation* de l'exegèse sociale qui est bien soutenu par l'hégémonie 1889, n'a plus grand avenir—mais d'autres autorités technocratiques prendront la relève" ("the contrivance of medicalizing social exegesis which is well supported by the 1889 hegemony, no longer has a great future—but other technocratic authorities will come to take up the relay") (1112). We are thus again confronted with the outmoding to the point of caricature of what contemporaries must have taken to be an existential characteristic and an "évidence" ("obvious fact") of daily life: what are we to do with errors of this kind, which are scarcely amenable to any imaginative act of the historical understanding?

The medical is at any rate a cluster of ideologemes which can in one way be studied in relative isolation; indeed, Angenot has devoted a spin-off volume, called *Le Cru et le faisandé* (*The Raw and the Gamy*), to doing just that, and it is one of his best and most readable. Here, however, he has a methodological warning for us:

> Il m'a semblé . . . que les caractères du discours médical sur l'hystérie par exemple ne sont pas intéro-conditionnés ni intelligibiles dans leur immanence. L'hystérie (le discours de Charcot et d'autres sur l'hystérie) parle d'autre chose que d'un désordre neuropathologique, de même que les discours de la polissonerie parlent d'autres choses encore que d'Eden prostitutionnel et de chronique du demi-monde. Ainsi encore le discours de terreur sur la masturbation, orchestré par les médecins, se lira dans un intertexte où, par "déplacement et condensation", il se fait homologue de la grande angoisse économique du gaspillage, de la dette publique, du déficit budgétaire, de la logorrhée des esthétiques décadentes, etc. (1080)

> (It has seemed to me . . . that the characteristics of medical discourse on hysteria, for example, are neither conditioned from within, or intelligible in their immanence. Hysteria [Charcot's and others' discourse on hysteria] speaks of something other than a neuropathological disorder, just as the discourses of smut speak of still other things than a prostitutional Eden and tenderloin chronicles. Thus again the terrorist discourse on masturbation, orchestrated by doctors, will be read in an intertext where, by

"displacement and condensation," it becomes the homologue of the great economic anxiety of waste, of public debt, of budgetary deficits, of the logorrhea of decadent æsthetics, etc.)

These mobile allegories, in which figures from one field offer themselves as tangible bodies for the spirits of another, at the same time that—as with the medical doctrines of "suggestion"—they do double duty as certified "scientific" explanations, Angenot has theorized in terms of discursive "migrations" (903), which one could ideally be in a position to map out according to their seasonal or sectorial rhythms. Clearly the medical sector is here and in this period a privileged one, which we cannot examine further in detail, save to add this interesting footnote on the development of the notion of an unconscious:

Ce qui me semble se produire en 1880–1890, date à laquelle la notion dans son imprécision devient "à la mode" chez les savants, c'est que "l'inconscient" va se séparer de l' "instinct", de l'activité végétative (dont il est encore proche chez von Hartmann) de ce qui chez l'individu relève de l'*espèce* dont il est membre, ou encore du "moi d'habitude" (Condillac), pour se mettre à désigner cette *chose* que révèlent l'hypnose, la suggestion, "un monde d'affections purement vitales" dont "nous ne percevons que le retentissement" car elles sont "hors du *moi*, mais le moi sympathise avec elles" (pour reprendre les termes de Maine de Biran dont les Français, par chauvinisme, font un précurseur). (422)

(What seems to me to occur in 1880–90, the date when the notion in its imprecision becomes "à la mode" among scholars, is that the "unconscious" is separated from "instinct," from vegetative activity [to which it is still close in the case of von Hartmann] from what in the individual depends on the *species* of which he is a member, or yet again from the "self of habit" [Condillac], in order to start designating this *thing* that hypnosis and suggestion reveal: "a world of purely vital affections" of which "we perceive only the echo" because they are "outside of the self, but the self sympathizes with them" [to take up Maine de Biran's term, whom the French, out of chauvinism, make a precursor].)

The privilege indeed of the medical figuration lies in the migration along with it of various levels of the body itself: thus on the one hand the dense realities of the individual body come to reinforce and to solidify the more disembodied figures of economic or social phenomena, while at the same time the concrete anxieties about the individual body itself add urgency to the more general national ones. Angenot points out that the omnipresent "Darwinism" of this period is scarcely drawn from Darwin himself, but rather from a long tradition of "social Darwinism" avant la lettre from Hobbes to Spencer (876): at any rate, it is certain that lived experiences of bodily illnesses, fever, deterioration, and even occasional convalescence, add power and content to the vaster collective and narrative fantasies of social Darwinism and a general crepuscular and entropic mood.

But now we face a significant problem: one which is both empirical, in the sense of the historical data themselves, and theoretical in terms of our models. For is this not—this belle époque which is also a fin de siècle—the well-known apotheosis of the bourgeois doctrine of progress, of triumphant Victorianism and of Utopias of wonder-working machinery in the far future, the golden age of European supremacy nourished—in different degrees by the different nation-states to be sure— by the certainty of infinite perfectibility and a historical *telos* as straight as an arrow? How then to imagine the coexistence of this euphoric doctrine of the bourgeoisie as the very goal and end of history with the other darker visions that Angenot documents in so much detail, and which seep, omnipresent, throughout all the fields and divisions of labor of "social discourse"? It will be too easy, but not at all wrong, to pronounce the word dialectic and to posit some profound "identity of identity and non-identity" between these two registers of value, which can only seem incompatible to the logician and the positivist; on the other hand the appeal to the dialectic is not meant to shut down explanation in some premature and facile way, but rather to authorize the invention of new models; and this is, I believe, what we find in Angenot. It will come as no surprise that in a work of this range, which seeks to organize so varied an array of contents, the theoretical interventions must be punctual and concentrated, intent on sorting out the irrelevant meanings of a term like "ideology" or marking references to theoretical authorities from Bakhtin to Bourdieu, but above all to the Montreal school of "social discourse" of which the present work is something like a monument.

I will at the risk of greatly oversimplifying it here hazard my own version of Angenot's theoretical solution to the problem we have raised—progress versus decadence—which involves I believe a crucial distinction between ideology—which is to say ruling class ideology—and hegemony in this textual sense of the omnipresent *doxa*, the "totalité du dicible, du narrable, de l'argumentable d'une société donnée . . . le réseau complexe de relations interdiscursives [qui] enserre tout énoncé, tout récit et leur donne du sens" (627) (the totality of the sayable, the tellable, of the arguable of a given society . . . the complex network of interdiscursive relations that box in any statement, any story, and give them meaning). (In addition, it should be noted that hegemony, in this sense, knows its own dual logic of identity and difference, "deux tendances [dont] l'une rassemble des facteurs de cohésion, de répétition métonymique de récurrence, de cointelligibilité, l'autre des facteurs de spécialisation, de dissimulation, de migration par avatars. . . ." [1096]. [two tendencies one of which brings together factors of cohesion, of metonymic repetition, of recurrence, of cointelligibility, the other, factors of specialization, of dissimulation, of migration by avatars].) This use of the term hegemony will perhaps surprise those who thought of Gramsci's idea in terms of social power rather than cultural strategy: it suffices to recall Angenot's insistence on the policing function of hegemony generally, which controls not merely the channels of communication but the very forms of expression themselves, and rules on what can alone be said—hegemony in this form, as the Foucauldian omnipresent system, is really at one with the totality of social discourse in the sense in which nothing other than itself could possibly have been enunciated there.

In that case, ruling class ideology will be something somewhat different, and perhaps not altogether coterminous with discourse at all and something closer to those mythological entities the sociologists used to call "values." In the present instance, we have to do with the great official ideologies of Jacobinism and republicanism and of progress: these are the class ideologies of a triumphant bourgeoisie, and they offer positive visions of the world (and indeed, I am tempted to say, properly Utopian ones, on which other future and different Utopias will nonetheless have to draw). But they do not in that sense inform everyday discourse:

> De façon mediée, la *doxa* reflète les luttes de classes sous forme de leurs résultantes et occultations dans les discours. L'idéologie dominante, officielle, est au contraire chargée d'une *mémoire*, de la préservation "religieuse" des plus anciens et plus légitimes préceptes idéologiques de la classe régnante, avec un bricolage, une mise à jour toujours précaire. L'idéologie dominante récapitule et adapte partiellement l'ontogenèse évolutive des formes idéologiques de

cette classe (esprit des Lumières, jacobinisme, libéralisme, humanitarisme quarante-huitard, saint-simonisme, positivisme . . .) Elle doit enfin remplir synchroniquement sa fonction de légitimation du pouvoir et de ses politiques. Elle a des monopoles, dans l'appareil scolaire par exemple, et joue un rôle d'apparat qui lui conserve un statut officiel. Mais elle a aussi une lourdeur spécifique, elle est constamment pénétrée par la *doxa* et obligée de composer avec elle et ses thèmes chargés d'actualité. Le rappport entre l'idéologie dominante et les effets déstabilisants de l'hégémonie est d'autant plus problématique que l'idéologie républicaine doit à la fois consolider et remotiver des thèses anciennes tout en faisant face à des "temps obscurs" où son amour de la Patrie est contesté par les forces nationalistes—boulangistes, son prétendu souci d'égalité par la montée des socialismes, des syndicalismes (sinon du féminisme) et son axiomatique du progrès par le concert décadentiste des lettres et des sciences. (732)

(In a mediated fashion, the *doxa* reflects the struggle of the classes in the form of their consequences and elisions in discourse. The dominant ideology, the official one, is on the contrary, entrusted with a *memory*, with the "religious" preservation of the oldest and most legitimate ideological precepts of the ruling class, always precariously adjusted and updated. The dominant ideology recapitulates and partially adapts the evolutionary ontogenesis of this class's ideological forms (spirit of the Enlightenment, Jacobinism, liberalism, 1848-style humanitarianism, St.-Simonism, positivism . . .) Finally, it must synchronically fulfill its function of rendering power and its policies legitimate. It has monopolies, in the school system, for example, and plays in pomps in order to retain its official status. But it also has a specific weight, it is constantly penetrated by the *doxa* and obliged to compromise with it and its themes of the moment. The relation between the dominant ideology and the destabilizing effects of the hegemony is all the more problematic as republican ideology must simultaneously consolidate and remotivate old theses while at the same time coping with "dark times" in which its love of country is contested by national-Boulangistic forces, its would-be desire for equality by the rise of socialisms, trade-unionisms [if not feminism], and its dogma of progress by the decadent conspiracy of letters and sciences.)

We are familiar with the prevailing narrative of bourgeois ideology, whose most influential versions can be found in Lukács' work on the one hand, and in Sartre's *L'Idiot de la famille* on the other: both posit the ways in which the universalizing doctrine of the Revolution—"liberté, égalité, fraternité"—which permits the class alliances that bring the bourgeoisie to power—

are increasingly undermined and ideologically discredited by the emergence of a new class whose presence will become inescapable by the time of the Revolution of 1848. This narrative, which underscores the failure of nerve, the internalized guilt, and the symbolic self-maceration, of ruling class or bourgeois intellectuals after 1848, is less effective in dealing with the persistence or survival of precisely that ruling class ideology itself: Angenot's more complex model thus has some advantages in accounting for the ideological double-bind of the period, certain both of its destiny—progress—and its fate—decadence. Meanwhile, we must also recall the often quoted remarks of Marx about the bourgeois revolutionaries of 1848: itself a two-stage narrative in which the revolutionaries of 1789 are filled with anxiety about the historical originality of their situation and their project, and give themselves courage by wearing ancient revolutionary costumes; while those of 1848 imitate this masquerade as a kind of fancy-dress ball and simulate, not the historical confrontation with the New, but rather the affect that resulted from it: a representation of revolutionary anxiety rather than the thing itself.

This is, I believe, the sense in which Angenot can deny the word ideology in its positive sense to the textual hegemony of 1889: ideology is in that sense the consciousness of a rising class, the ensemble of its values, its slogans, its Utopian visions, and there can thus be a genuinely bourgeois ideology only as long as the bourgeoisie remains an active social class in that sense. But this is no longer the case in our period.

> La vision du monde crépusculaire avec son pathos anxiogène, son ressentiment, ses mandats de reterritorialisation, *tient lieu* d'une idéologie bourgeoise (qu'on ne trouve guère esquissée que dans le saint-simonisme) qui aurait *aimé* et glorifié l'Effet-Capital jusque dans ses conséquences. L'hégémonie thématique qui domine en 1889 prétend aimer de tout son cœur ce que la "société moderne" vient fatalement désagréger, dégrader, déconstruire. Amatrice de progrès, mais atterrée par les décadences et les morbidités, nostalgique des axiologies précapitalistes, la vision du monde fin de siècle se présente comme une vaste *dénégation* qui cherche à réinstituer dans la "superstructure" ce que le capitalisme a pour vocation de dissoudre. (350)

> (The vision of a twilight world with its anxiety-producing pathos, its resentment, its mandates of reterritorialization, *takes the place of* a bourgeois ideology [which is hardly sketched anywhere but in St.-

> Simonism] which would have *loved* and glorified the Capital-Effect even in its consequences. The thematic hegemony which dominates in 1889 claims wholeheartedly to love what "modern society" has come inevitably to take apart, degrade, and deconstruct. Lover of progress, but floored by decadences and morbidities, nostalgic for precapitalist axiologies, the vision of the fin de siècle world is presented like a vast *denial* which seeks to reinstitute in the "superstructure" what capitalism undertakes to dissolve.)

This is also the sense in which Angenot reinterprets his own findings in the light of the question of modernity:

> La modernité, perçue dans ses dominantes culturelles opérantes, c'est le retour obstiné, bien que métamorphique, des mêmes résistances [au moderne], avec toutes sortes de formations de compromis qui neutralisent le novum en feignant de lui faire place. Le discours social "moderne" reste une dénégation du monde moderne . . . (1112)

> (Modernity, perceived in its operative cultural dominants, is the obstinate, though metamorphic, return of the same resistances [to the modern], with all kinds of compromise formations which neutralize the new while pretending to make room for it. "Modern" social discourse remains a denial of the modern world. . . .)

The discursive complex of this period then, with its various modernisms, is a *substitute* for bourgeois ideology and a systematic defense against modernity as such. In principle, this new and more complex theory of ideology (and its distinction from hegemony) ought to open up new perspectives on the periods that follow this one, whose modernities have so often been understood to cancel this era out and indeed to break their oppressive ties with this nineteenth century altogether (as we have seen). Whether Angenot's synchronic form allows us to glimpse those perspectives is a question we will only be able to raise after returning to his story rapidly to set in place its other two basic themes, that of the omnipresence of journalism and "publicistique" ("publicistics"), and that of the dominance of the "romanesque général" ("the general novelistic"), the narrative or novelistic paradigm.

The conception of the latter owes much to the work, no longer so widely read or influential, I think, of Charles Grivel, and participates in a more general poststructuralist suspicion of narrative that ranges from the general anticommunist critique of

Marxian ideas of a *telos* of history all the way to *Screen* magazine's denunciation of the ideological effects of Hollywood-type storytelling. I do prefer the latter to the former, not so much because I want to defend providential conceptions of history in general (I agree with Angenot that by *telos* is generally meant the teleological perspective of a specifically bourgeois notion of progress), but rather because I think that it is in the reduction of events to their individual dimension (as in Hollywood) that the vice of such storytelling lies. The collective also demands its forms of narrative, and it will have been clear that I want to consider *1889* itself as a kind of narrative, of a new type. But this is, I think, not Angenot's view, for whom the "gnoséologie" of the "generalized novelistic" is an "apparatus of resistance to other cognitive procedures" (197):

> Je pense que le "romanesque" a été dominant au XIXe siècle. Le discours social classique avait été oratoire; le XXe siècle devait être structural, nomothétique et relativiste . . . Les champs scientifiques en 1889 mettent de l'avant un paradigme— expérimental, moniste, organiciste, révolutionniste. Il faudrait toute une étude pour montrer combien le texte savant demeure cependant perméable à la narration expressive-romanesque. (198)

> (I think that the "novelistic" was dominant in the nineteenth century. Classical social discourse had to be oratory; the twentieth century was supposed to be structural, nomothetic, and relativistic. . . . Scientific fields in 1889 put forward a paradigm—experimental, monistic, organicist, and revolutionist. An entire study would be necessary to show how much scholarly texts remain however permeable to expressive-novelistic narration.)

The stakes of this particular form of *Ideologiekritik* need to be spelled out: it offers a research program of the greatest interest, particularly at a moment when the pendulum of intellectual fashion has begun to swing back towards some generalized valorization of narrative as such. At the same time, it directs our attention towards the contamination of nineteenth-century discourse in general by the narratives of journalism, of which more in a moment. But it would also seem to harbor a deeper hidden indictment of the æsthetic itself, insofar as one identifies that with narration (we will examine the analysis of poetry later on in connection with journalism). This would be the place, if we had time, to stage a debate about the work of Zola, so supremely representative, particularly in Angenot's account, of the *doxa* of contemporary social discourse. And it is certain that *La Bête hu-*

maine, with its multiple allusions to precisely the actualities of 1889, seems to fulfill the doubtful program Angenot ascribes to the novelist of this period:

> Le roman canonique fonctionne comme fournisseur bénévole de prestigieuses narrations anxiogènes répondant aux inquiétudes dominantes. Dans sa logique globale, il est au service du dispositif d'interprétation de la conjoncture, *ancilla doxae*. Dans la topologie interdiscursive, le roman opère la mise en connexion d'une série de thèmes journalistiques, venus de faits divers par exemple, et de thèses et axiomes venus d'esotérismes médical, philosophique et scientifique. Il s'agit de connecter l'actualité transitoire et la vérité éternelle. Le regard romanesque, en concurrence avec le regard médical et neurologique, *voit* alors une société de détraqués roulant vers toutes les déchéances et confirme ainsi ce que tout le monde redoute. (837)

> (The canonical novel functions as the benevolent supplier of prestigious anxiogenic narrations responding to the dominant preoccupations. In its global logic, it serves the moment's interpretive machine, *ancilla doxae*. In interdiscursive topology, the novel effects a connecting of a series of journalistic themes, coming from medical, philosophical, and scientific esoterica. It is a question of relating transitory current events and eternal truth. The novelistic gaze, in competition with the medical and neurological gaze, *sees* then a society of unhinged persons rolling towards every downfall, and thus confirms what all suspect.)

This is no doubt very much the sense in which the Zola of *La Bête humaine* can no doubt also be said to show "un joli flair doxique, la littérature à la mode n'étant souvent qu'un cocktail habile de *topoi* régulés par une protestation crépusculaire et confusionniste" (900) (a pretty doxic flair, fashionable literature often only being no more than a clever cocktail of *topoi* regulated by a twilight and confusionist protestation). But this text then no longer presents much similarity to the novel admired by Deleuze and Barthes and by Michel Serres (and for which I myself have a great fondness, I should add). I hope the divergence does not revive the ancient æsthetic problematic, however, in which literary value somehow derives from its unpredictable, that is to say, its natural energies (Kant's notion of genius): as we learn the detail of the period ever more closely, Zola's text seems to grow more and more transparent, we recognize more and more of its borrowings from actuality and the essential banality of its content, Zola's own intentions then take on form and seem to denounce their own vulgarity and sensationalism, and what was at first a kind of strange and inhuman meteoric apparition dissolves into a host of the most futile and obvious literary gestures. This is then contextualization with a vengeance, in which the contextualized object ends up being completely volatilized by the ever more completely researched context and by our own fuller knowledge. In that case, the task of the historian is truly to obliterate the past, to work through it in such a way that we no longer have to repeat it, very much in the spirit of Freud's talking cure; and to free us in a joyous and Nietzschean forgetfulness. Let the dead bury the dead: we shall see in a moment whether poetry fares any better.

And indeed with this particular novelist we are in any case very close to that immense new continent of journalism and of "publicistique" ("publicistics") about which *1889* also has so much to tell us: the new bourgeois "public sphere," not as it ought to have been, but as it really was. The statistics document an explosion in publications during this period, less in terms of book publishing (which saw a 20 percent increase over the preceding twenty years) than rather in newspapers and periodicals: thus, from 36 daily papers in Paris in 1870, the augmentation is such that by the year 1889 there are some 135, plus all kinds of specialized or ephemeral periodicals. Angenot takes an inventory of the division of labor represented by the genres of papers and their various kinds of "columns," as well as of the pressures on and tendencies of this writing (1104: crisis of ideological overproduction, false novelties, etc., etc.). The bulk of his extensive treatment of the press is however divided into what may be called the objective and the subjective dimensions of the phenomenon.

Objectively, what must be described is the way in which the press produces a whole new set of categories (or constructs them, if you prefer a less historical language): these categories are not directly ideological, nor are they purely imaginary or arbitrary: rather, they offer "schemata" (to use the Kantian term) for organizing experience as such and for deciphering the world. Henceforth, indeed, the interpretation of the world, the understanding of it, is condemned to pass through such categories (and this obligation, which cannot be circumvented, is another feature of the concept of hegemony). Thus, "la publicistique produit deux entités discursives correlées, l'Actualité et l'Opinion" ("publicistics produces two correlated discursive entities: News and Opinion") (505), categories which are obviously contested. "L'Actualité du *Temps* et du *Journal des*

Débats n'est pas celle de la 'presse à un sou' " ("The News of *Le Temps* and of *Le Journal des Débats* is not that of the "penny-press") (505); and by the same token, as we still know very well today, the struggle to characterize public opinion is often more important than the attempt to "influence" it, if indeed that notion has any coherent meaning when we are dealing with what Sartre would call a "serial" phenomenon par excellence. As for Actualité, the power to determine what counts as an event, the monopoly of this right to define and classify what happens as such, is a more subtle and intangible, yet perhaps even more significant new force, which reaches even more deeply into private life and has its say in the way people tell themselves their own biographical stories. "L'Actualité est ce que produit la rencontre inattendue sur une table de dissection doxique du réel imprévisible et de la nécessité idéologique." ("News is what is produced by the surprise meeting on a doxic dissection table of the unforeseeable real and ideological necessity") (597–98). Indeed it seems possible that the novel (whose external links with the press we have seen in naturalism, but which also mutates into a new psychological or intuitive genre in this period) will discover a whole new and perhaps more modern vocation when it begins to take as its deeper content the very categories of Experience and Event as such. As for the more obvious public forms of such categories, we need only to think of the concept of the "Affaire," as, along with the "scandal," it organizes information from the social sphere ("en 1889, huit affaires ayant toutes une composante de mystère et d'horreur occupent les journaux" [611] ["in 1889, eight affairs each having a component of mystery and horror are of concern to the newspapers"]), to grasp the shaping power of this new form of writing.

Its subjective dimension would then be constituted by the awareness people in general have of its historical novelty: that is to say, their willingness to act on the basis of what is perceived as a fundamental change. But how to decide whether this is a subjective or an objective matter? In one of the most interesting episodes of his exploration, indeed, Angenot comes to the matter of poetic production in this period, which can itself be thematized as it were objectively and subjectively, in the explosion of little magazines and esoteric presses on the one hand, and in the quality and themes of the poems themselves on the other. The picture one gets from Angenot's materials is one of an increasing saturation of public space by the public discourse of journalism and "publicistique," such that there is no longer any room for poetry as an autonomous discourse, or rather that poetry must open up a new space for itself: a hermetic space, outside the public sphere (or claiming to stand outside it), and ideologically disdaining everything marked popular or public (without that disdain necessarily taking on political and aristocratic or antipopular overtones).

The model is the one we have become familiar with in Bourdieu's sociology, namely that the primal driving force of every intellectual activity is to secure an institutional space in which it can exist and perpetuate its existence: once it thus rationalizes its own specialized activities (rationalization being used here in a non-Weberian and psychological sense), once it can motivate its own existence, then it can turn its attention to the content with which it is allegedly concerned. The Bourdieu approach is thus more than a mere sociology of the intellectuals themselves, but also cuts deep into the structure of the various specialized discourses. This is, for example, the spirit in which Angenot describes the related crisis of philosophy: whose traditional concerns have now been replaced by the rise of experimental psychology in a neighboring discipline, so that little more than a watered down Kantian ethics is left over for the philosophers until in this very year Bergson appears, with the splendor of the rising sun, and signals the possibility of a counterattack on experimental psychology in general and thus of an eventual *reconquista* (or as Angenot says more dryly "Bergson sauve les meubles" ("Bergson saves the furniture") [563]).

Poetry cannot pull it off in quite the same way, although its situation is equally imperiled: "Vers 1880, le discours social ne produit plus rien (ni épique, ni vision d'avenir, ni tragique même) qui puisse être reconnu par le poète comme potentiel de sublime. Le problème est alors de savoir *ce qui reste* à faire. Car la poésie, malgré son haut degré de discrimination sélective, se nourrissait du discours social. Il ne restait en effet que l'aventure de la folie ou l'autoreprésentation de la forme" ("Towards 1880, social discourse produces nothing [neither epic, nor a vision of the future, nor even tragic] that can be recognized by the poet as potentially sublime. The problem is then to know what remains to be done. For poetry, despite its high degree of selective discrimination, fed off of social discourse. In fact, all that remained was the adventure of madness or the self-representation of form") (818). This diagnosis, however, would seem rather to hold for literature in general; the poets themselves need to pursue a more specifically linguistic strategy and to talk themselves into believing that they can locate some nonsocial linguistic space, some pure language outside of social discourse:

> Le mandat qu'en tâtonnant se donnaient ceux que Verlaine appelait "les symbolos, les décardards", consistait à créer dans le discours social quelque chose qui *eut l'air* de n'en pas provenir. Si l'on veut voir une telle opération dans sa diversité révélatrice, il faut considérer globalement non seulement l'hermétisme de Mallarmé, mais aussi les "floupetteries" du *Décadent*, la wagnérisation de la prose de Peladan, les pastiches de la Pléiade chez les zélateurs de "l'Ecole romane", les divers procédés, "abstrus et abscons", de travestissement du discours social qui, dans leur concomitance manifestent la crise des lettres et la quête d'une autarcie, impossible et nécessaire, du poétique. La poésie rompt les ponts non par subversité, mais par fidelité à son mandat *traditionnel* que menace ce que Mallarmé allégorise comme "le Journal". (817)

> (The mandate that those whom Verlaine called "les symbolos, les décardards" had gropingly given themselves consisted in creating within social discourse something that *seemed* not to spring from it. If one seeks to see such an operation in its revealing diversity, it is necessary also to consider globally not only Mallarmé's hermeticism, but also the *Décadent*'s imitations of romanticism, the Wagnerization of Peladan's prose, the Pléïade pastiches by the zealots of the "Roman school," the various "abstruse and obscure" tactics for disguising social discourse which, in their concomitance, display the crisis of literature and the impossible but necessary self-sufficiency of the poetic. Poetry breaks bridges not by subversion, but by faithfulness to its *traditional* mandate which is threatened by what Mallarmé allegorizes as "the Newspaper.")

For anyone who, as I do, wishes to grasp literature and its forms in function of the situation literature confronts at a given historical moment, such an analysis is plausible indeed, and I don't wish to question it. But I do think it is important to point out that, in the very spirit of the Bourdieu analysis and in the light of the practical preconditions and requirements of his own project, Angenot has to think and show this. If the poets were, in other words and as it were in real life, to be granted some space and some language *outside* social discourse, then the very constructional principle of *1889* would be called back into question: "le discours social" ("social discourse") would no longer be a totality, and could no longer function as an absolute horizon.

But it certainly does so, and we need only to observe, as proof, the fateful reemergence of the august theological language that always tends to accompany the glimpsed emergence of that unrepresentable thing, the totality itself:

> "*In eo movemur et sumus*", dit Saint Paul: en lui nous évoluons et nous sommes. Le discours social est le médium obligé de la communication et de la rationalité historique, de même qu'il est instrument du prestige social pour certains, au même rang que la fortune et le pouvoir. En lui se formulent et se diffusent tous les "sujets imposés" (Bourdieu) d'une époque donnée . . . Pour qui ouvre la bouche ou prend la plume, le discours social est *toujours déjà* là avec ses genres, ses thèmes et ses préconstruits. Il va falloir se faire entendre à travers cette rumeur, ce brouhaha, cette facticité omnipresente. Nul ne peut se flatter de parler dans un vide, mais toujours en réponse à quelque chose. On songera à cet "et ego", moi aussi j'ai quelque chose à dire, si perceptible chez les "jeunes poètes", resolus à produire coûte que coûte de l'inouï. (1087)

> ("*In eo movemur et sumus,*" says St. Paul: in Him we evolve and we are. Historical discourse is the obligatory medium of communication and historical rationality, just as it is the instrument of social prestige for some, at the same rank as money and power. In it are formulated and are disseminated all the "required subjects" [Bourdieu] of a given period. . . . For anyone who opens his mouth or who takes her pen, historical discourse is *always already* there, with its genres, its themes, and its pre-constructs. It will be necessary to make oneself heard through this murmur, this brouhaha, this omnipresent facticity. No one can flatter himself that he is speaking in a void, but only in response to something. One will think of this "et ego," I too have something to say, so perceptible among "young poets," determined to produce, at whatever cost, something outrageous.)

Thus with a grand historical gesture, we find ourselves back in the universal stupidity of Flaubert, the inelectuable dizziness at human imbecility, the inevitable nausea of the social world and the world of speech itself:

> Thy hand, great Anarch, lets the curtain fall,
> And universal darkness buries all.

This perspective then inevitably exacerbates a question whose relevance it disputes in advance, and that is the question of the *novum*, of possible innovation, of the chance to say something new in the process of emergence. I have said that for Angenot the glimpse of novelty is a retrospective illusion: we know which seeds have grown and which have not, but this is a knowledge denied the contemporaries locked in their present of time.

There is an exception to this historical closure, and it suggests that if the better cannot be formulated here, then at least the worst can be so identified: this is the solidification of any number of the elements of this *doxa* into protofascism to come. It is a crystallization that will take place, unsurprisingly, around the name of Maurice Barrès; and what is constitutive of this grim *novum* is unexpectedly the falling away of all the pathos of the ideology of decline, at the same time that all its historical assumptions are retained, but now cynically and joyously:

> "Simon et moi nous comprîmes alors notre haine des étrangers, *des barbares*." Il le dit, mais ne dogmatise pas; il affiche la désinvolture d'une composition humoristique, en digressions et fragments. C'est le contraire de l'enquête systématique des poussifs naturalistes. Barrès réclame un lecteur que ne se prend pas pour un imbécile, qui devine autant qu'il lit. Le *mépris* forme l'*éthos* du roman et c'est un sentiment nouveau en littérature. Mépris de femmes, par exemple, mais sans avoir à le dissimuler derrière de poussiéreuses argumentations évolutionnaires. . . . En tout cela, Maurice Barrès c'est la *nouveauté*, un nouveau chant, cynique et allègre . . . le texte de Barrès représente la véritable originalité . . . (842)

> ("Then Simon and I understood our hatred of foreigners, *barbarians*." He says it, but he does not dogmatic; he displays the off-handedness of a humorous composition, in digressions and fragments. It is the contrary of the systematic studies of wheezing naturalists. Barrès demands a reader who doesn't take himself for an imbecile, who guesses as much as he reads. *Contempt* forms the *ethos* of the novel, and this is a new feeling in literature. Contempt for women, for example, but without having to hide it behind dusty evolutionary arguments. . . . In all this, Maurice Barrès is a *novelty*, a new song, cynical and light-hearted . . . Barrès's text represents true originality. . . .)

It is a breath of fresh air which will not particularly cheer the contemporary reader, a lone example of "subversion" and undermining which will not particularly help revitalize those concepts. Occasionally, in a kind of science-fictional mode, names from the future are also invoked—Proust, Kafka, Joyce, Musil (1111)—which can alternately serve as examples of method and of "le recensement et l'intérrogation accablée des 'idées reçues' " ("the inventory and overwhelmed questioning of 'received ideas' ") (1085), but also, no doubt, of the fresh air to be breathed in when we break this stifling historical window, and reach . . . what? A new age? An age of critical and satiric self-consciousness? Yet this startles one by positioning self-consciousness or reflexivity in another temporal world, an alternate universe: later on, over the horizon of our sight, which has been so oppressively limited to this year and this age, this nineteenth century. I wish therefore to ask two questions, the first of which has to do with "modernism" in its more Anglo-Saxon sense, and with the classical modernists in question. Is it possible that if we knew as much about their archive and their context as Angenot knows about 1889, the texts of Proust or Musil would also be observed to disintegrate into a tissue of stupidities and commonplaces; those of Joyce into masses of the most obvious intentions? Is it enough that the writers of this later modernist generation shun Zola's lust for the sublimation of the *fait divers* into literature, and his untimely (or even unholy) avowal of "la parenté qui existe aujourd'hui entre le reportage et le roman" ("the relation that exists today between reporting and the novel") (785)?

But surely the *doxa* of an age can suffuse the literary text in many other ways than in that of overt allusion; and in any case, the fascination with the new realm of "actuality" is surely itself to be thought of as a kind of dawning self-consciousness. Angenot himself quotes any number of sources indeed who fasten on the journalistic phenomenon—grasped as a historical novelty and innovation—for further proof of the decline of the West (1095). Is it only this insertion into the "romanesque" ("novelistic") of the period that deprives the writers of 1889 of their credentials as self-conscious critics and observers of the tendencies of the age?

Meanwhile, insofar as here finally "le discours social" ("social discourse") is inseparable from the mass "de l'imprimé" ("printed matter"), which is to say, of journalism, is this not a secret autoreferentiality of Angenot's text itself to have thus designated its own precondition, its own conditions of possibility and production? These questions are not merely the desperate objections one grasps at in order to find something critical to say about an achieved project of this magnitude; they are also the desperate attempts to keep the lid from closing, to forestall the grim closure of the synchronic and the definitive imprisonment in the past. Must literary history make antiquarians of all of us? Or does *1889* in reality not perform the more Nietzschean function of letting us forget the nineteenth century once and for all?

Notes

1. Claudio Guillen, *Literature as System* (Princeton: Princeton University Press, 1971).
2. Ezra Pound, *Kulchur* (New York: New Directions, n.d.), 96.
3. Roland Barthes, *Barthes par lui-même*, in *Œuvres complètes* (Paris: Seuil, 1993), vol. 3.
4. Walter Benjamin, *Gesammelte Schriften*, vol. 5 (Frankfurt: Suhrkamp, 1982), 495.
5. Marc Angenot, *1889: un état du discours social* (Montréal: Le Préambule, 1989). Page references to this volume are included within the text.

Part I
Within the Peripheries

Peripheral Publishing, or Is Tola Dorian Totally Boring?

MELANIE HAWTHORNE

THE FIRST PERFORMANCE OF VILLIERS DE L'ISLE-ADAM'S PLAY *AXËL* at the Théâtre de la Gaîté on 26 and 27 February 1894 has always stood as an important moment in symbolist history. Though the merits of the performance itself were much debated at the time, *Axël* was the "bible" of symbolism, some said,[1] and organizing a performance of the play was a significant undertaking regardless of its ultimate merits. There can be no doubt from a historical perspective that it was the answer to a prayer for symbolists and others in the avant-garde who were looking for a play that would do for symbolism what Hugo's *Hernani* had done for romanticism.[2] For Edmund Wilson, author of *Axel's Castle*, this play was the key to an entire generation of major modernist figures. Those involved in this project have, it would seem, earned an unforgettable place in literary history.

One of the figures who plays a major role in this story, along with Paul Fort, Paul Larochelle, and Aurélien Lugné-Poe, is Tola Dorian. Plans for a stage production of *Axël* had begun as early as 1891, but ran into difficulties. When Paul Fort announced his intentions to revive the Théâtre d'Art in 1893, it was the financial support of Tola Dorian that made this possible.[3] This time the production ran into opposition from other symbolists and poets, and a lengthy debate ensued in reviews and journals, culminating in Dorian's decision to stop rehearsals. Paul Larochelle, owner of three theaters on the Left Bank and also a friend of Tola Dorian's, took over the project and finally brought it to realization in 1894. Meanwhile, Paul Fort brought in Lugné-Poe to take over the Théâtre d'Art at Tola Dorian's request.[4] Lugné-Poe directed a production of Maeterlinck's *Pelléas et Mélisande*, with sets provided by . . . Tola Dorian.[5]

At first glance, then, the enigmatic figure of Tola Dorian seems to offer an eminent candidate for a feminist project of rediscovery. She seems to be everywhere—in casual references and notes—and yet nowhere, since she is never the object of study in her own right. Histories of symbolist theater such as Jacques Robichez's authoritative *Symbolisme au théâtre*, as well as the Pléïade edition of Villiers de l'Isle-Adam's work edited by Alan Raitt and Pierre-Georges Castex, all dutifully record symbolism's debt to Dorian. According to Robichez, "Amie de Victor Hugo [. . .], cette femme de lettres russe était liée avec Paul Larochelle" ("A friend of Victor Hugo's, this Russian woman of letters was linked to Paul Larochelle"),[6] while for the Pléïade editors, she is "une femme de lettres d'origine russe qui aimait les œuvres de Villiers" ("a woman of letters of Russian origin who liked the works of Villiers").[7] Such oblique references emphasize her exotic Russian origins along with her role as philanthropist and situate her in relation to famous men (Hugo, Villiers) while mentioning almost as an afterthought the fact that she was also a "femme de lettres," but these references always seem casually to imply that everyone already knows who she is and further comment is unnecessary. Being interested in *femmes de lettres* of the fin de siècle, I began the research for this article with the classic question: "who was that mysterious woman?" Research has offered a partial answer to that question, but more important, it has forced me to acknowledge some of the difficulties in the generally feminist project of the recovery of women writers as well as raise questions about the social construction of margins, peripheries, and centers.

But first, the "nuts and bolts" question: Tola Dorian? *Who*? Some people—such as the compilers of the British Museum catalog—think that the name was a pseudonym. It is an understandable assumption since it is at first difficult to see the connection between this unpretentious-sounding—if unusual—moniker and the person behind the golden mask, the princess Kapitolina Sergieevna (Mal'tsova) Meshcherskaya, born in 1841. And yet, unlike almost every other French woman writer of the nineteenth century, she did *not* operate under a pseudonym, for she acquired the name "Dorian" from her French husband, Charles Dorian, while "Tola" seems to be a diminutive—a common Russian custom—of her first given name, Kapitolina.

This shadowy historical figure was a forceful literary presence in turn-of-the-century Paris, not only as a philanthropist and patron of the arts, but as a writer in her own right. Her publishing career began in 1879 with the publication in Geneva of her poetry written in Russian, followed shortly after by translations into French of works by Shelley. Her translation of *Les Cenci* of 1883 was prefaced by Swinburne (whose personal copy of her 1894 volume of poetry *Vespérales* is now in the Library of Congress), suggesting that Dorian was an early conduit of influence between English æsthetes and French symbolists. Though not based on Dorian's translation, *Les Cenci* would be one of the first plays performed by the symbolist Théâtre d'Art in 1891.

In the course of her career, ended by her death in 1918, Dorian would dabble in a number of genres: poetry, short stories, and drama, as well as translations. The short stories remain the least successful—they are rather wooden, relying on a symbolist-style evocation of mood rather than on any subtleties of plot—or indeed sometimes any plot at all—for their effect. Her dramatic works, at least some of which were performed,[8] are also dated by their formulaic appeal to decadent æsthetics. *Domitien* for example presents the portrait of a cruel emperor who enjoys the spectacle of death for its own sake. A representative declamatory speech by the emperor reveals the limitations of Dorian's style:

> Ah! boire et posséder à pleine âme les tortures que je répands ou retiens à mon gré! Ah! faire mourir mille morts à la pensée vivante! Ah! rire et ne tuer que par l'effroi de mourir, volupté suprême! . . . Unique consolation des ennuis de vivre! (47)
>
> (Ah! to drink and to possess to the fullest the tortures which I spread or withhold as I please! Ah! to have living thought die a thousand deaths! Ah! to laugh and to kill merely with the terrifying thought of dying, the supreme pleasure! . . . The only consolation for the boredom of living!)

The succession of exclamations quickly becomes tiring.[9]

Somewhat more successful is her poetry. While a number of the poems are sentimental, a few enjoy some limited success, such as the following.

> Pas une étoile au ciel d'ébène,
> La lune énorme tout en sang . . .
> *Dans la chambre, éclairée à peine,*
> *J'écoute un sanglot, frémissant.*
>
> La lune énorme tout en sang,
> Sur la neige mate et blafarde . . .

J'écoute un sanglot, frémissant:
Pâle, une femme me regarde.

Sur la neige mate et blafarde
L'ombre s'étend des grands bois noirs . . .
Pâle, une femme me regarde,
Les yeux chargés de désespoirs.

L'ombre s'étend des grands bois noirs
Dans l'immobilité livide . . .
Les yeux chargés de désespoirs,
Elle prend la coupe et la vide . . .

Dans l'immobilité livide
Soudain s'enfle un long hurlement . . .
Elle prend la coupe et la vide:
Salut, dit-elle lentement . . .

Soudain s'enfle un long hurlement:
Un loup blessé se traîne et tombe . . .
Salut, dit-elle lentement:
Je bois à ce doux nid, la tombe!

Un loup blessé se traîne et tombe,
Il meurt: son œil cave reluit . . .
Je bois à ce doux nid, la tombe!
Pas un rêve, ô mort, dans ta nuit!

Il meurt: son œil cave reluit,
Son dernier cri s'étend à peine . . .
Pas un souffle, ô mort, dans ta nuit,
Pas une étoile au ciel d'ébène . . .[10]

(Not a single star in the ebony sky,
The moon enormous, covered in blood . . .
In the chamber, scarcely lit
I listen trembling to a sob.

The moon enormous covered in blood,
While on the dull and pallid snow . . .
I listen trembling to a sob
Pale, a woman looks at me.

While on the dull and pallid snow
Spreads the shadow of great dark woods . . .
Pale, a woman looks at me,
Her eyes are heavy with despair.

Spreads the shadow of great dark woods
In the still and ghastly night . . .
Her eyes are heavy with despair
She takes the cup and empties it . . .

In the still and ghastly night
A long howl swells up suddenly
She takes the cup and empties it
"Good-bye," she says slowly . . .

A long howl swells up suddenly:
A wounded wolf crawls along and falls . . .
"Good-bye," she says slowly:
"I drink to that sweet nest, the tomb!"

A wounded wolf crawls along and falls,
He's dying, hollow eyes aglow . . .
"I drink to that sweet nest, the tomb!
Not a single dream, o death, in your night"

He's dying, hollow eye aglow,
His last cry can be barely heard . . .
"Not a single breath, o death, in your night,
Not a single star in the ebony sky . . .")

In this poem, which clearly owes so much to poets such as Baudelaire and Verlaine, the use of italics divides the poem into two simultaneous narratives, one (unitalicized) describing an external landscape, the other (italicized) describing an interior in both senses of the word: a literal indoor setting "dans la chambre" ("in the chamber") but also, on a more metaphorical plane, the inner landscape of a human subject. The poem uses a rigorous pattern of repetitions to build dramatic effect. Each four-line verse of the poem is subdivided into two couplets, and the last line of each couplet becomes the first line of the couplet in the next verse, so that the second and fourth lines of the first verse (lines 2 and 4) become the first and third lines of the second verse (lines 5 and 7). The only exception to this is the variation in line 28. When it is repeated (as line 31), the word "souffle" ("breath") is substituted for "rêve" ("dream"). The major conceit of the poem is made clear in the last line (32) which, since it is the same as the first line, suggests not only a certain circularity but that, in true symbolist fashion, the exterior landscape has become the inner one. The evocation of landscape is seen to become the way of figuring inner human subjectivity.

But such success as this poem enjoys is all too rare in Dorian's work. Writing in 1928, the critic Henriette Charasson noted that "Ses vers, surtout parnassiens ennuient aujourd'hui" ("her verses, mostly parnassian, are tiresome today").[11] Though harsh, this assessment is correct in pointing out that Dorian's work is mostly derivative and has not succeeded in finding much of an audience today. But I shall return later to the question of whether her work is "boring" (one possible translation of "ennuient" in the quote above) and merely ask the reader to register here Charasson's choice of words.

The mediocrity of Dorian's work doesn't lend itself well to the case for her recovery today, though arguably she merits the kind of attention given to someone like Sylvia Beach for her prescient support of innovative literary ventures. But at this point it is necessary to complicate what so far has been a standard recovery narrative by closer examination of another aspect of Dorian's literary career. This examination is also intended to complicate the distinction between marginality and centrality.

In addition to writing and publishing her own work and underwriting theatrical performances, Dorian founded and edited a short-lived review, *La Revue d'Aujourd'hui*. This ephemeral yet curiously interesting journal which runs to only fifteen issues appeared between January and September 1890. It was thus an early rival to reviews such as *Le Mercure de France*, though it did not claim to be only a literary review, but a forum for all sorts of popular issues of the day. In addition to Dorian herself, who appeared on the masthead of the first issue under the rubric "Direction," the editorial staff included Rodolphe Darzens as "rédacteur en chef" ("editor in chief"). The son of a French businessman, Darzens was born in Moscow in 1865 and raised in Russia before returning to France, where he collaborated on a number of literary publications. The friend and disciple of Villiers de l'Isle-Adam, Darzens is remembered as an early editor of Rimbaud, whose unpublished poems he gathered together for an ill-fated edition in 1891.[12] From May 15 on, Léo Trézenik was added as "secrétaire de la rédaction" ("editorial secretary").

From the tone and content of some of the articles, one might conclude that *La Revue d'Aujourd'hui* has been consigned to the trash heap of history for good reason. Take, for example, the gossip section "jour par jour" ("day by day") of the second issue of the journal which appeared on 15 February 1890. Here, among other tidbits, the reader learns that on 3 February the public was treated to a performance of *Les Vieux Maris* by Antony Mars; that on 4 February J-H. Rosny's *Termite* was published; that on 5 February there was a performance of *Dimitri* at the Opéra-Comique (128). And so it continues.

But the section also contains an account of a duel which took place on 2 February between Camille Dreyfus, a journalist and politician, and the marquis de Morès.[13] No one would pay much attention to such *faits divers* today were it not that the marquis de Morès (1858–96) is now widely considered a key figure in the development of fascism in France. Recently resurrected by, for example, Zeev Sternhell,[14] who calls him the "organisateur des premières troupes de choc du socialisme national" ("the organizer of the first shock troops of national socialism"); though the marquis's troops wore flamboyant purple cowboy shirts and sombreros rather than the sinister black or brown shirts later associated with fascist sartorial discipline, the full importance of the marquis is only slowly emerging. Long known to Americans as an early ranching pioneer in the Dakotas, the marquis had a second, more sinister career as a political agitator. Among other things the marquis developed what he called the "doctrine du faisceau," the idea that anti-Semitism was the glue that would unite (bundle together, as in a "faisceau") the different sociopolitical classes to combat liberal democracy and bourgeois society in the name of nationalism.[15] The doctrine was published in 1894, which gives the marquis the rather dubious honor of founding what Alice Kaplan describes as the first "'faisceau' bound by racism."[16] An aristocrat himself, he rallied racist leagues referred to as "Amis" ("Friends") in the working-class suburbs of La Villette. In supplying the background to the 1890 duel, the author of "jour par jour" provides some information about the marquis, but it can also be supplemented from other sources: this "adventurer in four worlds" (as he is called in Gordon Wright's breathless boy's own story) was the son of the Italian Duke of Vallombrosa and educated at Saint-Cyr, one year behind Philippe (the future *maréchal*) Pétain. He resigned his commission in 1881, married Medora Hoffman, the daughter of a New York banker, and emigrated to New York in 1882. In 1883, he set off to try his hand as a cattle rancher in what was then the Dakota Territory (now North Dakota). At first things went well, and the marquis was poised to become "a tycoon of epic proportions—a frontier equivalent of the Fords, Rockefellers, and Armours."[17] He founded the town of Medora, built a chateau, and received guests such as Theodore Roosevelt (in 1884). As the author of "jour par jour" puts it: "Il réussit d'abord, malgré la résistance des cowboys indigènes qu'il dut combattre au péril de sa vie" ("he succeeded at first, despite the resistance of the indigenous cowboys with whom he had to fight at the risk of his life").[18] Yet after only a few years, he failed in his attempts to establish a meat-packing business in the Dakotas, one of a string of failures he would attribute to the powerful vested interests of Jews. After this, the marquis left America to dabble in railroads in Tonkin before returning to France where, according to "jour par jour," a promising political career awaited him.[19] It is true that he was more successful as a politician, but history is the worse for his success. Fortunately his career in politics was short-lived: his ranching experience may have given him some credence with the workers of La Villette, where the Paris *abattoirs* were located, but it did not stop him from being killed by Tuaregs on an expedition to the Sahara in 1896.

Given the support for the marquis and the anti-Semitic version of his adventures in *La Revue d'Aujourd'hui*, the identity of the author of the gossip section becomes a matter of interest and speculation. The section is signed "une vigie," but this self-styled "lookout"—whose name already announces the vigilante-style violence that would come to characterize elements of fascist militia—may well have been Tola Dorian herself.

The implications of the *faits divers* section of *La Revue d'Aujourd'hui* become even more troubling when juxtaposed with the "lead" article in that issue of the review, an article by Paul Adam entitled "L'Or des juifs" ("Jews' Gold"). This five-page polemic counters the argument that Jews excelled in banking because other professions were closed to them by arguing that "l'adoration et la conquête de l'or demeurèrent toujours le but religieux et sanctifié de la vie d'Israël" ("The worship and conquest of gold was always the religious and holy goal of the life of Israel").[20] Suspecting this truth, continues Adam, "la multitude a versé sa haine sur les gens dont les spéculations avilissent le travail" ("the multitude has poured its hatred upon people whose speculations demean labor") and "le peuple ne se trompe jamais dans cette juste haine" ("the people are never mistaken in this just hatred").[21] This invective which looks so extremist today (I hope) with its violent and unsubstantiated accusations nevertheless exemplifies a certain strand of fin-de-siècle thought, a strain of intellectual history which, it has been argued, starts as left-wing socialism but ends up as right-wing fascism. Adam's article illustrates a certain kind of logic which although resting on false assumptions appeared all too rational in its time: since the Jews had all the money, it was supposed, any program to redistribute wealth such as the socialist one would naturally target this group.

The anti-Semitism of Dorian's putative contributions is matched in other areas of her work. In *Domitien*, for example, the vestal virgin who becomes Domitien's wife and whose refusal to play politics ends up causing everyone's downfall is Cornelia, identified as a Jew. The plot of another play, *Le Précurseur*, while set in the Scottish highlands of James I, focuses on preserving the purity of some races over the "juif maudit" and the "marchands et les usuriers bouffis" ("merchants and bloated usurers") (212). The poem examined earlier ("Pas une étoile au ciel d'ébène") was first published in *Poèmes lyriques* by Marpon and Flammarion, who also published Edouard Drumont's virulently anti-Semitic works. As Willa Silverman has recently argued, such choices may be read as an indication of the publishers' political sympathies, in which case their support of Dorian may also carry political implications.[22]

What is troubling about this trend is that while *La Revue d'Aujourd'hui* may seem peripheral, ex-centric, today, it may not have seemed so to its contemporaries, to whom it appeared to be merely popular journalism. In addition to well-known but perhaps truly marginal figures such as Paul Bonnetain, Joseph Péladan, George D'Esparbès, and Pierre Louys, the review also boasted among its contributors a virtual "who's who" of late-nineteenth-century literature: Paul Adam, Paul Verlaine, Arthur Rimbaud, Stéphane Mallarmé, Villiers de l'Isle-Adam, Willy, Jules Renard, Maurice Barrès. The point is that while in some senses *La Revue d'Aujourd'hui* may be considered an example of "peripheral publishing," it was in a number of ways quite representative of its time and very much a part of the mainstream. The content of the journal did not attract any special attention; it was not denounced; collaborators did not withdraw their support. When the review folded, Dorian had no trouble finding alternative outlets for her work in other "respectable" journals such as the *Mercure de France* (one poem in May 1891; two poems in June 1892; a short story in May 1893; and so on) which also published her poetry (*Vespérales*, 1894). Nor have the other contributors to the journal been reevaluated retrospectively in light of their decision to publish in journals with suspect political affiliations in the way that Paul de Man's journalism, for example, has been scrutinized.

The case of *La Revue d'Aujourd'hui* thus illustrates a kind of falsely constructed marginality. We retrospectively construct it as peripheral, I think, because we need now to account for how we could have failed to notice the danger posed by such thinking in the past. We want some explanation of how we could have missed such things and how we could have lost sight of them in the present.

So far, though, this essay has focused on what we already know: what appears to be marginal is always already implicated in the construction of what is perceived as central. So my conclusion takes the reader back to the figure of Tola Dorian.

This essay was originally delivered as a conference paper. The evening before the conference, I was telling someone about the subject of my presentation. When I said it was about Tola Dorian, my interlocutor misheard me and thought I said it was totally boring. As with all parapraxes, the royal road of the unconscious directs us to what we really need to know. And I think what we really need to know is this: Is Tola Dorian totally boring? In some ways, perhaps, yes; but if, as Hannah Arendt has suggested, the face of evil always appears banal, it is precisely because she appears to be merely boring that it is dangerous not to pay attention to the Tola Dorians of history.

The case of Tola Dorian illustrates both the necessity for and the complications of recovery. It is hard to argue that such a person must be celebrated, yet the gesture of placing her always on the periphery as "the friend of Victor Hugo" or "the admirer of Villiers de l'Isle-Adam," which constructs her as a presence, but only a marginal one, seems a vain attempt at a kind of inoculation, submitting voluntarily to a small dose of a thing that is bad for you in the hope that this limited exposure will stave off a greater infection.

But if those who forget the past are doomed to repeat the past, we would do well to look beyond the periphery and remember Dorian's contributions to the mainstream popular press. Celebrating her is inappropriate because her work does at times seem boring, but to dismiss her because she was boring is to underestimate the implications of the mask of banality.

Notes

1. Alan Raitt and Pierre-Georges Castex, eds., *Œuvres complètes*, by Villiers de l'Isle-Adam, 2 vols. (Paris: Gallimard 1986), 1440.

2. Ibid., 1539.
3. Ibid., 1539; Jacques Robichez, *Le Symbolisme au théâtre: Lugné-Poe et les débuts de l'Œuvre* (Paris: L'Arche, 1957), 160.
4. Robichez, *Le Symbolisme,* 161, n. 23.
5. Ibid., 165–66. See also Octave Mirbeau's article "Pelléas et Mélisande" originally published in *L'Echo* (9 May 1893) and reprinted in *Gens de théâtre,* 105–9.
6. Robichez, *Le Symbolisme,* 160.
7. Raitt and Castex, *Œuvres complètes,* 1539.
8. *Mineur et soldat; drame en un tableau* (coauthored with J. Malafäyde) was performed at the Théâtre Libre, 13–16 March 1896.
9. In addition to the works compiled in the bibliography under the Dorian, Tola entry, and which are listed in library holdings today, the 1908 reprint of *Ames slaves* lists the following works: *Félicie Ariescalgheira* (Ollendorf); *L'Ensorceleuse* (Richard); *Virginité fin de siècle* (Mercure de France); *Mater* (Stock).
10. Tola Dorian, *Roses Remontantes* (Paris: P. Ollendorff, 1897), 57–60. An earlier version of this poem, without the use of italics, appeared in *Poèmes lyriques* (Paris: C. Marpon et E. Flammarion, 1888).
11. Quoted in Clarissa Burnham Cooper, *Woman Poets of the Twentieth Century in France: A Critical Bibliography* (New York: King's Crown Press, 1943), 134.
12. See the article by Jean-Jacques Lefrère in the "Dictionnaire des noms propres" in *Au Balcon, 1871–1914,* 1:6 (June 1995), 177–78.
13. Camille Dreyfus was, apparently, no relation to the more famous captain Dreyfus, but the life of the marquis de Morès did touch on that of the captain and his family at several points, according to Michael Burns.
14. See Zeev Sternhell, *La Droite révolutionnaire, 1885–1914: Les Origines françaises du fascisme* (Paris: Seuil, 1978), 178, 180–84, and 197–220.
15. Ibid., 180.
16. Alice Yaeger Kaplan, *Reproductions of Banality: Fascism, Literature, and French Intellectual Life* (Minneapolis: University of Minnesota Press, 1986), xxviii. See le Marquis de Morès, *Le Secret des Changes* (Marseille: Imprimerie marseillaise, 1894).
17. Gordon Wright, "Marquis de Morès, Adventurer in Four Worlds," in *Notable or Notorious? A Gallery of Parisians* (Cambridge: Harvard University Press, 1991), 77.
18. "Jour par jour," *La Revue d'Aujourd'hui* (Geneva: Slatkine Reprints, 1971), 127.
19. Ibid., 128.
20. Paul Adam, "L'Or des juifs," *La Revue d'Aujourd'hui* (Geneva: Slatkine Reprints, 1971), 65
21. Ibid., 67
22. "Gyp and Flammarion: A Marriage of Love or Convenience?" Paper delivered at Twenty-Third Annual Nineteenth-Century French Studies Colloquium, October 1997. My thanks, as always, for their help in the writing of this article go to Pamela Matthews, Mary Ann O'Farrell, and Margaret Waller, as well as to Deborah Harter for her inspiring misprision.

Asia in Pierre Leroux's Doctrine of Humanity

BRUNO VIARD

PIERRE LEROUX CAN ONLY PASS FOR A RETROGRADE THINKER in the wake of the antihumanism popular in France in the late 1960s;[1] indeed, the word *humanity* is one of the key words of the philosophy he liked to call the "doctrine of humanity." In his principal work, published in 1840 and entitled *De l'humanité*, we read: "Nul homme n'existe indépendamment de l'humanité, et néanmoins l'humanité n'est pas un être véritable; l'humanité, c'est l'homme, c'est à dire les hommes, c'est à dire des êtres particuliers et individuels"[2] (290) ("No man exists independent from humanity, and nevertheless humanity is not a real entity; humanity is mankind, that is to say human beings, that is to say distinctive and individual beings"). According to Leroux, individual human beings cannot be considered as separate from the human species that produces them and continues to nourish them for their entire lives, materially, emotionally, and intellectually. For no whole can be reified to the detriment of its parts as was the case for Marx or Durkheim: humanity is nothing without the individuals that compose it. The doctrine of humanity thus dismisses in advance two major trends in sociology that have come about since it was founded, methodical individualism and holism, without favoring one or the other. More precisely, as early as 1831, Leroux warned vigorously against the dangers of capitalist individualism and totalitarian socialism. His prophetic clear-sightedness is the main reason why I would like to reconsider the unrecognized inventor of what could today be labeled with the oxymoron *free-market socialism*, a doctrine currently repressed in a blind spot, too socialist under Napoleon III and too liberal under Lenin. This aspect of the problem will not concern me here.

The question of East/West relations needs to be perceived at the heart of the liberal and republican socialism that Leroux defended as a writer, as elected representative of the people in 1848, and as creator and editor of five newspapers and journals as well as an encyclopedia.

First of all, I must clear up a misunderstanding that Leroux's use of the word *East* might cause: Asia is what is in question. Leroux had no time for the picturesque Turkish-Arabic orientalism made fashionable by Hugo. When he wrote "Aux artistes" at the end of 1831, Leroux had just broken with Enfantin, the Saint-Simonian family, and "art engagé" ("engaged art") (before the term existed). He simultaneously rejected the Saint-Simonians' and republicans' "art with a purpose" and art for art's sake: "Je ne demanderai pas," he writes, "si on peut tirer directement d'un ouvrage une conclusion morale: mais j'écouterai l'impression qu'il fera sur ma vie. L'art, c'est la vie qui s'adresse à la vie" (115) ("I will never ask whether one can draw a moral conclusion directly from a work: but I will pay attention to the impression it makes on my life. Art is life addressing itself to life"). After 1830, art for the sake of art, precisely, did not address itself to life in dark years marked by disenchantment, individualism, and all-powerful money. What good was "la superstition de l'Arabe qui croit voir à travers la vapeur de sable que soulève le simoun, l'ombre de Buonaberdi debout sur le sommet d'une pyramide?" ("the superstition of the Arab who thinks he sees, through the screen of sand raised by the Simoom, the shadow of Buonaberdi standing on the summit of a pyramid"). Busy with the Peris, the Houris and the Djinns, Hugo "ne sait rien sur le berceau et la tombe" ("knows nothing about the cradle and the tomb").

> Ceux qui font de l'art uniquement pour faire de l'art sont comme des étrangers qui, venus on ne sait d'où, feraient entendre des instruments bizarres au milieu d'un peuple étonné, ou qui chanteraient dans une langue inconnue à des funerailles. Leurs chants ont beau être délicieux à mon oreille, le fond, le fond éternel de mon cœur est le doute et la tristesse. (117)

> (Those who create art only to create art would be like foreigners who, coming from who knows where, play strange instruments in the midst of a bewildered people, or who sing in an unknown language at a funeral. Even if their melodies delight my ear, the depths, the eternal depths of my heart are filled with doubt and sadness.)

Even so, and even if he rarely addressed the subject of Islam, Leroux defended the Koran against the simultaneous attacks of

Voltaire and the Church; building on the writings of his friend Alexandre Bertrand concerning ecstasy, he showed that, like Joan of Arc, Mohammed was "un dévot, un fanatique, un visionnaire, non pas un imposteur" ("a devout person, a fanatic, a visionary, but not an impostor").

> Le Coran est un hymne perpétuel sur l'unité et la puissance de dieu. [. . .] La réforme musulmane ne fut pas le fruit d'un mensonge, elle naquit et se propagea comme toutes les réformes religieuses, par les idées, en subjugant les cœurs et les intelligences, et non pas par une violence purement matérielle, par une violence purement physique. (77)

> (The Koran is a perpetual hymn on the unity and power of God. . . . The Muslim reform was not the result of a lie, it was born and propagated, like all religious reforms, from ideas, subjugating hearts and minds, and not by a purely material violence, by a purely physical violence.)

For obvious reasons of geographical distance, Europeans did not visit India and China as much as Egypt and Jerusalem, and their fascination with the former was smaller. However, Europe's cultural and religious references, spatial and temporal, were much more affected[3] by the discovery of Asia. As Roger-Pol Droit says, "la grande muraille d'Occident se fissura" ("the great wall of the West cracked") and "le roman familial de la pensée était à repenser" ("the family romance of philosophy needed to be rethought"). It is important to note[4] significant coincidences between political events (the Revolution and the Empire) and the discovery of Asia. A few reminders:

- -1771: Anquetil-Duperron's translation of the Avesta (the Zoroastrians' sacred book)
- -1785: the foundation in Calcutta of the Royal Asian Society of Bengal; Charles Wilkins's translation of the Bhagavad Gîta
- -1787: Charles Wilkins's translation of the Hitoupadesa
- -1793: Sylvestre de Sacy's key to the Pehlevi inscriptions (Iranian)
- -1795: foundation of the School of Oriental Languages in Paris, presided by Sylvestre de Sacy
- -1802: Anquetil-Duperron's translation of the Upanishads
- -1805: Colebrooke's important article on the Vedas (which would be translated by Rosen in 1830)

-1814: Abel Rémusat's appointment as first professor of Chinese and Tartar at the Collège de France.

It is difficult to pinpoint the origin of Leroux's interest in Asia. When he founded *Le Globe* at age twenty-seven, it was he who suggested this title to his colleague Paul-François Dubois. Furthermore, the avowal of faith which appeared at the beginning of the first issue announced that, while "current" literary criticism was characterized by parisianism and futility, *Le Globe* sought the universal and the useful. Leroux's first articles are reviews of books devoted to Asia: Turkey, India, Ceylon, Burma, China, but these books are disparaging in general and underline the backwardness and despotism of these countries. Leroux may have been influenced by Victor Cousin, the philosophic inspiration of *Le Globe* who (later, he would change) stated in his fifth and sixth university lectures of 1828:

> Nous sommes contraints de plier le genou devant la philosophie orientale et de voir dans ce berceau de la race humaine la terre natale de la plus haute philosophie. [. . .] On peut dire à la lettre que l'histoire de la philosophie de l'Inde est un abrégé de l'histoire entière de la philosophie.

> (We are forced to bow before Eastern philosophy and to see in this cradle of civilization the birthplace of the highest philosophy. . . . We can literally say that the history of Indian philosophy is an abridged version of the entire history of philosophy.)[5]

In Leroux's first noteworthy article on Asia, from 1826, "Du progrès de nos connaissances sur l'Orient," he develops a promising theme.[6] Dissipating the obscurity which prevents us from perceiving the annals of the Orient is supposed to lead to effects as important as those of the humanists during the fifteenth and sixteenth centuries: the founding of a new social order. In addition, Leroux did not accept the preconceived notion of "mollesse asiatique" ("Asiatic indolence") ascribed "à la race et au climat" ("to race and climate"). All this is empty of meaning, he says; if there is indeed a contrast between the stationary aspect of Asian civilization and the progressive character of Europe, it results from the caste system, a weight from which Europe had rid itself much earlier. Leroux concludes the article by predicting Asia's awakening.

A Universal Ethics

"Center everywhere, circumference nowhere"; the quotation from Pascal that Leroux uses to conclude his 1825 article, "De l'union européenne," could also apply to West/East relations. This is apparent in two texts which appeared in April, May, and June 1832, in the *Revue encyclopédique*. The first, entitled "De l'influence philosophique des études orientales," begins by recognizing the work of William Jones and the Academy of Calcutta: Leroux asserts "c'est l'Homère apporté en Italie à la prise de Constantinople" (119) ("it is like Homer brought to Italy at the fall of Constantinople"). One of the most important stakes in the cultural discovery of Asia is of course the new relationship that threatens to prevail between the traditional centers (Athens and Jerusalem) and their immense Chinese and Indian periphery. "La Grèce, mais ce n'était que le bord de l'Orient!" (121) ("Greece was only the edge of the Orient!") cries Leroux. The Greeks were naïve to have believed themselves aboriginal: "[d]écoupant leur mythologie du fond religieux de l'Orient" ("removing their mythology from the religious background of the Orient"), they made for themselves "un monde sans racines" (122) ("a world without roots"). They forgot that their word stems, their conjugations and declensions are the same as those of the gymnosophists of India, and that the same holds true for their art and their mythology.

The same could be said of Jerusalem, where again, the branch had been taken for the tree. Biblical societies were right to multiply translations of the Bible in all idioms and dialects: "C'est apporter son tribut à la grande bibliothèque de l'humanité où tout livre important sera traduit en toute langue" ("It is paying one's tribute to the immense library of humanity where every significant work will be translated in every language"). "Mais," Leroux adds, "il y a autre chose à faire de beaucoup plus utile pour le progrès général de l'humanité: c'est de faire connaître aux sectateurs mêmes de la Bible toutes les autres Bibles de l'Orient" (121) ("But, there is something even more useful to do for the general progress of humanity: to make the Bible's followers familiar with the other Bibles of the East"). "Nous voulons un panthéon plus vaste que le panthéon juif, un panthéon qui réponde à ce mot HUMANITÉ" (124) ("We want a pantheon larger than the Jewish pantheon, a pantheon that corresponds to the word HUMANITY").

The second article, "Des rapports de la doctrine de Confucius avec la doctrine de Jésus" ("On the connections between the doctrine of Confucius and the doctrine of Jesus"), proposes to demonstrate, starting from a word-for-word comparison between the Gospel and the Ta-Hio of Confucius translated by Guillaume Pauthier, that in bringing the ethics of the Gospel to the Chinese, the Jesuits only brought "ce qu'ils avaient déjà" ("what they already had"). Confucius was not the atheist that he had been lauded (or reproached, according to opinion) for being. The Tao, universal reason, was immanent to the world and humanity, and God was not yet an object of love separated from the world. It was to Confucius' credit not to have indulged in "ce dualisme qui est sensible dans l'Évangile de Jésus" ("the dualism evident in the Gospel of Jesus"). What Leroux preferred in the Gospels, and in particular in the Sermon on the Mount, was their ethics. Regarding ethics, five hundred years earlier Confucius had had the same intuition as Jesus. Do not do to others what you would not have done to you; do unto others what you would have them do unto you, suggested Tseng-Tzu, the disciple of Confucius who elsewhere defined a nation as brothers and sisters of different ages. Conclusion:

> A mesure que les figures orientales se dévoileront, celle de Jésus, sans perdre de son doux éclat et de sa rayonnante majesté, deviendra plus humaine. [. . .] Ainsi le point de vue de l'humanité changea quand l'astronomie eut appris aux hommes [. . .] que les étoiles dont les premiers hommes, pendant des siècles, faisaient le cortège du soleil et les signes de sa démesure, étaient aussi des soleils. (127–28)

> (As eastern figures unveil themselves, that of Jesus, without losing any of its soft radiance and majestic splendor, will become more human. . . . Thus humanity's point of view changed when astronomy had taught mankind . . . that the stars which humans, for centuries, had considered as part of the sun's celestial following and the symbols of its excess, were also suns.)

In a similar work, Leroux compared the Gospels to the Indian Hitoupadesa attributed to Pilpaï. In the adventures of the mouse Hiraniaka, the crow Laghou-Patanaka, and the tortoise Manthara, one finds the same surrender to creation, the same distancing from wealth, the same virtues of receptiveness to others as in the Sermon on the Mount. Leroux translated into French the text which Charles Wilkins had himself translated from Sanskrit:

> Vous perdez la vertu pour atteindre la richesse, dit la tortue, Manthara, et la richesse, quelque grande qu'elle soit, n'est jamais qu'une pauvreté. Ne vaut-il pas mieux s'éloigner d'un tas de boue que de se salir en s'approchant. Voyez les oiseaux de l'air: manquent-ils de nourriture? Voyez si l'herbe manque aux animaux des champs et si les poissons ne trouvent pas dans l'eau ce qu'il leur faut pour vivre. Ainsi partout Dieu a mis l'abondance. Quiconque amasse des richesses commence à craindre le magistrat, l'eau, le feu, les voleurs, et même ses proches, comme tout être enchaîné à la nécessité de vivre craint la mort. (482–83)

> (You lose virtue to obtain wealth, says the tortoise Manthara, and wealth, however great, is never more than poverty. Wouldn't it be better to keep away from mud than to get dirty by coming too close to it? Do the birds of the air lack food? See whether the animals of the fields lack grass or whether fish do not find in the water what they need to live. Thus everywhere God has placed abundance. Whoever gathers wealth begins to fear the judge, water, fire, thieves, and even his relatives, as every being chained to the necessity of life fears death.)

Jesus underwent Indian influence just like the Greek cynics;[7] his accomplishment is to have adapted this ethics to the West.

A Universal Metaphysics

Leroux's focus on the disappearance of the center/periphery antithesis has not only to do with moral questions; beyond the superficial diversity of dogmas and cults, it has also to do with discovering the unity of universal theology on an ontological level. Leroux's metaphysics concerns what he calls the trinity: a life at once triple and singular; a life is made up of interwoven sensation, feeling, and knowledge at the heart of a universal Being and at the heart of humanity with its singular individuals. All religions knew either through their own intuition or through communication with each other of the triplicity and the uniqueness of an immanent God. Leroux was not far from what in 1945 Karl Jaspers would call, referring to the sixth century B.C., *the golden century of the human spirit*. It is not possible to reproduce here Leroux's lengthy and learned demonstrations. I will say just a word about what he calls "hiéroglyphes verbaux" ("verbal hieroglyphics"): the name Jehovah without its consonants is IOA, identical to the Indians' sacred monosyllable AUM and the

Chinese trigrammatical I-Hi-Wei, according to Abel Rémusat's *Mémoire sur Lao-Tseu* (417); the AUM is found in the Christian AMEN (485–86). Western religion and philosophy not only do not possess a monopoly, but were in fact preceded and influenced by India and China. Moses owed a debt to Egypt, and the Essenians and Pharisees had learned of the soul's immortality in Persia during the captivity, Persia in turn having received its doctrines from India. Moses' Genesis is only "an abridged copy" of Manou's Genesis. It is thus an "affreuse impiété" ("terrible impiety") to restrict tradition to the Judeo-Christian line. "C'est comme si d'un bras de rivière, vous retranchiez et sa source et tous les affluents qui l'ont enrichi" (196) ("It is as if from the branch of a river, you were to cut away its source and all the tributaries that fed it"). The words *impiety* and *heresy* penned by Leroux, through an ironic and significant reversal of meaning, serve not to exclude, but to exclude the exclusion from humanity's (and not a popular sect's) point of view. Every manifestation of life is triple and one: the incarnations or "anthropomorphisms" that each religion has created under the names of Minerva in Greece, Brahma, Vishnu, Rama, Khrishna or Buddha in India, Lao-Tzu in China, Hermes or Thoth in Egypt, Jesus Christ for the Christians (see the article "Christianisme" in the *Encyclopédie nouvelle*) are of little consequence. It remains to "disanthropomorphize" Christianity (like other religions that have adopted a form of idolatry). "Vous êtes chrétiens, je suis humanitaire! Entre nous, il n'y a pourtant qu'un voile, un voile qui doit tomber, qui tombera, l'anthropomorphisme du verbe" (572) ("You are Christians, I am a humanitarian! Between us, there is only a veil, a veil that must fall, that will fall, the anthropomorphism of the word").

At the same time that he tried to find the tertiary vision of life in all civilizations and religions, Leroux identified another current which to him seemed fatalistic, the dualist current which anathematizes life in this world. This current also seemed to have an Eastern origin. Christian asceticism was not aware of propagating "un flot qui venait de plus loin" ("a flood which came from afar") through the mediation of the Essenians, Therapeutists, Pythagoreans, Cynics, Stoics, and Epicureans. "Les ascètes de notre Occident ne sont rien, ni pour le nombre, ni pour les pratiques, auprès des sannyasis de l'Inde" (189) ("The ascetics of our western world are nothing, either in number or in practice, compared to the Sannyasis of India"). Indian ascetics influenced Zoroastrianism which, in its turn, blended with Christianity to produce Manichaeism, which is prevalent in the theology of the Fall and original sin according to Saint Augustine: the world, life on Earth, the body, sex, were sin! A "mélange adultère" ("adulterated mixture") was produced when the doctrine of Moses and Jesus was contaminated by that of Zoroaster and Manes. It was the accomplishment of Saint Augustine to have "grafted" one doctrine onto the other.

The Question of Castes, a Significant Historic Discriminator

Two extreme tendencies were manifested in Germany.[8] Hegel on the one hand,[9] who sought to make Greece the mother of all philosophy and all humanity, and saw only stupefaction and superstition in India. For him, the principle of castes had irrevocably amputated Indian thought: liberty and intelligibility were missing; dreams and immobility prevailed. On the other hand, the German Romantics' lively fascination for India aimed at ousting the Jewish component of the Western tradition.[10] Following Herder, in 1803, Friedrich Schlegel wrote: "En Inde se trouve la source de toutes les langues, de toutes les pensées, et de toute l'histoire de l'esprit humain; tout sans exception est originaire de l'Inde" ("In India is found the source of all languages, of all ideas, and of the entire history of the human spirit: all without exception originated in India").[11] "Dans Mahâbhârata et le Ramâyâna, [Schlegel] voyait un Moyen Age aux formes d'éléphant" Heine ironically commented ("In the Mahâbhârata and the Ramâyâna, Schlegel saw the Middle Ages in the shape of an elephant").[12]

Leroux does not seem to have succumbed either to Western-centrism or to ingratitude or resentment against Greek or Hebrew origins. In this way, the text cited earlier which asked that justice be done to all of humanity's Bibles, shows how understandable it was that the Bible of Moses and Jesus was thought to have fallen from the sky because it spoke to man of "the human race" and not, as did Greek or Roman literature, of the passions of several thousand or several million men under this archon or Consul (122). Elsewhere ("De la recherche des biens matériels," 1846), he writes:

> S'il n'y avait qu'une seule palme à décerner, cette palme unique serait peut-être acquise à la nation qui a tiré du sein de l'Orient et du

fond des tabernacles les plus précieuses des vérités: l'unité de Dieu et l'unité de l'espèce humaine. (360)

(If there were only one laurel wreath to award, this sole wreath would perhaps be awarded to the nation that had torn from the heart of the Orient and from the depths of the tabernacles the two most precious truths: the unity of God and the unity of the human race.)

An allusion to the myth of Adam, who, far from being the accepted first human being, represents Universal Man, as individual as well as species (297). In another article, Leroux speaks of the "admirable legislation" (274) of Moses who, via the Sabbath, Passover, and the Jubilee, was able to reunite his people and block their tendency towards inequality and individualism. There are no castes in Mosaic legislation, and it is from "ce géant qu'on nomme Moïse" ("that giant named Moses") that Voltaire learned that Humanity exists. Moses too passed on the dogma of the unity of the human species, learned in the temples of Memphis and Thebes (295).

To show the consideration Leroux gave to Jesus would take an entire volume. I will merely make several observations. Once again, the emphasis placed on the unity of humanity is, Leroux claims, Jesus' principal merit and the mark of his superiority over Moses. For Leroux sees a contradiction in Passover, at once the symbol of the Jews' communion amongst themselves as well as the symbol of their separation from other peoples.

Les Juifs ont été la nation qui a pu à la fois émettre ce grand précepte de sociabilité: *Tu aimeras ton prochain comme toi-même,* et avoir en abomination tous les autre peuples. La fraternité des Juifs entre eux et leur distinction profonde des autres peuples, voilà les deux caractères de la législation de Moïse, et ils sont partout empreints dans la Bible. (272)

(The Jews were the nation that could announce this grand precept of sociability: *Thou shalt love thy neighbor as thyself,* while at the same time considering all the other nations abominable. The fraternity of Jews amongst themselves and their profound distinction from other peoples, are the two characteristics of Moses' legislation, and are found throughout the Bible.)

This is why Leroux sees progress in Jesus, about whom Saint Paul said: "In him, there is neither Jew nor Greek; neither slave, nor free person: neither man nor woman" (270). Neither West, nor East, one is tempted to add. What was the Eucharist for Leroux? A shared meal where women, slaves, and foreigners were all admitted, a huge innovation in the ancient world! By comparison to Christian feasts, the banquets of Plato and Aristotle were similar to our officers' mess or our gentlemen's clubs. And so Jesus' work could be compared to Buddha's: Buddha was the destroyer of castes and Jesus was "le Bouddha de l'Occident" (269) ("the Buddha of the West").

A brief parentheses here with regard to Buddha. Leroux hardly said more about this figure than what I have just mentioned. This is regrettable but can be easily explained: because of its quasi-disappearance in the Indian subcontinent, Buddhism was not known in Europe until fifty years after Hinduism, that is to say starting in the 1830s, thanks to the work of Abel Rémusat and Eugène Burnouf (1844: *Introduction à l'histoire du buddhisme* [sic] *indien*). Buddhism, because it fragmented the individual, was considered nihilist and skeptic and contributed largely to the end of European fascination with India,[13] Schopenhauer's appraisal adding to the general discredit of this wisdom. And Leroux did not have a chance to update his knowledge of Buddhism, later scarcely adding[14] to his 1826 article from *Le Globe*:

> Bouddha modifia les préceptes contenus dans les Védas, proscrivit les sacrifices sanglants, rejeta la distinction des castes. [. . .] Il voulut détruire cette odieuse inégalité que les prêtres attribuaient à Brahma; il voulut que chaque homme vît dans un autre homme son image et n'eût pour lui ni horreur ni mépris. (76)

> (Buddha modified the precepts contained in the Vedas, proscribed bloody sacrifices, rejected the distinctions between castes. . . . He wanted to destroy the odious inequality that the priests attributed to Brahma; he wanted each human being to see in another his own image without horror or scorn.)

It is essential to consider the diachronic parameter in the East/West problem which has, until now, been viewed above all in a geographic and spatial perspective. Let me take, for example, Plato's critique in the *Republic*, considered by Leroux in the article "Equality" of his *Encyclopédie nouvelle* from 1838. He especially reproached Plato for maintaining the principle of dividing humanity according to castes within his republic, even as he abolished hereditary castes.

> *Vous êtes tous frères!* quelle belle parole, et bien digne du précurseur du Christ! Socrate est admirable quand il rend cet oracle de la fraternité de tous les hommes. Il s'approche, dis-je, de Jésus. Mais remarquez qu'à l'instant même, la lumière qui l'éclairait s'obscurcit, et qu'il retourne aux Védas, au monde oriental, quand il ajoute: "*Mais parmi vous, les uns sont d'or, les autres d'argent, les troisièmes d'airain.*" (265)[15]
>
> (*You are all brothers*! such splendid words, and very worthy of the precursor of Christ! Socrates is admirable when he proclaims the oracle of mankind's fraternity. He resembles Jesus, I say. But notice that at the same time, the light that illuminated him darkens, and he returns to the Vedas, to the Eastern world, when he adds: "*But among you, some are gold, others silver, and still others lead.*")

Plato marked a progression compared to the old caste system which still remained in the East. But he was also left behind by the Gospels which initiated a fraternity without limits.

I should mention here the Essenianism to which Leroux devoted special attention and lengthy consideration in the same article "Equality," a consideration which can be summarized as follows: "Le mosaïsme développé devient l'essénianisme, et l'essénianisme est immédiatement contigu au christianisme" (274) ("Developed Mosaïsm becomes Essenianism, and Essenianism is immediately contiguous to Christianity"). The Essenians, from accounts by Joseph and Philo of Alexandria, celebrated a fraternal meal where bread was shared, which extended Passover and announced the Eucharist. If it is true that "Jesus was the greatest and the last of the Essenians" (275), this hypothesis, which has been the object of an important debate since the discovery of the Dead Sea scrolls at Qourâm in 1947, provides an important link between the Mosaïc and Christian religions, fueling the idea of progress in religious matters, and should force the renunciation of "la fausse opinion sur la perfection absolue du mosaïsme" (276) ("the false opinion concerning the absolute perfection of Mosaïsm") while showing the debt of Essenianism to Mosaïsm. Essenianism is even more than a link, it is a crossroads: in addition to Mosaïsm it is indebted also to the Zoroastrianism of Persia and Hinduism, since the name *Essenian* includes *sannyasis*, the name given to Hindu ascetics (486).

The fraternity of the Gospel contains however an imperfection in that it skips over the question of equality; and what is fraternity without equality? It was Rousseau who added equality (for which the Montagnards, and later, the Socialists fought) to Greek liberty and Evangelical fraternity. The doctrine of humanity was thus endowed with *perfectibility,* as Turgot and Condorcet proclaimed.

Such progress is neither linear nor automatic, for despite Buddha's reform, the East was still immobile, even if Leroux announced that its footsteps would soon join humanity's. On the other hand, despite the havoc sparked by the Gospel and the disappearance of slavery, Europe witnessed the perpetuation of the old caste system under the Catholic Church. Leroux was an unrecognized precursor of Georges Dumézil when he wrote, for example:

> Ces trois ordres, ces trois classes, on les retrouve dans l'Inde sous le nom de *brahmanes*, de *chatrias* et de *soudras*; en Égypte sous le nom de *prêtres*, de *guerriers*, et de *laboureurs*. Moins évidents et plus mêlés, quoique encore très évidents dans les républiques grecques et à Rome, ces trois termes sont reproduits dans le Moyen Age sous les noms de *clergé*, *noblesse*, et de *tiers état*. (261)

> (These three orders, these three classes, are found in India under the name of *Brahmans,* Chatrias and Soudras; in Egypt under the name of *Priests*, *Warriors*, and *Laborers*. Less evident and more mixed, while still very obvious in the Greek republics and in Rome, these three terms are reproduced in the Middle Ages under the names of the *clergy*, *nobility,* and the third estate.)

The article "Castes" from the *Encyclopédie nouvelle* provides a suggestive explanation: the celibacy of priests (to which Leroux was opposed) had the beneficial effect of permitting social mobility between castes, in opposition to their total petrifaction, hence the West's greater dynamism.

The East/West relation for Leroux was thus dialectic, the principal discriminating factor being the question of castes. I have considered three perspectives successively: moral, metaphysical, and social.[16] With regard to the first two concerns, India and China made no concessions to the Gospels: on the contrary, they preceded and influenced it. However, on the social level, under the successive effects of Christianity and of Enlightenment, Europe, by abolishing castes, regained the initiative and underwent more rapid change.

Notes

1. Antihumanism is in fact the common denominator of the fashionable philosophers of the 1960s and 70s; they themselves emulate German philoso-

phers, as Luc Ferry and Alain Renaut demonstrate (*La pensée 68. Essai sur l'anti-humanisme théorique* [Paris: Gallimard, 1985]). Althusser and Bourdieu are disciples of Marx, Foucault is a disciple of Nietzsche, Lacan is a disciple of Freud, and Derrida is a disciple of Heidegger.

2. The two works by Leroux to which reference is made are those published by the author, *De l'égalité* preceded by *De l'individualisme et du socialisme* (Geneva: Slatkine [Collection Fleuron], 1996) and *A la source perdue du socialisme français* (Paris: Desclée de Brouwer, 1997). References in the text are to *A la source perdue du socialisme français.*

3. See Léon Schwab, *La Renaissance orientale* (Paris: Payot, 1953), and Jean Biès, *Littérature française et pensée hindoue des origines à 1950* (Paris: Klincksieck, 1974).

4. Roger-Pol Droit, *L'oubli de l'Inde. Une amnésie philosophique* (Paris: PUF, 1989).

5. *Cours de l'histoire de la philosophie* (Paris: Pichon et Didier, 1829), 155, cited by Roger-Pol Droit, *L'Ouslide l'Inde.*

6. We find this idea in an article by J-J Ampère in *La Revue des deux mondes* in 1832, and in 1842, penned by Edgar Quinet in *Le Génie des religions*, chap. 2 reproduced in *Philosophie, France, XIXe siècle* (Paris: Le livre de poche, 1994).

7. In his thorough study, *Le Bonheur-liberté. Bouddhisme profond et modernité*, PUF, 1982, Serge-Christophe Kolm demonstrates the Indian and Buddhist influence on Heraclitus and the pre-Socratics, on Pythagoras, orphism, cynicism, skepticism, stoicism, and epicurianism, also on the Essenians (Saint Jean the Baptist) and emphasizes the role of mediator played by the Persians then by the missionaries sent by the Emperor Açoka in the third century to the centers of hellenism.

8. René Girard, *L'Orient et la pensée romantique allemande,* 1963.

9. Hegel, *Leçons sur la philosophie de l'histoire.*

10. Maurice Olender, *Aryens et sémites au XIXe siècle,* Seuil-Gallimard, 1989.

11. Cited by R-P Droit, *L'Oubli del'Inde.*

12. Ibid., p. 145.

13. Concerning this question, see Roger-Pol Droit, *Le culte du néant. Les philosophes et le Bouddha,* 1997.

14. See the article "Brahmanisme et Bouddhisme" in *L'Encyclopédie nouvelle,* 1836.

15. Plato, *The Republic,* book 3.

16. These three questions are linked for Leroux: from the ontological triad sensation-feeling-knowledge ensues a fraternal morale (feeling) that balances the liberty of each individual (sensation) and the equality merited by everyone (knowledge). Concerning this point see our *Sources*, pp. 36 and 249. In the same way, the trifunctional system of castes comes from a misconstrued and antiquated interpretation of the metaphysical triad: knowledge prevails for the priests, affectivity for the warriors, and sensation for the slaves.

Apologia and Ambiguity: Text and Image in the *Journal de l'Expédition des Portes de Fer*

GRANT CRICHFIELD

THE *JOURNAL DE L'EXPÉDITION DES PORTES DE FER* IS AN ACCOUNT of a military campaign led in October 1839 by the heir to the French throne, the Duc d'Orléans,[1] through northeastern Algeria to pacify it for permanent occupation. The Duc d'Orléans commissioned Charles Nodier to write a narration based on the notes which the prince had jotted down in the midst of the action; he appointed as well the painters Adrien Dauzats, Alexandre-Gabriel Decamps, and Denis-Auguste-Marie Raffet to illustrate the volume. Published in 1844, the book was presented as a commemorative gift to the campaign's participants.[2] Although this handsome tome's narrative was credited to Nodier, the onetime chief of the French romantics; and although it was profusely illustrated by Dauzats and Decamps, two of the foremost orientalist painters of the time, and by Raffet, a reputed military artist, it remains little known and virtually unavailable today. For several reasons the *Journal de l'Expédition des Portes de Fer* may draw our interest: the book's physical beauty; the artwork it contains; its place in the *œuvres* of Nodier, Decamps, Dauzats, Raffet; its associations with the Duc d'Orléans and the July Monarchy. Yet, above and beyond that, it presents important problems of authorship, of French textual and pictorial representations of Algeria and its conquest, and of relationships between text and image.

Although my discussion here concentrates on interactions between the narration and its illustrations, we need first to mention the status of the tome's author and especially Nodier's ambiguous role in the composition of the *Journal de l'Expédition des Portes de Fer*. The title page indicates that the volume was "Rédigé par Charles Nodier de l'Académie Française" ("Written up by Charles Nodier of the French Academy");[3] the Duc d'Orléans's son, Robert, later confirmed that "Un récit fut

. . . fait par M. Charles Nodier qui le rédigea après 1842, sur les notes du duc d'Orléans" ("An account was . . . done by Mr. Charles Nodier who wrote it up after 1842, from the Duke of Orleans' notes.")[4] However, Nodier's "Avertissement" remains incomplete because of his collapse in December 1843 and subsequent death in January 1844; doubt remains about the real authorship of the narration itself. For example, some Dauzats scholars suggest that the seriously ill Nodier was unable to write it;[5] that another person, perhaps Dauzats, played an important if indefinable role in the text's composition;[6] and that, in any case, it was Dauzats who saw the volume to completion and publication after Nodier's death.[7] Having sketched these problems and qualifications, I will nevertheless refer to the author and narrator as Nodier for the purposes of this discussion.

The Duc d'Orléans's own journal was published in 1890 by his son as part of the *Récits de campagne 1833–1841*;[8] a comparison between it and the *Journal de l'Expédition des Portes de Fer* shows that Nodier follows the prince's general chronology and structure of events, and stylistic differences between the texts are in most instances clear. Yet Nodier's narration in some cases parallels the Duc d'Orléans's literally or virtually word for word, for example the descriptions of "les ouvrages des camps de l'est" ("construction work on the eastern camps"; Nodier 97–98, Duc d'Orléans 134–35); but here, as usual, Nodier continues in his own words after a phrase or sentence or two. Thus, although a narrator's voice governs the *Journal de l'Expédition des Portes de Fer*, the prince's voice is clearly present throughout, if intermittently and unsignaled, like a palimpsest; a third voice, perhaps Dauzats's, may be blended in as well.

In the context of the norms of the numerous *voyages en orient* and other travel texts appearing in the third and fourth decades of the nineteenth century (and indeed in terms of his own functions as writer about his own travels in, for example, *Promenade de Dieppe aux montagnes d'Ecosse*),[9] Nodier's authorial role, his "modeste collaboration" (xii) vis-à-vis the *Journal de l'Expédition des Portes de Fer* is anomalous in important ways because he is an "interprète" (viii), a mouthpiece for another's thoughts in a volume not destined for commercial distribution. This writer's role is of course to be distinguished from that of the ghostwriter or collaborator who works with the living original source of the information or text(s). Unlike the traveler-writer who is twice an *actant* , that is to say the one who performs the peregrinations and also does the writing about them, here the *rédacteur* (author) becomes simultaneously both a reader-recipient of the Duc d'Orléans's notes and also a writer: it is he who gives new narrative shape to the information and texts received from the late prince. Thus, the authorial function becomes that of a reader(s) who performs a revisionist rewriting of text(s) by another person.

The reader, or *destinataire*, of the *Journal de l'Expédition des Portes de Fer* is defined not as the curious, anonymous public, as is typically the case for the travel narrative, but rather, for this commemorative book, as a small, specific, familiar group: the expedition's participants themselves. The narrator states, "le Duc d'Orléans résolut . . . de faire un livre, non pas historique, un livre littéraire, un livre poétique, . . . mais un livre privé, familier, écrit . . . pour ceux-là seulement qui y étaient désignés d'une manière plus ou moins directe par leurs emplois, par leurs grades, par le numéro de leur régiment" ("the Duke of Orleans resolved to create a book, not a historical one, nor a literary one, nor a poetic one, but a private, informal one, written only for those referred to more or less directly by their assignment, their rank, the number of their regiment"; vi–vii). In such a case, the excursion's members of course knew far more about the subject than did Nodier, who, in fact, had neither traveled with the prince's troops nor ever journeyed to Algeria or elsewhere in the Orient (among the several writers and artists who composed the volume, only Dauzats accompanied the mission). Published in France five years after the events, the narration really speaks to—and the illustrations are chosen for—memory; indeed, Nodier states the Duc d'Orléans desired a book which would be "orné . . . , élégant, presque magnifique," ("ornate . . . , elegant, almost sumptuous"), appropriate for a princely present to his officers, "pour leur rappeler sa mémoire quand il sera séparé d'eux" ("to recall his memory when he is separated from them"; vii). On the one hand, the volume promotes an embellished recollection of the expedition's drama and accomplishments and thus of its members' heroic deeds and contributions; on the other hand, the tome constitutes an exaltation of the now recently deceased Duc d'Orléan's superior qualities and ultimately those of the July Monarchy and its foreign policy. The *Journal de l'Expédition des Portes de Fer* is, then, an example of a representational practice which functions to engender certain kinds of personal and national memory in order to legitimize a particular regime and its conduct.

A major facet of the tome's representational strategies is the

193 images which appear frequently throughout the volume's 321 pages (often more than one per page) and which are emphasized by forty full-page plates ("grand-bois") and a two-page foldout map of the prince's route. Each signed by both the original "dessinateur" ("drawer") and also the "graveur" ("woodcutter"), the *grands-bois* are placed in physical and substantive juxtaposition to, and conversation with, the narration and also, occasionally, one another (when a number of images evoke the same subject, for example, Raffet's illustrations of African dances [Gravures 43–45]). As is typical for an illustrated book, the text never alludes to the artwork accompanying it; the images, however, represent people, places, and events mentioned in the text and are generally positioned in close proximity to the appropriate passage. Parallel to the narration, these images form a central representational structure that usually works in concert with the narration, but—significantly—one that is at times to some degree autonomous. My primary concern with the relationships between art and writing here is neither for *transpositions d'art* between text and image, nor for the deployment of one medium as referent for another (for example, Fromentin's journal about painting), nor for the one as intertext for the other (e.g., Gautier's evocations of orientalist painting in *Constantinople*);[10] my interest lies rather in the interactions between text and physically present image, understood as systems of visual and discursive representation of common referents external to the volume.

Because the forty full-page plates interspersed throughout the text call special attention to certain subjects, I will concentrate my discussion on these focal points. Overlaid with protective tissue indicating the illustration's title, and followed by a blank page (only the *grands-bois* are presented this way), they are in effect showstoppers. At first sight, each *grand-bois* , like most of the smaller images, merely seems to illustrate a given textual item in isolation from the rest of the pictures; however, an analysis of the whole series of full-page plates reveals a particular overriding structure for their choice of subject, place in the text, and point of view that may, but does not necessarily, coincide with the text.

Over the course of the first quarter of the text, the narrator recounts numerous elements important to the prince's expedition and typical for any voyage's beginning: the departure from Port Vendres, first sights and encounters in Algeria, descriptions of its population, geography, customs, and various logistical elements for the French. Most of these factors, however, are absent from the illustrations which, on the other hand, concentrate on a particular kind of subject: the lively Algerian culture now coming under French control, the vigor of its people, the characteristics of its natural settings. Among the first eleven of the full-page plates (through Gravure 47), just three depict the French, who, in each case are shown working in cooperation with the Algerians (e.g., Raffet's "Course à Mers-er-Ghin" [Gravure 14], "Revue à Alger" [Gravure 37]), or being welcomed by the City of Algiers (e.g., Raffet's "Bal à Alger" [Gravure 41]). Several early *grands-bois* represent important Algerian locales, for example, Dauzats's general view of "Oran" (Gravure 7) and the "Principale Mosquée d'Alger" (Gravure 32); another works in counterpoint to these depictions of grandeur by showing the humble buildings of the "Café à Douera" (Gravure 47). It is only in the early *grands-bois* that we see full portraits of Algerians (Raffet's "Le colonel Youssouf" [Gravure 18], "Mustapha-Ben-Ismaïl [Gravure 20]). Like the plates, the smaller images through Gravure 50 also concentrate overwhelmingly on Algerian subjects to the virtual absence of the French.[11]

As is generally the case throughout the volume, specific images do reflect particular textual passages;[12] and in many cases function to validate Algerian realities. Decamps's "Danse de Noirs" (Gravure 12), to choose a striking instance, provides a closely parallel visual depiction of the narrator's verbal description as well as an engaging sample of the volume's illustrations of Algerian life. The rigid verticality of Decamps's principal drummer, feet planted firmly on the ground, contrasts sharply with the lines of the chief dancer and the other musicians in the background. The instrumentalists, leaning with one foot lifted in synchronized movement to their music, frame the dancer who, instrument held over his head, one foot also raised, both feet turning, clothes flying, kicks up dust with his energetic movements. In the accompanying text, the narrator emphasizes similar points, "le tambour de la bande noire se plaça au centre d'un cercle formé d'une quinzaine de musiciens dansants, et y demeura seul, immobile et bruyant" ("the black band's drummer placed himself in the center of a circle formed by about fifteen dancing musicians and remained here alone, motionless and noisy"). One by one, they come to the center of the circle of dancing musicians to perform a solo, "Chacun de ces pas isolés se terminait par un tournoiement général d'une vivacité inexprimable" ("Each of his isolated steps ended by a general spin-

Fig. 1 "Danse de Noirs," Alexandre-Gabriel Decamps, *Journal de l'Expédition des Portes de Fer*, Gravure 12.

ning which was inexpressibly lively"; 21). Decamps repeats the narrator's emphasis on "cercle" and "tournoiement" by his use of circular forms (an element often noted in his orientalist œuvre): the dust clouds, the drums and instrument over the dancer's head, the heads and head-gear, the lines of the chief dancer's shirt and pant legs, the shape suggested by his raised arms, the arc of his body counterpointed by the background musician to our extreme right. These round forms counter the image's vertical lines and create a tension which suggests the dancers' energy, or "vivacité inexprimable" mentioned by the narrator. The first quarter of the *grands-bois* operate, then, to depict and very often valorize the places, culture, and people now being subdued by the French and also ultimately to underscore the significance of the Duc d'Orléans's successful foray through Algeria.

Between the first eleven and the last four plates, there occurs a shift in representational strategy. Most of the images throughout the middle of the tome alternately show not only Algerian people and places, but also the life of the French troops (e.g.,

Raffet's "Le Prince visite les hôpitaux" [Gravure 79], or "Le Prince et son état-major au bivouac" [Gravure 152]) and the drama, danger, glory, and import of the expedition. Raffet's depiction of Algerians rustling livestock in "Une razzia" (Gravure 66) is a good example of the numerous illustrations that present the kinds of people, situations, mysteries, and perils observed by the conquering French. "Razzia" accentuates speed and confusion: local men surround the animals and are chasing them to the left; the rustlers' rifles lean in the same direction to emphasize the movement of men, cattle, and sheep. Several French soldiers in the background, relatively immobile, observe the scene; the line of mountain peaks in the background repeats that of the crowd and observers, and above that, a dramatic, menacing storm cloud looms (and, in the narration, later catches up with them). The narrator describes the "spectacle" this way: because the thieves are galloping and turning about the animals, "A cette allure, les bestiaux font plus de deux lieues à l'heure; et c'est ce qui rend les vols de ce genre si fréquents et si faciles chez ces peuplades accoutumées depuis l'enfance à cet exercice" ("At this speed, the cattle do more than two leagues per hour, and that is what makes thefts of this type so frequent and easy for these people accustomed to this exercise since childhood"; 103). Dauzats's "Rue de Blidah" (Gravure 57) provides another particularly faithful illustration of the narrator's description of the towns and land the French now govern. The narrator states that Blidah is a city being rebuilt from an 1825 earthquake: "Ses maisons, qui ressemblent aux loges d'une ménagerie, se composent d'un simple rez-de-chaussée. D'un toit ou plutôt d'une terrasse à l'autre s'étendent des branches d'arbres, chargées de feuillages, qui entretiennent une constante fraîcheur . . . Les habitants accourent en foule, mais restent immobiles et silencieux" ("Its houses, which resemble loggias in a zoo, are made up of just a ground floor. Tree branches, loaded with foliage which maintains a constant coolness, extend from one roof or rather one terrace to another. . . . The residents rush up in a crowd, but remain still and silent"; 91). In his illustration, Dauzats reprises each element of the narration to create an evocation of a low, close, crowded, primitive, almost cavelike street; the people, several of whom are looking at the viewer, are almost all immobile, as if activity has ceased so the residents can contemplate the presence of the interloper, in this case defined contextually as the French.

As opposed to the first quarter of the volume, a significant

Fig. 2 "Une Rue de Blidah," Adrien Dauzats, *Journal de l'Expédition des Portes de Fer*, Gravure 57.

number (nine) of *grands-bois* that appear throughout the middle part of the tome (Gravures 48–179) portray the French staff, soldiers, and their activities. The reader encounters seven full-page individual portrayals of the "Prince royal" (Gravure 123) and his officers, always in uniform, on horseback, and full-length; these are certainly typical of and appropriate to a commemorative gift volume from commander to officers. Furthermore, through the middle section of the book, when the image depicts both Algerian and French people, the French are more frequently present in a more active way. That is to say, they are no longer merely observers in the background as is generally the case in the first quarter of the book; now they are most often interacting with the Algerians, or are clearly in control, just as the French army was gaining greater control over the country. An example is the "Distribution par les sœurs de Saint-Joseph" (Gravure 103, Raffet), in which French nuns, backed by soldiers, stand higher than the thankful Algerians accepting loaves of bread. Another good example is Raffet's *grand-bois*, "Les populations apportent des présents au Prince" (Gravure 90), in which Raffet illustrates the narrator's commentary on the strength of Algerian support for the new French supremacy,

"Ici les indigènes semblent avoir compris que notre autorité est plus douce à supporter que celle des Turcs, et ils s'y soumettent avec un empressement plein de zèle . . . Il est permis de croire que, dans cette partie importante de la conquête, les personnes nous appartiennent comme le sol" ("Here the natives seem to have understood that our authority is easier to endure than that of the Turks and they submit to it with a zealous eagerness. We can believe that, in this important part of the conquest, the people belong to us like the earth"; 136). Accordingly, in Raffet's image, the French military, on horseback, occupies half the image, the soldiers' height being greater than that of Maghrebins around them as well as at their feet and looking up to them. The native population is represented as laying gifts before the troops, offerings which suggest their desire to nourish the French presence: chickens, sheep, baskets of food.

Several series of plates placed through the middle of the volume merit special attention. First, a number of them depict Roman ruins encountered by the prince's troops: for example, Dauzats's series of precise reproductions of inscriptions found on stones there (Gravures 133–42)—every letter is clearly legible.[13] These images reflect a number of *lieux communs* (commonplaces) in French *récits de voyage en orient* (Oriental travel narratives). The author manifests a documentary or encyclopedic intention; the narration goes beyond recounting people and events in order to produce an organized and often analytical or scientific recording of artifacts which reveal historical, social, anthropological, or geological features of the region. The drawing of Roman inscriptions reveals as well an investment in the historical importance of the excursion through a discovery of evidence of antiquity in the very place where certain events happened, in this case, a reenactment of the conquests of the Roman army.[14] The Duc d'Orléans had in fact the idea to transport the ancient stones and an arch of triumph from Djamilah to Paris for erection as a monument to the Algerian achievements of his "armée d'Afrique" ("African army"; 203). The *grand-bois* of the "Arc de Triomphe de Djamilah" (Gravure 132, Dauzats), depicting the arch surrounded by the inscribed plaques which have fallen from it, immediately precedes and sets the context for the drawings of individual stones and thus further underscores their import. This account, and these images, of the discoveries made by the Duc d'Orléans's tour imbues it, and by association the prince himself and the policies of his government, with historical significance, justification, and virtue.

Dauzats's five-plate set of the dramatic and dangerous transit through the *Portes de Fer* composes the most famous and important of this volume's illustrations (Gravures 167–71). This is the high point of the expedition; the succinct narration and the series of *grands-bois* lead us step by step through the fearsome defile, reputed as impassable. The gorge's huge rocks form perpendicular walls as high as nine hundred feet, its five successive "gates" are as narrow as eight feet and oblige the troops to walk through one-by-one under the fear of an attack against which they would be defenseless (261–63). Dauzats's pieces emphasize the towering mountains; for example the "Portes de Fer, Premier défilé" (Gravure 168; this image is placed second in the series of five) is composed to throw focus on the troops—virtually minuscule in reference to their surroundings—disappearing into a menacing black hole formed by the jagged boulders. One of the stones looming over them, to their right, appears to be a fierce face, suggesting perhaps Algerians watching—as are we, or hinting even at the threat of ambush. The "Portes de Fer, Fond du ravin" (Gravure 170; this image falls next to last in the series) is placed before the troops' exit from

Fig. 3 "Portes de Fer, Premier Défilé," Alexandre-Gabriel Decamps, *Journal de l'Expédition des Portes der Fer*, Gravure 168.

Fig. 4 "Portes de Fer, Fond du Ravin," Adrien Dauzats, *Journal de l'Expédition des Portes de Fer*, Gravure 170.

the last *porte* and expresses the suspense of the operation: a barely perceptible cleft through the soaring walls hides the entire army of which not a member is visible here; the point of view is that of an observer apart from the *colonne expéditionnaire* and could again be that of watching Algerians. This successful passage constituted the excursion's military and political apogee: it meant that the French military had demonstrated its ability to go anywhere, and thus to control the northeastern portion of the country; the French were then able to integrate it into their domination of the Algerian west and center. Accordingly, these five full-page plates succeed one another closely, unlike any others in the volume;[15] it is the prominence accorded the images here as well as their representation of the seeming impenetrability of the massive barrier that communicates and underscores the drama, difficulty, and significance of the mission's achievement. Notably, the text does not echo the images here; while gripping, it is remarkably brief (only three pages: 260–63); it does not assign much more space or importance to this capital event than it does to several other episodes.

The concluding portion of the volume forms a counterbalance to the first series of images concentrating on Algeria and its inhabitants; here, text and image work in concert to portray the

French victory and its magnitude. All the tome's final four full plates are almost uniquely of French subjects, as are all the smaller images in the same portion of the tome (or last forty-two pages and their sixteen illustrations [Gravures 177–93]). The terminal *grand-bois,* Raffet's "Arrivée à Alger par la porte Babazoun" (Gravure 189), constitutes a summary of the kind of meaning which the volume seeks to confer on the expedition. The upper background of the image is composed of cheering Algerians on rooftops and city walls, all of which are commanded by the tricolor placed at the very apogee of the picture. At the walls' base, a group of immobile North Africans observes, perhaps unenthused but accepting of the new order. French soldiers, symbolically sitting higher than the jubilant crowd and echoing the dominance of the French flag, dominate the foreground; other groups of French *militaires,* civils (both men and women), and *Algérois* interact in friendship. The alliance among French civilian, military, and also Algerian interests is represented by the trio walking in unison, arm in arm, in the left foreground. They are virtually the only figures moving away from the crowd and facing the viewer (albeit obliquely), as if to pursue a new direction and to communicate directly to the outside

Fig. 5 "Arrivée à Alger par la Porte Babazoun," Denis-Auguste-Marie Raffet, *Journal de l'Expédition des Portes de Fer*, Gravure 189.

world the cooperative nature of the Duc d'Orléans's Algeria. Only two rifles are in sight, one held by an Algerian, the other by a civilian, none by the military; the populace is so happy with the new French regime that it can be trusted with arms, and the army, by the same token, does not need to carry them in the middle of the jubilant crowd. The message is apparent: the French pacification signals a new era of harmony and progress for the North African country, the Duc d'Orléans has accomplished the mission summarized by the narrator's sentence, "L'art de soumettre un peuple, c'est celui de s'en faire aimer" ("The art of subjugating a people is that of making oneself loved by it"; 99).

Although the illustrations I have presented so far generally reflect elements similar to the accompanying narration, some other images stand somewhat at odds with the text. We have seen the apparent differences in emphasis accorded the passage through the *Portes de Fer* in the brief textual description versus the series of five plates; a clear example of meaningful divergence between text and image is Decamps's "Arabes en embuscade" (Gravure 68). Here, the artist evokes a danger run by the

Fig. 6 "Arabes en Embuscade," Alexandre-Gabriel Decamps, *Journal de l'Expédition des Portes de Fer*, Gravure 6.

troops throughout the mission, but it is one that is not specifically described in any accompanying textual passage. Significantly, this image presents the situation from the perspective of the Arabs, rather than from that of the conquerors: two Frenchmen are standing at a distance, shooting into the sky, unaware of the four Algerians lurking in the foreground who are watching them through an opening in the low vegetation. Decamps's image is ironic, not only because it shows the French hunters as ignorant of the fact that they themselves are being hunted, but also because it presents the French being viewed by Arabs, as do a number of other illustrations; such representations oppose the hegemonic French point of view in both text and image. Another interesting example of important divergence between text and image is Dauzats's representations of the penetration into the Bey's Palace at Constantine ("Palais du Bey," Gravure 104). In the accompanying text, the narrator describes the French troops' arrival, emphasizes their feeling of relief in the palace's cool comfort, and relates as well the French sense of disappointment after analyzing the building as a less than perfectly designed palace (151–52). The artist, however, draws long, covered, arched, parallel corridors with a verdant arcaded courtyard to the right; a number of Algerians stand and sit about in the shadows, but no French people are present as they so often and symbolically are in other illustrations of the Algerian conquest. Dauzats gives us an image of the scene as it could have been beheld by the Algerians themselves or perhaps by the first Frenchman to enter the Bey's inner sanctum, but it is not an illustration of the narrator's description of the French presence and reactions after occupying this token of their conquest. Such images offer views that differ from the text and, in some cases, add surprising, possibly Algerian, points of view to this commemoration of colonial conquest.

Each of the artists contributes a particular vision and comment because each one portrays the kinds of subjects appropriate to his particular skill, experience, and reputation. None of Decamps's pieces depict the French; rather he paints the Algerians in their milieu, subjects he knew well and on which he had built his fame.[16] His striking and effective images convey a knowledge of and sympathy for North Africans and their environment, subjects he could portray without having accompanied the ducal tour. Among the three painters, Decamps's illustrations posit the most consistently a validation of the indigenous people, their traditions and mores, and the country's natural grandeur and architectural beauties. Almost without exception, Raffet's illustrations also are of subjects he knew best and which had made him a premier artist: military and battle scenes, portraits, uniforms and costumes; most of the depictions of the French are by him.[17] His illustrations very often show the prowess of the French military, the excitement of battle and conquest, the life of the officers to whom this volume is destined. For him too, these were images he could imagine and compose from his past work, without traveling with the prince's troops. Dauzats contributes illustrations of a variety of subjects, but like Decamps, virtually never of the French and rather, in general, of Algeria, its people, scenes specific to the expedition and whose accurate rendition required the artist be present.[18] Thus the impressive plates of the passage through the *Portes de Fer* are his, for example, as is the series of Roman inscriptions; he drew as well a great number of the depictions of the countryside and places visited by the expeditionary column; at the same time, he does relatively fewer portraits than the other two artists. Thus, subject, sympathy, tone vary among the three artists; their images, along with Nodier's text, contribute to the volume's polyphonic and polyscopic qualities.

Discontinuity and heterogeneity characterize the travel narrative, and are as well particularly suited to and typical of Nodier, who became over the course of his *œuvre* a master of the use of fragmentary, hybrid structures of many sorts and for all kinds of purposes and effects.[19] Raffet's, Decamps's, and Dauzats's illustrations do significantly more than provide a simple visual reflection of the expedition's progress as told by the narrator. They confirm as well tensions and discontinuities that are manifest within the French narrator's discourse, for example, portrayals of French political, cultural, military enlightenment and superiority on the one hand and, on the other, validations of Algerian monuments, cultural practices, individuals, and achievements. Furthermore, the volume's artwork in some cases moves beyond confirmative illustration of textual features to an opening of points of view because the images sometimes endorse Algerian points of view within the dominant textual and visual representations of the French conquest of the North African subject. The illustrations thus extend the plurality of voices and views present and contribute elements of variability to the hegemonic discourses and images of imperial might.

In the *Journal de l'Expédition des Portes de Fer*, composer(s) and painters produce what at first apprehension may seem a particularly monolithic manifestation of a certain facet of French orientalist practices: a textualization and visual representation of the ideologies of heroic adventure, colonialist expansion, dynastic legitimacy, and French power. But in spite of—and also because of—the identities and roles of the volume's note taker, writer(s), various artists, intended audience, and purpose, the *Journal de l'Expédition des Portes de Fer* constitutes something more than a unitary apologia of a prince's mission. Inevitably the tome exhibits characteristics of a collage, or an assemblage of visions, voices, modes of expression that inject significant discontinuous and ambiguous elements into an apparently unified presentation. Within the volume's overriding structure, then, instabilities both in and among text and images create heteroglossic spaces that are significant for French representations of its overseas project and of the Algerian other.

Notes

1. Orléans, Ferdinand-Philippe-Louis-Charles-Henri, Duc d'. 1810–1842. Eldest surviving child of King Louis Philippe and Marie-Amélie de Bourbon.

2. Charles Nodier, *Journal de l'Expédition des Portes de Fer* (Paris: Imprimerie Royale, 1844). Subsequent references to this volume will be included in the text.

3. All translations my own.

4. Ferdinand-Philippe-Louis-Charles-Henri, Duc d'Orléans, *Récits de campagne*, publiés par ses fils Le Comte de Paris et le Duc de Chartres (Paris: Calmann Lévy, 1890), xii. Subsequent references to this volume will be included in the text.

5. Nodier's health, never strong, deteriorated rapidly from the mid-1830s onward. By late 1836 he had a cataract and needed strong glasses to see; he had gone deaf in one ear and had only partial hearing in the other; he trembled violently when writing; and he walked laboriously. Throughout his life, he was plagued with weakness, rapid fatigue, irritability, nervousness, gastrointestinal upsets, and hypoglycemia; these symptoms may have been associated with Addison's disease, possibly inherited from his mother.

6. Ghislaine Plessier, *Adrien Dauzats ou la tentation de l'Orient. Catalogue raisonné de l'œuvre peint* (Bordeaux: Musée des Beaux-Arts de Bordeaux/William Blake and Co., 1990), 23.

7. See, for example, Plessier, *Dauzats*, 23, and Bruno Foucart, ed., *Adrien Dauzats et "Les Voyages pittoresques et romantiques dans l'Ancienne France" du Baron Taylor* (Paris: Fondation Taylor, 1990), 362. Plessier states however that the style of the *Journal de l'Expédition des Portes de Fe*r bears no resemblance to that of Dauzats and Dumas's *Quinze jours au Sinaï* (23), and she refers to Nodier as the volume's author (e.g., 60).

8. The volume contains an introduction by Robert d'Orléans, "Journal de l'Expédition de Mascara (1835)," "Journal de l'Expédition des Portes de Fer

(1839)" (pp. [83]-318), "Lettres diverses concernant l'Afrique," and two maps of Algeria.

9. Nodier stated that he wrote only the texts for the volumes on Normandy and Franche Comté, as well as prefaces for them. See Didier Barrière, *Nodier l'homme du livre. Le Rôle de la bibliophilie dans la littérature* (Bassac: Plein Chant, 1989), 212.

10. See my "Decamps, Orientalist Intertext, and Counter-Discourse in Gautier's *Constantinople*," *Nineteenth-Century French Studies* 21:3–4 (spring–summer 1993) for a discussion of Gautier's use of Decamps's orientalist painting as intertext for *Constantinople*.

11. Through Gravure 50 there are thirty-nine small images; two depict French troops in the center or foreground of the image; one other is of French boats; in four others French soldiers figure in the background only and are drawn more lightly than the Algerian subject.

12. The most literal reflection of the text is perhaps Decamps's vignette of the letter "A" (Gravure 25) for the beginning of the chapter on "Alger." The letter is composed of triangular forms, floating on water; it illustrates the sentence, "Alger a la forme d'un triangle dont la base repose dans la mer. . . ." ("Algiers has the form of a triangle whose base rests in the sea. . . ;" 45).

13. Though not *grands-bois*, these images are organized to occupy all of pp. 200 and 201 (except one line of text) and a portion of p. 199. Thus, pp. 200 and 201 become virtual *grands-bois*; this is the only instance in the volume of entire pages being devoted to technically smaller images. This choice and the organization of these illustrations highlight the inscriptions' special significance.

14. In a similar vein, the narrator likens the French troops to "les guerriers d'Homère" ("Homer's warriors" 38). Toward the end of the *récit*, another passage echoes a famous historical encounter specifically between French and Arabs: the Saracens' attack on Charlemagne's rear guard, led by Roland, which is evoked in the *Chanson de Roland*. As the Duc d'Orléans's column traverses one more difficult pass before regaining the safety of Algiers, the prince is informed that the rear guard is under attack. He immediately returns to it, and heroically leads it to victory (286–88). This triumph is of course an important difference between this excursion and the tragedy that befell Charlemagne's rear guard while returning through the Pyrenées from its campaign on foreign soil against the Saracens.

15. In one other instance, four *grands-bois* appear in rapid succession, but their subjects are miscellaneous rather than constituting a series: Gravures 104 ("Palais du bey" ["The Bey's Palace"]), 105 ("Les chutes du Rummel" ["The Rummel Waterfall"]), 106 ("Pont d'El Cantara" ["The El Cantara Bridge"]), all by Dauzats; and 107 ("Fantasia") by Raffet.

16. By the time Decamps's thirteen illustrations appeared in the *Journal de l'Expédition des Portes de Fer*, his oils, watercolors, pastels, and drawings had for a decade been considered by artists and writers a standard for the romantic orientalist style (Mosby, 1:4); he had already attained enormous commercial success as well. Like Dauzats, Decamps was one of the first European painters to travel extensively in the Orient (he spent a year [1828] in Smyrna from where he visited points in Asia Minor and eastern North Africa); in the 1830s and 1840s, he, perhaps even more than Delacroix or Géricault, established canonical visual representations of the Orient by such canvases as "La patrouille turc" (1830–31), "La défaite des Cimbres" (Salon of 1833), the "Sortie de l'école turque" (1841). Decamps remained throughout his life

(1803–60) the most famous of the French romantic orientalist painters. For example, at the Exposition universelle of 1855, Decamps exhibited forty-nine paintings, more than either Delacroix (35), or Ingres (41), or Vernet (22) (see Patricia Mainardi, *Art and Politics of the Second Empire: The Universal Expositions of 1855 and 1867* [New Haven: Yale University Press, 1987], 63), and he (with Delacroix and Ingres) was one of three given a retrospective in this Exposition. The international jury awarded Decamps a *Grande Médaille d'honneur* to recognize his position as chief of the French painters. His works were admired for their picturesque vision, use of nearly phosphorescent color, innovative techniques for the creation of effects of spontaneity, intense light, emotion. Today, art historians continue to consider Decamps the head, if not the best, of two generations of French orientalist artists. See Philippe Jullian, *Les Orientalistes. La Vision de l'Orient par les peintres européens au XIXe siècle* (Fribourg: Office du Livre, 1977), 52.

17. Raffet executed the largest number (ninety-two, or nearly half) of the images included in the *Journal de l'Expédition des Portes de Fer*. Unlike the orientalists Dauzats and Decamps, Raffet's reputation was built on pencil drawings, lithographs, and engravings of battle scenes and military subjects executed with much-admired finesse, vigor, and sometimes humor, often imbued with patriotism and poetry. Critics have remarked on his powers of observation and ability to depict manners and types as well a capacity to successfully include numerous figures and large spaces within a small-scale drawing. Examples of well-known works which earned great early success are, "Les adieux de la garnison," "Waterloo" (1830–31). Starting in 1825, he published popular albums of lithographs almost every year; from the early 1830s he became a sought-after illustrator of books, especially on the French Revolution and the Napoleonic legend, for example, Thiers's *Histoire de la Révolution* and Norvins's *Histoire de Napoléon*. Raffet was considered a master artist when he was selected to execute illustrations for the *Journal de l'Expédition des Portes de Fer*.

18. Dauzats had excellent working and personal relations with Nodier since their collaboration on the *Voyages pittoresques* (see below). He enjoyed good connections as well with the Orléans family at least since the success of his art-buying missions to Spain (1833, 1835–37) under the direction of the Baron Taylor (whom he met at Nodier's salon) for Louis Philippe's Spanish gallery at the Louvre. Dauzats's reputation for effective, precise, faithful drawings of architecture was in part established by his illustrations for Nodier, Taylor, and Cailleux's *Voyages pittoresques et romantiques dans l'ancienne France*. His stature as an orientalist painter was founded on the hundreds of drawings he contributed to Baron Taylor's *La Syrie, l'Egypte, la Palestine et la Judée* (1839), a result of their 1830 trip to obtain Mehemet Ali's permission to bring the Luxor obelisk to Paris. Still in 1839, another Dauzats orientalist book appeared, this time in collaboration with Dumas père, *Nouvelles impressions de voyage*. Quinze jours au Sinaï. Dauzats was at the height of his talent and fame when he created his eighty-eight pieces for the *Journal de l'Expédition des Portes de Fer*; some of his best oils (e.g., "Passage des Bibans") and watercolors (e.g., "Environs de Blidah," "Passage des Portes de Fer") come from his experience with the Duc d'Orléans's expedition into Algeria. During the 1840s he continued to paint and exhibit works based on his Algerian observations; among others, the five watercolors on the passage through the Gates of Iron (Salon of 1841); the *Place du Gouvernement à Alger* (1849). He also exhibited

such works at the Salons of 1844, 1845, 1861, and at Antwerp (1855), London (1862). Throughout his life, he had the friendship and respect of contemporaries like Hugo, Gautier, Delacroix, Raffet; he died in 1868 (born 1804). His talent as a gifted observer and his importance in the history of orientalist painting have recently been recognized, for example, by the exhibit organized by the Musée des Beaux-Arts de Bordeaux in 1990 and by Plessier's catalog of his paintings.

19. See Hélène Lowe-Dupas, *Poétique de la coupure chez Charles Nodier* (Amsterdam/Atlanta: Rodopi, 1995) for an excellent discussion of discontinuous elements in Nodier's *œuvre*.

The Socio-Politics of Orientalist Representations: Delacroix, Djebar, and *Les Femmes d'Alger*

SARAH DAVIES CORDOVA

SINCE REPRESENTATIONS IMPLY A VISION, A POINT OF VIEW, AN IDEOLOGY,[1] the result focuses the viewer's attention upon the relation between the portrayed and the general characteristics attributed to its class. Icons, as semantic and diagrammatic signs of religious or sociopolitical significance, in presenting the world, represent it with a homogeneous synthesis of chosen fragments of the real world. The visually-, verbally-, and/or movement-based work, drawing upon an intertextuality determined by the historical moment and the period's conventions, perpetuates even as it alters the mythic dimension of the represented.[2]

The issue of representation has very much been problematized in the news recently. The producers and consumers of such imprints, whether they be those surrounding the death of Lady Diana or, more to the point here, those dealing with the situation in Algeria have also been implicated. How does one perform representations? Headlines in France cry out: "Algérie, l'agonie" "Algeria, the agony" (*Evènement*, 43);[3] summons to respond to the atrocities perpetrated on the people of Algeria are heard on morning radio call-in shows; candle and torchlit marches silently and flamboyantly express the solidarity of some intellectuals and artists with the suffering Algerians;[4] television news announcers warn that the ensuing film footage may be inappropriate for some viewers. The schematic properties of these verbal and visual references to the Algerian predicament ally them with iconographic representations. These icons, which are reaching the French public, refer to or denote the massacres yet elide euphemistically or syncretically the reality of the carnage. They counter yet bolster statements like: "on l'a souvent dit—cette guerre n'existe pas car c'est une guerre sans images" "it has often been said—this war does not exist for it is a pictureless war" (*L'Evènement*, 3), statements that reiterate such clichéd idiomatic expressions as: "seeing is believing" whilst covering up the problematics of representation.

The most sold photograph about the recent events in Algeria was taken to illustrate reports of the 22 September massacre at Bentalha. Agence France Presse selected for commercialization from the collection sent in by Hocine, its only employee in Algeria, a photograph which newspapers and weekly magazines all over Europe and the United States bought and reproduced on their front pages.[5]

The photograph shows two women, with brown scarves covering their heads, against a blank, white, tiled wall, silently dumb: docile bodies responding to emotional pain. The one wearing a pale gray dress, whose scarf is untied, is supported by the wall and held up by the other in dark blue. Goskin Sipahioglu, who heads the photo agency Sipa, defends the judicious choice of this representation with: "les gens ne veulent pas voir du sang" "people do not want to see blood" (*Monde*, 12), thereby

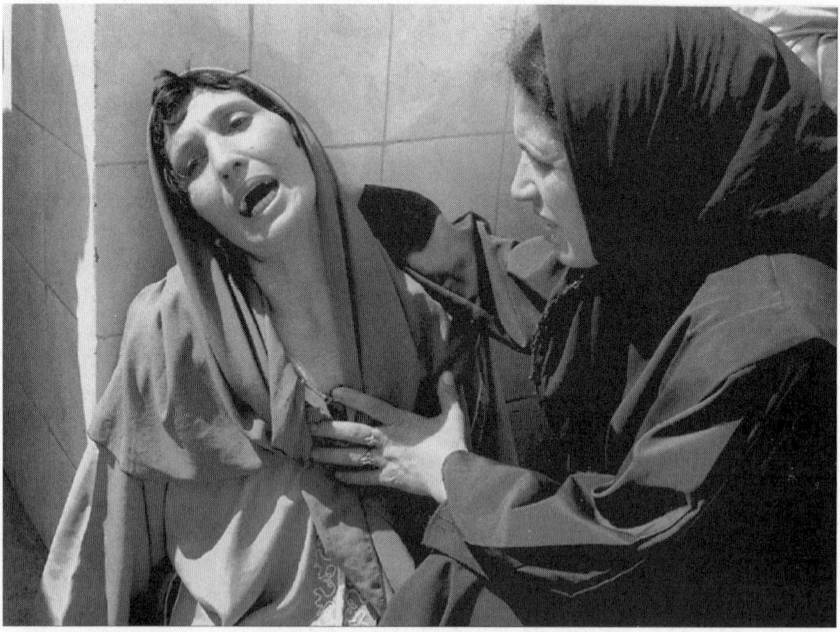

Fig. 7 Photograph from *Le Monde*, 9/12/97, pp. 5 and 12, Hocine, by permission of SARL Le Monde.

affirming the capitalist and economically-driven motivations of objective, informative publications. According to *Le Monde*, this photograph, of which a small, colored version appeared on the front page and a black-and-white large-scale one was reprinted on page twelve, says much more than any of rows of cadavers:

> C'est un cri de désespoir qui a éclaboussé la "une" des journaux, mercredi 24 septembre. C'est un regard, celui d'une femme comme déjà dans l'au-delà. C'est le portrait d'une mère à genoux, qui a perdu ses enfants, soutenue par une autre mère. C'est enfin une *Pietà* que l'on peut rapprocher d'une riche iconographie picturale, une madone en enfer. L'image est intemporelle, peu informative [. . .].
>
> Quand les repères s'évanouissent, il ne reste que la douleur du témoignage, si intense dans ce cliché qui émeut davantage qu'une série de cadavres alignés, au petit matin. (12)

> (It is a cry of despair that bespattered the front pages of newspapers on Wednesday September 24th. It is a look, that of a woman as though already in the hereafter. It is the portrait of a mother on her knees, who has lost her children, held up by another mother. It is finally a *Pieta* which one can place alongside a rich pictorial iconography, a Madonna in hell. The image is timeless, hardly informative [. . .].
>
> When the benchmarks melt away, there only remains the pain of testimony, so intense in this photograph which touches one more than a row of cadavers lined up, at daybreak.)

Alongside the visual prompt, words replace the mother's scream:

> Les mots, galvaudés ou trop faibles pour traduire l'horreur des tueries, ne suffisent plus pour rendre compte de la tragédie algérienne. Il reste les témoignages de quelques photographes. La détresse d'un regard, les stigmates de l'effroi sur un visage, en disent plus que les photos insoutenables des corps massacrés. (12)

> (Words, muddled or too feeble to translate the horror of the killings, no longer suffice to account for the Algerian tragedy. There remains the testimonies of a few photographers. The distress of a look, the stigmata of dread on a face, bespeak more than unbearable photographs of massacred bodies.)

A picture is worth a thousand words. The *pieta* image, according to *Le Monde*, is more acceptable than the reality of the massacres and of eviscerated pregnant women. It becomes a symbol, an emblem, an icon which calls out for compassion, which privileges emotion over information. Indeed the photograph was not even taken at Bentalha but at the Zmirli hospital in El Harrach, a suburb of Algiers, and it addresses the West, not the Algerians. No local newspaper carried Hocine's photograph. Rather than disseminating from the Métropole an image reminiscent of orientalist pictures of Algerian barbarism, the photograph with its title appropriates the colonizer's icon of the Madonna to represent the plight of Algerians today.

Imprinting or *stereo-typing* the image directly onto the viewer's imagination, eliminating the need for decoding, as Craig Owens has pointed out, is tantamount to visual subjection (195). As a "form of symbolic violence exercised upon the body in order to assign it a place and to keep it in place, the stereotype works less through persuasion (the goal of traditional rhetoric) than through deterrence [. . . .]. It promotes passivity, receptivity, inactivity—docile bodies" (194). The image effectively reduces viewer and viewed to unassuming positionalities of acceptance. Intertextual fragments, underlined by the caption: "Une madone en enfer" reconstitute in Hocine's photograph Western perceptions of woman as sufferer and define her in Christian terms. The *stereo-type* of these two Algerian women transports them into Biblical times and terms: the analogy of the Pieta iconicizes them as Virgin Mary and Mary Magdalene. They are not shown looking at the bodies of the woman on the left's eight massacred children or the other's murdered parents; nor can they be heard. In *Le Monde*, another's discourse—Michel Guerrin's text—is substituted for theirs. It alleges succinctly that words cannot recount the massacres and discusses over the remainder of the newspaper page the difficulty that male journalists encounter in reporting and representing the situation in Algeria. The stereo-type performs its subjection together with the "Madonna" categorization which ideologically censures the visualization as well as the women's own verbalization of the eradication of a family's entire generation.

Regard Interdit, Son Coupé

Forbidden Gaze, Severed Sound

Thus Assia Djebar[6] entitles her *Postface* to "Femmes d'Alger dans leur appartement" "Women of Algiers in their Apartment," in which she looks at the women portrayed in Eugène Delacroix's two identically-titled paintings. Written between 1959 and 1978, her volume of *nouvelles* published in 1980 after a ten-year break—a ten-year silence—examines the heritage of the 1830 French conquest of Algeria with women looking and speaking, breaking out of various subjections. In the *Ouverture*, Djebar announces that the *nouvelles* are "[. . .] quelques repères sur un trajet d'écoute, de 1958 à 1978./ Conversations fragmentées, remémorées, reconstituées . . ." (7) "[. . .] a few frames of reference on a journey of listening, from 1958 to 1978./ Fragmented, remembered, reconstituted conversations. . . ." (1). She hesitates however as to the tactics to employ in order to translate the orality of transmitted chains of echoes and sighs: "Mots du corps voilé, langage à son tour qui si longtemps a pris le voile" (7) "Words of the veiled body, language that in turn has taken the veil for so long a time" (1). The author broaches the problematics of representation which the emotional prompt of the Madonna image ignores or at least represses: "Ne pas prétendre 'parler pour' ou pis "parler sur," à peine parler près de, et si possible tout contre. . . (8) "Do not claim to 'speak for' or worse to 'speak on,' barely speaking next to, and if possible right up against. . . ." (2).[7] The *nouvelles* incorporate textual arabesques which link Djebar's transcriptions of these women's narratives to Delacroix's nineteenth-century orientalism and to one of Pablo Picasso's fifteen paintings of his predecessor's "Femmes d'Alger dans leur appartement." The *Postface* reads Delacroix's paintings from the vantage point of hindsight, of a historian and of a woman.

The first painting relates, for her, the dynamics of the women's relationship with their bodies and with their space, whereas the second portrays the women less like sultanas and more like prisoners:

> En Algérie, précisément, lorsqu'en 1830 commence l'intrusion étrangère—maintenue coûte que coûte aux seuils des sérails appauvris—, à l'investissement progressif de l'espace au-dehors, correspond parallèlement un gel de plus en plus sourd de la communication intérieure: entre les générations, et encore plus entre les sexes. (153)

> (In Algeria, it was precisely in 1830, when the foreign intrusion began—one maintained at all costs at the thresholds of the impoverished seraglios—that a deafer and deafer freezing up of indoor communication accompanied the parallel progressive conquest of

> exterior space: between generations, and even more between sexes.) (140)

The painted intertexts signify in 1979 a territorialized alterity which encompasses French colonization but also embodies the women's subjection to Algerian patriarchy:

> Ces femmes d'Alger—celles qui demeurent immobiles depuis 1832 sur le tableau de Delacroix—, s'il était possible hier de trouver dans leur fixité l'expression nostalgique du bonheur ou celle de la douceur de la soumission, aujourd'hui cependant, nous frappe au plus sensible leur amertume désespérée. (153)

> (These women of Algiers—those who have remained immobile in Delacroix's painting since 1832—, if it was possible yesterday to find in their fixity the nostalgic expression of happiness or of the mildness of submission, today however, their desperate bitterness strikes our most sensitive nerve.) (140)

Praising the paintings' enigmatic characteristics, which render the women simultaneously present and far off, Djebar's commentary accentuates the polyvalence of visual representation and underscores the dimensions and impact of temporal or historical and cultural difference. Mobilized rather than immobilized by Delacroix's imprinting of the women he saw in Algeria, Djebar subverts the stereotype, thus demonstrating that iconic discourses are neither singular nor fixed. Their interpretation depends upon the receiver's point of view, which impinges on its effect.

Taking my cue from Djebar, I reexamine Delacroix's two paintings to situate them within the context of a nineteenth-century France whose colonizing thrust continued to affect and effect the evolution of bourgeois ideologies. Much artistic attention was paid to representing the state and the nation and their spheres of influence and action throughout the period. Reaching for symbolic capital to express national stability and identity with, the interrogation of sex and gender and their social inscription resulted in an ideology of the feminine linked to the nation which the bourgeois monarchy of Louis Philippe expressly sought to marry with the masculine body of the state.[8] As a man of the French nation rather than a man of the State, Delacroix personified the aspirations and contradictions of his time.[9] His artistic renderings, the conception of which surpassed for him their execution, formulated the gendered division of state and nation together with representations of the citizenry's roles within the private sphere and the body politic (Larue, 71–72).

* * *

In 1832, Delacroix made an unprecedented visit to a harem on the way back to France after a trip to Morocco where, in conformity with French norms of the period, he had journeyed as the appointed artist to Count Charles Edgar de Mornay's embassy. As such, he participated in the failed French diplomatic and military mission that sought to assuage Sultan Moulay Abd al-Rahman's discontent at the French conquest of Algiers and to prevent an escalation of the Franco-Algerian conflict.

Upon reaching Algiers in June 1832, Delacroix expressed his desire to enter a harem—a site usually reserved for the women and children of a household to which were admitted only men of the immediate family—husband, father, and with more protocol adult brothers, and sons—as well as other women, including foreign women (see Lewis, esp. 238; Melman, part 2). M. Poirel, the chief port administrator, asked a former *raïs*—a captain of the high seas—turned bailiff cum odd-jobs-man. After much discussion, the *raïs* assumed his position of colonized and consented to allow the painter to "penetrate" his own home.[10] The first of Delacroix's paintings to reflect the colonizer's transgression of Algerian gendered spheres was exhibited at the Salon carré du Louvre in 1834, two years after his return to his *belle patrie*—his beautiful fatherland. Flaying harem myths, his representation of a "real" harem exposed for all to see a woman's world heretofore only imagined.

The canvas recombines elements from a variety of earlier sketches executed in Morocco and during his three-day stay in Algiers to reveal not a locale of eroticism but a milieu in which "docile" women socialize.[11] Three women recline on cushions at floor level, and a fourth stands, having crossed the room, and looks back and down at two of them, who chat and handle a *narguilé*, or water pipe whilst the third seems to be daydreaming. The detailed replication of the fabrics worn by the women and encasing the cushions as well as that of the jewelry, mules, carpets, and tiling on the floor and walls texture richly the interior space these women inhabit, grounding the representation in documentary realism.[12] Missing from Delacroix's painting are the children he would have seen according to Djebar's text:

> La maison se trouvait dans l'ex-rue Duquesne. Delacroix, accompagné du mari et sans doute de Poirel, traverse "un couloir obscur" au bout duquel s'ouvre, inattendu et baignant dans une lumière presque irréelle, le harem proprement dit. Là des femmes et des enfants l'attendent "au milieu d'un amas de soie et d'or." L'épouse de l'ancien raïs, jeune et jolie, est assise devant un narguilé. (146)

> (The house was situated in what used to be the rue Duquesne. Delacroix, in the company of the husband and undoubtedly of Poirel, walks down "a dark hallway" at the end of which, unexpectedly and bathed in an almost unreal light, the actual harem opens up. There women and children are waiting for him, "surrounded by mounds of silk and gold." The wife of the former raïs, young and pretty, is sitting in front of a narguilé.) (134)

The second version of "Femmes d'Alger dans leur appartement" was begun in 1846 and completed in 1849, seventeen years after the voyage. It re-presents the same scene but emphasizes the positioning of the harem at the end of the long, obscure corridor alluded to in Djebar's text, which draws upon the account of the visit by Delacroix's friend, Charles Cournault. Rather than having the observer share the room's floor with the women, the point of viewing is removed from their immediate surroundings. The enclosure is emphasized. In the 1834 version the door on the right, which draws the gaze back and out on a diagonal sight line, together with the contrasts of shadows and light, delineate the depth of the sitting space. The disappearance of the former and the reduction of light sources in the 1849 painting foreshorten and enclose the women's universe. "Cet effet de cadrage [Djebar points out] a pour [. . .] résultat: d'éloigner de nous les trois femmes qui s'enfoncent alors plus profondément dans leur retrait. . ." (148). "This framing effect [Djebar points out] has the [. . .] effect of distancing the three women from us as they pull away more deeply into their retreat. . . ." (136). The elimination of the (useless?) details concentrates the unity of the painting's effect. Delacroix himself felt that his style improved once he had forgotten the small details, once he was no longer seeking exactitude as a representation of the truth of reality.[13] The deemphasis of the realistic details directs the viewer's gaze to follow the curve of the bodies' arrangement in the room, initiated by the black servant's upper body twist, extended by her red headdress and the diagonal line of her arms. As her right arm draws and lifts a curtain up and away as if revealing the women, her left upper arm and elbow initiates a circular sweep which encompasses the three women at leisure. Furthermore, the standing woman, no longer an integral part of the grouping of women, serves as the accessory that enables the outsider's gaze. She draws the curtain which here comes between her and the sitting women rehearsing the unveiling "orientalist" cliché, and iconicizing the stolen glance: "Ce tableau lui-même est un regard volé" (Djebar, 149) "This painting itself is a stolen glance" (137).

Regardless, the two "Femmes d'Alger dans leur appartement," especially when taken together, do not simply reproduce the orientalist topos of the transgressive male gazing at an *odalisque* set out against an imagined harem backdrop. The attribution of an identical title to the two paintings emphasizes the ambiguity of the represented. Such a repetition, such a stereotyping, dissimulates the origin of their inspiration by dissociating the signifiers from their signified Algerian setting. Two questions, one lexical, the other syntactical, come to mind. First, why is "appartement" substituted for harem, a word derived from the Arabic "haram" or "harim" which signifies unlawful, protected, sacred, what is forbidden (*Petit Robert*; *Larousse*).[14] In its secular usage, "haram" refers to the separate, protected part of a household where women, children, and servants live in seclusion and privacy (see Croutier, 17), apart from the *serenlik* where the men gather. Instead of the descriptor "harem" being used, it is translated or rather conveyed etymologically into French with the lexeme "appartement," which is derived from the Italian "appartare," to separate. The *Larousse* suggests that the usage of "appartement" in French dates back to Catherine de Vivonne, who devised the Hotel de Rambouillet's interior as several groupings of rooms; and that by the nineteenth century, the term "appartement" designated one or several divisions inside one residence in which persons lived apart. Hence the paintings of Delacroix resituate the women in a contemporary French environment. The Orient is therefore less a place than an artistic and sociopolitical topos which here blurs the cultural habitat reference by situating the women in, at the very least, a lexically French milieu.

The second question addresses the identity of the women in the painting and the manner in which they are referred to in its title. Who are these "femmes" in their apartment? The absence of any article in the title, ironically repeated in the eponymous title to Djebar's *nouvelles*, points to their position as representatives for a class of subjects. The term "femmes" surprises after the orientalist *défilé* of paintings with such titles as "orientale" or "odalisque." Yet the three sitting women hardly resemble the *odalisques* portrayed by Ingres, Decamps, and later by Gérome, or Manet for instance. They are not Turkish "odalik," enslaved chambermaids serving women in a harem. They do represent women from Algiers, and if the records of Delacroix's visit to the home of the French administration's bailiff are accurate, they belonged to the bourgeoisie. Djebar identifies the woman handling the *narguilé* as the Raïs' wife. Cournault asserts that the women were warned of the visit and so donned their most beautiful clothes. Delacroix himself is reported to have exclaimed upon seeing the women:

> C'est beau! C'est comme du temps d'Homère! La femme dans le gynécée s'occupant de ses enfants, filant la laine ou brodant de merveilleux tissus. C'est la femme comme je la comprends. (Djebar, 165)
>
> (It's beautiful! It's as in Homer's time! The woman in her gynaeceum looking after her children, spinning wool or embroidering splendid fabrics. That is woman as I think she should be!) (153)

With this problematic exclamation, the prying French painter transports the women to an almost atemporal milieu of domesticity. The erasure of the Algerian women's individual subjectivities universalizes and essentializes them. They are assigned to the general category of Woman, one which Delacroix has no problem understanding.

The comparison to women of Homer's time repeats the colonizing and appropriative gesture of Algerian similitude to the foundations of French culture. Tahar Ben Jelloun interprets "c'est beau comme au temps de Homère" "it's beautiful as in Homer's time" to signify that what impresses Delacroix is the presence of antiquity in the Maghreb (prologue, n.p.).[15] The colonized serve as models for their French counterparts, as purer models of an Occidental society predating modernization and industrialization. Rather than actually translating the perceived opacity of Maghrebi cultures, Orientalism delineated the recognizable in the inscription of the Other. French choreographic, literary, and visual artists more often than not depicted their own desires and values within an Oriental context. Hence, as John MacKenzie points up, a theory of cultural cross reference may be more pertinent than a theory of "Otherness" when looking at orientalist representations (50).

Over the course of the nineteenth century, the French cultural preoccupation with defining a new coherent national identity instantiated once again the emblematization of the Oriental.[16] This obsession extended to the question of sexuality. As political, industrial, and urban mutations impacted cultural and economic constructions of society, gender specific ideologies differentiated the body politic from the private domain. The transformation of mankind into humankind which eighteenth-century medical and anatomical research set out with its recasting of the one sex–two gender model as a two sex–two gender paradigm brought about a profound malaise about womanhood and femininity (Laqueur, 149–243). Such revisions together with the postrevolutionary upheavals blurred traditional definitions of male subjectivity and created anxieties about female spheres of influence. The ensuing sexualization of space—inner space, the home is reserved for women; outer space, the workplace and government for men—which Djebar also stresses as a configuration of traditional Algeria, served as a strategy for containing female power and defining feminine subjectivity. Such a division also demarcated male and female ideological roles within the bourgeois polity so that the notion of Nation was associated with women as the mothers and educators of the citizenry and that of State with men as the voters and administrators of France.

"Orientalist paintings" MacKenzie states "celebrate separation of male and female spheres in the Arab world and hold up this ideal for emulation" (58). These imaginary Western representations of harems also actualized woman as powerful and dangerous for the Western male. Delacroix's "Femmes d'Alger" confront the sexual connotations of the *odalisque* stereotype. They delineate the French obsession with docile female bodies but instead of displaying an eroticized scenario, they iconicize an ideology of feminine domesticity.[17]

The æsthetic distance which exists between the sketches and the paintings as well as the elapsed time between the trip and the finished works intimate the allegorical moves at work in the production of "Femmes d'Alger dans leur appartement." If, as Walter Benjamin reemphasized, allegory as defined by Quintilian signifies other talk or talk of the other,[18] these paintings "other talk" of the colonized Algerian women on one level, and on another, talk of the other as French domesticated woman. They allegorize with woman as private subject and public image, the domestication of bourgeois women. Delacroix's paintings execute a social model for women's behavior.

Victor Hugo mused in the 1829 preface to his "Orientales": "pour les empires comme pour les littératures, avant peu peut-être l'Orient est appelé à jouer un rôle dans l'Occident" "for empires as for literatures, before long perhaps the Orient will be called on to play a role in the West" (581). To this intertextual observer, the title's metaphorization of Delacroix's "appartement" scenes presents an equivalence between the harem and the domestic interiors of French bourgeois homes. The reiteration of the harem of female bodies seeks neither to portray nor to essentialize the real women at the *raïs*' home. Rather it enacts a Foucauldian notion of management of women. Delacroix's painting does not simply colonize the intimate space of the harem with a misrepresentation of the Orient and an appropriation of non-European women but reproduces French bourgeois ideology. The Métropole's periphery models the domestic subject of empire or the private sphere of French bourgeois women, secluded and receiving, quietly attending to homely tasks. Although the redoubled title refers to the Algerian women Delacroix saw and literally stereotyped in his two paintings, it also alludes to French women and their status and place in society. His second painting with its lack of ethnographic specificity could represent a Parisian living room. As the detailed perception of the harem habitat recedes over seventeen years, what occurs can be referred to, in light of Gayatri Chakravorty Spivak's work, as "the reciprocal effect of Empire on the home population" (Mackenzie, 21). Orientalism, a response to the desire to refigure the French nation, observes a form of endomorphism.

Just as Delacroix's "Femmes d'Alger dans leur appartement" were produced with a French public in mind, Hocine's "madone en enfer" was distributed with a Christian audience in mind.[19] Whether disseminated by Delacroix or by Agence France Presse, the images of the women of Algiers reinforce Western culture, its social codes and mentalities. The paintings and the photograph, these maps of interactions as Edward Said might mark them, stage a one-way ideological traffic of identities and gender roles (20).[20] And yet, as Djebar points up in her *postface*, the women in the paintings are talking and the preceding *nouvelles* inscribe stories which detail their own feminine spaces and activities. Similarly, the women shot (I use the term purposefully) for the "madone en enfer" photograph have other discourses and narratives—political, social, corporeal, cultural, religious, philosophical, scientific, fictional, gendered—to hold and recount:

> N'entretenant avec nous, spectateurs, aucun rapport. Ne s'abandonnant ni ne se refusant au regard. Etrangères mais présentes terriblement dans cette atmosphère raréfiée de la claustration.[. . .]
>
> Ces femmes [. . .] ne cessent de nous dire, depuis, quelque chose d'insoutenable et d'actuellement présent. (Djebar, 148–49)

> (Entertaining with us spectators, no rapport. Neither abandoning themselves to the gaze nor refusing it. Strangers, but terribly present in the rarified atmosphere of confinement. [. . .]
>
> These women [. . .] have never stopped telling us since, something unbearable and so very much about the present.) (136)

These passages, which refer to the women portrayed by Delacroix, seem nevertheless just as applicable in the context of the women in Hocine's photograph. Orientalist endomorphism, under a variety of different guises, perpetuates the sociopolitical problematics of representation.

Notes

1. As Althusser has shown, ideology does not represent the workings of the actual relations that regulate the lives of individuals but their imaginary affiliations to the relations they experience (165).

2. To situate the issue of representations briefly, I am borrowing from Sander L. Gilman's introduction to "Black Bodies, White Bodies: Toward an Iconography of Female Sexuality in Late Nineteenth-Century Art, Medicine, Literature," esp. 223–24. "Icon" is used as in C. S. Pierce's semiotics and in talking about Byzantine art to refer to a certain verbal or imaged diagrammatic/schematic symbolization in paintings, photographs, and texts which exhibits an ideological or mythical sign-posting.

3. Translations of passages from *Le Monde* and *L'Evènement* are my own.

4. Television and radio reports of the Algerian Daylight march replayed an interview with the French actor Boringer, who wanted his presence to be seen symbolically as a lit candle. Others wanted light to signify life and knowledge.

5. The Algerian author of this portrait only gave his first name. Although journalists are not formally banned from reporting and photographing, the police make their work very difficult, not allowing them on the scene, confiscating equipment and film, and accusing them of selling out, of being traitors and enemies of Algeria. Hocine affirms that on this occasion: "J'ai dû être interpelé quatre ou cinq fois par des policiers en civil, au point de ne pouvoir sortir mon boitier" "I must have been questioned four of five times by plainclothed police, to the point that I could not take out my camera." An Algiers

photographer, also present, was molested, insulted, and had his rolls of film confiscated (*Le Monde*, 12). The risks are great for all photographers, but especially those not working for Algerian newspapers. However, those who continue to try to witness the event deem valid the poet Tahar Djaout's assessment of the situation before his death in 1993: "Si tu parles, tu meurs. Si tu te tais, tu meurs aussi. Alors, parle et meurs" "If you speak out, you die. If you remain silent, you die also. So speak out and die" (quoted in *L'Evènement*, 44). According to *Le Monde*, the photographs in the Algerian press graphically show the massacres.

Hocine, whose photograph won first prize in the 1997 World Press Photo Competition, now faces defamation charges. "Within months" of the photograph's appearance in the world's presses, the Algerian weekly *Horizons*, "described as pro-government," "mounted a campaign" stating that Hocine had staged the photo and that "the unnamed woman did not exist." The woman then identified herself as Umsaid and denounced the caption as erroneous. Even though Agence France Presse issued a correction, Umsaid, represented by the lawyers for *Horizons*, filed suit in July 1998 claiming that "Hocine and the news agency exploited her suffering." From National Public Radio's *Morning Edition*, Dean Olsher reporting, 10 September 1998.

6. I draw the translations of Assia Djebar's text from Marjolijn de Jager's work. Where I have altered the latter's text I have tried to remain closer to the original text, which makes, however, for a less smooth style.

7. Although Djebar's rich text elaborates historicized narratives which speak of the strategic movements Algerian women have performed in the public sphere, my work here does not address the body of the collection's *nouvelles* but explores the issues that the author raises in her *ouverture* and *postface*.

8. See Leora Auslander for a succinct presentation of the changing forms of representation and definitions of citizen after the 1789 Revolution (101–2) where she states that: "[t]he State came to be understood as a constructed object (man-made quite literally) while the nation was equated with the natural, feminized, domestic world. . . . The hyphen [in "nation-state"] was not there accidentally; contemporaries thought that for the state to be secure, for the votes of its male citizens to be properly cast, nation was also necessary. Women were to be members of the nation—"nationals" representing their families . . . socially" (102).

9. Detached from political involvement, Delacroix nevertheless pursued a career which repeatedly sought official recognition. After eight attempts he was finally elected to the Institut. Although only elected to the Académie des Beaux Arts in 1857, his achievement was marked in 1855 at the Exposition universelle, where thirty-six of his canvases were exhibited.

10. Charles Cournault, Delacroix's friend and a frequent traveler, noted how the painter had gained access to a harem: "[Delacroix] désireux de visiter l'intérieur d'une maison où il pût dessiner des femmes mauresques, ce qu'il n'avait pu faire à Tanger où il n'avait pénétré que chez les israelites, prie [sic] M. Poirel de lui en faciliter les moyens. On fit venir le Cahouch de la direction, sorte de factotem qui remplit l'office d'huissier près des administrations. Après de longs pourparlers, M. Poirel obtint de lui qu'il conduirait clandestinement Eugène Delacroix dans sa propre maison. . . . Delacroix exécute d'après [les femmes], des croquis à l'aquarelle qui lui servirent plus tard à peindre son tableau des Femmes d'Alger" "desirous to visit the interior of a

house where he would be able to paint Moorish women, which he had not been able to do in Tangiers where he had only entered the homes of Israelites, [Delacroix] asked Mr Poirel to make it possible for him. The management's Cahouch, a sort of odd-job man who functioned as the administration's bailiff was called for. After lengthy negotiations, Mr Poirel had him agree to lead Eugene Delacroix secretly into his own home. . . . Delacroix executed several water-color sketches of [the women] which helped him later with his painting of the Women of Algiers" (Lambert, 11).

11. See for example: the lead pencil and watercolor study "Femme arabe assise sur des coussins" (Louvre RF 4185e), with its numerous color notations and the woman's identity Mounay ben sultane written in (Delacroix probably remembered or even used this sketch as the basis for the figure of the woman resting on the pillows on the left of the painting); the one of two Algerian women (Louvre RF 4185a) representing Moûni and Zohra Bensoltane; and the drawings of the Jewish women seen in Morocco.

12. Although obviously an interior space, the open door at the back of the room together with the black maid's trajectory towards a possible other room, signal a certain freedom of movement rather than the orientalist version of the harem as a women's prison.

13. As Edgar Pisani underlines: "[c]e qui surprend . . . c'est la distance esthétique qui existe entre les croquis saisis sur le vif et le vaste tableau plus élaboré mais aussi le temps qui s'est écoulé entre le voyage et l'essentiel de l'œuvre. En allant des uns aux autres, chacun se demandera ce qu'il préfère de l'improvisation souvent intimiste ou de la reconstitution où la lumière éclate" "[what] surprises . . . is the aesthetic distance which exists between the sketches drawn on the spot and the vastly more elaborate painting but also the time which elapsed between the trip and the most important works. Moving to and fro between them, everyone will ask himself which he prefers: the often intimate improvisation or the reconstruction with its explosion of light" (Préface, n. p.).

14. The sacred area around Mecca and Medina for instance is *haram*, closed to all but the Faithful. The term would also be applied to the women that a stranger must not see.

15. Similarly, Alain Daguerre de Hureaux emphasizes: "L'Orient tel qu[e Delacroix] le perçoit est surtout un lieu préservé, où s'épanouit une antiquité revivifiée" "The Orient as [Delacroix] perceives it is above all a preserved place, in which a revivified antiquity blooms" (71). Ben Jelloun admits that Delacroix's work ". . . est un miroir légèrement déformant, réfléchissant une nature brute . . . des couleurs qui ne correspondent pas à la réalité" ". . . is a slightly deforming mirror, reflecting a savage nature . . . colors which do not correspond to reality." He adds: "un créateur n'est pas un copieur de la vie, il ne représente pas la réalité" "a creator is not a copier of life, he does not represent reality" (Préface n. p.).

16. Since the Middle Ages, the North African and Arabian cultures have repeatedly served as points of comparison and as scapegoats for the French.

17. Louis Philippe, the bourgeois monarch, was so taken with the 1834 version of "Femmes d'Alger dans leur appartement" that he bought it.

18. See Chris Bongie's discussion (22–23) of Benjamin's definition of allegory in *Gesammelte Schriften* (666; 681).

19. Indeed, Benjamin shows that "allegory itself was sown by Christianity" (*Origin*, 224).

20. Said calls for studying the map of interactions, "the actual and often productive traffic occurring on a day-by-day, and even minute-by-minute basis among states, societies, groups, identities" (20). To begin to understand the nineteenth century's colonizing desire, he suggests looking at the cultural documents of the period to make explicit the relationships between the power considering itself at the center and what it situated at its peripheries.

L'Éducation nationale and Salvation through Literature

M. MARTIN GUINEY

HISTORIAN EUGEN WEBER ONCE WARNED THAT ONE CAN EASILY overestimate the importance of education in the history of the French Republic, since that same history is written almost exclusively by academics. It is indeed tempting to write a narrative in which one's own profession is the conquering hero, a temptation university professors rarely have the opportunity to resist. Since the birth of a fragile Republic after the *débâcle*, however, the French University has practically not ceased to write its own *De Bello Gallico*. National education came into prominence as a topic of political debate immediately upon the founding of the *Convention Nationale*; France's chronic lack of a fully developed and implemented public education policy was the rationalization which emerged from the intense national self-analysis following 1871; and finally, the school became the locus as well as the instrument of France's return to cultural and political dominance: *veni, vidi, vici*. My essay will examine not only the incongruity of academics claiming relevance as agents of historical change, but the even greater one of having the traditionally most disinterested field of academic inquiry, literature, claim a place in the vanguard of the Republican struggle for legitimacy.

The early 1880s were a symbolic turning point in the history of the Third Republic from the perspective of national educational policy. As everyone knows, Jules Ferry's laws went into effect and, in their wake, many secondary events occurred, such as the founding of the *Alliance Françoise* (1883), or the appearance of a relatively new type of publishing venture: the anthology of French literature, combining excerpts of literary texts with historical and pedagogical commentary, designed for use in the secondary school classroom. La Librairie Belin, which published its first edition of the popular primary school reader *Le Tour de la France par deux enfants* in 1877, and La Librairie

Hachette, which already had specialized in school textbooks as well as scholarly research on education, were two of the first companies to take advantage of the importance of a new category of books written for and about the recently regenerated institution of national education. Some *manuels* from this period which I will discuss are Wilhelm Rinn's *Littérature, composition et style* of 1880, Louis Liard's *Lectures Morales et Littéraires* of 1882, Charles Bigot's *Le Petit Français*, an elementary school reader of 1883, Philibert-Soupé's *Analyse des ouvrages français* of 1888, and Edouard Roehrich's translation of *La Chanson de Roland, à l'usage des écoles* of 1885. All translations of the French quotes from these works are my own.

Contemporaneous with the rapid growth of this new market created by governmental policy was a plethora of pamphlets, speeches, more or less scientific studies defending particular educational ideologies that fell into three basic categories: defense of the Church, advocacy of a mostly leftist utilitarian concept of education, and the defense of the Republic itself which, I argue, consisted of a dialectical synthesis of these two extremes. One of the many academics who provided Republican educational policy with its scientific rationale was the philosopher Alfred Fouillée of the Sorbonne whose wife, born Augustine Tuillerie, had written *Le Tour de la France par deux enfants* (1877) under the pseudonym G. Bruno (for Giordano Bruno, in homage to an earlier professor of the Sorbonne who sought to reconcile the worldly and the spiritual). In 1891, Fouillée published his answer to both the utilitarian and the Catholic factions: *L'Enseignement au point de vue national* (*Education from a National Perspective*) chez Hachette, of course. The purpose of my essay is to delineate the Third Republic's attempt, both in theory and in practice, to enlist literature in support of its claim to legitimacy. In brief: literariness, the quality which is presumably unique to canonical texts, functions as the source of the aura of authority that, when it is manifest, sanctions the exercise of political power, especially of political power which has explicitly relinquished the rule of force in favor of representative democracy. To put it differently, in their attempt to put forth and to regulate the notion of literariness, the pedagogues of the Third Republic derived political capital from the exploitation and dissemination of the belief that literature is *sui generis*, that it manifests the absolute yet secular value that alone can provide the State with the means to replace the spiritual authority of organized religion as well as the physical authority of tyranny.

Of course, literature was one of several subjects that constituted the raw material of primary and secondary public education. Furthermore, most of the political arguments put forward to promote education, such as the claim that Prussia defeated France because of the higher degree of education of its troops, certainly did not appear to imply that literature should be a privileged subject ahead of, let us say, math and geography. In fact, a large portion of public opinion, members of the radical leftist opposition as well as free-market advocates, adopted in the 1880s the utilitarian argument that the State should put purely strategic economic concerns above all others when supporting education, and require only applied sciences, modern languages, and any other subject which had a direct impact on France's competitiveness in the world. Raoul Frary, a left-wing journalist, published this thesis in a book called *La Question du latin* in 1885, and the title became a catchphrase for the debate, not only over Latin's status as an obligatory component of the *baccalauréat*, but more generally over the question of whether the disinterested study of literature, either classical or modern, was still sufficiently relevant after the *défaite* to deserve its position as one of the pillars of national education. I believe that what might seem like a rather insignificant question—whether access to the *baccalauréat* and the social status it conferred ought necessarily to require study of ancient Greek or Latin—in fact stood for a much larger and more significant question: should the State be in the business of supporting, much less privileging, *any* field of study which did not have a direct, measurable impact on national prosperity and influence worldwide?

The defense of Latin and of its close relative, the study of literature, gradually came to distinguish staunch supporters of the Republic from their political adversaries, including the inheritors of the legacy of 1848 and of the *Commune*. The question I am interested in is the following: why did the Third Republic muster a vast array of political and academic figures to defend literature's position at the very center of the educational enterprise? Ferdinand Buisson's monumental *Dictionnaire de pédagogie* (1882–1911), the founding of the prestigious *Revue pédagogique* and *Revue Internationale de l'Enseignement*, all of which take for granted the centrality of literature in education, represent an unprecedented mobilization of the academic elite. The obvious answer, that literature is an important constituent of national identity, is insufficient: something other than a modern *Défence et illustration de la langue française* is at work.

To answer this question I will first look at how Edouard Roehrich, in his introduction to his translation of *La Chanson de Roland*, justifies its use in classes for students who have not even attained the *lycée* level. His text was therefore intended for a wide audience, encompassing future *lycéens*, as well as future students of *enseignement spécial* and even individuals who would not continue their education longer than was required by law:

> [Les enfants] vivent parmi nous comme des étrangers. Nous autres adultes, parents et professeurs, hommes d'action et savants de cabinet, nous n'avons guère de prise sur eux parce que nous pensons autrement qu'eux. Notre culture met une trop grande distance entre nous et nos enfants. Mais ceux-ci pensent et sentent exactement comme pensaient et sentaient nos ancêtres à l'époque où la culture moderne n'existait pas.[1]

> (Children live among us like foreigners. We adults, parents and teachers, men of action and scholars, have little hold over them because we think differently than they. Our culture puts too great a distance between our children and us. But they think and feel exactly as our ancestors thought and felt before the existence of modern culture.)

The implication of Roehrich's statement is quite clear. Children are, figuratively speaking, foreigners, as well as primitives. The claim that medieval literature is more accessible to them because they are so much more like people in the Middle Ages than modern adults, supports an enterprise in which the child, in the process of acquiring a chronological knowledge of literature, gradually loses his alien status. What we have is a process of initiation which resembles at times a related, but fundamentally different process: spiritual conversion—but here it is conversion of a secular kind, therefore one that defies precise definition. To begin to describe it, one could say that secular conversion, like religious conversion, refuses to acknowledge faiths that compete for the child's allegiance. Roehrich admits as much when he states outright in his teacher's manual that the only verse of the *Chanson de Roland* which he omitted from his translation was the one most expressive of Christian fanaticism, the one describing the revenge of Charlemagne's army on the city of Cordoba and which deals, not coincidentally, with conversion: "En la cité, il n'est pas un païen qui ne soit tué ou devenu chrétien." ("In the city there is not one pagan who was not killed or become a Christian.")[2]

The mention of *Roland*'s role in the curriculum raises an important question relative to the construction of national identity in the classroom from a Republican perspective. As a subject of study, isn't history the most appropriate means of creating a sense of national destiny, and of reinforcing the legitimacy of republicanism as the telos of the narrative that begins: "Nos ancêtres les Gaulois . . ."? This is true, and the history class in the Third Republic school repeatedly asks the student outright to make a leap of faith, a suppression of the rational process, that is akin to religious initiation as represented by Catholic traditions such as catechism, first communion, confirmation. I will mention two examples that show the school requiring the student to believe that the value of French history is other than the values of strength and virtue, a belief that was especially important given the recent history of an illegitimate regime followed by *la défaite*. When Mme Fouillée, in *Le Tour de la France par deux enfants*, describes Vercingétorix throwing his weapons disdainfully at the feet of Julius Cæsar,[3] she asks rhetorically: "Enfants [. . .] demandez-vous lequel de ces deux hommes, dans cette lutte, fut le plus grand?" ("Children . . . ask yourselves which one of these two men, in this struggle, was the greatest?")[4] In my second example, Charles Bigot takes the paradox even further in his textbook for advanced primary schoolchildren, *Le Petit Français*:

> La France a de graves et insupportables défauts, dont aucune leçon ne l'a bien corrigée. Elle est légère, vaniteuse, téméraire dans la bonne fortune, prompte à s'abandonner dans la mauvaise. Elle a été querelleuse souvent, arrogante plus d'une fois, injuste à l'occasion. Elle a aussi abusé de la force contre des faibles, accablé et opprimé, fait sentir au vaincu le poids de son talon. Elle t'a fait sa confession sans réticence quand tes maîtres te racontaient son histoire.[5]

> (France has serious and intolerable faults, of which no lesson has cured her. She is frivolous, vain, foolhardy when her fortunes are good, quick to be discouraged when they are bad. She has often been quarrelsome, sometimes arrogant, at times unjust. She has also abused of her strength against the weak, burdened and oppressed, and has made the vanquished feel the weight of her foot. She has given you her confession without reticence whenever your teachers were telling you her story.)

The structure of the confession, curiously inverted in this passage in which the classroom is the place where the nation seeks absolution for its sins from its future citizens, and the act of faith demanded in order to interpret France's history as glorious, even, and perhaps especially, in its moments of physical and even moral weakness, are essential elements of the *culte laïque*. But they are matters of doctrine, which is to say, they speak to the content of Republican secular ideology, and not so much to its practice. And yet it is in the practice, I would argue, that the power of such ideology to evangelize, so to speak, manifests itself. My approach to the study of the school system assumes that the practice within which the initiation/conversion takes place is, primarily, the teaching of literature.

The spiritual authority of religion seems most closely related, in the pedagogical sphere, to the "literariness" of literature, one aspect of the school curriculum that escapes rational analysis. When attempting to define this quality, the pedagogues of the Republic could only make arbitrary statements, such as Louis Liard's following claim in his anthology *Lectures morales et littéraires* (which has a dual table of contents: one which lists works of literature according to time period, another which lists them according to moral categories: *courage, patriotisme, fidélité,* etc.): "[l]es grands écrivains sont aussi les meilleurs maîtres de morale et de patriotisme, ceux dont la leçon saisit le mieux les âmes." ("Great writers are also the best teachers of morality and patriotism, those whose lesson best touches the soul.")[6] It is important to recognize here that Liard does not state that all great literature is inherently moral, an impossible claim regardless of how strongly one desires to make it, but merely that literature, when it happens also to be moral and patriotic, is best suited to transmit those values to the student. It is on this purported ability of literature to be the best vehicle for moral instruction that I now want to concentrate.

Alfred Fouillée, who spent part of his career elaborating a philosophical justification for the educational policy of the Third Republic, brought up the *Question du Latin* in 1891 (which suggests that the controversy was still raging almost ten years after Frary's book appeared) in *L'Enseignement au point de vue national.* In order to understand his point, one must realize that an objection made against classical studies, and through them implicitly against any obligatory subject which did not have utilitarian ideals as its purpose, was that only wealthy people could afford to study a dead language which could not provide anyone with a living wage, with the exception of the (already) very small number of classicists able to make it their profession. In fact, making the teaching of Latin one's profession was in itself a source of ridicule. Maupassant published in 1886 a short story called *La Question du Latin* in which the protagonist is a pathetic Latin teacher, a caricature of the person whose physical ineptitude is exceeded only by his professional irrelevance. It is not clear from the text itself why Maupassant called his story *La Question du Latin*, since the polemic by that name plays no role in the plot. The narrator merely uses it as a pretext to initiate his narrative: "Cette question du latin, dont on nous abrutit depuis quelque temps, me rappelle une histoire, une histoire de ma jeunesse." ("This question of Latin, by which we have been bored for some time, reminds me of a story, a story from my youth.")[7] In the context of the 1890s, however, in which *la question* revolved around the relevance of Latin to the modern world, it is quite clear that Maupassant meant for the title to underscore how hopelessly out of touch with practical reality—and good, modern business sense—his classically-trained protagonist really was. His story and the caricature it contains illustrate how popular the notion of Latin as an antiquated, useless subject had become.

This view of Latin (and literary studies in general) as a mere badge of social distinction derived in large part from the Jesuit tradition of teaching Latin rhetoric, or the ability to write and speak the language with *no* reference to classical literature, except for the very narrow purpose of emulating the style of a few famous Roman orators. The Latin (or Greek) whose status in the *lycée* Alfred Fouillée defends is something altogether different:

> Leur vertu mystique, si on entend par là une influence latente parce qu'elle est profonde et vitale, vient de tous ces liens invisibles qui nous rattachent à l'antiquité et qu'ont noués, renoués vingt siècles. Vertu toute naturelle et non surnaturelle, analogue à celle de l'hérédité, de la race, de la nationalité.[8]

> (Their mystical virtue, if by that one understands a latent, because deep and vital, influence, comes from all those invisible links which attach us to antiquity and which twenty centuries have created and recreated. This virtue is completely natural and not supernatural, analogous to the virtue of heredity, race, and nationality.)

And later on:

> M. Raoul Frary aura beau dire qu'il comprend toutes les cultures, sauf celle du bois mort, [la littérature classique] est une des principales racines mères dont la sève vient encore se mêler à celle de l'arbre entier et contribuer à sa floraison perpétuelle.[9]

> (Mr. Raoul Frary can well say that he understands all cultures, save the culture of dead wood, [classical literature] is one of the primary roots ("mother roots") of which the sap continues to mingle with that of the entire tree to contribute to its perpetual blossoming.)

Fouillée's organic metaphor for the history of literature is Darwinian, but the use to which he puts it is definitely not a scientific, in the sense of materialistic, proposition:

> Si la théorie de l'évolution, appliquée aux problèmes de l'enseignement, n'a encore donné que des conclusions très générales et souvent peu nettes, c'est qu'on a négligé d'introduire le moyen terme nécessaire entre l'humanité et l'individu, à savoir la nationalité.[10]

> (If the theory of evolution, applied to problems of education, has so far only led to very general and vague conclusions, it is because one has neglected to introduce the necessary middle term between humanity and individual, which is to say nationality.)

We are once again confronted with Roehrich's thesis that the history of culture is, in a sense, teleological. It is not strictly evolutionary in the sense that it changes perpetually in response to historical, as compared to biological forces, but rather in that it represents the transition between two different states, understood as akin to foreign and native, as well as primitive and cultured. It is exactly like another kind of evolution, which is both a continuum and a metamorphosis: the transition from child to adult. Another way to express this notion of conversion from one state to an entirely different one might be: it is impossible to be just a little bit French.

The inherent contradiction of the spiritual positivism that Fouillée expounds is one that he shares with Taine and Renan, two other evangelists for the cult of positivism who sought to reconcile the spiritual with the scientific and the historical. Quite simply, the positivist ideal is similar to, and supportive of, Republicanism. Both seek to ground their legitimacy in reason, either the reason underlying the scientific method, or the principle according to which a nation can legally arise from the equitable distribution of power through universal suffrage. In each case, it would seem, the institutions in question sacrifice the power to convert, understood as a process that exceeds the domain of reason. The genius of the Republican policies on education was the ability to recognize that sacrifice, and in that recognition to avoid making it. To the extent that the canonical status of literary works is itself a matter of faith, it helps the State in its attempt to elevate the secular to the atemporal. It at least symbolizes, if it does not actually resolve, the paradox of taking an evolutionary (Darwinian) model of culture and turning it into a teleological one. All that is required is the agreement on the part of the student of literature to ask any and every question about his or her subject of study except one: what makes literature literary?

The controversy surrounding the status of Latin in the curriculum, which has erupted sporadically in France numerous times since the 1880s, is so important because Latin is seen as the vanguard of Republican education. If eliminated or marginalized by the stewards of national education, it will signal the beginning of the end of education's moral authority, and hence of its power to convert. Here is Fouillée again:

> L'éducation n'a pour fin ni de faire parler les langues vivantes [. . .] ni de faire lire couramment les langues mortes [. . .]. Sa fin, encore une fois, est la culture des forces intellectuelles, en vue de la nation et de la race: les langues ne sont que des moyens; [. . .] les langues mortes sont de bons moyens, à la condition qu'elles soient étudiées *littérairement*.[11]

> (Education has as its end neither to make one speak modern languages, neither to make one read dead ones. . . . Its end, once again, is the culture of intellectual forces for the sake of the nation and of the race: languages are but a means; . . . dead languages are a good means, provided they be studied *literarily*.)

To understand what Fouillée means by the term "*étudier littérairement*," one must be familiar with the conflict, throughout the Third Republic, between "*histoire littéraire*" and "*critique littéraire*," analyzed by Antoine Compagnon in *La Troisième République des lettres*. Fouillée falls into the camp of the *critiques*: ". . . l'esprit doit être un instrument, non un magasin d'antiquités . . ." ("the mind must be an instrument, not an antique shop"),[12] and: "Ce n'est pas, tout au moins, en racontant l'histoire de la peinture qu'on fera des peintres." ("It is certainly not by telling the history of painting that one will create painters.")[13] Fouillée rejects both the Jesuit tradition of Latin rhetoric and the growing tendency to substitute the study of literature with the study of literary history, a sort of erudition for its own sake which might be posited as being at the opposite extreme of Jesuit pedagogy. The transformative power of literature depends upon the school's willingness to require students to demonstrate the literariness of texts to themselves, which makes Fouillée's position similar to the Protestant attack on the Catholic concealment of scripture from the faithful, its replacement of the Word of God with images and glosses. The French literary canon, as it is ratified by the institution of *l'éducation nationale,* shares in major respects the function of scripture in religious practice, and the school is the closest that the Third Republic can come to spreading the news of its advent to the population. The debates over Latin and over literary history were, in some ways, akin to certain issues dividing the Church from its Protestant offshoots, with the difference that the Republic contained within its ranks partisans of all sides of the theological debate. Both the utilitarians, who believed in individual salvation through one's ability to contribute to the general economic prosperity, and the literary historians, who believed in the inviolability of the mystery of the literary text to such an extent that they removed it from view, were up against the spiritual positivism argued for, and I think ultimately achieved, by Fouillée and the philosophers of *l'éducation nationale.*

In Fouillée's terms: "considérée philosophiquement, la grammaire a sa moralité" ("considered philosophically, grammar has its own morality.")[14] There is an ethics of language, governed by rules of clarity which are themselves derived from the study of literature, echoed by Wilhelm Rinn in *Littérature, composition et style*: "[les règles] apprennent à perfectionner [les dispositions naturelles] par la pratique et par l'étude des meilleurs écrivains." (". . . rules teach one to perfect [one's natural dispositions] by practice as well as by the study of the best authors") (10). In his conclusion, Fouillée states that ". . . les objets essentiels d'études *intensives* sont: la littérature, la théorie générale des sciences, la philosophie." ("the essential objects of education are: literature, the general theory of sciences, philosophy.")[15] Nothing that is utilitarian, nothing that places rote memorization over the disinterested exercise of the mind, belongs in the school. This is a seductive model indeed, for those of us who teach the humanities in a world in which the utilitarian ethos is as dominant as ever. According to such a model, not only are the sciences and humanities good preparation for the demands of the global economy, they are the *only* truly appropriate preparation.

To convince anybody of this argument, much less achieve the social consensus that alone creates change in a democratic society, however, a major task lay ahead: there needed to be a massive assimilation of the fundamental articles of faith upon which Fouillée's vision depended. The history of the Third Republic, particularly of its educational policy, teaches us that such can occur, but that it is a never-ending process that is vulnerable to moments of great collective doubt. What makes this a matter of faith, which is to say, that part of it which no scientific method can adequately explain, is well expressed by Professor Philibert-Soupé in the section on seventeenth-century literature in his 1888 anthology: *Analyse des ouvrages français.* Needless to say, the belief in the seventeenth-century as the apogee of French literary style was and is a pillar of the educational system. Philibert-Soupé justifies this exalted position in the following terms: "Ce fut pour les lettres, les arts et même les sciences une époque privilégiée, où la raison, le bon goût, le beau style égalèrent et parfois surpassèrent le génie et l'inspiration." ("It was for literature, the arts, and even science, a privileged era, in which reason, good taste, and beautiful style equaled and sometimes surpassed genius and inspiration.")[16] It is in that final claim, that the achievements due to formal aspects of classicism not only equaled but even surpassed those due to genius and inspiration, that the article of faith that is unique to Republican education appears. For it is in the process of demonstrating what cannot be demonstrated, that literariness is most clearly present in the victory of *visible* style over *invisible* inspiration, that the task of the *professeur de français* or the *professeur de rhétorique* both resembles and diverges from that of the parish priest he was called upon to replace.

Notes

1. Edouard Roehrich, trans., *La Chanson de Roland: traduction nouvelle à l'usage des écoles précédée d'une introduction sur l'importance de la Chanson de Roland pour l'éducation de la jeunesse* (Paris: Fishbacher, 1885), 6.

2. Ibid., 40.

3. This passage from *Le Tour de la France par deux enfants*, suggesting the superior greatness of Vercingétorix in spite of, and perhaps because of, his defeat at the hands of the Romans is very effectively parodied in the opening sequence of Goscinny and Uderzo's *Astérix le Gaulois* in which we see a hulking giant of a Vercingétorix casting his weapons, not at, but *on* the feet of a minuscule Julius Caesar.

4. Alfred Fouillée, *L'Enseignement du point de vue national* (Paris: Librairie Hachette, 1909), 138.

5. Charles Bigot, *Le Petit Français* (Paris: Weill et Maurice, 1883), 79.

6. Louis Liard, *Lectures morales et littéraires* (Paris: Belin, 1882), I.

7. Guy de Maupassant, *Contes et Nouvelles* (Paris: Albin Michel, 1959–60), 565.

8. Fouillée, *L'Enseignement,* 150.

9. Ibid, 158.

10. Ibid., 131.

11. Ibid., 297.

12. Antoine Compagnon, *La Troisième République des lettres: de Flaubert à Proust* (Paris: Seuil, 1983), 314.

13. Ibid., 323.

14. Fouillée, *L'Enseignement,* 305.

15. *Ibid.*, 380.

16. A. Philibert-Soupé, *Analyse des ouvrages français indiqués aux programmes du baccalauréat ès lettres (première partie) des baccalauréats ès sciences complet et restreint, de l'enseignement secondaire spécial, de l'enseignement secondaire des jeunes filles et de l'enseignement primaire supérieur* (Paris: Foucart, 1888), 34.

Part II
Beyond the Peripheries

Aerial Misses and Spectating Messieurs: The Paradox of the Lady Acrobat in the French Fin de Siècle

JENNIFER FORREST

ACCORDING TO THE AMATEUR CIRCUS PERFORMER AND CIRCUS historian Henry Thétard, the evolution of the European circus, from Phillip Astley's codifying of the modern format in 1770 to the twentieth-century version, possesses three more or less distinct periods: the period of English dominance from 1770 to 1840, that of French dominance from 1840 to 1880, and that of German dominance from 1880 to the 1940s. Phillip Astley's circus had taken over the attractions presented at the "music-houses" and incorporated them into the program that had formerly only featured equestrian acts. French dominance of this form of entertainment corresponded to the dominance of permanent circuses throughout France, but particularly in Paris. In the Paris of the 1840s there were three permanent circuses: le Cirque Olympique, l'Hippodrome, and le Cirque des Champs-Elysées. The foundation of the latter in 1841 marked the period when Paris was "la capitale du cirque" ("the circus capital"),[1] offering "un spectacle luxueux, grandiose, goûté de toutes les classes de la société, aussi bien de l'aristocratie que du populaire" ("a luxurious, grandiose spectacle, enjoyed by all social classes, by the aristocracy as well as the working classes").[2] The decline of the permanent circus began in the 1880s with the competition created by the music halls, where acts featured in the circus began to appear regularly on bills. It is with this period of the entertainment's decadence, however, that coincides a peculiarly fin de siècle appreciation of the circus, and of the lady aerialist in particular, through her ability to embody the æsthetics of simulation.

Between roughly 1880 and 1910 the lady acrobat, especially the flying woman, appealed strikingly to the French imagination, and we can further account for her ability to fascinate fin de siècle artists and *littérateurs* in the general highlighting of aerial acts in the permanent circuses, hippodromes, and music halls. Tightrope and high-wire acrobatics, and the flying and solo trapezes, were, and continue to be, "exercices gracieux" ("graceful exercises") dominated by women, leaving floor work to men for whom the display of their "vigueur musculaire" ("muscular strength") counted more than "la grâce souple" ("supple grace") in the execution of a trick (Thétard, 2:154).[3] Another explanation for her popularity comes from Le Roux who claims, however erroneously, that the true female acrobat was more an exception than the rule; the attraction was rather in her *beauté plastique* ("physical beauty") and circus directors counted on the appeal of a half-nude female performer's physical charms to compensate for her lack of real talent. Even when her skill is equal to that of a man, Le Roux as spokesman for his generation says that "nous préférerons toujours l'exercice de la femme à celui de l'homme" ("we will always prefer the exercise of a woman to that of a man"). He explains this preference by citing that the pleasure of watching the execution of a trick is augmented by "le plaisir général que cause en toute occasion l'exhibition d'un corps féminin parfait. Ce plaisir très vif n'est pas, chez nous autres modernes, uniquement intellectuel et moral: il y entre un peu d'émotion physique, de désir, d'amour . . ." ("the general pleasure that on each occasion the exhibition of a perfect feminine body causes. This keen pleasure is not, among us other moderns, solely intellectual and spiritual: a little physical emotion, desire, and love play a part. . . .") (Le Roux, 141–42).

He was not alone in his preference for the lady acrobat. In painting, the lady acrobat figures prominently in Edgar Degas's *Miss Lala au Cirque Fernando* (1879), Henri de Toulouse-Lautrec's *Au Cirque Fernando* (1888), and Georges Seurat's *Cirque* (1890–91), the celebrated study of the female equestrienne. And, however peripheral, in the left-hand corner of Manet's *Un Bar aux Folies-Bergère* (c. 1882), a lady acrobat's lower legs in tights, her feet in bright green boots, balance on a trapeze swing. Among Jules Chéret's many circus posters featuring female acrobats one finds his 1880 depiction of Miss Lala at the Folies-Bergère, and his 1886 work for the Nouveau Cirque. The most courted of the lady acrobats were the aerialists, and it is no wonder that other popular entertainments offered flying women in the manner of the female trapeze artist. In 1892–93 in the fairground circuit and in 1896 at Paris's Alcazar d'été, the acrobat-illusionist Marie Fourrier combined the thrills and chills of the circus trapeze and tightrope/high-wire acts with that of mechanical theatrical illusions in her role as "Miss Aérogyne" or the flying woman. She had many fairground and music hall imitators: Ethéra at the Palais de l'Art Nouveau, Magneta at the Amphithéâtre, Miss Beauty "femme volante" ("flying woman"), Mlle Myrtha, "Aérolithe Reine des Airs" ("Aérolithe Queen of the Air"), and Erolyna.[4]

The lady acrobat's ability to fascinate the fin de siècle artist and *littérateur*, however, draws less upon the era's efforts to construct and perform sexual difference in the unmistakable display of a half-nude female body (as in the 1890s version of the burlesque, and in the trapeze striptease) and more upon the circus's uncanny way of facilitating the creation of an alternate universe, one epitomized by the chameleon sexuality of the lady acrobat's body during a performance. Whereas the male acrobat of the fixed circus's heyday appealed to artists and poets in his ability to give the illusion of passing into another reality, the lady acrobat, because of her power visibly to change sex, will dethrone him, and will offer herself to the fin de siècle as living proof of that other reality.

Gendering the Trapezist's Body

In a journal entry dated 21 November 1859, Jules and Edmond de Goncourt expressed their preference for the circus over all other forms of entertainment. At the time, the French circus was at the height of its success, and all of Paris made it the rage:

> Nous n'allons qu'à un théâtre. Tous les autres nous ennuient et nous agacent. Il y a un certain rire de public à ce qui est vulgaire, bas et bête, qui nous dégoûte. Le théâtre où nous allons est le cirque. Là nous voyons des sauteurs et des sauteuses, des clowns et des franchisseuses de cercles de papier, qui font leur métier et leur devoir: le[s] seuls talents au monde qui soient incontestables, absolus comme des mathémathiques ou plutôt comme un saut périlleux. Il n'y a pas là d'acteurs et d'actrices faisant semblant d'avoir du talent: ou ils tombent ou ils ne tombent pas. Leur talent est un fait.
>
> Nous les voyons, ces hommes et ces femmes risquant leurs os en l'air pour attraper quelques bravos, avec un remuement d'entrailles, avec un je ne sais quoi de férocement curieux et, en même

> temps, de sympathiquement apitoyé, comme si ces gens étaient de notre race et que tous, bobèches, historiens, philosophes, pantins et poètes, nous sautions héroïquement pour cet imbécile de public.
>
> Au fait, savez-vous que c'est la plus grande supériorité de l'homme sur la femme, que le saut périlleux?[5]
>
> (We go to only one theater. All the others bore us and irritate us. There is a certain audience laughter at what is common, low, and stupid, which disgusts us. The theater where we go is the circus. There we see male and female tumblers, clowns, and women acrobats leaping through circles of paper, who do their craft and their duty: the only talents in the world which are incontestable, absolute like mathematics or rather like a[n aerial] somersault. There, there are no actors and actresses pretending to have talent. Either they fall or they don't fall. Their talent is a fact.
>
> We see them, those men and women risking their bones in the air to snatch some applause, with a stirring in the bowels, with a fiercely strange, and, at the same time, warmly commiserating je ne sais quoi, as if these people were of our race and as if all of us, mugs, historians, philosophers, stooges, and poets, were leaping heroically for that imbecilic audience.
>
> By the way, do you know that the [aerial] somersault is the greatest superiority of man over woman?)

The pleasure that the Goncourts experience at a circus performance is unlike any other, because, while they admire the talent and skill displayed by circus performers as others do that of actors, dancers, and other artistes, the circus offers them a surplus delectation in the danger to which its members expose themselves with each execution, and in the mathematical precision to which this greatest of risks enjoins them. Indeed, the circus spectacle springs from the very peril that awaits all circus performers, from the clowns to the wild-animal tamers to the equestrians and the aerialists. The chronicler of Parisian fin de siècle spectacles, Hugues Le Roux, compels his reader to admit that, "Je nourris, vous nourrissez comme moi, l'espoir qu'un jour nous verrons peut-être manger un dompteur. C'est une aventure qui arrive quelquefois, plus souvent qu'on ne croit" ("I nourish, you nourish like me, the hope that one day we will perhaps see a[n animal] tamer eaten. It is an adventure which sometimes happens, more often than we think.") (112–13). And the novelist and critic Jean Lorrain brazenly confesses that the intense attraction of watching Miss Jessica on the high wire resides in the awareness that she could fall to her death:

Les dix minutes durant lesquelles Jessica balance, dans le vide, l'offrande de sa nudité quasi divine en son étroite trousse de gaze d'or, le corps de l'acrobate peut vingt fois trébucher et venir s'écraser devant ces fauteuils d'orchestre qui flambent et halètent, les yeux rivés sur elle. Il y a de la cruauté et du malaise dans l'involontaire plaisir qu'on prend à regarder ce supplice aérien d'un svelte corps de femme. C'est ce danger qu'elle court qui nous épanouit l'âme, c'est l'angoisse de son âme à elle qui nous fait si délicieusement haleter et frémir.[6]

(The ten minutes during which Jessica balances, in empty space, the offering of her almost divine nudity in her close-fitting tights of gold muslin, twenty times the acrobat's body can stumble and fall before those orchestra seats which blaze and pant, eyes riveted on her. There is cruelty and discomfort in the involuntary pleasure that one feels in looking at this aerial torture of a slender woman's body. It is this danger that she is in that makes our souls swell, it is the anguish of her own soul that makes us gasp and shudder so deliciously.)

Indeed, Lorrain's circus thrills derive from his knowledge that Miss Jessica could fall to her death, perhaps even from his conviction that she *should* fall. His pleasure comes not, however, from the risks that just any circus acrobat takes, but from those precisely that Miss Jessica assumes as a symbol of her gender, here figured as transgressive because as a woman she was assumed to be somehow not quite up to the task. The spectator that Lorrain represents imagines that she is wracked by "suffering" and "apprehensions," and he relishes the sight of her as she hovers precariously over the abyss: "Ce sont toutes ces choses horribles, jointes à l'impression de sa faiblesse, de son sexe et de sa beauté, qui font la cuisine infâme de notre plaisir de spectateurs" ("It is all these horrible things, together with our own impression of her weakness, her sex, and her beauty, that make up the foul cuisine of our pleasure as spectators") (203). Of course, if he wasn't merely projecting emotion onto Miss Jessica and really perceived fear in her face, Lorrain was probably dupe of a planned error. To heighten spectator anxiety, circus performers deliberately wove serious mistakes into their choreography. As Hugues Hotier notes, "ces manquements sont volontaires et répétés, soigneusement à chaque représentation" ("these errors are voluntary and carefully repeated at each performance") (15).[7] Lorrain's perverse desire to see Miss Jessica plunge to the ground considered in conjunction with the Goncourts' comment that it is the *saut périlleux* ("somersault") which reveals incontrovertibly the superiority of men over women enables us to see the circus *piste* ("ring") as the privileged place where the balancing act between life and death also puts a critical difference on display: sexual, professional, and sociocultural or "racial," to use the Goncourts' term. At the circus, the Goncourts have us understand, an essential distinction is made between men and women, circus performers and actors, artists and "cet imbécile de public" ("that imbecilic audience"), a distinction visible to, and appreciated by the discriminating spectator.

The circus then and now does codify the performance of difference through a makeup, costume, and gesture designed to æsthetically emphasize the body, in men their muscles, in women their shape. Male performers, however, function as the zero-degree in opposition to which the signifying effects of circus performance are constituted, and the circus code correspondingly requires female performers to distinguish themselves from male acrobats by exaggerating the attributes of their sex. For example, while acknowledging that a costume exaggerates a performer's physical qualities according to whether s/he is a man or a woman, under the category of "Maquillages et Perruques" ("Makeup and Wigs"), Hugues Hotier identifies only those æsthetic traits that refer to the female performer and discusses how she is to differentiate herself from her nonsexed male counterparts: "sexualisation (mise en valeur des chevelures, des bouches, des yeux . . .)" ("sexualization [emphasis on the hair, the mouth, the eyes. . . ."). And in the category "Gestes" ("Gestures"), Hotier cites only the following æsthetic characteristics: "galbe des jambes féminines souligné par l'avancée d'une jambe légèrement pliée en repos sur la pointe du pied tandis que l'autre pied est à plat sur le sol, bras levés et doigts tendus, geste rotatif du poignet, lenteur, décomposition" ("curve of the feminine legs emphasized by putting forward a leg slightly bent in a rest position on the point of the foot while the other foot is flat on the ground, arms raised and fingers stretched, rotating motion of the wrist, slowness, decomposition"): male poses do not even warrant description (12). As regards the construction of gender during a performance, Peta Tait notes that "[i]n solo trapeze performance on the bar, which is largely the domain of female aerialists, feminine identity is signified at strategic points throughout the routine, with legs together, feet and arms extended in balletic poses." For the flying trapeze artist, however, gesture and pose can only come into play "at the beginning and end of the trick."[8] At those moments when gender can be encoded for the spectator, the female flier puts "her hands up, her head back, one hip forward and her weight on one leg." The male flier too has his own prescribed gestures—he stands with "a hand or hands up, his shoulders back, his torso extended as he rotates his body towards the audience"; the female flier distinguishes herself from the male by differentiating the entirety of her *beauté plastique* ("physical beauty") from his muscular chest and shoulders, enjoining the spectator to contemplate her from the tips of her fingers down to the arch of her nonweightbearing foot.[9]

Gender, however, disappears completely in flight, revealing the flying trapeze as a weak spot in the circus's ability to construct sexual identity according to universally adopted norms of circus behavior. From the benches below, the spectator may be unable to distinguish the male performer from the female performer in flight and may thus experience a certain discomfort. For the fin de siècle spectator, the exposed stitches in the circus's otherwise seamless efforts to make difference seem both natural and visible are the entertainment's most intriguing features. While the difference between men and women, circus performers and actors, artistes and spectators, is revealed (or, more appropriately, performed) at strategic moments in an act, the ambiguous sexuality of the lady acrobat in flight specifically identifies her gendered gestures as empty signs that, only once she assumes them, actualize difference and subjectivity. On the other hand, the lady acrobat in flight betrays the artificiality of the feminine poses that she adopts to frame the stunt, and undermines the gender that her movements and attire are at pains to construct.

The Male Acrobat as Metaphor for the Poet

It was during 1859, the year of the Goncourt journal entry cited earlier, that the French acrobat, Léotard, whose name is synonymous with the aerialist's trademark costume, invented the flying trapeze (Thétard, 2:134). At the close of the season of the flying trapeze's début, there were already a number of Léotard imitators. Before long the flying trapeze was featured on the standard circus program, as would the fixed and the aerial bars, innovations that would follow soon after. Although from its modern inception the circus program modified old or added on new acts, 1840 marks the infancy of aerial act innovations, beginning with the fixed trapeze and the aerial rings. By 1860 aerial acrobatics were by far the most popular acts (Thétard, 2:25–26). And although equestrian and aerial acrobatics were both disciplines whose rapidly evolving techniques continued to transform circus repertoires, fueled by the intense competition between performers to outshine their rivals and command the highest salaries, the Goncourts' journal entry marks the moment when the circus will begin to take advantage of the soaring popularity of aerial acrobatics by showcasing such acts while relegating equestrian feats to a less central role.

Whether male or female—but particularly when they are male—the stunts performed by the circus acrobats of Théophile Gautier's theater reviews, of Théodore de Banville's *Odes funambulesques* (1857), of Baudelaire's *Le vieux saltimbanque* (1861), of Mallarmé's "Le pitre châtié," the first version of which dates back to 1864, and in many respects of Edmond de Goncourt's *Les Frères Zemganno*, are allegories of the verbal feats accomplished by the poet/writer, for whom the creation of a work of art is not, as the Goncourts state, just a "métier" ("craft"), but a "devoir" ("duty") as well. The lightness of a body tumbling on the ground, but especially that of the acrobat at the moment he springs upwards from the trampoline,[10] the quest for ever greater height, and the necessity for technical precision serve as parallels of the poet's own efforts to surpass his own weighty corporeality and the heaviness of the real and attain a lightness of being that could only be the result of the creation of something seemingly effortless, something beautiful, something precise, something totally divorced from mundane human concerns: a work of art.

In the Goncourt journal entry, the circus acrobat's play before the audience also functions as an analogy for the gymnastics the artist and the writer are forced to perform for their own public, a monkey show that the acrobat transcends the moment he soars high, "tout en faisant la grimace aux bourgeois, aux 'assis' " ("while making faces at the bourgeois, to those seated"). The circus acrobat's talent is absolute because he must be precise in his every movement. And whereas actors and actresses pretend to have talent, the acrobat plays with his own life; his performance is absolute because the *saut périlleux*—the meat of equestrian, ground, and aerial acrobatics—makes the stakes particularly high. The *saut périlleux* also makes of the circus "une excellente école de moralité" ("an excellent school of morals") (Le Roux, 180). Le Roux challenges those who circulate vicious rumors about acrobats to admit that, "dans ces occasions mortelles, ils admiraient le surprenant courage dont ces parias font preuve" ("on these deadly occasions, they admired the astonishing courage of which these pariahs give proof"). The myth of moral degeneracy simply does not hold up before the facts of acrobatic life; "cette habileté," he insists, "ne s'acquiert point sans vertus quotidiennes, dont la moindre est la tempérance, et la plus admirable, une persévérance qui passe l'imagination" ("this skill is not obtained without daily virtues, the least of which is temperance, and the most admirable, a perseverance which exceeds the imagination") (Le Roux, 179). As the Goncourts surmise, "ou ils tombent ou ils ne tombent pas. Leur talent est un fait" ("either they fall or they don't fall. Their talent is a fact").

In the concluding pages of *Portrait de l'artiste en saltimbanque (Portrait of the Artist as Acrobat)*, Jean Starobinski suggests that circus performers, particularly clowns, represent through their movements—jumping through paper hoops while standing on a horse's back, springing dizzyingly upwards from the trampoline, turning somersaults in the air—the miraculous passage into the beyond, or into *a* beyond. For later poets like Rilke in his fifth elegy or Apollinaire in his "Crépuscule"/"Twilight," Starobinski finds that the world of the *saltimbanque* is symbolically "posé entre ciel et terre, entre vie et mort, plus près de la mort que de la vie, et où tout s'ordonne autour du secret d'un passage" ("placed between heaven and earth, between life and death, closer to death than to life, and where everything is arranged around the secret of a passing over") (131). If the acrobat's leap into the emptiness of the space overhead does not end in the transcendence of material being, it nevertheless partakes of the spectator's desire to "dépasser le monde, ou plus exactement d'introduire dans le monde le témoignage d'une passion *venue d'ailleurs* ou *visant un ailleurs* . . ." ("go beyond the world, or more exactly to introduce into the world the testimony of a passion come from elsewhere or aiming at an elsewhere") (136). For the Goncourts in their journal entry and for Starobinski, it is the senselessness of the threat to their lives that these performers face daily that lends itself to the production of a meaning that the spectator discovers there (141). The allegory of acrobats who madly risk their lives just for the sake of a few "bravos" from "cet imbécile de public" elevates society's other outcasts to the status of heroes, whose own seemingly empty and absurd gestures assume great signification.

There exist also the allegories of the acrobat no longer at the height of his/her powers, of the acrobat fallen from a fickle public's favor, or the disorienting image of the acrobat's surprising lack of vitality offstage, as in Toulouse-Lautrec's *Clownesse assise* (1896). In Baudelaire's old, decrepit, forgotten, and forlorn *saltimbanque* who is long past his performing years, the narrator sees "l'image du vieil homme de lettres qui a survécu à la génération dont il fut le brillant amuseur; du vieux poëte sans amis, sans famille, sans enfants, dégradée par sa misère et par l'ingratitude publique, et dans la baraque de qui le monde oublieux ne veut plus entrer" ("the image of the old man of letters who has outlived the generation of which he was the brillant entertainer; of the old poet without friends, without family, without children, degraded by his misery and by public ingratitude, and in whose stall the forgetful world no longer wants to enter"). Baudelaire emphasizes the capriciousness and inconstancy of public recognition through the tragically ridiculous figure of the acrobat wearing a comic costume that reflects necessity more than art. But as Starobinski points out, the pitiful scene is complicated by the misguided pretensions of such a has-been trying to recapture, if not his past, then at least his public (99).[11]

Finally, although the Goncourts' 1859 journal entry mentions *sauteuses* ("female tumblers") and *franchisseuses de cercles de papier* ("women acrobats leaping through circles of paper"), seemingly expressing admiration for the accomplishments of all performers in the profession, male and female, they end their argument supporting circus entertainment over that of the theater with the very unexpected comment: "Au fait, savez-vous que c'est la plus grande supériorité de l'homme sur la femme, que le saut périlleux?" ("By the way, do you know that the [aerial] somersault is the greatest superiority of man over woman?"). This question makes it clear that probably all the allegorical renditions of the acrobat made by Banville, Gautier, and the Goncourts, respond to the peculiar way that the circus plays with gender. Because the "presentation of circus acts . . . was designed to maximize the impression of extraordinary [physical] feats," even the display of gender through a female acrobat's "gestures, poses, and costume" worked inversely to emphasize masculinity. Thus, even though the nineteenth-century circus was that place where women, especially in the latter half of the century, rivaled men in performing athletic exploits of daring and endurance, the socially gendered maleness of their exposed muscular bodies and their acrobatic prowess identified them with masculinity.[12]

The Masculine Effect

While Hugues Le Roux claims that the male spectator's pleasure in watching the execution of the trick may pale demonstrably before the lure of the seminudity of the lady acrobat, the two are in reality inseparable, at least for the format and period under discussion. The female performer's allure comes more from the amalgamation of seemingly dissimilar elements in her body; she is identified as woman by name, costume, and gesture, but she communicates maleness through her ability. The sight of just any half-naked woman does not possess the power to create desire in the fin de siècle male spectator, as Le Roux makes clear in his interview with the Volta brothers, who claim that "La femme est mal faite" ("Woman is badly proportioned"):

> Ce n'est pas un objet d'art, mais d'utilité. Regardez ses hanches qui débordent la ligne tombante des épaules, écrasent les jambes trop courtes, brisent la proportion. Tout cela appelle le mensonge de la robe et défend l'exhibition de la nudité. Au contraire, ce poids de la vie, ce poids de l'amour que la femme porte dans ses flancs, l'homme le soutient sur ses épaules. La femme boite grotesquement enceinte et déformée. (199)

> (She is not an object of art, but of utility. Look at her hips, which extend beyond the slope of the shoulders, squash the too-short legs, and destroy proportion. All this calls for the deception of dresses and prohibits the showing of nudity. On the contrary, that weight of life, that weight of love that women carry in their lower body, men carry on their shoulders. Pregnant and deformed, women limp grotesquely.)

The lady acrobat, who wears the *maillot de soie* ("silk leotard") like all circus performers to facilitate the unencumbered execution of a trick, has no recourse to "le mensonge de la robe" ("the deception of dresses"), and yet she is hardly "déformée" ("deformed") as in William Volta's description. Trained in acrobatics since her tender years, the nineteenth-century lady acrobat's physique differs little from that of those men whose slighter builds destine them for tricks demanding nimbleness rather than physical strength. Gender, Le Roux implies, is determined more by the nature of the stunt than by a performer's actual sex:

> Il y a, en effet, dans tout couple d'acrobates, un mâle et une femelle, le héros fort, le porteur, en argot, 'l'homme de dessous,' celui qui soutient le poids de tout l'exercice, celui auquel 'l'homme de dessus' confie sa vie. Celui-là, c'est le plus jeune, le plus souple, le plus gracieux. (201)
>
> (There is, in effect, in each acrobatic couple, a male and a female, the strong hero, the carrier, in slang, "the man underneath," the one who bears the weight of the whole exercise, the one to whom "the man on top" trusts his life. The latter is the youngest, the most flexible, the most graceful.)

Before the development of his Herculean physique, an *homme de dessous* ("a man underneath") like Hippolyte Triat may have performed in travesty in his youth (he was called *Isela)*, and an *homme de dessus* ("a man on top") like Olmar Kingsley may have opted to create for himself a female persona (he was known as Miss Ella) (Thétard, 2:33, 62). Young girls, too, cross-dressed, as did the youngest of the Seven Craggs, "gentlemen acrobats" (Le Roux, 222, 4). Female *Hercules* ("strongmen") like Athléta and her three daughters, Sandwina, Miss Vulcana, and Adriana, however, did not assume male identities, but neither were they the object of the fin de siècle male spectator's fascination (Thétard, 2:74–75). The unusual *frisson* produced in the spectating Monsieur as he watches the lady acrobat owes to much more than the sight of a woman like Miss Jessica in Lorrain's article, half-naked and socially encoded as weak and fragile, braving dangers associated with male activity. Miss Jessica must have played at "suffering" and having "apprehensions," to heighten the spectator's sense of her superhuman accomplishment at the end of her act. The desire he experiences must therefore be of another order.

On the one hand, the desire which briefly surfaces in Le Roux's discussion of the acrobat is, if not entirely homoerotic, then narcissistic in nature. In Edmond de Goncourt's *Les Frères Zemganno* (1879), Nello and Gianni Zemganno form a self-sufficient couple of the kind described by Le Roux, with Nello, who even has "une bouche de femme" ("a woman's mouth"), occupying the role of *femelle/homme de dessus*. Women envy Nello's beauty "pour ce qu'elle empruntait, pour ce qu'elle dérobait à la beauté de la femme" ("for what it borrowed, for what it stole from women's beauty") (Le Roux, 182–83). For Le Roux, it is perfectly understandable how *l'homme de dessous* who contemplates the beauty of his more lithe partner "passe de la notion de cette beauté au désir de cette beauté, c'est-à-dire à l'amour" ("passes from the notion of this beauty to the desire for this beauty, in other words to love"). He is quick, however, to prevent any "vilaine équivoque" ("sordid misunderstanding"): the physical demands made on the acrobat, he informs us, make this love, or "presque toutes ces amours" ("almost all these loves"), chaste (200–201). According to the mythology of the acrobat, chastity is a condition imposed by the physical exertions and rigors of the acrobat's life. What about the love that the spectator experiences? According to Jean Starobinski, there is narcissism as well for the spectator/poet of the art for art's sake aesthetic who identifies with the acrobat, who, "sous les yeux du public auquel il s'exhibe, poursuit sa propre perfection à travers la réussite de l'acte prodigieux qui met en valeur toutes les ressources de son corps" ("under the eyes of the audience before whom he displays himself, pursues his own perfection through the success of the prodigious act that emphasizes all the resources of his body"). He adds that, if the poet perceives androgyny in the acrobat, it is "moins une constatation 'objective' qu'une projection imaginative" ("less an objective observation than an imaginary projection"), a projection that will assume mythic dimensions.

Narcissistic desire, however, belongs to the poet as he describes the feminized male acrobat, not to the masculinized lady acrobat. Edmond de Goncourt's *Les Frères Zemganno* stands at the divide between the literary and artistic community's earlier privileging of the male clown and *saltimbanque* ("acrobat"), as represented by Nello and Gianni Zemganno in Goncourt's novel, and their election of the lady acrobat to the gallery of valid literary and artistic models, as represented by the temperamental and self-serving, but immensely fascinating equestrienne, la Tompkins. The earlier romantic poet had identified with "le bouffon, le saltimbanque et le clown" ("the buffoon, the acrobat, and the clown") as the "images hyperboliques et volontairement *déformantes* que les artistes se sont plu à donner d'eux mêmes et de la condition de l'art" ("hyperbolic and voluntarily deforming images that artists enjoyed giving of themselves and of the state of art") (Starobinski, 9). The later ironic and playful *littérateur* will dispense with identification and depose the male *saltimbanque*, replacing him with the lady acrobat, particularly the flying woman. For Starobinski, when *l'homme de dessus* is a masculinized woman, the spectator betrays a masochistic desire for "des persécutrices idéales" ("ideal women persecutors"), for the femme fatale (49, 55). Her attraction lies, he claims, in her being not only "différente de toutes les autres femmes" ("different from all other women"), but "secrètement différente de son apparente féminité" ("secretly different from her apparent femininity"). Starobinski attributes her ability to be different from herself in the poet's mind to an association of physical metamorphosis with physical agility, and in the eyes of the spectator this allows her to assume "un rôle sexuel changeant" ("a changing sexual role"); she is first victim by her sex, but she becomes executioner by her ability to become (an)other (51–52). The great majority of fictional fin de siècle lady acrobats are not, however, sexually destructive women in the way described by Starobinski. He has, nevertheless, discovered in her apparent ability to change—not only from one sex, but also from one race into another as well—the source of the desire that the male spectator experiences upon seeing her perform.

Young Flaubert seems to have loved above all other performers the *danseuse de corde* ("tightrope dancer") precisely for these reasons. He enumerates her feminine qualities, which he links solely to her attire and accessories: the long earrings that sway with her movements, the necklace that strikes her chest, the sound that her spangled dress makes as she flies through the air, the sight of the feathers of her turban as they touch the ground when she is upside-down. But he also recalls how "[son] esprit se tourmentait en songeant à ces cuisses de formes étranges, si bien serrées dans des pantalons roses, à ces bras souples" ("[his] mind was tortured by dreams of those strangely formed thighs, fitted so snugly in pink trousers, of those supple arms") (Starobinski, 48). The suppleness of her arms, and especially the form of her thighs as revealed through pink tights, however, are strange, creating an effect of sexual ambiguity for the reader. Literary scholars like Naomi Ritter have interpreted this androgynous aerialist as a "metaphor for the mystery of the artist himself," and the difficult task the artist experiences in balancing two contraries. For Ritter in her study of Picasso's *L'acrobate sur la balle* (1905), the artist's inherent duality produces a series of oppositions: professional vs. personal, adolescence vs. adulthood, boy vs. girl, perhaps too, the visually weighty corporeality in the acrobat's muscular build vs. the gravity-defying agility in the trapeze act. Starobinski identifies these contraries as life and death, earth and heaven, the possible and the impossible.

But androgyny and duality are not the natural states of the artist and that androgyny is resolved into the masculine in the male spectator's mind during the course of an aerialist's act. Such is the case in des Esseintes's experience of Miss Urania, the American circus star "au corps découplé, aux jambes nerveuses, aux muscles d'acier, aux bras de fonte" ("with a lithe body, sinewy legs, muscles of steel, arms of cast metal") in Huysmans's *A rebours*:

> Peu à peu, en même temps qu'il l'observait, de singulières conceptions naquirent; à mesure qu'il admirait sa souplesse et sa force, il voyait un artificiel changement de sexe se produire en elle; ses singeries gracieuses, ses mièvreries de femelle s'effaçaient de plus en plus, tandis que se développaient, à leur place, les charmes agiles et puissants d'un mâle; en un mot, après avoir tout d'abord été femme, puis, après avoir hésité, après avoir avoisiné l'androgyne, elle semblait se résoudre, se préciser, devenir complètement un homme.[13]

> (Little by little, while he was watching her, strange ideas arose; as he was admiring her suppleness and her strength, he saw an artificial change of sex take place in her; her graceful leaps, her insipid and affected female charms increasingly faded away, while there developed in their place, the agile and powerful allure of a male; in a word, after having been at first a woman, then, after having hesitated, after having bordered on the androgyne, she seemed to make up her mind, to take shape, to become completely a man.)

In des Esseintes's description, Miss Urania's transformation from woman into man entails only a momentary hesitation in the vicinity of androgyny, but never a lengthy stay. Des Esseintes and Flaubert's overdetermined feminine indicators—the "singeries gracieuses" ("graceful leaps"), the "mièvreries de femelle" ("insipid and affected female charms"), the bracelets, earrings, and spangles—are there to augment the masculine effect.

Travesty is an old circus tradition, and the travesty of a male as a female occurs most often, perhaps, for the purpose of enhancing the spectator's gendered perception of the perils to which the acrobat exposes him/herself. Henry Thétard notes that, "[I]l est bien évident qu'un travail assez ordinaire pour un homme paraît presque remarquable quand il est facilement accompli par une femme . . . ou par un homme habilement grimé en femme" ("it is quite obvious that a task that would be rather ordinary for a man seems almost astonishing when it is easily accomplished by a woman . . . or by a man cleverly made up as a woman") (2:61). Although most male travesties eventually revealed their identities—either at the end of the act, like the American Barbette in his strip-tease at the Cirque Médrano and the Folies-Bergère during the 1920s, or when they married women, as did the American "equestrienne" Miss Ella—the "female gymnast" Miss Lulu, who debuted in Paris in 1870, never did settle the question of her true sexuality. The degree of difficulty of her aerial feats—the *saut en fusée* ("rocket jump") at twenty-three feet above the ground, and possibly even the triple *saut périlleux* on the flying trapeze (according to Thétard, she turned most likely, however, into the net)—suggested that she was a male acrobat (Thétard, 2:62). Every contemporary critic who discussed Miss Lulu—and anyone who saw photographs of her, for that matter—remained convinced, however, that she was a man. Miss Lulu's exceptional accomplishments aside, aerial and equestrian feats performed by male travesties tended to heighten competition with female acrobats to the point that the latter pushed themselves to achieve the same degree of endurance and intrepidity as their male counterparts, continually blurring the neat distinction between the abilities of male and female bodies.

On the one hand one can say that the female travesty of pre-1890 burlesque shows raised many of the same questions as those regarding the sexual identity of the lady acrobat. Some contemporaries, disturbed at the sight of women playing men's roles and wearing pseudo-men's costumes that revealed their legs and arms, wondered if the burlesquer had difficulty recuperating her identity offstage.[14] Robert Allen comments in *Horrible Prettiness* that, "So long as women portrayed dramatic characters, what a 'woman onstage' signified could be more or less controlled through the words written for her by the playwright. But when women appeared in spectacle pieces—whether ballet or equestrian drama—their bodies, not someone else's words, bore the burden of signification."[15] While the talking female burlesquer wore flesh-colored tights and leotards like the dancer and the acrobat, Allen says she distinguished herself from them by aggressively assuming her gaze, a combination that disturbed many male spectators who wanted the activity of gazing to be unidirectional. And when the burlesquer was silenced in the 1890s and turned into the stripper, the show of her legs worked to announce and display, and no longer to blur sexual difference. As the female aerialist could not really possess a disruptive gaze because she needed to concentrate on movements that if badly executed could end in her death, she could possess a disruptive power through the masculine appearance of her arms and legs and through the danger and skill of her exploits. As Peta Tait contends, the female aerialist's show of arms and legs "weakens and disrupts social belief in an innate and fixed identity defined by sexual difference" ("Danger," 43).

The history of the saucy burlesquer reduced to striptease artist seems to be also that of the lady acrobat in filmic versions of the female trapeze artist. The latter no longer threatens because she is not a real acrobat and therefore does not possess threatening muscles; what remains are the actress's very feminine legs. Striptease and trapeze do ironically come together in the Edison Manufacturing Company's 1901 film *Trapeze Disrobing Act*, where two men in a loge watch a woman on a trapeze strip. In her discussion of this film, Judith Mayne comments appropriately "there is little doubt about the intended audience for this spectacle." Nor is there any doubt that the trapeze striptease is intended to reveal a female body.[16] On the surface, the same is true for Georges Méliès's *Le Brahmane et le papillon* (1901), in which a brahmin/Méliès orchestrates the transformation of a caterpillar into a hand-size butterfly-woman who flies through the air. Lucy Fischer in her study of *The Vanishing Lady* (1896), Méliès's first "substitution trick" film, states that since the trick film derives from the "antecedent tradition of theatrical magic," or illusionism, the "dominance and immutability of that paradigm . . . makes one begin to suspect that sexual role-playing is *itself* at issue in the rhetoric of magic, and that perhaps in performing his tricks upon the female subject, the male magician is not simply accomplishing acts of prestidigitation, but is also articulating a discourse on attitudes toward women."[17] In illusionism and in the Méliès trick film, Fischer notes, woman is a decorative object that is acted upon by a conjuring magician: the latter makes her disappear and reappear; he shrinks her or enlarges her; he dismembers her and reassembles her, the latter sometimes from nonhuman objects (341). Fischer interprets all this as not only "demonstrating the male sense of power over the female," but also pointing as well to "certain deep-seated male anxieties concerning the *female's power over him*" (emphasis in the original). In his book on Méliès, John Frazer's comments on *Le Brahmane et le papillon* echo Fischer's when he describes this two-minute film as a Pygmalion and Galatea scenario gone wrong.[18] In the second half of the film, the Brahmin's creation ends not only by turning on her creator, but also by thoroughly humiliating him in true femme fatale fashion:

> The Brahmin decides to capture this lively insect. He wraps her inside a striped cloth. Assistants arrive and the cloth is removed. The butterfly has become an oriental princess. Struck by her beauty the Brahmin kneels and kisses her foot. To his surprise she puts her foot on top of him, changing him into a caterpillar. The triumphant woman leaves with the assistants. The miserable caterpillar crawls away after her.[19]

While carrying all the telltale traits of Fischer's reading of the Méliès substitution film, there are also elements that are strangely reminiscent of des Esseintes's efforts and ultimate disappointments regarding Miss Urania. The transformation of the butterfly-woman into an oriental princess ultimately draws upon the signifying register belonging not only to the lady acrobat, but also to the circus performer in general.

Starobinski holds back from assigning any fixed meaning to circus performers because he concludes that their "raison d'être" must be the total absence of signification: "C'est seulement au prix de cette *vacance*, de ce *vide* premier qu'ils peuvent *passer* à la signification que nous leur avons découverte. Ils ont besoin d'une immense réserve de non-sens pour pouvoir passer au sens" ("It is only at the price of this *vacancy*, of this *void* that they can *pass* into the signification that we have perceived in them. They need an immense reserve of non-meaning in order to pass into meaning") (Starobinski, 141; emphasis in the original). Peta Tait too sees a *vide* ("void") in the circus performer's lack of determining sexual indicators when in flight, as well as "fluid and changing significations" permitting otherwise marginalized ethnicities to deconstruct their identity all while performing racial and sexual difference,[20] making the circus the privileged place of the production of another kind of meaning.

Artifice and the Radical Otherness of the Lady Acrobat

"Les gens du voyage" ("circus travelers"), as circus performers refer to themselves, are not "de notre race" ("of our race"), the Goncourts inform us in their journal entry, however much we as spectators identify metaphorically with the death-defying feats they perform to please "cet imbécile de public" ("that imbecilic audience"). Indeed, the circus performer is *not* of our race, and in more than one respect as far as the spectator is concerned: first, Edmond de Goncourt's novel *Les Frères Zemganno* and the writings of other novelists and poets will identify the circus performer with bohemians/gypsies, as people of a certain ethnic group. Second, the life of the circus performer has been and continues to be led at the extreme margins of ordinary existence, on the one hand because of their perennial ambulatory existence, and on the other hand because of the rigid demands made on their bodies by their profession; they have sacrificed normal lives to their art. For example, Jean Lorrain assumes that acrobats like Miss Jessica are "virginale et chaste (chaste comme ils le sont forcément tous et toutes dans le métier)" (203) ("virginal and chaste [chaste as all of them, men and women, must necessarily be in the profession]"). Third, as in paintings like Picasso's 1917 *Rideau de scène pour Parade* or Toulouse-Lautrec's 1896 *Clownesse assise*, or even Baudelaire's poem "Le vieux saltimbanque," which represent the other side of the spectacle, we find that there is no other side. Regarding the traveling circus Yoram S. Carmeli notes that even when circus people are photographed or portrayed in their offstage mode, they are still always onstage. In circus books, she continues, "There are no photographs which depict off-stage and home life *un*related to the show, immune from exhibition to the public. It is also typical that there are no pictures of circus people mingling with townsfolk inside the tent," nor are there any "pictures depicting circus folk intermingling with townsfolk outside the circus grounds."[21] The absence of noncircus related photographs does not reflect the image that circus performers strive to produce of themselves; on the contrary, any image deviating from the mode of performance disappoints the expectations and desires of circus fans. Le Roux, invited to the wedding of an animal trainer's daughter, expresses surprise and frustration at the sight of a room filled with very middle-class *dompteurs* and *dompteuses* (male and female "animal tamers"): "Ils n'avaient cru devoir revêtir,—et dans mon for intérieur je le regrettais bien,—ni leurs pourpoints pailletés ni leurs bottes à l'écuyère. Ils portaient tous le frac et les gants mauves" ("They didn't think it necessary to put on,—and in my heart of hearts I really regretted it—either their spangled doublets or their riding boots. They all wore tails and mauve gloves."). He turns to the description of the wedding gifts which alone are capable of compensating for the lack of circus pomp in the guests' attire; the bride received four lions, a small panther from Java, two rattlesnakes, and a hairless rabbit, "curiosité inconnue jusqu'à ce jour" ("a curiosity unknown until then") (Le Roux, 104). In the absence of standard circus uniforms, Le Roux has to reconstruct the circus through the exotic animals that constitute the animal tamer's dowry. Des Esseintes too seeks to recreate the circus arena experience in his courting of Miss Urania; for the encounter to be of an ideal nature, Miss Urania must stay in character well beyond the performance in the ring. Fourth, the concept of race applies equally to the high rate of intermarriage within the great circus families like the Chiraninis, the Renzes, and the Guerras, as to the not so infrequent marriage of equestriennes and aerialists to aristocrats. The most talented and famous of the circus performers during the eighteenth and nineteenth century belonged to great circus dynasties under whose tutelage their noble offspring learned their trade literally from earliest childhood. Circus people created an alternate world. And fifth, and perhaps most important, circus performers play before crowds who are significantly enticed by the notion that a number could end in their death. The delicate balance between life and death indicates an existence led on the edge where few outside the circus would dare to venture.

Circus spectators seek out mythical figures capable of superhuman feats. Circus performers, therefore, don't need to pass into the beyond: they are the beyond, the distant, the inaccessible, the exotic, the other. As the previous examples demonstrate, the ideal otherness achieved by the circus performer is only partially racial in reality, but performers and circus directors did, and still do, exploit race and its potential for exoticism. The celebrated Miss Lala of Degas's painting and of Chéret's posters, for example, was advertised as "la Vénus des Tropiques" ("the Venus of the Tropics").[22] But race is not the only factor in creating the atmosphere of otherness. Travesties like Miss Lulu, "the female gymnast," and Miss Ella most certainly profited from preconceptions about what the gendered body can do. Whereas writers who patronized the circus during its prime used the male acrobat as a symbol of their own quest for transcendence, writers and artists during its decline expected the lady acrobat to actualize transcendence through the otherness of her body. So, although the feminization of des Esseintes through his idealization of the masculinized Miss Urania can be read in terms of gender ambiguity and its relation to the dilemma of the artist vis-à-vis his public, it is more probable that the transformation that the encounter with her permits is the same sought by Baudelaire's protagonist from "La Fanfarlo." At the sight of the nudity of his beloved, Samuel Cramer cries out: "Je veux Colombine, rends-moi Colombine; rends-la-moi telle qu'elle m'est apparue le soir qu'elle m'a rendu fou avec son accoutrement fantasque et son corsage de saltimbanque" ("I want Colombine, give me Colombine; give her to me as she appeared to me the evening she drove me mad with her bizarre costume and her acrobat's bodice").[23] Des Esseintes and Samuel Cramer both want their performers to stay in character, a character to which they will be forced to physiologically adapt, to become themselves other so as not to "coïncider avec [leur] présence corporelle" ("coincide with [their] bodily presence") (Starobinski, 66). Only the shifting, signifying register of the circus, isolated in the lady acrobat in flight, allows des Esseintes to subvert the real and replace it with an alternate reality.

Notes

1. All translations from the French are my own.

2. Henry Thétard, *La Merveilleuse Histoire du cirque*, 2 vols. (Paris: Prisma, 1947), I:85. Subsequent references to this work will appear in the text.

3. See also Hugues Le Roux, *Les Jeux du cirque et de la vie foraine* (Paris: Plon, 1899), 164–65. Subsequent references to this work will appear in the text.

4. According to John Frazer, Marie Fourrier's aerial performance also made her the "progenitress of a long line of stage and screen fly-by-wire ladies," including those in Georges Méliès's early trick films *La femme volante/Marvelous Suspension and Evolution* (1902), and *Le brahmane et le papillon/The Brahmin and the Butterfly* (1901). It is more likely, however, that the flying women that populated the paintings, literature, fairground attractions, and early films reflect the circus's privileging of aerial acts and the spectators' awe of the trapeze artist's death-defying feats. See also Jacques Deslandes and Jacques Richard, *Du cinématographe au cinéma 1896–1906*, vol. 2 of *Histoire comparée du cinéma*, 3 vols. (Paris: Casterman, 1968), 183, 209–11.

5. Edmond and Jules de Goncourt, *Mémoires de la vie littéraire, 1851–1865*, ed. Robert Ricatte, 3 vols. (Paris: Laffont, 1989), 1:491.

6. Jean Lorrain, "L'Acrobate," in *Une Femme par jour*, ed. Michel Desbruères (Saint-Cyr-sur-Loire: Christian Pirot, 1983), 202–3. Subsequent references to this work will appear in the text.

7. Hotier calls the planned error a "transgression" of the rules established by the circus, with transgression incorporated into circus code for the purpose of enhancing the pleasure of the spectator.

8. Peta Tait, "Danger Delights: Texts of Gender and Race in Aerial Per-

formance," *New Theater Quarterly* 12:5 (1996): 43. Subsequent references to works by Peta Tait will be included in the text.

9. The more difficult it is for the spectator to tell male from female performers, the greater the effort to make the lady acrobat signify the feminine. For example, one of the exemplary women chosen as witnesses for the defense by Eve Banner (Katherine Hepburn) in *Adam's Rib* (Cukor, 1949) is a former tumbler and trapeze artiste who, because of weight gain, now works as the supporting strong arm of the circus's human pyramid. She tells the jury that she is part of a trick where, to the amazement of the audience, a *hercule* ("strongman") who picks up a three-hundred-pound dumbbell with one arm is subsequently picked up by none other than herself and poised with ease in the air. She notes that the only way that spectators know that she is a woman is by her seminudity. I would add that it is also because of the way her costume invents a female form. Without a costume to encode her sexuality, she implies, audience members would be at a loss to distinguish her from her male counterparts.

10. Jean Starobinski, *Portrait de l'artiste en saltimbanque* (Geneva: Skira, 1940), 38. Subsequent references to this work will appear in the text.

11. There are real-life counterparts to Baudelaire's *vieux saltimbanque* such as Mme Saqui, the star *danseuse de corde* ("tightrope dancer") whose career, "[c]ommencée souls la Révolution" ("begun during the Revolution"), as Henry Thétard recounts, ". . . s'épanouit sous Napoléon . . . demeure glorieuse sous la Restauration, décline sous Louis-Philippe et finit, lamentable, dans les hippodromes en plein air du Second Empire, à la Porte Dauphine et au quai de Bercy" ("blossomed under Napoleon . . . remained glorious during the Restoration, declined under Louis-Philippe and finished, lamentably, at the Porte Dauphine and the quai de Bercy"). Even in his gentle treatment of the aged Mme Saqui, he describes her as *demi-momifiée* ("half mummified") (2:118).

12. Indeed, male transvestites tipped the balance even further towards the masculine by forcing lady acrobats to achieve the same level of mastery, even if it meant going beyond what they considered the their bodies' abilities: "Une grande émotion se manifesta vers 1852 dans ce gracieux petit monde du panneau quand vint sur le continent européen la célèbre Miss Ella qui, nous le savons, était un jeune garçon. Les étoiles du moment, Catherine Renz, Catherine Carré, Virginie Blennow crevaient successivement vingt 'ballons' ou cerceaux de papier, et voilà que miss Ella en crevait cinquante et, en plus, tournait les saut périlleux comme un collègue masculin. . . . L'émulation produit des miracles. Catherine Renz, Catherine Carré, d'autres encore, arrivèrent à crever les cinquante ballons et à tourner les sauts périlleux sur panneau.

"Désormais, l'audace de l'écuyère voltigeuse ne connaîtra plus de bornes et, peu à peu, la danseuse équestre fera place à l'acrobate sur panneau ou cheval nu.

("Towards 1852 there was great excitement in the graceful little world of circus-riding when the celebrated Miss Ella, who, as we know, was a young man, came to the European continent. The stars of the moment, Catherine Renz, Catherine Carré, Virginie Blennow burst through 20 successive 'balloons' or paper hoops, and now Miss Ella went through fifty and, in addition, turned somersaults like a masculine colleague. . . . Rivalry produced miracles. Catherine Renz, Catherine Carré, and even others, succeeded in going through fifty hoops and in turning somersaults on the saddle.)

("Henceforward, the female circus rider's daring would know no limits and, little by little, the equestrian dance will make room for the acrobat on saddle or bareback." (Thétard 2:178–79).

13. Joris-Karl Huysmans, *A rebours*, ed. Marc Fumaroli (Paris: Gallimard, 1977), 210.

14. Robert C. Allen, *Horrible Prettiness: Burlesque and American Culture* (Chapel Hill: University of North Carolina Press, 1991), 134.

15. Ibid., 81.

16. Judith Mayne, "Uncovering the Female Body," in *Before Hollywood: Turn-of-the-Century American Film*, ed. Jay Leyda and Charles Musser (New York: Hudson Hill, 1987), 65.

17. Lucy Fischer, "The Lady Vanishes: Women, Magic, and the Movies," in *Film Before Griffith*, ed. John L. Fell (Berkeley: University of California Press, 1983), 340.

18. John Frazer, *Artificially Arranged Scenes: The Films of Georges Méliès* (Boston: G. K. Hall, 1979), 86–87.

19. Ibid., 87.

20. Tait, "Danger," 45.

21. Yoram S. Carmeli, "Text, Traces, and the Reification of Totality: The Case of Popular Circus Literature," *New Literary History* 25, no. 1 (1995): 185.

22. Eric Darragon, "Pégase à Fernando: A propos de *Cirque* et du réalisme de Seurat en 1891," *Revue de l'Art* 86 (1989): 56 n. 27.

23. Baudelaire, *Œuvres*, 1:577.

Powerless in Paradise: Zola's *Au bonheur des dames* and the Fashioning of a City

ROSEMARY LLOYD

THE ENORMOUS INTERNATIONAL RESPONSE TO THE MURDER OF fashion designer Gianni Versace in July of 1997 draws attention to the fact that of all the arts, except perhaps music, fashion is the one with which the average person is now most familiar. As Baudelaire emphasizes in his praise of makeup and in his personal dandyism, fashion is what allows us to recreate ourselves according to a certain image, to escape from the limitations imposed on us by nature, and to some extent too, to diminish the control exercised over us by culture. What changed it from the domain of the elite and brought it into the very heart of popular culture was, of course, the Industrial Revolution and specifically the invention of the sewing machine, created by Singer in 1851. That invention, together with a sea change in the concept of shopping, from individual specialized shops to the vast emporium and department store, lies at the core of Zola's capitalist paradise, *Au bonheur des dames* (*The Ladies' Paradise*).

Within the context of peripheries and centers, the novel occupies a pivotal position. Through the extended metaphor of clothes allowing access to women's hearts and men's pocketbooks, and through its narrative structure of the outsider moving ineluctably to the center while the building itself spreads out and up to swallow an entire neighborhood, indeed an entire way of life, it reveals a deeper meaning, according to which modern life, especially the modern city, has destroyed former distinctions between peripheries and centers, and among social strata, so that all seems now surface. As Oscar Wilde might say (indeed, as Oscar Wilde did say): what is interesting is not the face behind the mask but the mask itself. Yet the novel is also particularly eccentric both within late-nineteenth-century norms and within Zola's own production: at a time of high misogyny it replaced the male hero epitomized by Rastignac—the outsider who through the intermediary of a fairy godfather, Vautrin, dominates the city and its society—by a woman who single-handedly transforms much of that society and comes to govern it in very different ways. While Mouret does of course follow the pattern handed down by Balzac and many others in that he comes in from outside and with the help of Hartmann, the novel's Haussmann figure, appears to take control of society, all he does, and this despite the novelty of his vision, merely achieves a replication of the hierarchical structures: Denise, on the contrary, works to flatten hierarchical structures and thus effects far more wide-reaching social changes.

This shift in social structures, and indeed in the categories in which commodities had previously been placed, is reflected in the parallel that is established with the visual arts, for *Au bonheur des dames* also reveals Zola vying with his artist friends not so much through the topoi of the landscapes and cityscapes that dominate *Germinal* or *L'Assommoir*, for instance, as through still life. Moreover, whereas in *Le Ventre de Paris* his still lifes, focused as they are on food, have an element of the classic in them, here he moves into the still life underworld of underwear, descending even further into the depths of what Norman Bryson, in his study *Looking at the Overlooked,* explores as rhopography. And whereas Zola habitually follows, or at least exploits, contemporary medical and scientific convictions to posit woman as deviant, and femininity as both illness and weakness, here he situates the woman at the center of the new world of commerce, a world, moreover, that not only legitimizes but depends on female desire, although that desire is constantly channeled away from direct sexuality towards the attributes and outcomes of sexuality.[1] Where contemporary constructions of gender punished desire in mothers, while alienating from the center of power those women who failed to assume their destiny as reproductive systems, desire becomes an essential element of the exchange mechanism driving the new society, and Denise, as surrogate mother to her brothers, is both allowed to desire, and gains her power from her refusal to succumb to desire. *Au bonheur des dames* appears to present us with a text that examines changing power structures in a rapidly changing world, and especially the question of woman's role, a text in which underdogs and underwear finally have their day.[2]

In considering how this novel explores the question of shifting power, across classes and between the sexes, I want to look at the interface of two domains linked by the mechanism of metonymy: first, that which replaces the church with the department store, Christian mythology with a more primal mythology of fecundation and growth; and secondly that of still life painting, which, as Bryson reminds us, operates by uniting three cultural zones: the life of the table and the interior; the domain of sign systems which encode the subject matter in ways that relate it to other cultural concerns; and the technology of painting, the material practice and its semiotic processes.[3] Mouret's displays, evoked by Zola in a series of virtuoso still lifes, focus on the life of the domestic interior, encoding it through the unexpected juxtapositions of lace and umbrellas, shoes and corsets, in ways that reflect on the rapidly increasing diversity of contemporary urban life.[4]

In many ways, *Au bonheur des dames* looks back to the first novel of the series, composed some ten years earlier, *La Fortune des Rougon*, with its problematic imbrication of religious and political power structures. If party politics wins out over the Church in the earlier novel, they could not in themselves replace the function of the Church, especially in controlling and organizing the force of women at an age when politics sought merely to exclude women from any kind of role. With the rise of that microcosm of the city, the department store, the Second Empire—or at least Zola's Second Empire, finds a role for woman, one that recreates and transforms certain Catholic structures, but that also draws on more ancient and pagan rites, while legitimizing and channeling aspects of female and even maternal desire.

The department store itself becomes the new cathedral, built on a blood sacrifice, that of Mouret's first wife, as ancient societies sacrificed the corn king, the green man, or the wicker man to ensure a fruitful growing season. The vaults and arches of the new store, its vast windows, and its metallic naves all make it, as Zola tell us, "la cathédrale du commerce moderne," ("the cathedral of modern business") (258/234), [5] the temple in which Mouret, like a jealous god, could hold woman at his mercy. Mouret himself becomes both god and priest of his new religion, attracting confessions of unbridled desire from his wealthy clientele. Whereas *La Fortune des Rougon* followed Michelet in presenting the priest and confessor as the agent of the destruction of families, supplanting the husband with a stronger force, here the store (and Mouret as its metonym) takes over that role. In a conversation between Mouret and Hartmann, Zola suggests the complicity of political and mercantile power in their exploitation of woman:

> Tout y aboutissait, le capital sans cesse renouvelé, le système de l'entassement des marchandises, le bon marché qui attire, la marque en chiffres connus qui tranquillise. C'était la femme que les magasins se disputaient par la concurrence, la femme qu'ils prenaient au continuel piège de leurs occasions, après l'avoir étourdie devant leurs étalages. Ils avaient éveillé dans sa chair de nouveaux désirs, ils étaient une tentation immense où elle succombait fatalement.[. . .] En décuplant la vente, en démocratisant le luxe, ils devenaient un terrible agent de dépense, ravageaient les ménages.
>
> (Everything else led up to it, the ceaseless renewal of capital, the system of piling up goods, the low prices that attracted people, the marked prices that reassured them. It was Woman the shops were competing for so fiercely; it was Woman they were continually snaring with their bargains, after dazing her with their displays. They had awoken new desires in her weak flesh; they were an immense temptation to which she inevitably yielded [. . .]. By increasing sales tenfold, by making luxury democratic, shops were becoming a terrible agency for spending, ravaging households.) (110/76)

Mouret's sole passion becomes his longing to conquer woman, woman in general and Denise in particular. It is part of the slippery nature of this kind of discourse, constantly crossing between secular and religious connotations, that even the word passion in the previous sentence is not just imbued with the sexual meanings that jostle for our attention but is also freighted with the more specifically Christian meaning of Christ's suffering, as though Mouret is not merely building a mercantile empire but also erecting a system of signs which will confer godhead on him. Yet metonymy, like the shift from Christian to pagan values, suggests that Mouret as the new king of commerce is replaceable, and that his godhead may rapidly be conferred on the next in line.[6]

Zola seems to delight in stretching the parallels between store and cathedral to their fullest extent. In doing so, he suggests the degree to which Mouret's initial concept has gained a life of its own, gone beyond him to exceed his reach and challenge his power. Just as medieval cathedrals frequently include a labyrinth (one that leads the faithful through a maze to heaven) so the *Bonheur* contains a complication of stairways and corridors, a series of rooms and attics, that leads to a far-off department where Denise occasionally meets Deloche in secret, out of sight of prying eyes. As the store moves from the margins of society to its center, it brings with it its own margins, beyond even peripheral vision of the center.

If Mouret's office at the top of the stairs had previously allowed him, like Frollo overlooking the parvis of Notre Dame or the priest watching from the pulpit, to be all-seeing as well as all-powerful, now the complete assimilation of store and cathedral appears to have enforced the inclusion of this hidden corner, where his vision and his power are limited. And the discourse of commerce and religion, once it has been shared with Hartmann, also goes beyond Mouret's grasp, so that he finds the rival store, *Les Quatre Saisons,* not only given political power by Hartmann's indiscriminate bestowal of his favor, but being officially blessed by the bishop of La Madeleine, the church whose very name suggests desire, in a ceremony which as Zola puts it had resulted in "une pompe religieuse promenée de la soierie à la ganterie, Dieu tombé dans les pantalons de femme et dans les corsets" ("all the pomp of the Church was paraded through the silk and glove departments, God circulated among women's knickers and corsets") (406/394).

But if god has been brought down to the level of women's knickers and corsets, it is in part because he was always already there, in the person of Mouret himself, in his persona as god the artist. Where Claude Lantier is Zola's image of the failed artist, Mouret, paradoxically, appears as supremely successful artist, even though (or perhaps because) he is working in the rhopographic medium not just of still life, but in the lower reaches of still life. Where still life that presents food can be re-encoded as a commentary on the male world of luxury and power, a commentary moreover that bestows permanence on the fleeting, Mouret's displays tend to focus on the specifically feminine—silks, linen, children's clothes, and bedroom furnishings—and must, in order to function as creators of appetite and desire, always be ephemeral. Yet these elements of what would otherwise be regarded, in a phallocentric vision, as unimportant, assume, through the coding system that drives the whole novel, the function of symbols of ultimate power. At the same time as he moves Mouret from the peripheries of still life painting to the center of high finance, Zola of course also maneuvers to move himself from the weak position of entertainer and novelist to that of powerful, scientific analyst of social movements.[7]

How much Zola would have reveled in the current renovation

of London's major department store in which El Fayed has translated that Mecca of merchandise to a fantasized Egypt! After all, he had already achieved the same effect himself with Mouret's first great display, the one that used carpets from the Levant to create an Oriental salon: "Cette tente de pacha somptueux était meublée de fauteuils et de divans, faits avec des sacs de chameau, les uns coupés de losanges bariolés, les autres plantés de roses naïves. La Turquie, l'Arabie, la Perse, les Indes étaient là. On avait vidé des palais, dévalisé les mosqués et bazars. [. . .] Et des visions d'Orient flottaient sous le luxe de cet art barbare, au milieu de l'odeur du pays de la vermine et du soleil" ("The sumptuous pasha's tent was furnished with armchairs and divans made from camelbags, some ornamented with multicolored lozenges, others with simple roses. Turkey, Arabia, Persia, the Indies were all there. Palaçes had been emptied, mosques and bazaars plundered. [. . .] Visions of the Orient floated beneath the luxury of this barbarous art, amid the strong odor which the old wools had retained from lands of vermin and sun") (121/88). The coding here is straightforward: Mouret uses images of male wealth and status to attract money. Later, as the power of the department store grows, the displays become increasingly feminized and use a different set of codes, but they all speak the same word or set of words: desire and satisfaction. As Mouret's sexual desire for Denise reaches its highest point, the displays evoked speak increasingly less of the clientele than the shop owner. Thus Denise and her brothers walking through the shop in search of blouses traverse the women's underwear department: "Le déshabillé galant commençait, un déshabillé qui jonchait les vastes pièces, comme si un groupe de jolies filles s'étaient dévêtues de rayon en rayon, jusqu'au satin nu de leur peau" ("But beyond them the luxury *déshabillé* began, a *déshabillé* strewn across the vast galleries, as if an army of pretty girls had undressed as they went from department to department, down to their satiny skin") (420–21/409). Carnal desire here moves rapidly into the purity reconferred on the desiring woman by motherhood in a metonymic representation that points forward to cubist's fragmentation of the viewed object, but that also suggests the absent object of desire in a symbolism reminiscent, curiously enough, of Mallarmé, who after all reveals in his letters to Zola that he was fully aware of overlapping purposes, even if Zola himself failed to recognize these parallels between his work and the poet's. The fragmentation of the female body displayed in the department store and by extension in the way in which she is regarded merely as a source of finance in the economy the store depends on is also reflected in Robert Altman's movie *Prêt à porter*, when one of the fashion designers is asked how he perceives his ideal woman. Clad in a kilt, and having just staged a fashion show the purpose of which is to bring back the bustle while retaining the miniskirt, he offers the following reply: "I think that my ideal woman has a bust, and a waist, and hips, and she isn't shy about her shoulders. I think shoulders are very fresh this year. Oh and legs. It's not essential that she have legs, but oh! it's wonderful if she does."

Yet while Mouret's consummate artistry and his understanding of desire enable him to transform the lowly form of still life into high art, the despised domains of the feminine into the prime source of enrichment, he in turn is transformed by desire, brought down from his position of dominance to one of impotence, from center to periphery: "Mais c'était surtout pendant son inspection quotidienne des magasins qu'il sentait sa misère. Avoir bâti cette machine géante, régner sur un pareil monde, et agoniser de douleur, parce qu'une petite fille ne veut pas de vous! Il se méprisait, il traînait la fièvre et la honte de son mal. Certains jours, le dégoût le prenait de sa puissance, il ne lui venait que des nausées, d'un bout à l'autre des galeries" ("But it was during his daily tour of inspection of the shop that he felt his misery most. To have built this gigantic machine, to reign over so many people, and to be in agonies of suffering because a little girl rejected him! He despised himself; he was pursued by the fever and shame of his affliction. On some days he felt disgusted with his own power, feeling nothing but nausea as he went from one end of the galleries to the other") (351/334). Mouret here is feminized by his subjection to Denise, to the point of hysteria, and the store itself, initially a projection of his desire for status and money, now becomes a projection of his pain, trembling and panic-stricken as he suffers the ravages of jealousy.[8] Whereas his displays function by metonymy and metaphor, tropes that work to deny or at least diminish unicity by focusing on the endless transferability of meaning, Mouret is forced to acknowledge Denise as individual, irreducible to the category of shop girl.

As desire threatens to become destruction, Eros changing masks with Thanatos, Mouret's domination of the crowd weakens as he places himself at the mercy of that voice of the crowd, gossip.[9] Again the movie *Prêt à porter* sheds a lurid not to say

Lurex light on this subjection to the voice of the mass. Discovering that her son has sold her fashion logo to of all things a Texas boot maker, *Prêt à porter*'s female fashion designer responds to an act that not only barters her identity, but that strikes at the very heart of fashion-making, which is predicated on constant change, for the point about a Texan boot is that it must always be a Texan boot, not a moccasin or slipper. Her response takes the form of a fashion show in which all the models, with the exception of the extremely pregnant model who wears a bridal veil, promenade completely naked. Anouk Aimé's voice-over as she introduces the show promises "something completely new" in an accent that leaves open the possibility that she has actually said: "completely nude." The nude show allows the movie to reach a closure as problematic as that of Zola's novel. Both end with a vision of female power but both are forced to stop at that point: after the nude fashion show there is nowhere else to go. Variations on the theme, the staple of fashion design, are not possible in this case. Nudity is a degree zero, an absolute that either limits power to a single unrepeatable moment, or equates power with powerlessness. Similarly, the abrupt ending of *Au bonheur des dames*, providing as it does a perfect example of an oxymoron—a Zola happy ending—leaves us with a series of questions concerning the nature and future of power, especially in the changing context of the nineteenth-century city. Did Zola stop because he was unable to envisage the changes in society that would be implicit in Denise's continuing hold on power, or was it because it is so obvious that the happy ending has no future in a happy continuance? The novel's first word is "Denise," its final word is "toute-puissante," all powerful: in focusing on the circle this appears to offer, we might forget a conversation that takes place in the middle of the book, where Hartmann, contemplating Mouret's planned mass seduction, warns: "Vous savez qu'elles se rattraperont" ("You know, they'll have their revenge"). Mouret's response is a gesture of disdain, explained by the narrative voice in these terms: "Quand il aurait tiré d'elles sa fortune et son plaisir, il les jetterait en tas à la borne, pour ceux qui pourraient encore y trouver leur vie" ("When he had extracted his fortune and his pleasure from them, he would throw them on the rubbish heap, for those who could still make a living out of them") (111/77). Yet, with Denise won, what power remains to Mouret? The driving force behind the expansion of his empire has been the desire to seduce, but once this is achieved, what next? What the novel seems to suggest is that the *bonheur* of the title must always be a destination, not an arrival point, that power in the new mercantile economy and in the new, destratified urban society, is dependent on a constant expansion that privileges the plural over the individual, the *dames* over Denise, the mass over Mouret, the margin over the center. As so often with Zola's endings, narrative strategies, whether perceived as drawing on the metaphor of entropy, as David Baguley suggests, or as dominated by the metonymic trope of displacement, conflict with the political and scientific messages of the diegesis to present a conclusion fraught with contradictions, and one that has powerful implications for his vision of the future of city life.

Notes

1. For useful background on this see Brooks (*Body Work: Objects of Desire in Modern Narrative* [Cambridge: Harvard University Press, 1990]), Flynn (*Reflections on Gender and S????*), and Keller ("Pious Pathologies: Medical and Religious Discourse in the Female-Centered Narratives of Emile Zola,"),

2. For a different reading of the power structures in this novel, see Bell, who in my view underplays the implications of the abrupt ending.

3. See N. Bryson, *Looking at the Overlooked,* 14. (Cambridge: Harvard University Press, 1990).

4. Illuminating readings of shopping as motif can be round in Bowlby and Schor (1993).

5. Emile Zola, *au bonheur des dames* (Paris: Flammarion, 1971), 258; Emile Zola, *The Ladies' Paradise,* trans. Brian Nelson (Oxford: Oxford University Press, 1995), 234. Subsequent page references to Zola's *Au bonheur des dames* will be included in the text; the first reference will be to the French edition, the second to Nelson's English translation.

6. David Baguley's exploration of the motif of entropy (*Naturalist Fiction: The Entropic Vision* [Cambridge: Cambridge University Press, 1990]) provides a useful context for this depiction of Mouret.

7. See Robert Lethbridge's persuasive exploration of Zola's artist envy. (" 'Le Delacroix de la musigne': Zola's Critical Conflations," in *Le Champ Littéraire* [Amsterdam: Rodopi, 1996]).

8. The question of hysteria is interestingly explored in Janet Beizer's *Ventriloquized Bodies* (Ithaca: Cornell University Press, 1994).

9. In this regard, I have found Patricia Spack's book on gossip particularly helpful.

Artful Shenanigans: Painting, Prostitution, and Cinema in Jean Renoir's *La Chienne*

JOHN ANZALONE

DÉDÉ, SMALL-TIME PIMP, IS LOOKING FOR THE SCAM THAT WILL allow him a big-time score. Lulu whores for him, sleeping with older men to keep her darling Dédé in fancy clothes and drinks in the cafés where he loses all his money at cards. For a none-too-bright con artist, the big time can be elusive, but Dédé has an idea. Maurice Legrand, the cashier Lulu is sleeping with, is also a painter. Legrand has decorated the love nest in which he has set her up with some of his artwork, which his shrewish wife derides as "(s)es sales tableaux . . . du bric-à-brac" ("his filthy paintings . . . just junk").[1] Easy money, thinks Dédé, and walks off with two canvases. When Gustave, his skeptical crony, points out that no one will want the paintings because none of them are signed, they devise a front. They invent a painter whom they call Clara Wood (after a horse Gustave has just lost a bundle on) to be played by Lulu, and they hit the streets in search of a witling. What they find are accomplices.

In the subsequent sequence in the Wallstein gallery, they meet an art critic and a dealer only too happy to fall in with the scam. That sequence ends with the four plotters gazing at the paintings and then at one another, in a wry image of recognition that reveals to the viewer their familial resemblance. It also concludes the lengthy exposition of Jean Renoir's first sound film *La Chienne* (1932); in many respects it constitutes as well the film's core, where all its significant themes are joined. The multiple deceptions fueling the plot merge to impart upon it an irresistible momentum that will first cause the action to take off towards a vaudeville, comic high, then to careen with brutal suddenness into somber and tragic farce. A rich fabric of deception is woven by the three major characters whom we watch delude themselves into believing they are pulling a fast one, when all the while they do no more than play out the stereotypical triangle of the pimp, his whore, and her fool. So well-worn is this schema, in fact, that the film's celebrated prologue, played on a Punch and Judy stage, presents its trio of protagonists in purely generic terms as "Lui, elle et l'autre, comme toujours" ("he, she, and the other guy, as usual") (7).

But it is crucial to our understanding of this film in Renoir's *œuvre* that it achieves its special energy only once painting is joined with prostitution in the scam Dédé sets in motion. The deceptions we have witnessed since the film's opening sequences attain a far deeper complexity, once a series of private manipulations becomes public with the complicity of the marketplace. "De nos jours, tout le monde ment" ("these days, everybody lies"), said Renoir himself in the role of Octave, in one of the best-known lines of *La Règle du jeu*. But what does it mean to this particular filmmaker when the lies center on painting, art, and artistic ownership? A particularly wicked irony emerges from the glance of recognition that closes the sequence, when a beautiful, slow, forward tracking shot closes in to bare the mutual connivance of not one but two sets of pimps setting out on an elaborate swindle via the commodification of art.

La Chienne is the adaptation of Georges de La Fouchardière's successful if mediocre novel of 1930. The sometimes farcical turns of the plot, the sudden, violent death of Lulu at the hands of a Legrand made desperate and bereft at the loss of his illusions, the grotesque mistaken identity climax by which a hapless Dédé is found guilty and executed for Legrand's crime all come right from the novel. In it, Legrand is the ready and willing fool who allows his paintings to be appropriated without a murmur, as long as he believes Lulu loves him.[2] But the elements of the story taken directly from the novel have no more than a surface effect on the issues concerning art and painting raised by this sequence in the film.

La Fouchardière had adopted the unusual narrative strategy of having each of his characters speak in the first person to recount his or her part of the story. If the prostitution of painting contributes to the complexity of the novel's plot, it does so without a shred of the irony so evident throughout the film; it certainly had no particular biographical ramifications for the novelist. The film on the other hand, keeps the viewer far from first person confessions. The mise-en-scène relies on thorough, studied instances of distanciation. Critical moments or scenes are elided, emotional impacts deemphasized. The film announces its ironic, self-conscious stance vis-à-vis its subject at every moment, beginning with the narrative framing device of puppet show prologue, where the viewer is warned that there will be no easy conclusions, but instead a recommendation from the outset to look closely, to look in depth, and to listen.

With the coming of sound, Jean Renoir began the elaboration of a visual signature that used the availability of this new addition to the cinematic medium in startlingly original and influential ways, a fact well documented in the critical literature devoted to him.[3] But another factor is at work in his evolution at this stage in his career. For the son of Pierre-Auguste Renoir, the impact of the direct experience of impressionism and of the art world generally were far more significant factors in the redefinition and refinement of his mise-en-scène throughout the thirties than is commonly acknowledged in film history. References do occur occasionally in the literature to Jean Renoir's "impressionism," especially with reference to his 1936 adaptation of Guy de Maupassant's *Une Partie de campagne*. But with the exception of Alexander Sesonke's subtle observations here and there throughout his book, and of Jean-Louis Leutrat's occasional remarks in his recent, crackling essay on *La Chienne*, no extant study deals at any length with Renoir's sometimes pointedly self-conscious exploitation of painterly surfaces and effects. Whenever they occur, Renoir's allusions to painting inevitably recall his constant exposure to and experiences of visual art in the milieu of his father. More important, they extend deeply into his practice of his own medium, in terms of both continuities and distinctness.

But in fact, whenever attempts have been made to connect this self-described "man of the nineteenth century" with the art and culture of that century, it has always been to literature that critics have referred. There is no doubt that Renoir was French cinema's greatest interpreter of the realist-naturalist school of fiction. Drawn to the novels of Flaubert, Maupassant, and Zola, he absorbed thoroughly the naturalist conventions of scrupulous documentation and strict observation of milieu, often using sound, in effect, as a leveling or layering medium to present several worlds in relationship or collision with one another. At least two of his films of the thirties, *Toni* (1934) and *La Bête humaine* (1938), can be understood as attempts to create a cinematic equivalent of the naturalist novel.[4] At the same time, these two films are *visual* masterpieces: they demonstrate a remarkable range of tones and an expressive use of composition that we can appropriately describe as Renoir's palette. The bright sun of the *midi* in *Toni* is used consistently to illuminate a dark tragedy by the relentless discovery of dangerous sensuality in painterly tableaux. The many compositions using locomotives, smoky train yards, and vast stations in *La Bête humaine* can hardly fail to recall one of the favorite themes of impressionism's period of social observation. Even the richness of the black, white, and gray palette of *La Règle du jeu* (a film initially intended for color photography, and Renoir's avowed retreat from naturalism) brings photography and landscape painting together in ways that surprise and delight.

But if there is one film that stands out as an openly self-conscious statement about Renoir's artistic inheritance from painting, that film is *La Chienne*. It is the only film of Renoir's entire career which makes explicit and reiterated visual as well as textual references to the world of painting, to the painterly canvas, to portraits and to still life. The allusions are constantly ironic, becoming acerbic with the sequence in the gallery. That Renoir devoted such attention, and deepened with such unmistakable gusto what is hardly more than a simple plot device in the novel underscores the complexity of his attitude toward painting. Admiring and frankly imitative on the one hand, it displays conflict and unease as well. That ambivalence has never really drawn much attention, which is both natural and curious. Natural, because Renoir's relationship to Auguste Renoir as he presented it in his long memoir *Renoir, My Father*, was "wonderfully sane (and) perceptive," as Terrence Rafferty aptly noted in a *New Yorker* portrait of the director.[5] Curious, because no one would deny that even "wonderfully sane" relationships are more complicated than they appear.

Clearly, the film itself invites us to consider painting, prostitution, and cinema as closely entwined. Painting is first presented in *La Chienne* as a private act by which reverie and aspiration find expression in a world of incomprehension, persecution, and even frank hostility. Once it becomes linked with prostitution, however, both attain the aura of inevitability appropriate to accessories of tragedy and death. For painting carried tremendous freight throughout the film: initially, it is the revelation of Legrand's unspoken longings. It decorates Lulu's apartment thus standing in for the absent Legrand, only to become the barter Dédé extorts so that Legrand may keep his whore. It is when

Lulu throws this arrangement in his face by crudely nagging him to finish a painting she wants to sell that he kills her; in the final sequence of the film, Legrand's portrait recedes in the back seat of an automobile as a grim and paradoxical reminder that the rise of an artist has been stamped "paid in full" by the fall of a man. At the very least, a close examination of how the medium of cinema joins painting with prostitution will allow us to revise our sense of *La Chienne*'s originality, by demonstrating Renoir's need to acknowledge the art of his father even as he asserted his independence from it.

A shot near the conclusion of the gallery sequence makes that assertion explicit. The pimps have come to discuss painting with two higher-class purveyors. The topic of discussion is painting, the subtext is prostitution, but the self-conscious subject is cinema itself. When Dédé and Gustave arrive in the gallery, the paintings they bring are placed on the floor, facing away from the viewer. Langelar, the art critic, entertains the men's proposition, but the viewer's attention is directed away from the already deemphasized paintings towards the rear of the shop where the dealer Wallstein is looking for a receipt he can't seem to find. During the entire gallery sequence we never once see the paintings the pimps have bought. When Legrand subsequently discovers in the very next sequence that his work is being exhibited and sold under someone else's name, the paintings we do see are not the ones we witnessed Dédé remove from Lulu's apartment. In fact, the shot is composed deliberately to draw the viewer's gaze away from the foreground discussion and towards Wallstein in the rear. Dédé and Gustave lean against the wall on the left, with Langelar standing opposite them, against the wall on the right, forming a central tunnel down which the viewer's gaze travels towards Wallstein. Attention returns unequivocally to the subject of painting only once Wallstein is drawn out of the back room. Even then, the quartet seems more interested in the coup they're about to make than in the paintings themselves. Thus, the dialogue here speaks to the viewer of painting, just as the composition of the sequence borrows from painting, while the dynamics of the shot itself speak instead of cinema.

That duality of painting/cinema is reinforced immediately when, in the very next sequence, Maurice Legrand passes in front of the gallery and discovers one of his paintings in the window. The painting is a portrait of a woman at a window frame and we have glimpsed it twice previously; first, when Legrand's

Fig. 8 ***La Chienne*, Jean Renoir, Braunberger-Richébé.**

wife berates him for wasting time on his painting, and second as the establishing shot of our first look at Lulu's love nest. In neither case do we see the entire painting, as we do here, now publicly displayed. Scholars have noted how frequently Renoir constructed his films by concerted use of repetition, reflection, and reprise, and La Chienne provides a textbook demonstration of this preference. A subtle variation of the shot of Legrand looking at this portrait in Wallstein's window is indeed reprised later in the film when, during its epilogue, a now destitute Legrand stops in front of a gallery on the Avenue Matignon to contemplate another woman in a scene of intimacy. This time he gazes at the *Femme à sa toilette* of Auguste Renoir. Beyond the fillip the viewer experiences upon recognizing the artistic lineage inscribed in this reiteration, the two paintings attain analogous status by virtue of subject matter and of parallel mise-en-scène, and last, but especially by their participation in the system that transforms art as private, personal expression into art as commodity.

That we are to identify Maurice Legrand as a serious painter is vouchsafed for us in a similar fashion. From the first he is pre-

Fig. 9 ***La Chienne*****, Jean Renoir, Braunberger-Richébé.**

sented as misunderstood, a victim of his talent for seeing beyond appearances that both the dialogue and his painting suggest in the film's earliest sequences. The artwork itself is associated with advanced painting by virtue of the *Woman in the Window*'s resemblance to similar representations of women in domestic scenes by Vuillard or Matisse, for example, both of whom are mentioned in the novel.[6] Renoir himself seems to have intentionally imitated a specific tableau when he shows first Gustave and Dédé playing cards in a café, and then Legrand and his wife's first husband, Alexis Godard, in paired shots that are strongly reminiscent of Cézanne's *Les Joueurs de cartes*, a painting he is known to have admired.[7] Furthermore, Legrand is involved in another pairing of shots at the opening and then at the close of the film, both of which show his self-portrait, first while he is painting it, and then in the epilogue as that very same portrait is purchased by a wealthy collector and removed from a gallery adjacent to the one exhibiting the Renoir bather. The painting, stolen from its creator, has appreciated enormously in value as Legrand has gone from bourgeois

Fig. 10 ***La Chienne*****, Jean Renoir, Braunberger-Richébé.**

respectability to the classless, homeless status of the down and outer in the distinctive trajectory the film stages.

When we look at the first sequence of the self-portrait, then, we are seeing Legrand at the height of his creative power. As he contemplates himself in the mirror we see him in three planes: his head and upper body from behind, his image in the mirror, and between them, the portrait itself. He portrays himself as smartly dressed and coifed, and in a self-confident attitude he only displays once he has made his connection with Lulu. The camera then pans right to reframe the scene in profile as we are allowed to look out the window and across the courtyard into the apartment where a little girl, whose voice we have been hearing all along, is singing. The reprise of the multiple framing of a portrait again moves us visually from the realm of painting to that of cinematic depth of field photography, whose use in the sound film Renoir pioneered in France in the thirties, beginning precisely with *La Chienne*. We have already witnessed dynamic framing in the gallery sequence. It is used as a signature compositional device throughout *La Chienne*, recurring in every critical sequence and with particular emphasis in the scenes where

Fig. 11 ***La Chienne*, Jean Renoir, Braunberger-Richébé.**

Legrand discovers Lulu in bed with Dédé, and when he murders her. Of course, framing can arguably be claimed as one of cinema's most important debts to painting; the continuous take here may be read as an acknowledgment of that fact by Jean Renoir.

Legrand stops painting shortly after meeting Lulu. His art, hitherto his only means for release, dwindles as he focuses increasingly on her. The film is nearly incoherent about the evolution of his relationship with her. He is at first portrayed as canny, resourceful, and clear-thinking about everything, including Lulu. He is masterful in disguising his passion and his thefts from his wife and his coworkers. Renoir's use of dialogue and especially of the patois that he pointedly taught actress Janie Marèze lets us hear that Lulu is lower-class, and there is no question for the viewer that Legrand "hears" her that way too, that he understands the foolish things she first says to him with the same gentle derision as the viewer. He also is initially aware of Dédé as her *souteneur*, having after all met both of them when he intervened as Dédé tried to beat her up. But all of this lucidity simply disappears from the narrative and from his character

Fig. 12 ***La Chienne*, Jean Renoir, Braunberger-Richébé.**

as the film progresses. Similarly, it is to say the least astonishing that he meekly acquiesces in the swindle that passes his paintings off as Clara Wood's. The film first expresses the power of prostitution in this way: Legrand falls under the sway of what he imagines Lulu to be, and it renders him truly inept by cutting him off from his art, his true avenue of imaginative expression and investment, even as the product of that imagination is prostituted to the marketplace.

As with much else in *La Chienne*, however, the film presents two distinct visions of prostitution. The literal prostitution of Lulu to Legrand on Dédé's behalf is by far the simpler of the two, since it does not spill outside the confines of the novel's stereotypical plot. Lulu's status as a loose woman bothers Legrand little until the dramatic scene of disillusion. At the height of his triumph over his hectoring wife, he steps out into the rainy night of his ultimate betrayal, and stumbles into the revelation of the true nature of a relationship to which he has become willfully blind. Only then does he call Lulu a *chienne*. His self-delusion is the only reasonable explanation that the film offers for

Fig. 13 ***La Chienne*****, Jean Renoir, Braunberger-Richébé.**

his docile, passive acceptance of the theft of his art, which the viewer greets with similar docility.

Not so, the director, however. There is only one explicit instance in the film where Lulu is seen prostituting herself in a demeaning way to yet another older man (we know that she has already left an elderly man for Legrand). Significantly, it involves her pretending to be Clara Wood in order to swindle a potential client who wants a portrait of himself. Since she cannot paint him, she ingratiates herself by snuggling up to him at a party as the dealer and the art critic wryly note: "Sacrée Clara! Autant qu'elle s'y prenne comme ça . . ." ("Jesus, that Clara! Well, she might as well do it like that . . .") (17). What follows is an extraordinary shot that once again puts prostitution and painting squarely in the context of cinema. A fade to black is followed by the depiction of the result of the illicit transaction: at Dédé's offscreen dictation, Lulu signs the check she has seduced the client into giving her. The fade-in gives us a shot that is repeated with variations several times in the course of the film: a close-up image, held for a brief length of time in a tight frame, where compositional elements very distinctly recall the

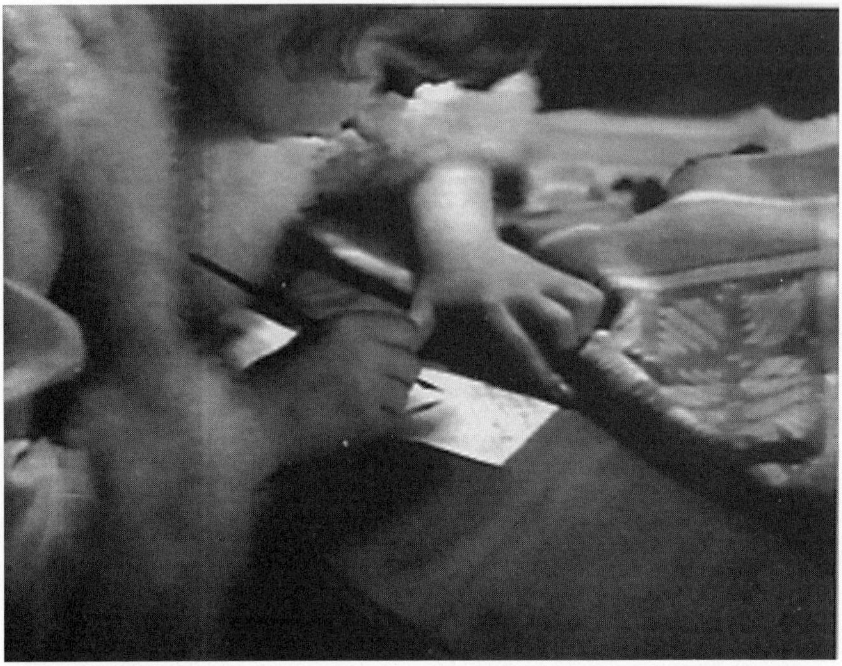

Fig. 14 ***La Chienne*, Jean Renoir, Braunberger-Richébé.**

painterly still life. In the critical literature, such shots are traditionally associated with the *effet de réel* or reality effect of the mise-en-scène, and with Renoir's acknowledged mastery at creating settings, milieus and atmospheres out of the humble objects of daily life. But they also self-consciously exploit a painterly esthetic. Note in this still of the check-signing the extraordinary use of the tablecloth, which answers the textures of Lulu's feathery robe (the semiotic of the prostitute) with the folds and pleats of the type of cloth used as a prop in still-life paintings of fruit, vegetables, or bread. That this effect was intentional is vouchsafed by Lulu's gesture at the end of the take. Having finished signing the check on the wooden table surface, she restores the tablecloth to its customary position, smoothing it out as she rises. The close-ups also demonstrate an instance of perhaps the most fertile yet underappreciated "impressionism" in Renoir's cinema, that of sound: voices and ambient sounds are heard, experienced *sur le vif*, or in the moment, as the camera executes a leisurely backward tracking, expanding the frame to the broad, open mise-en-scène of realist cinema.

The prostitution motif thus achieves its maximum ambiguity

and impact in the film not in the sexual transactions between the three protagonists, but in the prostitution of art, which is always presented in a way that underscores at the same time the problematic relationship of painting to cinema. Prostitution, the middle term of this uncomfortable *ménage à trois* is ultimately canceled out, just as Lulu dies by Legrand's hand. The final close-up of an object uses one last time the pleated cloth of the still life as a cushion for the blade with which Legrand strikes her a moment later. The prostitution of art so genially expressed by the art critic Langelar ("Vous savez, les peintres, c'est nous qui les faisons" ["You know, we're the ones who make painters"]) (14) can then be read in terms of the questions Renoir confronted in the making of cinema as a visual art form with its own problematic status as a commodity in the marketplace. "What is art?" asked Baudelaire, quickly answering: "Prostitution."

Even a cursory overview of Renoir's career in the thirties points up his regular difficulties with producers. By the time of *La Chienne*, he was already a director with a reputation for artistic independence and correspondingly expensive habits. The

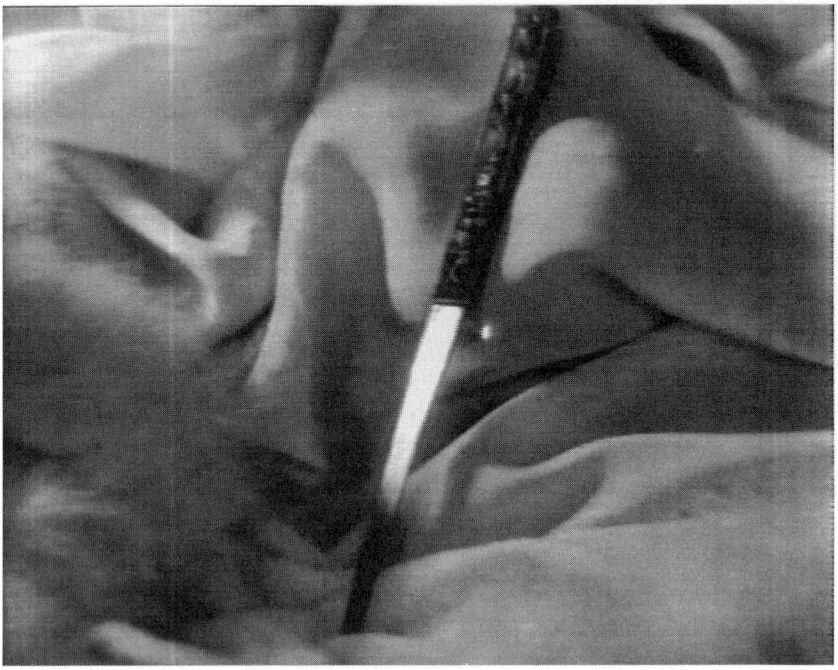

Fig. 15 ***La Chienne*, Jean Renoir, Braunberger-Richébé.**

filming of *La Chienne* resulted in quarrels with his producers that would be repeated in varying forms and degrees throughout the decade. To cover his part of the costs of his 1928 silent adaptation of Zola's *Nana*, perhaps the greatest of all nineteenth-century novels of prostitution, Renoir had to sell off some of the paintings he inherited from his father. And his memoirs of Pierre-Auguste Renoir's career include several discussions of frauds and swindles that, not surprisingly, bear a profound resemblance to the scam we began with in the gallery sequence.[8]

La Chienne has been rightly seen as Renoir's brilliant foray into a new order of realist mise-en-scène that used sound to exploit continuous takes. But it also stages a series of self-portraits in which the son of a great painter inscribes into his work his own image as a cinéaste in a rapport with his father that is certainly more richly ambiguous than has until now been proposed. One final, unintentional framing device emphasizes the connection in a startling and moving way. Just before Legrand stops to admire Auguste Renoir 's *Femme à sa toilette*, a luxurious roadster convertible pulls up in front of a gallery. As the

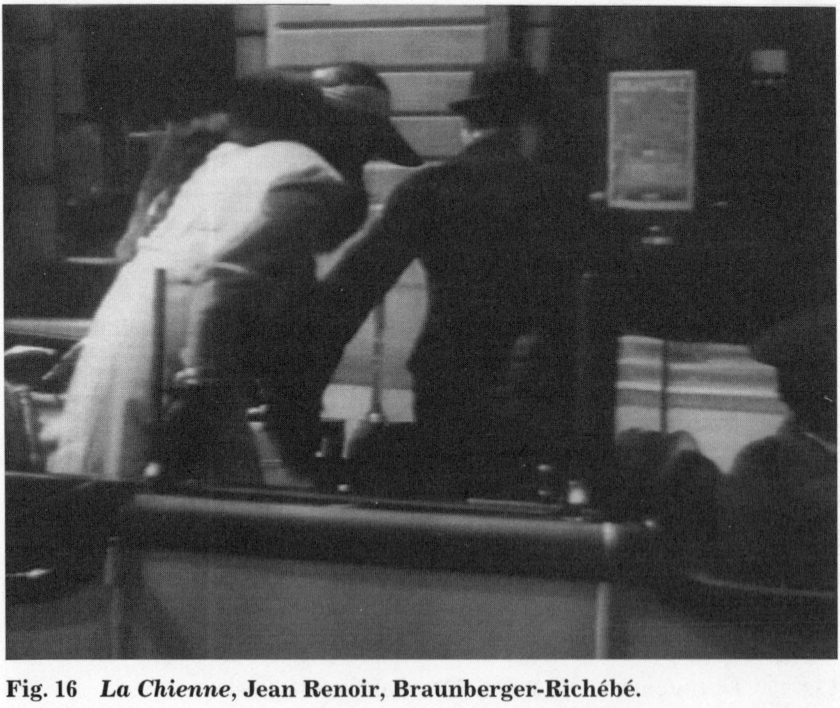

Fig. 16 ***La Chienne*, Jean Renoir, Braunberger-Richébé.**

Fig. 17 *La Chienne*, Jean Renoir, Braunberger-Richébé.

Fig. 18 ***La Chienne*, Jean Renoir, Braunberger-Richébé.**

wealthy patrons rise to get out of the car, the gentleman's black coat turns the car window into a reflecting surface. In this sudden mirror we glimpse the furtive image of Jean Renoir himself (lower right corner of the car window). Soon thereafter the image of the painter, the self-portrait of Maurice Legrand, emerges from a gallery. Gently placed into another convertible, it recedes into the distance and into invisibility, leaving only the cinema.

Notes

1. All quotations from *La Chienne* are taken from the découpage intégral published by *Avant-Scène, cinéma* 162 (October 1975). Subsequent references to the script will be given in the text of the article. Translations are taken from the subtitles of *La Chienne*; other translations are the author's.

2. The novel was published in translation by Alfred Knopf in 1932 under the remarkably apt title *Poor Sap*.

3. Based on his brilliant if thoroughly unconventional handling of the soundtrack of *La Chienne*, Renoir was approached by engineers from Western Electric who thought him capable of hastening the technological evolution of film sound, and so offered him use of their most state-of-the-art equipment.

Dudley Andrew, *Mists of Regret: Culture and Sensibility in Classic French Films* (Princeton, NJ: Princeton University Press, 1995), 104.

4. Renoir himself described *Toni* as "un film qui correspond à une de mes crises de réalisme aigu" ("A film corresponding to one of my acute attacks of realism"). Jean Renoir, *Entretiens et Propos* (Paris: Cahiers du Cinéma, 1979), 134. Cf. also Leo Braudy's contention that the true heir to the naturalist novel was realist cinema. "Zola on Film: Ambiguities of Naturalism," *Yale French Studies* 42 (1969): 74 ff..

5. Terrence Rafferty, "The Essence of the Landscape," *New Yorker*, 25 June 1990, 86.

6. These allusions were clearly taken seriously by Renoir, who commissioned paintings for the film that are evident pastiches of contemporary artists. Unfortunately, no one seems to know who executed the paintings, nor what became of them after the filming. Jean-Louis Leutrat, *La Chienne* (Belgique: Editions Yellow Now, 1994).

7. "Cézanne ouvre une fenêtre sur des joueurs de cartes, et les gens qui habitaient autour de ces joueurs de cartes, dans la ville d'Aix en Provence, il leur a fallu cinquante ans pour le voir, mais au bout de cinquante ans, ils disent: tiens, oui, ces joueurs de cartes sont comme ça, je n'avais jamais vu qu'il y avait des reflets de telle couleur dans la peau de ces joueurs de cartes, et cette révélation les ravit" ("Cézanne opens a window to reveal card players. The people who lived near these card players, in Aix en Provence, needed fifty years to see it, but at the end of those fifty years, they said: 'Say, that's right, Card players are like that—I never noticed that there are hints of this or that color on the skin of those gamblers.' And the revelation tickles them"). Renoir, *Entretiens*, 104. On the theme of prostitution among the Impressionists, see Hollis Clayson, *Painted Love: Prostitution in French Art of the Impressionist Era* (New Haven, CT: Yale University Press, 1991).

8. In particular the instances in which Renoir *père* willingly colluded with people clearly out to swindle him by retouching the obvious "unsigned" frauds they brought him, and then affixing his signature. Jean Renoir, *Renoir, My Father* (Boston: Little, Brown, 1962), 268 ff.. It is impossible not to see in such anecdotes a model for Legrand's otherwise puzzling behavior, nor to miss the echoes of Dédé and Gustave's first conversations in preparing their scam: Dédé: "Mais qu'est-ce que tu rigoles, mon vieux! Il y a de l'argent à gagner dans les tableaux comme dans tout!" . . . Gustave: "Oh, dans les tableaux il n'y a qu'une chose qui compte, c'est la signature! Et comme la signature que tu mettras sera pas connue, j'ai bien peur qu'on t'en offre des haricots!" ("Dédé: 'Hey, what are you laughin' about pal? There's money to be made in paintings just like anything else!' . . . Gustave: 'Oh, with paintings the only thing that counts is the signature. And since no one will know the signature you use, I doubt you'll get any more than a hill of beans!' ") (14).

A Bat's-Eye View of the Republic; or Victor Hugo in Gotham City

ILLINCA ZARIFOPOL-JOHNSTON

I BEGIN WITH A PEDAGOGICAL ANECDOTE. I TEACH AN UNDERgraduate course on literature and popular culture. In it, the students read Hugo's *Notre-Dame de Paris*, and watch Disney's *The Hunchback of Notre-Dame* (1996) and Tim Burton's 1989 movie hit, *Batman*. In addition to the customary papers and exams, students are required to keep a weekly journal in which they record their impressions and observations concerning the week's assignments, lectures, and discussions. In their journal entry for the *Batman* week, the students almost unanimously note that, at first, they could see *no* connection between Hugo's novel and Burton's movie. Throughout most of the movie, they wondered—and probably worried—why I had assigned *Batman* in conjunction with *Notre-Dame*. It was not until the end of the movie that they saw the writing of Hugo on the wall, or rather, on the screen.

Here is a brief narrative of what the students saw in the movie's closing sequence: at the end of a civic parade that has gone awry, the Joker shoots down the Batmobile with a huge gun he pulls out of his clownish pants. The Batmobile crashes in front of Gotham City Cathedral, and Vicki Vail, dressed all in white, her long, blonde hair flowing, comes running to it in her dainty, white pumps. She fears for the life of her lover, Bruce Wayne, alias Batman. As she strains to see through the blinding smoke, she hears a sinister voice whispering, "Darling, I've got to take you to the church on time." It is the Joker, who is pointing his big gun at her head; he motions her to move away from the Batmobile and towards the church door. Then, with Batman in pursuit, the Joker drags the reluctant Vicki up a long flight of stairs to the cathedral's bell tower. The police arrive on the scene as well but their attempt to follow is thwarted by the Joker who sprays the metal screws holding the bell in place with a liquid hidden in a flower he wears on his lapel, and melts them, dropping the bell on the policemen below. They abandon the pursuit. Batman, however, reaches the top of the tower and fights two spectacular fights with the Joker's bodyguards, while the latter waltzes with Vicki in the moonlight. The dance and all the fights in this sequence are choreographed around the figure of a leering gargoyle crouching on the rooftop, the movie's visual citation of Violet-le-Duc's famous gargoyle from the towers of the Notre Dame cathedral in Paris. Once the bodyguards are defeated, Batman and the Joker finally face each other. Before they come to blows, the two have a duel of words during which their father-child relationship is firmly established. "You made me," says the Joker to Batman, referring to the vatful of chemicals into which Batman once threw him, disfiguring his face into a permanent joking leer. Batman replies, "You made me first," referring to the Joker's murder of his parents. During the fight that follows, the protagonists repeatedly fall off the cathedral tower, hang precariously suspended on a ledge of crumbling stones, or try to scramble back to safety. Their struggle is also dominated by the immobile figure of the crouching, mocking gargoyle. The Joker's planned escape in a helicopter becomes his deathtrap. While he attempts to climb the ladder sent down from the helicopter to rescue him, Batman ties him unawares to one of the gargoyles whose weight, as it breaks away from the wall, pulls him down into the gaping void. Batman and Vicki Vail are not spared a last-minute scare as they fall off the crumbling ledge, and only manage to escape when the iron hook at the end of Batman's utility belt catches onto another gargoyle. Thus the gargoyle plays the deus ex machina part, literally killing the Joker while saving Batman and his girlfriend, who, after their fall, dangle in a tight embrace at the end of the rope that saved their life.

The movie's closing sequence, which is twenty-five minutes long, thus taking up about a third of the entire movie time, activated in my students' mind one of *Batman*'s hidden, but as I shall argue, central, intertexts: Hugo's *Notre-Dame de Paris*. In the final standoff between Batman (played by Michael Keaton) and his archenemy, the Joker (Jack Nicholson), with Vicki Vail (Kim Basinger) their female prize between them, on top of Gotham City's immense, dilapidated, Gothic cathedral, the students recognized fragments, albeit scrambled and distorted, from the final scenes of Hugo's novel: Quasimodo hurling Frollo to his death from the tower of Notre Dame; Esmeralda, a *creat-*

ura bella bianco vestida, being dragged, limp and defenseless, to her death up the ladder to the scaffold; Esmeralda dangling or "dancing" at the end of a rope and Quasimodo's marriage-in-death, all juxtaposed on earlier but equally climactic scenes from the novel, such as Quasimodo swinging on a rope to save Esmeralda from doing *amende honorable*, and Quasimodo melting lead to pour down on the attackers of Notre Dame to stop their advance.

Working their way backwards from this scene, the students were able to establish a number of connections between the movie and the novel. Just to state the most obvious ones: first, the pairs of protagonists, Quasimodo and Claude Frollo, and Batman and the Joker, have a "monstrous" character but with interesting reversals: Batman has Frollo's dark, erect, and sinister (caped rather than robed) figure, whereas on the Joker's face is permanently stamped with Quasimodo's (or Gwynplain's) disfiguring "grimace." Visually, the movie is very explicit at the end: the monster that links Batman to the Joker is the crouching, winged gargoyle who provides the focal point around which the two opponents revolve in their final confrontation, each alternately identifying with the grotesque statue as they take turns standing by it or moving around it as if they were—Batman with his pointed horns/ears and flying cape and the Joker with his grimacing face—the statue itself come to life.

Whereas Batman's brightly clad comic book competitors, Superman and Captain America, have an unambiguously positive superhero status, Batman's all black costume in the movie (rather than the traditional blue and gray shades of his comic book versions) introduces him as a figure of darkness with an indeterminate status—is he friend or foe, angel or demon? If we watch the movie without "traditional"—i.e., comic book—associations, it is not immediately apparent that Batman is good, and in his dark costume, reminiscent of Claude Frollo, Dracula, or even the Phantom of the Opera, he brings terror rather than relief to the audience. Like Frollo, Batman is power-hungry, obsessed with reading pictures that will allow him to control the world, the TV screens studding the walls of his Batcave having replaced the bas-reliefs of Notre Dame. But it is the chaos-wreaking Joker who has a degree in both chemistry (read alchemy) and art, and whose motto could very well be Frollo's famous phrase, "this will kill that," since he has a fondness for cutting up photographs, vandalizing works of art, and jamming TV programs, not to mention killing people! Like Frollo, Batman sublimates his sexual urges into nightly chores; he is a sort of repressed freak, "borderline, pathological, obsessive," in the words of Frank Miller, whose revival of the comic book character as *Dark Knight* in 1985 influenced Burton.[1] Whenever Vicki Vail sexily and generously offers herself to him, Batman invariably replies: "I have work to do." Of course, it does not do Vicki any good, as it did not do Esmeralda either, when all that pent-up sexual energy she craves for and chases after throughout the movie is transferred to the grotesque person of the Joker, Batman's alter ego. But, as my students coolly remarked, "She got what she deserved. She was too eager."

The central female figures, Esmeralda and Vicki Vail, are both virginal and victimizable, a feature stressed in the movie by Vicki's white bridal outfits in key scenes such as the one I have just described. Both texts have an outside observer/spectator type figure, whether poet-philosopher Pierre Gringoire, Esmeralda's juggling partner and ineffectual husband, or a newspaperman, like Alexander Knox, Vicki's professional partner. The plot revolves around the conflict between legitimate and illegitimate authority, insurgency and political terrorism (king vs. people in *Notre-Dame de Paris*, the mayor of Gotham City vs. Mafia-type criminals plotting to take over the city); there are popular street carnival and crowd scenes in both. The centers of action are contained within a small city perimeter, defined by the cathedral of Notre Dame, Place de Grève, and the Palais de Justice in the novel, and the Gotham City Town Hall, Gotham City Cathedral, and the mean streets in between described by *Batman* comic books' editor Dennis O'Neil as "Manhattan below 14th St. at 3:00 a.m. November 28 on a cold year."[2] The streets, with their steaming manholes, the dark and dangerous figures lurking in the shadows, look, in the words of the publicity blurb for the movie, "as if Hell has erupted through the sidewalk," and they are strongly reminiscent of the streets of Paris through which on a cold and wet January night Gringoire gropes his way into the Court of Miracles. Moreover, both *Notre-Dame* and *Batman* rely heavily on repeated (literary or visual) "descriptions" of a grotesque, Gothic urban landscape (heavily stylized, and hybridized with art deco and futuristic architecture in *Batman*). Last but not least, the trope of *spectacle*,—whether it's Gringoire's stodgy play, the contest of grimaces, the popular street carnival whose centerpiece is Esmeralda's dance in the novel, or Gotham City's anniversary parade complete with balloons and floats, or the TV news and ads in which the broadcasters and actors suffer and die from a face-distorting disease—is essential to the articulation of the two works.

But, beyond scenes, plot, and characters, the film and the novel also relate intertextually in their meditation on the history of urban civilization, cultural revolutions (the printing press vs. TV), and on human sexuality and violence. Hugo's somber novel is about the death of one (oppressive) civilization (signified by the cathedral and its malevolent priest), and the birth of another civilization, more progressive and more democratic, heralded by the invention of the printing press. Burton's *Batman*, however, is a film about the end of all culture and civilization, especially one that is liberal and democratic—an apocalyptic nightmare to Hugo's dream of a future republic. As one commentator put it, "Batman only works if the world really sucks."[3] Burton's movie portrays a violent and chaotic world taken over by crime, money, corruption, and surveyed by the omnipresent and impersonal eye of the TV camera. The film has Hugo's signature all over it, but it heavily stresses the pessimistic, doom and gloom aspect of Hugo's novel summed up in the word *anankè*, without the novel's open-endedness towards a future of freedom in which the "birds" of free thought will scatter over the face of the earth. The movie takes a cynical, dystopian view of the future in which no responsible social action is possible: the future is *us*, and in each one of us there is a "batman," i.e., a lonely, scared, violent and paranoid child who dreams up dark fantasies of revenge. Thus a vastly popular pop culture product projects a vision of the ruination of civilization and proposes as "solution" what amounts to a strongman, fascist response to the future of civilization: one kind of mutant battling another (Batman versus the Joker).

This particularly bleak reading of Hugo's novel in Burton's movie is reinforced by another mediating intertext, cited in the movie's final scene, the lonely, chimera-like gargoyle contemplating the city of Paris from the towers of Notre-Dame, a reproduction of Violet-le-Duc's modern gargoyle constructed during the restoration of Notre-Dame which began in 1844. This gargoyle was most famously reproduced in Charles Meryon's 1853 etching, originally called *La Vigie* (The Lookout), then *Le Singe de Notre-Dame*, and finally *Le Stryge*. "Le stryge" is usually translated as "vampire" but it derives from the Latin *striga*, which means "predatory night-bird" (and once we've said "predatory night-bird," the "bat" cannot be far behind). The inscription that goes with Meryon's picture, "Insatiable vampire

Fig. 19 ***Le Stryge*****, Charles Meryon, by permission of Yale University Art Gallery, the gift of "A Lover of Prints, in grateful recognition of the Founder of the Etching Collection."**

l'éternelle Luxure / Sur la Grande Cité convoite sa pâture" ("Eternal Luxury, [that] insatiable vampire covets its prey over the great city") spells out the subject of his etching which is also the subject of the movie: the gargoyle is a personification of the city's corruption, sizing the city up as if it were a prey to feast on.

This grotesque figure activates in the audience's cultural memory the connection with *Notre-Dame de Paris*, the novel best known for the mysterious, chimeric hunchback who, like a gargoyle come to life, haunts the summits of Notre Dame and strikes terror into the hearts of the public at large. But the gargoyle also plays a central part in the movie's visual rhetoric. It is, as I have noted above, the common link between the two protagonists, the Batman and the Joker, who in the final scene take turns identifying with it. More important still is the gargoyle's function as watcher or overseer of a dark, dystopian cityscape. In it culminates the trope of spectator/spectacle developed throughout the movie: reality is represented as pictures, the past as treasured pictures in a museum called the Fluggelheim, the present, sometimes as photographs in newspapers and magazines, but mostly in TV shots, which Batman and the Joker obsessively watch and manipulate—besides fighting, watching TV is their main activity in the movie. The former arranges the pictures into coherent narratives about dangerous plots (his hidden TV cameras constantly record the happenings in the world outside his cave, and from this cache of electronic documentation, Batman selects and retrieves the information he needs to fill in the gaps of some plot or other), the latter distorts and destroys any semblance of coherence, continuity, and established reality. Thus the watchers watch a world that is not only corrupt but also corruptible, being only a projected, artificial image of itself. It is not surprising then that the last image of the movie is that of Batman's erect, dark figure on top of one of the city's skyscrapers, watchful and as still as if he were made of stone, the newest, postmodern version of the gargoyle, both witness to the corrupt world below and its dark avenger.

In his book *The Mysteries of Paris and London*, Richard Maxwell discusses the close relationship between Meryon's *eau-forte* and Hugo's novel, focusing especially on the former's "status as a kind of historical discourse" analogous to Hugo's famous disquisition chapter, "Ceci tuera cela."[4] Maxwell points out that the optimistic thrust of Hugo's vision of the future, "le nouveau monde qui sortira de ce chaos verra en s'éveillant planer au-dessus de lui, ailée et vivante, la pensée du monde englouti" ("the new world that will come out of this chaos will see as it awakens the thought of the submerged world soaring above it, winged and alive")[5] is transformed in Meryon's picture into a gloomy prediction:

> . . . the gargoyle is the witnessing "new world," but what he witnesses, above all, is an act of surveillance directed against himself. . . . He [i.e., Meryon] elides the Utopian implication that—after the unspoken deluge—an enlightened survivor will realize that nothing has perished, that nothing could possibly perish. The gargoyle is neither enlightened nor elated: he awakes to a staring madness, persecuted rather than saved by the world that surrounds him. This is a bird's-eye view that would turn the most prehensile monster to stone, freeze him in his place with fear.[6]

The movie's last image of Batman-turned-gargoyle achieves precisely that: it turns the monster to stone on his watchtower, it "freezes" him in place with horror. It replaces Meryon's chimera with a postmodern demon-figure but it preserves its sinister connotations, and together they "kill" Hugo's gargoyle. In this new gargoyle, we read the movie's prediction of a dismal future. For, though it may not be immediately apparent to everyone, to be in the hands of a humorless, obsessive, and violent control freak such as Batman is almost as bad as to be the victim of the Joker's black humor. Batman is the personification of what for Michel Foucault in *Discipline and Punish* is the new model for modern power, the totalizing system of knowledge called "panopticism," a term borrowed from Jeremy Bentham's Utopian prison, the Panopticon (. . .) . Batman's dark, soldierly figure keeping night duty on the city's towers calls forth the image of the prison guard in his watchtower as much as he invokes images of sentinels on the walls of a fortress.

One example given by Foucault to illustrate his concept of the Panopticon is the city struck by plague, an "enclosed, segmented space, observed at every point, in which . . . the slightest movements are supervised, in which all the events are recorded . . . all this constitutes a compact model of the disciplinary mechanism . . . of an omnipresent and omniscient power."[7] Orwellian in its vision, Foucault's example accurately describes the situation Gotham City is in, eaten up by crime as if by the plague, and monitored by Batman's conspicuous cameras. But Foucault, as Maxwell points out, "functions within a well-established tradition of French culture," and suffers, like Meryon, from postrevolutionary depression.[8] It is therefore not surprising that he "is attracted to the same motifs as Meryon:" "the malign 'lookout' whose existence as a horror apart seems certain but who then is revealed as one of us; the panoramic observers—birds or books, documents with wings—who scatter this way and that, apparently far more mobile than a human spy could ever be; the difficulty of locating power in any one place."[9] In a similar vein, one could speculate that what attracted Burton to Meryon's figure was its potential to function as an icon of horror, and that the vesperal, *noir Batman*[10] with its gloomy view of reality may very well be a symptom of post-Thatcherite/post-Reaganite depression.

It should be clear from what I've said so far that popular culture texts such as Burton's *Batman* reward those in the audience who possess a high degree of cultural sophistication. They are bristling with cultural allusions, references, symbols begging to be interpreted. Thus the audience who must learn how to read them engages in a hermeneutic enterprise not unlike Claude Frollo's efforts to decipher the hieroglyphic inscriptions on the walls of Notre Dame. Directors and audiences alike become semioticians.

Hugo's novel is the intertext that generates all the other Gothic citations that run through the movie and culminate in the final scene's setting of the cathedral with its winged gargoyles. The cathedral itself is a mix, as Jim Collins points out in an article on narrative structure in *Batman*, between Notre Dame of Paris and Gaudi's *Sagrada Familia* in Barcelona.[11] Gotham City is a mix of medieval and futuristic architecture that also invokes Fritz Lang's *Metropolis*;[12] medieval-looking Wayne Mansion has an impressive collection of medieval armor; a chemical plant looks like a medieval fortress; and the hero-villain pair, like Quasimodo and Claude Frollo, have a doppelganger relationship.

But besides Hugo's *Notre-Dame*, the scene from *Batman* alludes to other texts such as *Dracula*, for example, in the representation of Batman as a "dark knight," a mysterious vampire bat. This darkly romantic or Gothic view of the character bypasses the lighter, sunnier *Batman* of the fifties' comics and the campy *Batman* of the sixties television series to return to the original comic book character created in 1939 by artist Bob Kane and writer Bill Finger. The original Batman was itself an intertextual cross between Douglas Fairbanks's Zorro and Rolland West's 1930 detective-horror movie *The Bat Whispers*, while the original Joker was inspired by a still shot of Conrad Veidt in the 1928 movie adaptation of Hugo's novel *L'Homme qui rit*.[13] But as Collins notes, besides these infinitely spiraling allusions to other *Batman* texts and the Gothic tradition, there are also allusions "not so explicitly associated with the Gothic."[14] Burton's movie also "steals" specific shots from Hollywood films: from *Vertigo,* the high-angle shots of flights of stairs in the tower, the woman going upstairs to meet with danger, the hero following to save her, from North by Northwest, the hero and the heroine hanging side by side off the wall of the Mount Rushmore monument, and from *Blade Runner,* the final confrontation.[15] In a lighter, parodic vein, the movie also makes a passing reference to *My Fair Lady* when the Joker tells Vicki that he has "to take her to the church on time."

For Collins, "the narrative structure of *Batman* is founded on a hybrid repertoire, calling up and/or abducting motifs from cinematic and non-cinematic texts alike—comic books, Hollywood films, nineteenth-century novels, medieval architecture."[16] Such a mixture of genres, forms of discourse and different media points to this movie's "hyperconsciousness," i.e., its "awareness of [. . .] antecedents and [. . .] rivals in the marketplace," which, according to Collins, is a "distinguishing feature of recent popular narrative," known as "meta-pop."[17] The movie's conflicting technique of simultaneously "calling up" and destroying cultural references is reflected in the dramatic tension between the Joker's habit of erasing or "cutting up" the past—in one scene he is shown cutting up photographs, surrounded by scattered bits and pieces of pictures—and Batman's compulsive retrieving and reconstituting of the past—in his Batcave, he is shown watching images recorded by his secret TV cameras in order to figure out criminal plots.[18]

This technique of erasure and reinscription which results in a hybrid narrative structure is also the main feature of Hugo's *Notre-Dame de Paris*, a book built on the effaced trace, "le fragile souvenir" ("the fragile memory")[19] of a Greek inscription (*anankć*) already erased from the wall of Notre Dame. By pointing to an effaced inscription as the origin of *Notre-Dame*, Hugo implies that the novel has two authors: the (dead) writer of the original inscription on which "on a fait ce livre" ("this book was written") and himself, "l'auteur de ce livre" ("the author of this book") in whose work the only trace of the original writing lives only as a "fragile souvenir." He thus gives *Notre-Dame* a paradoxical origin in another's writing, thereby doing away with traditional notions of originality. Hugo makes hybridization the main structural and compositional principle of the novel summed up in the ambiguity of the famous phrase "ceci tuera cela." ("this will kill that"). The dialectic between the two terms, "ceci" and "cela," as put into play by the future form of the verb *tuer*, "tuera," suggests an indefinitely postponed but nonetheless mortal struggle for supremacy between two structuring meanings, be they *ananké* and freedom, theocracy and democracy, architecture and the printing press, Romanesque and Gothic, epic and drama, Homer and Walter Scott, past and present, Frollo and Hugo. For Hugo, modern, new writing is hybrid writing and he illustrates it in spectacular fashion with his own hybrid novel. The relation of mutual interdependence and self-mirroring which exists between Hugo's novel and his theory of hybrid writing, made explicit in two architectural metaphors, the cathedral of Notre Dame and the tower of Babel, emphasizes how central the idea of a hybrid poetic work was to Hugo's æsthetics at the time he was writing *Notre-Dame*.

The "hyperconsciousness" exhibited by meta-pop texts such as *Batman* about their status as hybrid cultural products, "mobile signifiers, subject to further rearticulation as they circulate throughout disparate cultures, or more accurately, different micro-cultures,"[20] strongly resembles Hugo's self-conscious æsthetics of hybridity as they are set forth in *Notre-Dame de Paris*. Thus one could say that *Batman* adopts and adapts not only Hugo's scenes, characters, and themes, but also, more important, and in a more fundamental way, his theory of art. Hugo's novel and his literary Tower of Babel are constructed, hybrid texts in which earlier literary works and traditions coexist and interact, where, as he put it about the Tower of Babel, "chaque œuvre individuelle, si capricieuse et si isolée qu'elle semble, a sa place et sa saillie . . . Depuis la cathédrale de Shakespeare jusqu'à la mosquée de Byron, mille clochetons s'encombrent pêle-mêle sur cette métropole de la pensée universelle. . . . Le genre humain tout entier est sur l'échafaudage" ("every individual work, as capricious and isolated as it might seem, has its place and its niche. . . . From Shakespeare's cathedral to Byron's mosque, a thousand bell-turrets crowd pell-mell into this metropolis of universal thought. . . . The entire human race is on the scaffolding").[21] Like Hugo's Tower of Babel, meta-pop texts such as *Batman* are endowed with cultural memory, they are aware that "popular culture has a *history*: earlier texts do not simply disappear or become kitsch, but persist in their original forms as well as diverse reactivations that continue to be a source of fascination for audiences, providing pleasure in the present and forming a fundamental part of cultural memory."[22] Hugo's novel is a central element in this cultural memory, an observation which reconfirms John Ruskin's cranky, Joker-like insight about *Notre-Dame*—though not his negative evaluation: Ruskin is referring to the realistic novel of urban mysteries, but we could extend his term to popular culture often dismissed as mindless, when he identifies *Notre-Dame de Paris* as "the head of the whole cretinous school . . . the renowned novel in which the hunchbacked lover watches the execution of his mistress from the tower of Notre-Dame."[23]

Notes

1. Christopher Sharrett, "Batman and the Twilight of the Idols: An Interview with Frank Miller," in *The Many Lives of Batman: Critical Approaches to a Superhero and His Media,* ed. Roberta E. Pearson and William Uricchio (New York: Routledge, 1991), 38.
2. Bill Boichel, "Batman: Commodity as Myth," in *The Many Lives of Batman,* 9.
3. William Urichhio and Roberta E. Pearson, "I'm Not Fooled by That Cheap Disguise," in *The Many Lives of Batman,* 202.
4. Richard Maxwell, *The Mysteries of Paris and London* (Charlottesville, VA and London: University of Virginia Press, 1992), 232.
5. Victor Hugo, *Notre-Dame de Paris* (Paris: Garnier-Flammarion, 1967), 206.
6. Maxwell, *Mysteries,* 233.
7. Michel Foucault, *Discipline and Punish: The Birth of the Prison* translated by Alan Sheridan (New York: Vintage Books, 1979), 197.
8. Maxwell, *Mysteries,* 237.
9. Ibid., 237.
10. James Bollella, "The Aberrations of Good and Evil: A Vesperal Perspective on Societal Decay in Tim Burton's *Batman,*" in *Film and Society: Proceedings of the Eighth Annual Kent State University International Film Conference,* 1990, 134.
11. Jim Collins, "Batman: The Movie, Narrative: The Hyperconscious," in *The Many Lives of Batman,* 164–81.
12. Bob Kane, *Batman and Me: an Autobiography* (Forrestville, CA: Eclipse Books, 1989), 148.
13. Ibid., 38.
14. Collins, "Aberrations," 169.
15. Ibid., 169.
16. Ibid., 169.
17. Ibid., 165, 170.
18. Ibid., 168.

19. Hugo, *Notre-Dame,* 30.
20. Collins, "Aberrations," 167.
21. Hugo, *Notre-Dame,* 210–11.
22. Collins, "Aberrations," 171.
23. John Ruskin, *The Works of John Ruskin,* ed. T. Cook and Alexander Wedderburn (London: George Allen, 1908), 35.277.

Part III
Balzac's Centers and Peripheries

Balzac's Bretons: Racism and National Identity in *Les Chouans*

MARIE-PIERRE LE HIR

AT THE ORIGIN OF THIS ESSAY IS THE INTRIGUING OBSERVATION that the process of national unification that occurred in post-revolutionary France did not only produce, as expected and often noted, cultural homogeneity but also cultural difference. The basis of this observation is the comparative analysis of early postrevolutionary representations of Brittany in nineteenth-century French drama with later ones. In plays performed on Parisian stages during the Empire and the Restoration, the issue of Breton identity is never at stake because the criteria used to define that identity are superficial at best: some characters are identifiable as Bretons but usually only because their geographic place of origin is mentioned. No linguistic or cultural traits are offered to justify this categorization and therefore to provide a sufficient basis for classifying them as a group different from other provincials.[1]

By midcentury, by contrast, the codification of cultural markers (language, dress, manners, etc.) is such that any confusion between Bretons, Auvergnats, or Savoyards is no longer possible. Moreover, claiming such identities has by then also become the norm for authors as well as for characters.[2] Chateaubriand's treatment of Brittany over the course of his literary career encapsulates this fascinating development. In *René* (1802), Brittany is evoked as "*une province reculée*" ["a faraway province"] but not even mentioned by name whereas in *Mémoires d'Outre-Tombe* (1848–50) the author not only claims his Breton identity, but he also describes Brittany (Combourg, Saint-Malo, etc.) in uniquely vivid terms.[3]

Published in 1829, Balzac's *Les Chouans* represents a foundational text in the history of literary representations of Brittany insofar as it marks the crucial, intermediary stage between these two moments, the turning point after which Breton identity is no longer simply posited in literary texts, but rather defined in rich, original terms—in stark contrast with the earlier period. As interesting as these representations of Bretons and Brittany are, however, my main concern is to understand the process that led to their emergence. For instance, there are good reasons to expand the examination of national identity in *Les Chouans* beyond the Breton question not only because the novel has long been hailed as the first literary work about the French Revolution, but also because identities are always constructed in relation to other identities. In this case, my working hypothesis will be that the Breton material Balzac created in *Les Chouans* served to address the question of French national identity obliquely: appearances to the contrary, what is at stake in the novel is not only how to define Breton identity, but also how to define French national identity.

With its center of interest on the counterrevolution, *Les Chouans* represents an attempt on Balzac's part to come to terms with the French Revolution—if only because it is difficult to imagine how the novelist could possibly describe the Chouans' ferocious resistance to the new political order without wondering out loud about the origin of the conflict. Historically, the Chouans refused to recognize the legitimacy of the First Republic and fought the revolutionary armies because their goal was to preserve the old identity of the nation, an identity based on the alliance of God and the king, of Catholicism and monarchy. At the core of the novel, then, is the opposition between two "ideas" of France, two different conceptions of French national identity.

As has often been noted, the narrator in *Les Chouans*—and the author in the preface—seems to position himself on the side of modernity, to advocate values associated with the new political regime: in the struggle between past and present, the victory of the Republican army led by Hulot over "le dernier des Chouans" seems to symbolize the ineluctable march of progress, the triumph of the forces of civilization against "féodalité" ["feudalism"] and "superstition" which the Chouans embody.[4] What needs to be emphasized, however, is that the novel does not really follow this logical *political* plot: it does not present the struggle between Chouans and revolutionaries as a civil war,[5] as a conflict between two *French* political enemies fighting to impose their own conception of French identity, but rather between two distinct peoples, two distinct races.

Balzac's Bretons: Myths and Stereotypes

Balzac's reluctance to handle the Western insurgency in political terms is apparent from the start. In the opening pages, the detailed physical description of the Breton conscripts being led away from home by the *bleus*, the revolutionary army—most of them against their will—serves to introduce two important notions. First, that Bretons are no more interested in defending the French nation than they are in political change: supporters of the status quo, they are fundamentally indifferent to politics. Second, that *based on the way they look*, they belong to a culture that is profoundly different from French culture.[6] This initial positing of cultural difference has a direct impact on the further development of the novel: it leads to an overemphasis of cultural concerns at the expense of political ones. As a result, the novel shifts from the expected political questions—e.g., how can the Chouans' preference for the old Regime be explained?—to cultural ones: why do Bretons reject a French identity—"nos lois, nos mœurs, notre habillement, nos monnaies nouvelles, notre langage" ["our laws, our customs, our dress, our new coins, our language"][7]—that is in every respect superior to the one to which they clinging? What prevents Bretons from understanding the obvious, namely how much they would benefit from adopting our new ways? Why do they so stubbornly refuse to let go of their outdated traditions and values? The answers to these questions are also developed in the first chapter of the novel and reflected upon in the preface: the Chouans are Bretons, not French, they belong to a different race, to a more primitive race.

This argument is first presented in the passage that begins with the etymology lesson on the word "*gars*" (38), a lesson meant to recall the common Celtic origin of the two races: "La Bretagne est, de toute la France, le pays où les mœurs gauloises ont laissé les plus fortes empreintes, [. . . une] province, où de nos jours encore, la vie sauvage et l'esprit superstitieux de nos rudes aïeux sont restés flagrants" ["Brittany is the part of France where the customs of the Gauls have left the strongest imprint, [. . . a] province where, even to our days, the savage life and superstitious mind of our primitive ancestors have remained flagrant"] (39). Clearly, the function of this reminder is not to emphasize similarities, but on the contrary to better mark the distance that separates the French from the Bretons: originally part of the same "species" ("*nos* rudes aïeux"—"*our* primitive ancestors"), the French have evolved into something newer and better, the Bretons have not. A comparison with another novel on Brittany Balzac wrote several years later confirms this interpretation since in *Béatrix* the notion of a common origin for the Bretons and the French is altogether abandoned. Describing the family of Baron du Guénic, the Breton archetype that reappears in *Béatrix* after *Les Chouans*, he writes: "Vieux comme le granit de la Bretagne, les Guaisnic ne sont ni Francs, ni Gaulois, ils sont Bretons, ou pour être plus exact, Celtes," (49) ["As old as the granite of their country, the Guaisnics are neither Franks nor Gauls, they are Bretons, or more precisely Celts"]. But in *Les Chouans* already, this "time-gap theory" receives reality status in three ironclad verdicts that seem to push Brittany further out of time with the repetition of each "là": "Là, les coutumes féodales sont encore respectées. Là, les antiquaires retrouvent debout les monuments des druides. Là, le génie de la civilisation moderne s'effraie de pénétrer à travers d'immenses forêts primordiales" (39). ["There the feudal customs are still respected. There the antiquarian finds the druids' monuments still standing. There, the genius of modern civilization stands aghast at the thought of penetrating immense primeval forests."] Like Hegel's Africa, Balzac's Brittany is thereby confined out of history.

Balzac's main argument to anchor his "time-gap theory" is the thesis of Breton eternal resistance to change. Resistance to change is presented as the organizing principle of Breton life and culture in areas ranging from politics (acceptance of the status-quo), to psychology—Balzac mentions "l'entêtement du caractère breton" ["the obstinacy of Breton temper"] in his preface (504)—and, as we will see, religion. In the dichotomy that serves to construct French and Breton identities in opposition to each other, with immobility on the Breton side and progress on the French side, the notion of resistance to change is given a powerful expression in the granite image noted earlier. Its most forceful illustration is Baron du Guénic's petrifaction in *Béatrix*—"En lui, le granit s'était fait homme" ["In him, granite had turned to man"] (58). But the image of the "druids' monuments" already fulfills the same function in *Les Chouans* since it cannot fail to bring to mind "menhir"—"long stones" in Breton, or monumental, elongated blocs of granite—and "dolmen"—"flat stones" in Breton, or altar-shaped configurations of the same granite. Elegantly but unambiguously, the evocation of Brittany's mysterious, prehistoric roots conveys the notion that the presence of the Breton people in the modern world is just as incongruous as that of the megaliths they are compared to.

Having established the primitivism of the Breton race through archaeological and geological images, Balzac then turns to a more powerful register to define this primitivism, zoology. Comparing Bretons to American Indians, he begins by pointing out that it is one thing to find a primitive race in Canada, and quite another to find it in the middle of Europe. And yet, in spite of its privileged position in Europe, Brittany has failed to evolve: "[e]ntouré de lumières dont la bienfaisante chaleur ne l'atteint pas, ce pays ressemble à un charbon glacé qui resterait obscur et noir au sein d'un brillant foyer" (39–40) ["surrounded by lights whose beneficent warmth never reaches it, the province is like a frozen coal that would remain hidden and black in the midst of a glowing hearth"]. This "fact" is then offered as a testimony to the crucial role of race in human history. The argument, clearly articulated in *Béatrix*, that "le caractère d'immuabilité que la nature a donné à ses espèces zoologiques se retrouve là [en Bretagne] chez les hommes" ["The character of immutability that nature has given its zoological species is found there among human beings"] (46) is given expression in *Les Chouans* through the repeated animal images used to characterize Bretons, goats in particular, but also dogs, and wild animals in general, "de semblables bêtes" ["such animals."] More specifically, Bretons are said to lack what distinguishes animals from human beings, intelligence: they are "plus pauvres de combinaisons intellectuelles que ne le sont les Mohicans et les Peaux rouges de l'Amérique septentrionale" ["poorer in intellectual means than are the Mohicans and Redskins of North America"] (39). Conversely, they share with them an animality difficult to reconcile with the most basic human values: "dureté" ["harshness, cruelty"], "entêtement brutal" ["brutal obstinacy"], "incroyable férocité," ["incredible ferociousness"].

The primitive intelligence[8] of the Bretons makes it easier to understand why they are so easily manipulated by their unscrupulous leaders, aristocrats,[9] and priests who have their own material interests at heart rather than the political and religious principles they claim to defend. Abbé Gudin's criminal abuse of power[10] consists in appealing to and thereby reinforcing the Bretons' natural instincts rather than in instilling in them the sense of human dignity nature has denied them. Instead of denouncing the horrors of "cannibalism,"[11] instead of educating

Bretons to respect the sanctity of life, of helping them become true human beings, Gudin takes advantage of these primitive qualities—when he promises indulgences in exchange for the murder of Republican soldiers, for instance. The horror of the crimes committed by Bretons on fellow human beings (Pille-Miche's attempted rape and murder of Marie de Verneuil, and her subsequent sale to Marche-à-Terre; the roasting M. d'Orgemont's feet, the beheading of Galope-Chopine with an axe and the posting of his head by his door) is only matched by the total lack of remorse that follows such crimes.[12] The fact that Bretons are presented as "victims," that their lack of "physical or moral progress" is attributed to leaders who betrayed the civilizing mission they had been entrusted with, only confirms the nature of the mission itself: to contribute to the evolution of a primitive race. Race, in short, impacts on Breton behavior in two ways according to Balzac: it limits these people's intelligence and it deprives them of moral sense. Hence the double wish formulated in the preface "pour l'amélioration physique et morale de la Bretagne!" ["for the physical and moral betterment of Brittany"] (504). If the thesis of Breton racial inferiority is particularly powerful in *Les Chouans* because of the strategic place of articulation it occupies at the beginning of the novel, a related contention ends up playing a more crucial role not only in Balzac's "demonstration" of Breton racial inferiority but also in the global thematic economy of the novel: that Bretons do not have enough intelligence to understand religion, that the religion they practice is not really Catholicism.

Catholicism: The Hidden Stake in Balzac's Conception of National Identity

Balzac's treatment of Catholicism in *Les Chouans* is ambiguous at best. On the one hand, religion is viewed as the obligatory road to moral progress—the road Bretons would take if their religious leaders did not betray their mission. But on the other hand, a doubt is constantly cast on the Bretons' ability to be good Catholics: in Brittany, Balzac claims in the preface, "la superstition *remplace* la morale du Christ" ["superstition replaces the morals of Christ"] (my underlining, 5). Apparently forgetting that *Le Génie du Christianisme* (1802) was written by a Breton, Balzac returns to this notion time after time throughout the novel, mobilizing a variety of images to illustrate the distinction he seeks to establish between real religion and Breton religion.

The image of the "monuments of the druids" for instance draws from the two central dichotomies that structure the opposition between French and Breton: immobility instead of progress, since, as we already saw, it implies that like these monuments, the Breton race has been frozen in time; but also "superstition" instead of real faith, insofar as the word "druids" functions as a reminder of the Bretons' non-Christian origins. In his comments on the Guénic family in *Béatrix*, the narrator elaborates on this point, emphasizing the common primitive qualities of Breton race and religion: "Ils ont dû être druides, avoir cueilli le gui des forêts sacrées et sacrifié des hommes sur des dolmens" ["They must have been druids, they must have gathered mistletoe in sacred forests and sacrificed human beings on dolmen"] (49). The notion that the past still informs the present, that these ancient religious practices still influence the Bretons' relation to religion, is thereby instilled. It further serves to explain their fatal attraction to the letter, rather than the spirit of Catholicism: they are drawn to the irrational; they confuse religion and superstition.

A first case is made against young Breton women who lure Republican soldiers to their death but fail to feel any remorse whatsoever because there is no relation for them between religious worship and ethical behavior: "[. . .] elles allaient en pélerinage avec leurs pères et leurs frères demander des ruses et des absolutions à des vierges de bois vermoulu. La religion, ou plutôt le fétichisme de ces créatures ignorantes désarmait le meurtre de ses remords" ["they went on pilgrimages with their fathers and brothers to ask Virgins of rotten wood to teach them new wiles and to give them absolution. In the religion, or rather the fetishism of these ignorant creatures murder and remorse were dissociated"] (42). While the terms "creatures" and "ignorant" function as reminders of the primitivism of the race, the word "fetishism" and the plural in "virgins" posit the survival, within contemporary religious practices, of ancient polytheist rituals. The misappropriation of the Catholic pilgrimage by these primitive creatures highlights the fundamental incompatibility between "our religion" and "their fetishism": true religion never condones murder, and yet these young Breton women use theirs to plan it. Murder itself cannot fail to provoke remorse in a truly religious person, and yet remorse is foreign to them. Breton religion, in short, might look Catholic but it is not.

In *Les Chouans*, in fact, the most obvious proofs of Breton Catholicism are systematically reinterpreted as deviations from it. In the gesture of a Chouan who is about to die and grabs his rosary to say a last prayer, for instance, Balzac sees "un fanatisme obscur" ["a baffling fanaticism"] (70). The devotion granted to local saints such as Sainte-Anne d'Auray or Saint Labre is constantly ridiculed as a superstition (89, 113). The practice of burning a candle in exchange for a saint's fulfillment of a wish is also dismissed as a narrow-minded accounting that misses the point.[13] The custom of dancing as soon as mass is over is offered as evidence of the superficial character of Breton faith, of its lack of spirituality.[14] Moreover, the fear of ghosts, the confusion of idolatry and pious veneration are presented as evidence of Catholicism's contamination by primitive, pagan beliefs.[15] At mass in the forest, when the priest's "véhémence du débit [est] le plus puissant des arguments pour persuader ses sauvages auditeurs" ["the priest's forceful delivery is the most powerful argument to convince his half-savage listeners"] (329), Bretons remain untouched by the beauty of the rite itself, but they are deeply moved by the "miracles" mentioned by Abbé Gudin in his preach, the resurrection of Marie Lambrequin, the apparition of Sainte-Anne d'Auray, and the miraculous healing of Marche-à-Terre's mother. They believe that their priests have supernatural powers, that guns blessed by them will not miss their target, and that every enemy killed will bring them closer to heaven's door. Even in an "évoluée"[16] like Francine, who has spent seven years in Paris and forgotten most of her native language, *bas-Breton*, the race betrays itself, "superstition" prevails over religion (332).

Balzac's systematic effort to dissociate true Catholicism from superstition is remarkably clever. Since all the points mentioned above are actually part of the Catholic ritual, Catholicism itself should be criticized as superstition, but the focus on the allegedly erroneous practices of a particular ethnic group preempts such a critique. The fact that Balzac does not hesitate to scapegoat the Bretons just to prevent a direct critique of Catholicism should suffice to indicate how much is at stake here. Conversely, once the notion sets in that the racial characterization of the Bretons actually plays an ancillary role in the novel, it becomes easier to resist a reading so masterfully imposed by a compelling imagery[17] and to wonder what is at stake here. Why does Balzac, against all historical evidence to the contrary, refuse to admit Brittany into Christianity? Why is it so important for him to distinguish between Catholicism and Breton pseudo-Catholicism? Drawing from Pierre Birnbaum's insights in *"La France aux Francais!" Histoire des haines nationalistes,* I would like to suggest that these discursive moves represent an attempt, on Balzac's part, to reconcile two conceptions of French identity that are usually seen as antagonistic.

Birnbaum convincingly argues that the political stake of the "guerre des deux France" ["war of the two Frances"] that lasted from the French Revolution to the Third Republic, and of which the Chouan's insurgency was the first and probably most bloody episode, was to determine which definition of French national identity would prevail: "[I]l s'agit très largement de savoir si la France fonde toujours son identité propre sur le catholicisme ou si elle s'engage dans la construction d'un ordre politique tourné vers un autre universalisme, celui de la Raison, au regard duquel tous les citoyens abandonnent dorénavant leurs valeurs, du moment qu'ils entrent dans l'espace public" ["It is primarily a matter of knowing whether France still grounds its own identity in Catholicism or whether it has committed itself to the construction of a political order based on a different universalism, the universalism of Reason which requires all citizens from now on to abandon their values whenever they enter public space"] (10). During the radical phase of the Revolution, this question had received a clear answer: the new universalism of the Republic demanded the abolition of the Old Regime, the disappearance of both "feudalism" and "superstition." The struggle against "superstition" was therefore a struggle against the *Catholic* identity of France.

From that vantage point, the function of the racial Other in *Les Chouans* becomes clearer: the recourse to race makes it possible to free the term "superstition" from its original meaning, Catholicism; in other words, to reconcile a liberal rhetoric of denunciation of "feudalism" and "superstition" with a more conservative agenda. On the one hand, denying Bretons the status of real historical players, refusing to present them as conscious advocates of the old universalism enables Balzac to blur the political stakes of the struggle between Chouans and Republicans and to bypass the question Birnbaum identifies as central. On the other hand, Balzac's theory of race makes it possible to work through the question of French identity without having to raise it explicitly: to show what Bretons lack, namely Reason and

Faith, is just another way of defining French national identity Balzac's way, that is as a reconciliation of "le progrès des lumières" [Enlightenment] and of "la charité catholique."[18]

French National Identity in *Les Chouans*

Commenting on the revisions made by Balzac from one edition of the novel to the next, Roger Pierrot concludes: "*Le Dernier Chouan* a été écrit par un libéral favorable aux bleus, il est corrigé par un défenseur du trône et de l'autel" ["*The Last Chouan* was written by a liberal who supported the revolutionaries, it is revised by an advocate of the throne and the altar"].[19] As my examination of the hidden importance of Catholicism in *Les Chouans* suggests, however, the contrast between these two political positions might not be as clear-cut as it first appears. The question that needs to be examined, then, is whether such a defense of the old identity of France, of "throne and altar," of "feudalism and superstition," can already be found in *Les Chouans*.

That Balzac conceived of French identity as the reconciliation of Reason and Faith is already suggested by his comments on the duc d'Aiguillon in the 1829 preface to the first edition of the novel (504–7). The passage, in which Balzac recalls how this governor of Brittany attempted to modernize the province in 1761 but failed because of the "local patriotism" of the Breton nobility, shows that for the novelist, the idea of progress was not necessarily coupled to that of political Revolution: "progrès des lumières" ["enlightened progress"] and Catholic monarchy were not, or at least did not have to become, mutually exclusive terms.[20]

If this reconciliation seems possible, however, it is because Balzac singularly limits the concept of "progrès des lumières." As presented in *Les Chouans*, Enlightenment is viewed positively only as long as it relates to the material side of life, to progress in agriculture, communications, commerce, etc. As a system of values and beliefs, by contrast, it is labeled "philosophie moqueuse" ["scoffing philosophy"] and presented as a destructive social force. Count de Verneuil, Marie's father, has lost his heart and his soul to it: "l'esprit avait desséché tous les cœurs" ["wit had withered all hearts"] (365). From Balzac's perspective, then, the notion that the universalism of reason could replace the universal principles of Christianity would simply seem preposterous: the two do not appear to be commensurate systems of values. Such is indeed the position Balzac defended later in life when his political conservatism took the form of an embrace of the legitimist monarchy and of a more pronounced Catholicism. In a famous passage in *Béatrix*, for instance, the narrator, raging against the democratic principle of "l'égalité moderne" ["modern equality"], denounces the social evils that cannot fail to appear "dès qu'une nation a très impolitiquement abattu les supériorités sociales reconnues" ["as soon as a nation has very unwisely eliminated superior beings recognized as such by society"]. "En proclamant l'égalité de tous, on a promulgué la déclaration des droits de l'Envie" ["In proclaiming equality for all, one has promulgated the declaration of the rights of Greed"], he concludes (328).

Balzac's critique of the principle of social equality deserves to be seen as an illustration of the shortcomings of the universalism of reason: the idea might sound good, but its consequences are disastrous, he implies. His fundamental distrust in man's ability to come up with great ideals and to live up to them is discernible when he argues that what was thought to be a Declaration of the Rights of Man was nothing more than a Declaration of the Rights of Greed. His analogy speaks for the necessity to have something bigger than man preserve values and ideals, namely institutions such as the Church and the monarchy. But it also exemplifies the incompatibility that exists, for him, between the two forms of universalism since, from his point of view at least, the product of man's reason (the Declaration of the Rights of Man) is nothing else but sin (greed).

In "Making the Revolution Private," Gabriel Moyal convincingly argues that the same mode of thinking is already at work in *Les Chouans*, particularly in Balzac's "idealization of the monarchy's role as symbol of unity and as preserver of abstract, spiritual values."[21] Balzac's treatment of the Bretons might provide the best shortcut illustration of his deep conviction that men are not equal, but another notion reinforces it: the idea that nobility is a grace, that it comes as the result of innate qualities, of birth, of destiny, and not of personal merit. For if all characters are judged and ranked on Balzac's social scale according to their ability to fulfill noble ideals (honor, disinterest, courage, distinction, etc.), not all of them have the same shot at greatness. From Balzac's vantage point, those who fail to recognize this crucial point are just poor imitators.

In the crucial scene at Vivetière manor where the two conflicting political identities of France oppose each other in the persons of the Republican Captain Merle and the Royalist Marquis de Montauran, Marie de Verneuil does not opt only for "un homme, un roi, des privilèges" ["a man, a king, privileges"]. She also votes against "ces troupiers français, qui savent siffler un air au milieu des balles et n'oublient pas de faire un lazzi sur le camarade qui tombe mal" ["those French privates who know how to hum a tune when the bullets are whistling and inevitably crack a bad joke when a comrade falls in a strange way"] (222), that is against a vulgar, common, democratic vision of France. What the Republicans lack, across the board, is distinction. Hulot, Merle, and Gérard are not entirely different from Montauran since they too have courage, integrity, intelligence, and faith in their mission. But they possess these qualities to a lesser degree, in a more vulgar register. Once in the presence of "supériorités sociales reconnues" ["superior beings recognized as such by society"]—whether at the Vivetière, or, for Hulot, in the presence of the Comte de Bauvan at Marie de Verneuil's dinner table—they are dwarfed.

At the top of the social ladder Alphonse de Montauran stands for a younger duke of Aiguillon, a Royalist hero who embodies the spirit of "patriotisme national"—as opposed to the "patriotisme local" of the other Breton nobles. The ideal symbiosis between monarchy and religion—"Le roi, c'est le prêtre et je me bats pour la foi" ["The priest is the king, and I'm fighting for my faith"]—Montauran sees the world according to that grid only: whether he loves or loathes Marie de Verneuil depends entirely on the authenticity of her birth. Moyal points out that Balzac's idealized depiction of Alphonse de Montauran as the noble defender of the crown and the faith is set against the background of a modern world in which materialist values dominate. The lesson to be learned when the clash between these two worldviews cannot be avoided—when Montauran asserts himself against his selfish, greedy Breton officers, for instance—is not, however, that Montauran's position is "anachronistic," that he should realize "that the monarchy has long ago forfeited the ideals which [he] wants to defend," as Moyal points out.[22] Rather, that rallying to the defense of these ideals is all the more pressing.

This is certainly what Marie de Verneuil does in the novel and it is of particular significance because she holds the symbolic key to Balzac's understanding of French national identity.[23] As her sociohistorical trajectory indicates, Marie is an allegory of

France: caught between, on the one hand, her natural tendency "pour tout ce qui était religieux et vrai" ["for all that was spiritual and true"] and, on the other hand, the "philosophie moqueuse dont s'enthousiasmait la France" ["the scoffing philosophy that thrilled France at the time"] (365), she commits the double error of marrying Danton and of fighting the Chouan war on the wrong political side. But she redeems herself through her unconditional love for Montauran; through her subsequent marriage to him; and finally through the sacrifice of her life to her noble husband, dying as Francine observes, in a state of sainthood.[24]

As unrealistic as it may seem, the moment Marie falls in love she gives up her own values, she stops being a Republican and becomes a Royalist and a fervent Catholic. Her transformation does not come as a result of a learning process, of an enlightenment, but rather, of sentiment pure and simple, of love, that is of blindness. Balzac's noble characters are not subject to the logic of education, of progress, but to that of grace. Each of Marie's steps toward "sainthood" is marked by a spiritual epiphany, her lone rebirth to faith during the first part of the mass celebrated by Abbé Gudin in nature; her exchange of vows with Montauran during a secret and dangerous wedding mass.

As his presence at this most sublime moment in the novel indicates, Baron du Guénic also deserves to be seen as one of these "supériorités sociales reconnues" since he too follows the logic of love, not the logic of reason. Like these other "superior" beings, du Guénic has a very clear sense of himself and of his place in the world—which is what Montauran actually praises when he singles him out as the only disinterested man among his officers. Ostensibly a critique of his peers' ridiculous material ambitions, du Guénic's ironic answer to Montauran—"Ma foi, marquis, ces messieurs ne me laissent que la couronne de France, mais je pourrais bien m'en accommoder" ["Well, marquis, these gentlemen leave me nothing but the crown of France, but I could manage to put up with it"] (343)—is also a stigmatization of their complete disrespect for social hierarchy; a critique, in other words, of the contamination of their minds by a prevailing and dangerous egalitarianism. In du Guénic's vision of the world, all one needs to know is one's place and function.[25] Can we argue, then, as Moyal does, that "precisely because it is irrational, because it is capable of sustaining contradictions, sentiment provides a more solid grounding for political allegiance than reason"?[26] Whether it is the case or not, it is certainly the point Balzac is making.

At one level, the story of Marie's return to the solid values of monarchy and religion functions as an account of France's reconquest of its "wholeness." It is therefore as much a historical commentary on the country's evolution from revolutionary "error" to monarchical wisdom as an indication of Balzac's political preference "pour le trône et l'autel." At another level, we may wonder whether the old universalism of the Catholic monarchy does not stand for something bigger than the nation itself. Montauran's "cosmopolitan royalism"[27] would certainly point in that direction, not only because he is at the same time Breton, French, and *émigré*,[28] but also because, as Moyal argues, "the unity and sovereignty of France, is, for him, irrelevant." If monarchy matters, it is as "the symbolic preserver of a spiritual unity, the guarantor of individual integrity against the encroachment of materialism."[29]

In a more subtle way, Marie's story recounts a challenge all Balzacian characters are confronted with: how to negotiate the traumatic turn to modernity at the personal, psychological level, how to "make the revolution private."[30] Moyal's analysis is particularly useful to understand their helplessness as well as Balzac's anger at seeing society ruled by the "material interests" of "financiers and bankers." The scandal, as seen by Moyal from Balzac's perspective, is that "[u]nder their near-hegemony *abstract values and ideals* which invariably come into conflict with material interests *come to be seen as matters of private conscience and are gradually excluded from influence or effect on social or political behavior.*"[31]

Balzac's perceived relegation of the most noble human aspirations to the private sphere brings to mind Birnbaum's observation that the new universalism of reason requires modern citizens to learn to distinguish between their public and their private lives, their public and private (religious) values. The novelist's nostalgia for the mythical time when things were transparent and human beings whole is clearly related to this difficult learning process. But his pessimistic outlook also seems to be linked to his failure to imagine the possible survival of "abstract values and ideals" in a secular public sphere: chasing Christianity out of the world of power is equated with renouncing all ideals and values, with abandoning it to material interests alone. Like Alphonse de Montauran and Marie de Verneuil, who are incapable of conceiving of solutions that would preserve the boundary between their private desires and their political ideals, Balzac has not yet understood the lesson of the new universalism. On the contrary: as Moyal points out, the idea that the values and ideals he cherishes could become a matters of private conscience, that they could be excluded from direct influence on social and political behavior is for him still simply "delirious."[32]

Seen that way, Balzac's political position in *Les Chouans* appears far less liberal than it has usually been assumed. If the crucial question with regard to French national identity is whether Catholicism can be relegated to the private sphere or not, Balzac's answer is "no, it cannot." During the Restoration, of course, true liberals saw things differently: by the time *Les Chouans* was published, Charles X's rigid and total commitment to Catholic France had given the liberal opposition fresh ammunition in its struggle against the Church. Once again, "Catholicism" and "superstition" had come to mean the same thing. Balzac borrows this liberal rhetoric of denunciation of "superstition," but by redirecting its focus from the general (Catholicism) to the particular (the Bretons), he is able to conceal the conservative politics the novel actually supports while at the same time presenting a friendly, liberal front.

Conclusion

A central claim of my essay has been that it is more relevant to examine Balzac's racial and racist characterization of the Bretons in *Les Chouans* for its ability to reveal the unsettling of a doxic assumption within French society—as a symptom of deep-seated anxieties about French national identity—than for its truth value about Breton identity. Nonetheless, I would like to conclude on a cautionary note and warn that the impact of Balzac's Breton stereotypes should not be underestimated. As fictional as Balzac's myth of Breton identity might have been, it had real, long-lasting effects.

Because Breton's characters are the only ones in the novel described with "une rigueur, une brutalité déjà naturaliste" ["a severity, an already naturalist brutality"],[33] it is difficult not to read *Les Chouans* as a novel about race. Balzac was certainly not the first to point to Brittany's economic backwardness or to identify cultural elements that made it different from the rest of France. Many others before him had pointed to these differences as serious obstacles to its complete integration into the modern French nation. But he was the first to argue that the Chouans' refusal to embrace the ideals of the Revolution could be explained through racial difference; that their failure to side with the forces of modernity and progress resulted from a lack of intelligence and moral sense only too understandable in a primitive race; in short that they were not French, because they belonged to a different race.

Yet for all its superficial explanatory power, Balzac's theory of racial incompatibility between the French and the Breton offers serious shortcomings. Even if we leave aside the important, historical role many Bretons played in the French Revolution,[34] the myth of a Breton race is based on a notion of linguistic and cultural homogeneity that cannot be sustained. Balzac presents Brittany as linguistically homogeneous—assuming, for instance, that *bas-Breton* is spoken everywhere in Brittany, including in Fougères[35]—although the province has been divided linguistically between a western Breton-speaking and an eastern French-speaking part (where *Les Chouans* actually takes place) at least since the Middle Ages.[36] Moreover, even if the term "Breton" is used to refer to inhabitants of both regions, the term "Chouans" has a wider extension since it also includes people south of the Loire, the Vendéens. How to fit them in Balzac's "Breton race" is therefore unclear.

As ludicrous as it might therefore seem, Balzac's early recourse to race in his treatment of Breton characters deserves to be remembered for several reasons. First, because it had an impact on French literature itself: after 1830 it became customary for writers from Brittany not only to claim their Breton identity, but also to write about Brittany, largely in an effort to erase the stereotypes of Bretons as uncivilized savages and to produce gentler counterstereotypes. These reactions are at the origin of a new type of literary production, regional literature. Second, and from a more theoretical perspective, highlighting Balzac's early recourse to race in *Les Chouans* is also a way to provide contrary evidence to one of E. J. Hobsbawm's claims in *Nations and Nationalism*, namely that "it has not often been recognized how late the ethnic-linguistic criterion for defining a nation actually became important"[37]—by which he means after 1870. Hobsbawm's attempt to establish various historical stages in the discourses on national identity—by linking specific criteria such as "the ethnic-linguistic criterion" to specific historical contexts—seems to me questionable. If such an evolutionist, historicist perspective recognizes the arbitrariness of the criteria used to define national identity, it nonetheless overlooks an essential dimension of that arbitrariness, namely the openness and availability of these principles of vision and division with regard to future uses, in other words, their ability to be endlessly recycled.

Notes

1. See Marie-Pierre Le Hir, "Génèse des stéréotypes sur la Bretagne: la contribution du theater," paper presented at the Nineteenth-Century French Studies Colloquium, Toronto, 1996.

2. See Catherine Bertho, ':'L'Invention de la Bretagne: Génèse sociale d'un stereotype," in *Actes de la Recherche en Sciences Sociales* 35 (1980): 45–62.

3. See Marie-Pierre Le Hir, "Landscapes of Brittany in Chateaubriand, Balzac, and Flaubert," in *West Virginia Philological Papers* 37 (1991): 20–31.

4. "[. . .] dans *Les Chouans*, Balzac a pris parti pour les Bleus, laissant clairement paraître la raison de sa préférence; avec les colonnes républicaines, c'étaient la civilisation, le progrès économique, en un mot l'avenir qui s'éfforcaient de pénétrer dans l'Ouest sauvage" [". . . in *Les Chouans*, Balzac sided with the Blues, clearly indicating why he preferred them: with the Republican armies it was civilization, economic progress, in a word the future that were trying to penetrate into the wild West" (Donnard, 427).

5. In his introduction to the first edition (1829), Balzac does use the expression "guerre civile" [civil war] to describe the Vendée wars (504).

6. In his analysis of the same passage, James Hamilton praises Balzac's "insight of a sociologist" (661) when he classifies Breton conscripts into three groups, each corresponding to a different social class. Where Hamilton sees heterogeneity, however, I see cultural homogeneity since the most salient characteristic of the Breton group as a whole is to be different from the French—or rather to represent a radical departure from the Parisian norm in term of dress-code. Moreover, the differences among Bretons Hamilton interprets as indicators of social class can just as well be taken as indicators of various degrees of "barbarity." The uneven allocation of space in the description of these three groups lends supporting evidence to this interpretation. The first two categories—which Hamilton himself calls the "primitive" and "half-barbarous" (661)—occupy pages of description, whereas the third, the category of city dwellers—who represent this modern, progressive Brittany all too absent in the novel—is granted only a few lines. This cursory mention of the presence of a few Republicans among the Bretons does not suffice, therefore, to instill the possibility of political divisions among Bretons—and therefore the thought that Bretons might be political beings—or consequently, to dispel the impression that the Bretons form a culturally homogeneous group, radically different from the French.

7. Honoré de Balzac, *Les Chouans, ou la Bretagne en 1799* (Paris: Gallimard, 1977), 47. Subsequent references to this text will be included in the text; translations are by the author.

8. Comments on the Bretons' lack of intelligence are too many to quote.

Here are a few examples: "Plus loin, deux autres officiers paraissaient vouloir apprendre à quelques Chouans plus intelligents que les autres, à manœuvrer deux pièces de canon" ["A little farther, two other officers seem to be trying to teach a few Chouans, who were more intelligent than the rest of them, how to manipulate two cannons"] (335). "Nous avons agi en vrais Bretons, nous nous sommes battus avant de nous expliquer" ["We acted as true Bretons: we fought first and then we talked"] (389).

9. Montauran is not excepted from the condemnation. When the comte de Fontaine asks: "Qu'espérez-vous faire avec de semblables bêtes?" ["What do you hope to achieve with such animals?"] Montauran's answer shows that he is also conscious of using the Bretons: "[Ils seront bons à] plonger mon épée dans le ventre de la république. . ." [("They'll come in handy when it's time) to plunge my sword in the belly of the Republic" (244).

10. Gudin is presented as "un de ces jésuites assez obstinés, assez dévoués peut-être pour rester en France malgré l'édit de 1763 qui les en a bannis. Il est le boute-feu de la guerre dans ces contrées et le propagateur de l'association religieuse dite du Sacré-Cœur. Habitué à se servir de la religion comme d'un instrument, il persuade à ses affiliés qu'ils ressusciteront, et sait entretenir leur fanatisme par d'adroites prédications" ["a Jesuit, obstinate, or perhaps devoted enough,—to remain in France in spite of the decree of 1793, which banished his order. He is the firebrand of the war in these regions and a propagandist of the religious association called the Sacred Heart. Trained to use religion as an instrument, he skillfully feeds his followers' fanaticism in his shrewd sermons and has them convinced that they will resuscitate"] (209).

11. During the torture scene of Monsieur d'Orgemont, Marie is horrified by the Chouans' "cruauté de cannibales" ["cruelty of cannibals"] (278). Later, she tells the Comte de Bauvan : "[. . .] vous faites ici une guerre de cannibales" ["the war you are fighting here is a war of cannibals"] (315).

12. Following Galope-Chopine's gruesome murder, "les deux chouans se lavèrent les mains sans aucune précipitation, dans une grande terrine pleine d'eau, reprirent leurs chapeaux, leurs carabines et franchirent l'échalier en sifflant l'air de la ballade du Capitaine" (413) ["the two Chouans took their time washing their hands in a large pot full of water, picked up their hats and their guns and then left through the gate, whistling the " 'Ballad of the Captain' "].

13. "Grâces à Saint Labre à qui j'ai promis un beau cierge," Galope-Chopine says to his wife, "le Gars a été sauvé! N'oublie pas que nous devons maintenant trois cierges au saint" ["Thanks to Saint-Labre to whom I owe a candle, the gars is safe. Don't forget that we now owe three candles to the saint"] (407).

14. "Ignorez-vous que les Bretons sortent de la messe pour aller danser!" ["Don't you know that the Bretons go dancing as soon as they leave the church!"] 287).

15. It is interesting to note that the poor artistic quality of religious artifacts is used to reinforce the notion that Bretons revere saints as they would idols. It is the case, for instance, with the pitiful reproduction of Saint Labre owned by Barbette, or with her "bonne vierge en plâtre colorié" ["colored, plaster cast of the good Virgin"] (300).

16. Frequently found in Francophone literature from Africa, the term "évolué(e)" describes indigenous people who, like Francine, have been assimilated into the dominant culture with a certain degree of success.

17. Not that I want to underestimate the "reality effect" of such racist repre-

sentations on readers and critics alike. Donald Aynesworth, for instance, in his 1986 article on *les Chouans* talks about "the prestige which the rector enjoys among *these primitives*" [my underlining] (45).

18. Honoré de Balzac, *Béatrix* (Paris: Garnier-Flammarion, 1979), 329.

19. Roger Pierrot, Notice to *Les Chouans ou la Bretagne en 1799*, by Honoré de Balzac (Paris: Gallimard, 1977), 483.

20. Seen that way, the depiction of Bretons as savages primarily sheds new light on the magnitude of the local nobility's betrayal of its task: it is its failure to live up to the ideals of the monarchy and the Catholic faith, including its refusal to embrace "progress," that caused the Revolution and led the nation to question the very principles on which its identity was founded.

21. Gabriel Moyal, "Making the Revolution Private: Balzac's *Les Chouans* and *Un Episode sous la terreur*," *Studies in Romanticism* 28, no. 4 (winter 1989): 616.

22. Ibid., 614.

23. Noting that "[t]he unity of the Nation is [. . .] primordial for Marie," Moyal continues, "[i]n her strongest argument against Montauran's cosmopolitan royalism she presents herself personifying France, as the motherland torn apart by its squabbling children" (614).

24. "C'est une sainte!" ["She is a saint!"] Francine exclaims.

25. As a Breton, du Guénic is subject to the same stereotypical, racist treatment as other Breton characters, but the feeling that in spite of his "stupidité" ["stupidity"] he belongs to the "chosen ones" is unmistakable in the following description: "Cette physionomie [. . .] offrait comme toutes les figures bretonnes groupées autour du baron, des apparences sauvages, un calme brut qui ressemblait à l'impassibilité des Hurons, je ne sais quoi de stupide, dû peut-être au repos absolu qui suit les fatigues excessives et qui laisse alors reparaître l'animal tout seul. La pensée y était rare [. . .]. Les Institutions, la Religion pensaient pour lui. Il devait donc réserver son esprit, lui et les siens, pour agir, sans le dissiper sur aucune des choses jugées inutiles, mais dont s'occupaient les autres. Il sortait sa pensée de son cœur, comme son épée du fourreau, éblouissante de candeur, comme était dans son écusson la main gonfalonnée d'hermine. Une fois ce secret deviné, tout s'expliquait. On comprenait la profondeur des résolutions dues à des pensées nettes, distinctes, franches, immaculées comme l'hermine." ["This face (. . .) offered, like those of all the Bretons gathered around the baron, a sort of savage appearance, a stolid composure resembling the impassiveness of the Hurons, with a hint of stupidity, due perhaps to the total slump that follows excessive fatigue and then allows the animal alone to reappear. Thought was rare. (. . .) Institutions, Religion thought for him. Like his kin, he had to save his mind for action, not to waste it on anything deemed useless—other people took care of that. He drew his thought from his heart as he drew his sword from his scabbard, it dazzled in its candor as did the hand wrapped in ermine in his crest. Once this secret was understood, everything made sense. One understood the depth of resolutions based on thoughts as clear, distinct, straightforward and immaculate as ermine] (*Béatrix*, 59).

26. Moyal, "Making the Revolution Private," 612.

27. Ibid., 614

28. "Son exaltation consciencieuse [. . .] faisait de cet émigré une gracieuse image de la noblesse française" ["With his expression of exalted devotion [. . .] this emigré was a graceful image of French nobility"] (*Les Chouans*, 65).

29. Moyal, "Making the Revolution Private," 614.

30. "The characters in *La Comédie humaine* appear to cling desperately to a sense of individual wholeness which they see as continuous with their social responsibilities while they are besieged by a society which pressures them to systematically shed the remaining abstract spiritual values which have sustained them until the Revolution and beyond. In the place of these values, money and material property increasingly dominate and control all the activities and all the concerns of individuals within society. Though Balzac's France still clings to its symbols and theoretically remains a constitutional monarchy, its true rules are its bankers and financiers. Under their near-hegemony abstract values and ideals which invariably come into conflict with material interests come to be seen as matters of private conscience and are gradually excluded from influence or effect on social or political behavior" (601–2).

31. Moyal, "Making the Revolution Private," 601–2, my underlining.

32. Ibid., 622.

33. Pierre Gascar, preface to *Les Chouans ou la Bretagne en 1799*, by Honoré de Balzac (Paris: Gallimard, 1977), 14.

34. The fact that the Club des Jacobins was created in Rennes should suffice here as a reminder that not every Breton was a Chouan.

35. When Barbette asks the Republican men disguised as Chouans where they are from, Balzac betrays his assumption of linguistic homogeneity by having the "deux ou trois Fougerais" ["two or three inhabitants of Fougères"] answer "en bas-Breton" (393).

36. One should also take into consideration the internal linguistic division of the Breton-speaking region, given the great number of Breton dialects that existed, as well as, in more recent history, the opposition between French-speaking (or bilingual) towns and a Breton-speaking countryside.

37. E. J. Hobsbawm, *Nations and Nationalism Since 1780: Programme, Myth, Reality* (Cambridge: Cambridge University Press, 1990), 102.

Napoleon's Compass: The Third Term of History in Balzac's *Les Chouans*

MARY JANE COWLES

BALZAC'S HISTORICAL NOVEL *LES CHOUANS OU LA BRETAGNE en 1799*[1] stages the conflict between the ragtag but savage Royalist forces of peasant Brittany, commanded by the dashing and idealistic Marquis de Montauran, and the half brigade of Republican troops led by the stalwart Hulot. Mediating these two forces, these two ideologies, these two heroes, is Marie de Verneuil, a government spy, who falls for her intended victim, Montauran. The intrigue of the novel weaves between these two poles, advancing in a series of arabesques as Marie espouses alternatively the cause of her beloved and that of the Republic. It is appropriate then, as Claudie Bernard points out,[2] that the novel is doubly dated, hesitating between a sense of promise and a sense of decline: the beginning of an era in the eyes of the Republic—"Dans les premiers jours de l'an VIII, au commencement de vendémiaire" ("In the early days of the year VII, at the beginning of Vendemaire")—and the end of a year, of a century, of an era for the legitimist historian—"ou, pour se conformer au calendrier actuel, vers la fin du mois de septembre 1799" ("or towards the end of the month of September 1799, reckoning by the present calendar").[3] The simultaneous presence of the dawn and dusk of political orders is also suggested in a certain hesitation concerning the subtitle: *La Bretagne en 1800* of the original edition of 1829 became *La Bretagne en 1799* in the Vimont edition of 1834 (Frappier-Mazur, 1660).

FROM PERIPHERY TO CENTER

If, as Bernard states, "le mythe de la Révolution est un mythe centralisateur par excellence"[4] ("the myth of the Revolution is a centralizing myth above all") with Paris as its privileged setting, Balzac's choice of Brittany as the site of his drama marks it as ex-centric, not only for its profusion of barbarous local color, but also for its peripheral position. Brittany and the Vendée are the "Ouest" ("West") to Paris's center, and the further the protagonists travel on the road from Paris to Fougères, the more labyrinthine the landscape becomes.[5] But of course, by choosing Brittany and its borderlands (such as Alençon) as the *sole* locus for his novel, Balzac inverts the terms of "center" and "periphery." "La place que la Bretagne occupe *au centre de l'Europe* la rend beaucoup plus curieuse à observer que ne l'est le Canada" (emphasis mine) ("The fact that Brittany is situated in Europe makes it very much more interesting than Canada") (918/15), writes Balzac, a statement which elicits the following note from Lucienne Frappier-Mazur in the Pléïade edition: "Une telle localisation géographique paraît étrange" ("Such a geographic placement seems strange") (1699). Strange indeed—but particularly apt for the purposes of Balzac. The domain of the Chouan is a world unto itself where communication with the "outside" is especially problematic. "Entouré de lumières dont la bienfaisante chaleur ne l'atteint pas, ce pays ressemble à un charbon glacé qui resterait obscur et noir au sein d'un brillant foyer" ("It is surrounded by enlightenment, but the beneficent warmth never penetrates it; the country is like some frozen piece of coal that lies, a dim black mass, in the heart of a blazing fire") (918/15). Brittany constitutes a center in which Royalists are as cut off from the authority of the exiled Louis XVIII as Republicans are from the decrees of the Directoire. Hence throughout the early pages of the novel, in which, as Kadish shows, the reader shares the "outsider's" perspective of the Republican soldiers (46, 48), a sense of confusion and isolation reigns. The Chouans regularly intercept military dispatches (922/18), and the government of the Directoire in Paris is of no help at all. "En effet, le gouvenement, n'ayant ni troupes ni argent dont il pût disposer à l'intérieur, éluda la difficulté par une gasconnade législative: ne pouvant rien envoyer aux départements insurgés, il leur donnait sa confiance." ("The government, as a matter of fact, had neither troops nor money available for the prosecution of civil warfare, so the difficulty was evaded by a bit of bombast on the part of the Legislature. They could do nothing for the revolted districts, so they reposed complete confidence in them") (909/5). To add to the confusion, the government leadership is unstable. Bernadotte has quit as war minister, and the rest of the "pentarques ou pantins" are neither especially trustworthy nor competent. "Hulot ne recevait aucune réponse aux demandes et aux rapports réitérés qu'il adressait à Paris. Ce silence étonnant annonçait, sans doute, une nouvelle crise révolutionnaire" ("Hulot's repeated reports and appeals received no reply from Paris; some fresh revolutionary crisis, no doubt, caused the astonishing silence") (957/57).

The silence, which is the consequence of Brittany's distance—real and moral—from Paris, sets the stage for Bonaparte's arrival on the political scene with the coup d'état of 18 Brumaire. The Parisian theater of political action, however, operates on a distant periphery. In this respect, Balzac goes one step further than Walter Scott's model of the historical novel as analyzed by Lukács.[6] Not only are the important historical figures not the central figures of the action, in *Les Chouans* they do not appear at all. Thus Bonaparte, though often named, remains mysterious and inaccessible. Preoccupied with Germany and the Italian campaign, at times absent from Paris, the figure of Bonaparte functions at a remove even beyond the periphery. Yet from that liminal moment of the text at the very end of the first chapter, the shadow of the First Consul constitutes a third term in the confrontation of Republican and Royalist ideologies. This presence, which partakes of both Republican concepts and absolutism, both a new order and a reedition of the past, is significantly embodied in a proclamation[7] emanating from the diegetic periphery (Paris) to its center (Brittany) and articulated in terms of an act of reading and a visual icon:

> "Tiens, regarde, reprit La-clef-des-cœurs en montrant en tête de la proclamation une grossière vignette où, depuis peu de jours, un compas remplaçait le niveau de 1793. Cela veut dire qu'il faudra que, nous autres troupiers, nous marchions ferme! Ils ont mis là un compas toujours ouvert, c'est un emblème.
>
> —Mon garçon, ça ne te va pas de faire le savant, cela s'appelle un problème [. . .] reprit Beau-pied [. . .].
>
> —C'est un emblème.
>
> —C'est un problème. [. . .]." (960).

> ("Now look here," went on Clef-des-Cœurs, pointing to a rough vignette at the head of the proclamation, where a pair of compasses had in the past few days replaced the plumb-line level of 1793. "That means that we soldiers will have to step out. That's why the compasses are open; it's an emblem."
>
> "No, my boy, you can't come the scholar over us. That thing is

called a problem. I served once in the artillery," he added, "and that was what my officers fairly lived on."

"It's an emblem."

"A problem.") (60)

When the two soldiers appeal to their superior Gérard to adjudicate, the idealist Republican gravely replies, "C'est l'un et l'autre" ("It is both the one and the other").[8]

Emblem

The compass as the symbol of a Napoleonic system is indeed both an emblem and a problem. First, as emblem, it is significant that the compass replaces the principle of equality represented by the carpenter's level. Rather than serving as an instrument to level a hierarchical society, the compass divides up space, defines territories, measures ambitions. It is more the tool of the conqueror than that of the builder of the new Republican society. In this regard it is of interest to compare a passage from a somewhat later text by Balzac, *Un Drame au bord de la mer* (1835):

> Les jeunes gens ont presque tous un compas avec lequel il se plaisent à mesurer l'avenir; quand leur volonté s'accorde avec la hardiesse de l'angle qu'ils ouvrent, le monde est à eux. Mais ce phénomène de la vie morale n'a lieu qu'à un certain âge. [. . .] Après cet âge rapide comme une semaison, vient celui de l'exécution. Il est en quelque sorte deux jeunesses, la jeunesse durant laquelle on croit, la jeunesse pendant laquelle on agit; souvent elles se confondent chez les hommes que la nature a favorisés, et qui sont, comme César, Newton et Bonaparte, les plus grands parmi les grands hommes. (10:1159)

> (The young for the most part delight to measure the future with a pair of compasses of their own; when the strength of the will equals the boldness of the angle that they thus project, the whole world is theirs. But this phenomenon of mental existence takes place, however, only at a certain age, [. . .]; it passes as swiftly as the sowing time, and is followed by the age of execution. There are in some sort two periods of youth in every life—the youth of confident hopes, and the youth of action; sometimes in those whom Nature has favored, the two ages coincide, and then we have a Cæsar, a Newton, or a Bonaparte—the greatest among great men.) (1)

This is not the celebration of equality but the cult of genius. The ability to measure and define, to imaginatively stride across one's future ("j'arpentais mon avenir" ["I paced out my future"]) is itself a process of intellectual conquest. Gaëtan Picon finds in this passage "un dynamisme horizontal non moins vigoureux et obsédant, la marche dans la vie, d'obstacle en obstacle,—pas du promeneur dans les rues de Paris, piétinement d'un détachement militaire, [. . .] marche du « réquisitionnaire» dans la petite ville endormie . . . " (141–42) ("a no less vigorous and obsessive horizontal dynamism, walking in life, from obstacle to obstacle,—not the stroller's in the streets of Paris, but the stamping of a military detachment, (. . .) the marching of 'conscripts' in the sleepy small town. . . .") In this way, the meaning of the "emblem" returns obliquely to the "interpretation" given by the soldier La-clef-des-cœurs: "Cela veut dire qu'il faudra que, nous autres troupiers, nous marchions ferme!" ("That means that we soldiers will have to step out"). By referring to Hulot's favorite expression for marching, "ouvrir le compas" ("opening the compass") in which the soldier's long open stride imitates the two extended arms of an open compass, La-clef-des-cœurs evokes that other quintessential of conquest, movement through space. Movement is certainly present to an unusual degree in *Les Chouans*, from the march of armies, to numerous carriage rides crisscrossing the same terrain, to Marie de Verneuil's frequent forays into the countryside surrounding Fougères. Constant movement in space doubles Marie's arabesques of sentiment in the psychological domain and works generally toward the same goal of conquest and domination. And as emblem, the compass foreshadows Napoleon's very real domination of Europe.

Additionally, as an instrument of measurement, the compass symbolizes the triumph of rational science, and hence implies the reversal of a divinely-sustained hierarchy. Where once Atlas's shoulders or God's open palm may have provided the measure of the world, that power is now given to the scientist, the engineer, the strategist. The order of the ancien régime and the equality of the Republic are replaced by a military technocracy whose standard of measure is merit and ambition.

Problem

Significantly, it is because the compass is an emblem that it becomes a problem as well. Indeed the compass participates in a whole network of problematized readings. As Pierre Barbéris writes, "Ainsi la lecture du réel, révélé par l'effort même de la lecture comme essentiellement problématique, est bien au centre de la production romanesque et de l'écriture du *Dernier Chouan*"[9] ("Thus the reading of the real, revealed by reading's very effort as essentially problematic, is right at the center of novelistic production and the writing of the *Last Chouan*.") For example, Hulot must see through Marche-à-Terre's demeanor in order to recognize that an ambush is imminent (916, 921/13, 18). Hulot's soldiers "regardèrent alternativement la vallée du Couesnon, les bois de la route et la figure sévère de leur commandant, en tâchant d'y lire leur sort," ("looked by turns along the valley of the Couësnon, at the woods along the road, and at their commandant's stern face, trying to guess what the experienced sportsman means") (925/23), and they use the intonations of Hulot's "Tonnerre de Dieu" as "un sûr thermomètre de la patience du chef" ("indicated . . . like the degrees of a thermometer, the amount of patience left in their chief") (961/61). Marie must read letters, real and forged, as well as smoke signals to confirm a rendezvous with her lover, and even God is presumed to read the sacred heart tattoos the faithful Chouans have inscribed upon their chest. The problematic nature of the *compass* derives from the fact that it must be read and interpreted; unfortunately there are not enough clues to make the meaning clear. Of course, in this particular example, the fact that the interpreters of the message are all illiterate ("pas un d'eux ne savait lire" ["no one among them could read"] (960, 60) renders the scene comical, but at the same time exemplary. The soldiers who scrutinize Napoleon's compass are not much better off than the Royalists and Republicans who try to divine, from the little information they have, what the first consul's positions will be. When news of the events of the 18 Brumaire reaches the military leaders of the West, it seems magical, prophetic, suspenseful: "ces chefs n'en furent que plus impatients d'être délivrés de la responsabilité qui pesait sur eux, et devinrent assez curieux de connaître les mesures qu'allait prendre le nouveau gouvernement" ("they grew impatient of the heavy responsibilities that weighed upon them, and eager to hear what steps the new government meant to take") (957/57). After reading the first consul's proclamation to the troops, Hulot exclaims, "Quel compère! [. . .] il sonne la messe et il la dit. Est-ce parler, cela?" ("What a fellow! [. .] first he rings the bells for Mass, and then he goes and says it. Isn't that plain speaking?"), to which the well-educated, idealist Gérard replies: "Oui, mais il parle tout seul et en son nom" ("Yes, but he speaks for himself and in his own name") (960/59).

Clearly, Hulot's reading of Napoleonic discourse, like his captain Merle's, reveals his faith in the general's efficacy, and his comic use of the metaphor—"il sonne la messe et il la dit" ("he rings the bells for Mass, and then he goes and says it")—suggests that his allegiance to an anticlerical, egalitarian Republic will bow before a certain military ethic and the man he *believes* Napoleon to be. Indeed, despite his forthright manner, he is willing to resort to disguise and even begrudgingly recognize Marie de Verneuil's strategic capabilities as a spy in service to the Republic. As Jeannine Guichardet points out, "fidèle à sa lecture naïve des événements, Hulot n'a vu en [Napoléon] que son semblable, un homme issu de la Révolution" ("faithful to his naïve reading of events, Hulot only saw his likeness, a man born of the Revolution, in Napoleon") (162). And certainly the majority of the troops (like Merle) represent the same stance. The adjutant Gérard on the other hand, true to the principles of the Republic and politically more astute, glimpses in Bonaparte the Napoleon-to-be. His concern about Bonaparte's personal ambition explains his response to the soldiers: the first consul's compass *is* an emblem and a problem. Consequently, it is indeed symbolic that Gérard is one of the first to fall in the events following the 18 Brumaire, a fact which Courteix repeatedly stresses in *Balzac et la Révolution française* (86, 291): it would have been impossible for Gérard to reconcile his Republican ideals with an allegiance to the general who would be emperor.

But it is not only with respect to his leadership qualities or his personal ambitions that the characters of *Les Chouans* attempt to decipher Bonaparte's intentions. The Royalists are at least as nervous and hopeful about the possibilities the first consul represents as are the Republicans. The number of questions, suppositions, speculations, or threats revolving around Bonaparte makes it clear that the rules of the game have suddenly changed. "Ne va-t-il pas, dit-on, arrêter l'effet des lois contre les émigrés?" ("Do they not say that he is about to repeal the law against the Emigrants?") asks Mme du Gua, posing as the mother of a disguised Montauran (985/84). The miser d'Orgemont tells Marie "[. . .] un décret des Consuls, que j'ai lu dans *Le Primidi de l'Ille-et-Vilaine*, vient d'arrêter les séquestres" (". . . a decree putting a stop to the sequestrations. I saw it in the paper, in the *Primidi de l'Ille-et-Vilaine*") (1089/198). Montauran asks the Chouan priest, Abbé Gudin, "Ignorez-vous aussi que MM. Hyde de Neuville et d'Andigné ont eu il y a cinq jours une conférence avec le Premier consul sur la question de rétablir Sa Majesté Louis XVIII" ("Do you really not know that MM. Hyde de Neuville and d'Andigné had a conference with the First Consul, five days ago, over the question of restoring his Majesty, Louis XVIII?) (1089–90/199). At the Chouan assembly and ball in Saint-James, one of the leaders of the revolt demands to be given the title "M. de Cottereau" and the rank of colonel, or threatens to surrender to Bonaparte (1127/240). At the same gathering, some of the nobles dismiss Bonaparte by comparing him to his predecessor Marceau; but those who had already fought against the Republican forces alone understand the current crisis and, "sachant que s'ils parlaient du Premier consul et de sa puissance à leurs compatriotes arriérés, il n'en seraient pas compris, tous causaient entre eux [. . .]" ("were aware of the real gravity of the crisis, and they knew that they should be misunderstood if they spoke of the First Consul and his power to their countrymen who were behind the times. So they talked among themselves. . . .") (1131–32/245). Hulot complains of Corentin, "Si le Premier consul m'écoutait [. . .] il laisserait ces renards-là combattre les aristocrates, ils sont dignes les uns des autres [. . .]" ("If the First Consul were to take my advice . . . he would leave this kind of fox to fight it out with the aristocrats—they would be well matched. . . .") (1149/265). Even Marie's watchdog, the astute and ruthless Corentin, misjudges Bonaparte: "Il n'a fait sans doute le 18 Brumaire que pour obtenir des Bourbons de plus forts avantages en traitant de la France avec eux" ("He arranged the 18th Brumaire because, no doubt, he wished to obtain the best possible terms from the Bourbons, in treating with them as to France") (1153/269).

Despite all the attention, opportunism, and anxiety surrounding Bonaparte, it is notable that few if any of the actors of this drama seem to have the "right" reading of his intentions, and most of the accounts come to us thirdhand. To a large extent the conflict, which is reputed to oppose two principles, has degenerated into a struggle of personalities (see Gabriel Moyal, "Making the Revolution Private"). This, in turn, throws into greater relief the fact that virtually all action of the novel, and certainly the resolution of the larger political dilemma, is in suspense, awaiting the first consul's decisions. The diegetic center turns all eyes toward the shadowy figure on the periphery, upon which their future depends.

Interestingly, one of the questions about which characters in the novel speculate most is that of the first consul's relationship to women. For the naïve Hulot, Bonaparte has a no-nonsense approach to women that embodies Republican virtue, quite unlike the dallying of the ancien régime that even Danton and Barras were guilty of: "Voyez le Premier consul, c'est là un homme: pas de femmes, toujours à son affaire. Je parierais ma moustache gauche qu'il ignore le sot métier qu'on nous fait faire ici" ("Look at the First Consul now, that is a man for you; no women, always at work. I would wager my left moustache he knows nothing of this foolish business") (964/63), referring to his orders to obey the commands of a mere woman, Fouché's spy Marie. Significantly, Hulot shaves his beloved moustache in the last chapter of the novel when he goes undercover as a false "Chouan." For Captain Merle, though, only the most beautiful woman could be Bonaparte's wife: "[. . .] c'est la femme la plus belle que j'aie jamais vue! [. . .] C'est la femme du Premier consul, peut-être?" (". . . she is the handsomest woman I ever set eyes on! . . . Perhaps it is the First Consul's wife") (971/71). Others are not quite so dazzled as Merle, but still closely connect Marie with Bonaparte. At the Chouan ball in Saint-James, one of the women guests snidely comments: "Croyez-vous qu'elle vienne ici pour traiter au nom du Premier consul?" ("Do you think that she can have come here to treat with us in the name of the First Consul?") (1136/250) and one of Marie's dancing partners flatters her by saying, "Le Premier consul nous envoie des ambassadeurs bien dangereux" ("The First Consul is sending us very formidable ambassadors!") (1136/251).

It is natural enough for the actors of this drama to link Marie and Bonaparte. Even if we learn early on that Fouché might send a woman to trap Montauran, it is only after the 18 Brumaire that he puts his plan into action. Bonaparte seems to share Marie's indeterminacy in choosing sides in the conflict: he is head of the Republican army, of course, but has also initiated dealings with the aristocrats. But they share another trait as well. One of the underlying questions that gives the plot several of its numerous twists and turns is the question of Marie's identity. Is she a real de Verneuil or just an impostor, a little courtesan from the Paris opera? Indeed, Montauran's love for her seems to hinge on the revelation of that secret, the truth of her legitimacy. Not surprisingly, she is both legitimately who she says she is, and illegitimate, since she is the natural daughter of the Duc de Verneuil. In this regard a certain parallel with Bonaparte again emerges: neither the true representative of the Republic nor a ruler whose authority is an integral part of the social structure of the ancien régime, his only legitimacy flows from his power and his will. Like Marie, his personal destiny takes precedence over political stakes.

But the parallel between them ends there. Because Marie is at the center of the action, she only catches glimpses of its shape and meaning. Ironically, it is only when in the thick of the "bocage" ("grove") , following the high earthen walls topped with hedges which block all perspective, that Marie can begin to "read" the meaning of the Chouan war. The full meaning, however, is something only genius can decipher: "Elle admira le génie du ministre qui devinait du fond d'un cabinet le secret de la paix. Elle crut entrevoir les considérations qui agissent sur les hommes assez puissants pour voir tout un empire d'un regard, et dont les actions, criminelles aux yeux de la foule, ne sont que les jeux d'une pensée immense" ("She admired the genius of the minister who had discovered the clew to a peace in the depths of his cabinet. She thought she had gained an insight into the nature of the considerations which sway men who have ability enough to see the condition of an empire at a glance. Their actions, which in the eyes of the crowd seem to be criminal, are but the partial manifestations of a single vast conception") (1115/227–28). As much as Marie successfully manipulates others, as much as she has the illusion of control, she ultimately falls prey to her own passions, and does so because those very passions play their role in some vast machinery set in motion by Napoleon and his minister Fouché. As Corentin observes:

> Employer habilement les passions des hommes ou des femmes comme des ressorts que l'on fait mouvoir au profit de l'Etat, mettre les rouages à leur place dans cette grande machine que nous appelons un gouvernement, et se plaire à y renfermer les plus indomptables sentiments comme des détentes que l'on s'amuse à surveiller, n'est-ce pas créer, et, comme Dieu, se placer au centre de l'univers? . . . (1148)
>
> (To make a dexterous use of the passions of men and women, as so many springs which can be set in motion for the benefit of the State; to set in position all the wheels in the mighty piece of machinery that we call a government; to take a pleasure in setting within it the most stubborn sentiments, like prisoners [sic; "triggers" would be better] whose action one can amuse one's self by controlling; is not

all this the work of a creator? Is it not a position like God's in the center of the universe?) (263–64)

If we follow Corentin's logic, then notions of a natural center and periphery are irrelevant. The positions of center and periphery are reversed yet again, not in terms of space, but in terms of thought. It is the dispassionate application of a "pensée immense" ("vast conception") that creates a center anywhere, even "au fond d'un cabinet" ("in the depths of [his] cabinet"). That "pensée immense" is the ideal compass with which to take the measure of ambitions, tracing a circle "dont le centre est partout, la circonférence nulle part" ("whose center is everywhere, and circumference, nowhere").

Notes

1. All references to *Les Chouans* are from vol. 8 of the Pléïade edition of *La Comédie humaine* (Gallimard, 1977); subsequent references will be found in the text; references to other works by Balzac are taken from the same edition and will likewise be found in the text.
2. Claudie Bernard, *Le Chouan romanesque: Balzac, Barbey d'Aurevilly, Hugo* (Paris: Presses Universitaires de France, 1989), 181.
3. *Les Chouans*, 905. Translations are from the Saintsbury translation, and page references will henceforth be indicated in the text, first to the French text, then to the translation.
4. Bernard, *Le Chouan*, 73.
5. See Doris Kadish, *The Literature of Images: Narrative Landscape from Julie to Jane Eyre* (New Brunswick, NJ: Rutgers University Press, 1986).
6. Gyorgy Lukács, *The Historical Novel*, trans. Hannah and Stanley Mitchell (Lincoln: University of Nebraska Press, 1983), 38–39.
7. See Donald Aynesworth, "The Making and Unmaking of History in *Les Chouans*" for a discussion of what he considers the failure of Napoleonic discourse.
8. Jeannine Guichardet also discusses this image in "Le maréchal Hulot," 154–55.
9. Pierre Barbéris, *Lectures du réel* (Paris: Editions Sociales, 1973), 290.

Territorial Peripheries: Balzac's Forests

MICHAEL TILBY

WITH IMPROVED COMMUNICATIONS AND THE SUCCESSFUL NAPOLEONIC prescriptions for local government, nineteenth-century France was an age which witnessed the destruction of peripheries as part of a movement towards inclusion and centralization. Locations that were formerly peripheral came to entertain a new relationship of resemblance with the center, one which replaced the oppositions on which the notion of the peripheral depended. Yet this process towards uniformity did not always enjoy an unimpeded course. Its inherent artificiality and ambiguity may most obviously be seen in its increasing identification with a questionable colonialist ideal. Even on a more limited scale, it was accompanied by a countermovement of displacement and redefinition that illustrated just how deep-seated remained the need for a notion of the peripheral. Arguably, the dual nature of this process was never more apparent than during the July Monarchy, the era that was contemporaneous with Balzac's reflection on the changing socioeconomic realities of postrevolutionary France, yet within the latter's lifetime there remained much within the topography of France and its various constituent regions to sustain the love of dramatic contrast that was the cornerstone of both his thought and his æsthetics. The privilege of constituting the center was frequently observed to shift, with new centers—and thus new peripheries—establishing themselves through the outcome of power struggles, however parochial. Taking an example from one of Balzac's own novels, *Les Paysans*, the hierarchy separating La-Ville-aux-Fayes from Soulanges, and Soulanges from Blangy was not, the Balzacian narrator tells us, determined once and for all by the origins of these villages but was the result of political and economic factors new to the age.

Among the various generic locations affected by this changing perception of the peripheral was the forest. Within the overall landscape, the forest was traditionally the embodiment of the peripheral and to that extent it played a key role in the collective psyche. By nature labyrinthine, it was the prime location identified with the experience of losing one's bearings and, as such, was an exemplary source of terror. Its heart was frequently represented as a realm of darkness, a center from which the circumference was imperceptible, and which, in its most complete state, was no less enclosed with regard to the sky above than it was horizontally. Both in the chronicles of the law courts and in fictional representations, the forest was associated with violent crime, as the location of murder, armed robbery, and sexual aggression. Even those with a legitimate purpose associated with the forest, such as woodcutters, were often accorded the role of bogey or scapegoat. It is no coincidence that, in some Romance languages and dialects at least, the forest dweller is synonymous with the foreigner or stranger.

Although the number of novels by Balzac in which the forest is a prominent location is relatively small, they span his entire career, from certain works signed "Horace de Saint-Aubin" and *Le Dernier Chouan* in the 1820s to such works of his maturity as *Une Ténébreuse Affaire*, *Le Curé de village*, and *Les Paysans*. Given the thrust of the argument that follows, recognition of Balzac's awareness of the changing reality of the forest in historical terms needs to be conceded from the outset. For there can be no doubt that his depiction of the forest is a valuable documentary source. The lawbreaking activities of the peasants in *Les Paysans*, for example, have an established pedigree; the parallels they present with the grievances contained in the *cahiers de doléances* of 1789 are striking. Research by a modern historian of the forests of Burgundy into the crimes committed against the forest in the second half of the eighteenth century leads to a picture which likewise bears a close resemblance to the view presented by Balzac's unfinished novel, to the extent of the *estaminet* being seen as the center of the violent discontent and the forest keepers as surrogates for the landowner in the war waged by the peasantry.[1] Such continuity may, nevertheless, be regarded as an indication of Balzac's reactionary bias when set alongside Theodore Zeldin's analysis of the conflict, according to which it was increasingly the landowners who emerge as the lawbreakers:

> Until the 1830s villages had little hope of preventing the descendants of their feudal lords from usurping common rights in the woodlands around them, which meant so much to the poor; but

after that date an increasing number of communes brought lawsuits against the rich and more often than not won them. Poor communes could not afford the legal fees—but the richer ones were able to carry on the struggle, not only against the lords but even to extend it against the state also, which tormented them with its Forestry Code and its endless taxation.[2]

Yet if Balzac's peasants are, at one level, part of a continuum that stretches back beyond the revolution, *Les Paysans* shows an acute awareness not only of the adverse effect of the revolution on French forestry but also of the way the forest in subsequent decades was brought entrepreneurially within the economic system of the bourgeoisie. (It might be noted in this connection that the first schools of forestry in France date from 1825.) If the forest was one of the principal locations in which the conflict between *château* and *chaumière* was discernible, the Restoration was the period in which that opposition, the terms of which echo throughout *Le Curé de village* in particular, became increasingly problematic. As Balzac shows in the case of General Montcornet, the Napoleonic nobility, especially when represented by high-ranking army officers *en disponibilité*, constituted in relation to land ownership an unwelcome element of instability. Taken as a whole, *Le Curé de village*, with its promotion of science and religious faith allied in the service of economic progress, and *Les Paysans*, with its emphasis on the devastating effects of the forest's being reclaimed by the purchasers of ever smaller plots, serve as eloquent, contrasting illustrations of an ideal and its denial.

My concern in this essay, however, is to trace Balzac's representation of the forest, not in relation to the author's explicit themes but in terms of his implicit response to it as a peripheral location. The investigation will inevitably broaden to encounter a world in which boundaries in general are no longer sacrosanct. More challengingly, it will also encounter the way the Balzacian novel questions the conventional fictional narrative on which it is based, in order to evolve a new kind of novel that can accommodate the incompatibility of the nonfictional (the realm of verifiable historical, economic, and legal facts) and the fictional. Such an investigation is part of a wider concern to understand the ways in which the didactic dimension of the Balzac novel consists of more than the incorporation of a freestanding nonfictional theme, the nonfictional elements becoming part of the fabric of the text, even in the case of those passages that might seem to constitute interpolated lectures but which, in fact, can be shown to fulfill a more sophisticated role in terms of poetics than is often assumed.

At this point, account has to be taken of the fact that, in addition to being a historically evolving phenomenon that compels a documentary investigation, the forest was also a literary and artistic entity which, though well established, was likewise receptive to a change in the prevailing æsthetic sensibility. For it will be seen that, in customary fashion, it is to these stereotypes that Balzac in his maturity will continue to turn in his need to fictionalize the nonfictional. In practice this means that Balzac allots himself the task of marrying the social and historical dimension of his subject to the formal restraints of a novel form whose unsatisfactory origins in the simple adventure story become increasingly manifest as the *Comédie humaine* progresses.

In the Gothic novels whose schemata served as fundamental reference points for Balzac's earliest novels, especially those of Mrs. Radcliffe and Ducray-Duminil, the forest was an obvious stage for the production of terror. A novel such as Radcliffe's *The Romance of the Forest* conveys in suitably heightened form many of the traditional characteristics of the forest previously recalled. The imprisoning effect of the forest on a virginal heroine is followed by the expected scene of abduction, though terror is by no means the prerogative of the female cast; the earliest evocation of fear at becoming lost in the forest is allocated to two of Radcliffe's male characters, who despair of extricating themselves and who suffer from "apprehensions of banditti [that] were very sanguine."[3] The Gothic forest nonetheless establishes itself as the epitome of ambiguity, in that it is also susceptible of a portrayal in terms of luxuriance, solitude, and various other components of Romantic beauty. Radcliffe's heroine ventures forth into the forest and delights in the sensuous experience it offers. In terms of the plot, the forest offers a refuge for (the admittedly criminal) La Motte. It also contains within its midst a ruined Gothic abbey. In other words, with the arrival of the Romantic world picture, the forest acquires an additional, sublime dimension. As Chateaubriand, in *Le Génie du christianisme*, felt able to proclaim: "Les forêts ont été les premiers temples de la Divinité et les hommes ont pris dans la forêt la première idée de l'architecture." ("The forests were the original temples to the Divinity, and mankind derived from the forest its first idea of architecture").[4] The forest duly became a favorite scene for the landscape painter, whether members of the German Romantic school or representatives of the new French school such as Paul Huet. In these higher forms, as in the more narrowly Gothic depictions, the Romantic writer or artist was irresistibly attracted to the forest's contradictory physiognomy, its almost meteorological ability to metamorphose instantly from being the embodiment of radiant charms to being synonymous with menace; and to its capacity to unite these contrasting effects in such ambiguous states as melancholy. Such a picture, which was the context the young Balzac inherited from his reading, indicates that the peripheral location of the forest was no longer necessarily a space in opposition to the self, but one in which emotional self-awareness could be experienced to a heightened degree through intimate acquaintance with one's surroundings.

A survey of the evolution of Balzac's representation of the forest reveals a movement from the more or less conventional representation in *Le Vicaire des Ardennes*, in which fiction does not meet History and is unaffected by it, to *Le Curé de village* and *Les Paysans*, in both of which the central topography consists of a tripartite relationship between chateau, park, and forest. That the mature Balzac novel grew out of a constant reworking of the stereotypes that formed the basis of the novelist's earliest fictions is confirmed by the links discernible between the *Scènes de la vie de campagne* and the *romans de jeunesse*, the memory of which would have been revived for their author by Souverain's republication of the works of "Horace de Saint-Aubin" in 1836–37. In addition to the return, in *Le Curé de village*, to the concern which the young Balzac had displayed in *Annette et le criminel* with religion and prayer in the context of crime and repentance, a cabaret with the punning name "Le Grand I Vert" appears in both *Le Vicaire des Ardennes* and *Les Paysans*. The *Paul et Virginie* motif which features so prominently in all but name in *Le Vicaire des Ardennes* is explicitly evoked in *Les Paysans* as well as in *Le Curé de village*. The figure of the stoic Republican first introduced in the form of Véryno in *Le Centenaire* reappears in *Les Paysans* in the person of Niseron, and is continued more generally through the concern in the *Scènes de la vie de campagne* with that rare phenomenon, the faithful *intendant*.

Balzac's depiction of the forest in *Le Vicaire des Ardennes* and *Annette et le criminel* is essentially conventional in its role as an adventure story location. The Château Durtal recently acquired by the former pirate Argow is situated at the edge of the forest, which had been the case with the chateau in *The Romance of the Forest*. (Montalt tells Madame La Motte: "I have a chateau near the borders of the forest.")[5] In *Annette et le criminel*, the forest of Saint-Vallier near Valence is frequented by brigands and is the scene of a holdup of a carriage by night. This forest, like the Ardennes forest, is emphatically vast, and, in accordance with the superlative mode that connotes the fictionality of the adventure story, Argow's henchman Vernyct assembles his men "dans l'endroit le plus épais d'une forêt" ("in the densest part of a forest").[6] It is expected that Jeanneton will experience fear in such a location; she is asked by one of the customers of the «Jolie Hôtesse»: "Mademoiselle [. . .] vous ne craignez donc rien dans cette maison si voisine de la forêt, et dans laquelle il est arrivé tant de malheurs?" ("Doesn't it scare you, Mademoiselle, living in this house so close to the forest, where so many misfortunes have occurred?")[7] On the other hand, if, in *Le Vicaire des Ardennes*, Joseph gets lost in the forest, the latter location also provides him with a means of escape as well as being home to the woodcutters who, in this fiction at least, are given the role of protectors:

> Joseph, élevé dans les forêts et les montagnes, était beaucoup trop agile pour qu'aucun de ceux qui le pour-suivaient pût l'approcher. Mélanie que ce combat avait rendu tremblante comme les feuilles qui restaient encore aux arbres, vit, avec joie, son frère disparaître dans la forêt . . .
>
> (Joseph, having been raised amidst forest and mountains, was far too nimble for any of his pursuers to catch up with him. Melanie, whom the sight of the struggle had caused to shake like the leaves that remained on the trees, was filled with joy as she watched her brother disappear into the forest.)[8]

At the same time, the forest is a source of Romantic delight for Joseph, albeit in the most cliched of terms:

> . . . les ruines de l'ancien château lui offraient une scène qui plaisait à sa mélancolie. Du tertre où il se plaçait, il apercevait la vaste forêt des Ardennes qui semblait une couronne posée sur la tête des aimables collines qui formaient la vallée circulaire d'Aulnay. A ses pieds, un lac factice, assez vaste, le séparait des débris romantiques de l'antique forteresse dont il ne restait que des tours carrées, solidement bâties, que l'on n'avait pas pu démolir. La mousse, le lierre

couvraient toutes ces ruines et les eaux du lac environnaient cette île pittoresque.

(. . . the ruins of the ancient castle presented a scene pleasing to him in his melancholy state. From the knoll where he stood, he surveyed the vast Ardennes Forest, which was like a crown placed round the head of the lovely hills that formed the circular Aulnay valley. Below, a man-made lake of some size separated him from the romantic remains of the ancient fortress, of which there now stood only its square-shaped towers, which had been solidly built and had resisted all attempts at demolition. Moss and ivy covered the entire ruins, which formed a picturesque island surrounded by the waters of the lake.)[9]

As for the religious topos recalled earlier in the example taken from *Le Génie du christianisme*, it is present in *Annette et le criminel* in the sermon of the Abbé de Montivers:

Entrez dans une vaste forêt? Au crépuscule, qu'elle soit épaisse et que ses arbres forment une colonnade végétale et tâchez de ne pas trembler, car ce sentiment est le premier principe de la prière, prenez garde! Vous vous prosternez alors devant toute la nature représentée par cette voûte de verdure, là, vous touchez encore à Dieu.

(Should you go into a vast forest at dawn and find it dense, its trees forming a colonnade of greenery, endeavor not to tremble, for such a feeling is the starting point for prayer. Be on your guard! For you are prostrating yourself before the whole of Nature represented by this verdant ceiling, and there, you are close indeed to God.)[10]

Yet in both these early novels the positive and negative attributes of the forest are randomly distributed as discrete, purely surface elements which fail to come together to produce that sense of ambiguity which forms a large part of the attraction of the exemplary Gothic fictions.

That said, there is, however, in *Le Vicaire des Ardennes* one depiction of Aulnay and its backdrop, which, while again conventional, may possess more significance than is at first apparent. At an early stage in the novel, the elderly curé Gausse is roused to lyrical heights on the subject of his parish:

—M. le maire voulait dire que notre pays est délicieux: en effet, la vaste forêt des Ardennes couronne de tous côtés nos montagnes, et ses arbres semblent une foule réunie dans un amphithéâtre, pour jouir du spectacle de notre joli vallon. La petite rivière qui y serpente l'anime par ses détours; ces chaumières irrégulièrement placées, ce clocher gothique qui les domine, le château qui finit le village, son beau parc, les ruines du lac; tout ici est enchanteur . . .

(His worship the Mayor was implying that our village is delightful. The vast Ardennes Forest indeed crowns our mountains on all sides. Its trees are like a crowd gathering in an amphitheater in order to enjoy the spectacle of this pretty valley of ours. The winding little river provides interest with its twists and turns; the cottages dotted about, the imposing Gothic belltower, the castle at the edge of the village, its fine park, and the lakeside ruins, everything is enchanting.)[11]

Ostensibly this is an æsthetic idyll, a landscape composition. With the hindsight provided by the *Scènes de la vie de campagne*, still greater significance is apparent in the impression it exudes of social harmony. In this naïve vision, not only is everything in exactly the right place, the separate identity of *château* and *chaumière*, of park and forest is explicitly established. Implicit in the likening of the trees to "une foule réunie dans un amphithéâtre" is the sense of a desire for the populace to be submitted to an imposed order. Very soon after, there is reference to the church in Aulnay containing the entire population of the village.

The fact remains that by the time Balzac returns to the forest in *Le Curé de village*, his experience in refashioning stereotypes into complex figures saturated with competing levels of significance causes the forest to take on a radically new complexion that nonetheless never quite disguises the fact that it is a location inherited from the Gothic story of adventure. Explicitly, *Le Curé de village* depicts the economic transformation of an unproductive forest. Yet what distinguishes "la grande forêt dite de Montégnac" from its predecessors in the *romans de jeunesse* is the fact of its being a multifaceted textual entity that is responsible for the novel having a resonance independent of its more didactic purpose.

The forest of Montégnac remains the conventional location of terror. It is a particularly inaccessible forest: "les sentiers étaient à peine tracées dans ces montagnes inhabitées" ("the paths had scarcely been marked out in these unpopulated mountains").[12] Farrabesche warns the wandering Véronique: "vous êtes séparée par plus de deux lieues de toute habitation" ("you are more than two leagues from the nearest dwelling") (764). Her keeper Colorat's Christian name is Jérôme but, unlike his illustrious namesake, he is ill at ease in the deserted, rocky clearings, being described as "[e]ffrayé surtout des clairières semées de roches granitiques qui nuançaient de loin cette immense forêt" ("terrified, above all, by the clearings strewn with granite rocks which relieved from afar that vast expanse of forest") (761). The traditional association of the forest with crime remains and, as usual, is identified first of all with highwaymen:

> Souvent les voitures, les voyageurs, les piétons avaient été arrêtés au fond de cette gorge dangereuse par des voleurs dont les coups de main demeuraient impunis: le site les favorisait, ils gagnaient, par des sentiers à eux connus, les parties inaccessibles de la forêt. (708)
>
> (Often coaches, travelers, and those on foot had been held up in the depths of that dangerous gorge by robbers whose exploits remained unpunished: they were abetted by the location and made off into inaccessible parts of the forest along paths which were well known to them.)

The forest is also the home of the dreaded chauffeurs whose activities are so graphically described to Véronique by Jérôme Colorat. Yet Balzac has here found a way of moving beyond the Gothic scenario of the innocent victim falling prey to the *hors-la-loi*, and without having recourse to the Byronic figure of the noble brigand. Not only is the forest of Montégnac the habitat of two unrelated criminals, Tascheron and Farrabesche, before becoming the property of a third, Véronique herself, the stereotype is defamiliarized by the unique circumstances in which these characters committed their criminal acts and by the fact of their crimes belonging to a now distant past. The forest becomes the locus of the acts of repentance by two of them, rather than being associated purely with their criminal phase. The memories set in train by the visual aspect of the forest are essential to the act of repentance. When the Abbé Bonnet draws a comparison between the variations (*inégalités*) within the mass of trees and "la vie sociale," Véronique observes bitterly: "Il en est *que la serpe de la femme qui fait du bois* arrête dans la grâce de leur jeunesse" ("There are those who are cut down in the prime of their youth by *the woman gathering wood with her billhook*") (758). On another occasion, the channels formed by the melting snow on the mountaintops appear to her in the form of human scars (762). Farrabesche refuses the chateau farm Véronique offers him in order to remain "l'homme de la forêt," where he is now a force for good (831). The forest itself, in other words, is accorded a crucial role in taking the reader from the realm of superstitious fear to the certainties of religious faith.

The actual facts of the crime, at least as far as Véronique's precise involvement is concerned, are never allowed to become the central concern and this receives its poetic reflection in what otherwise would have been a purely clichéd dimension of the forest's description, namely its silence. This evocation of silence—"ce beau spectacle muet, d'ailleurs: pas un oiseau, la mort dans la plaine, le silence dans la forêt" ("that beautiful spectacle was, moreover, without a sound: not so much as a bird, a deathly hush in the plain, and in the forest, silence") (758)—is a reflection of an example of another kind of silence, those textual silences in Balzac so much admired by Proust. For despite the dramatic public confession Véronique makes immediately prior to her death, there remains at the heart of the novel an enigma that is never fully resolved. In keeping with the secrecy of the confessional, only the Abbé Bonnet, we assume, knows Véronique's full story.

Moreover, the process by which the forest becomes the externalization of a state of mind is given universal expression in the course of the principal description of the Montégnac forest:

> Il n'est pas un site de forêt qui n'ait sa signifiance; pas une clairière, pas un fourré qui ne présente des analogies avec le labyrinthe des pensées humaines. Quelle personne parmi les gens dont l'esprit est cultivé ou dont le cœur a reçu des blessures, peut se promener dans une forêt, sans que la forêt lui parle? (762)
>
> (There is not a single forest setting that does not have its meaning, no clearing or thicket that fails to offer analogies with the labyrinth of human thoughts. What individual is there of an educated mind or whose heart has been wounded who can wander in a forest without its speaking to them?)

For the purpose of the present discussion, it is not so much the verifiability of this statement that is important as its status as the expression of a principle by which Balzac is able to integrate his geographical setting with all the other dimensions of his fiction that are productive of meanings.

To the gaze of Bonnet and Véronique, the late-afternoon forest in autumn appears as a masculine entity (tree-names in French are, of course, of a convenient gender in this respect) attracting a female caress ("la forêt de Montégnac sur laquelle cette lueur glissait comme une caresse" ["the Montégnac Forest, over which this light glided like a caress"] [757]) which, at a level deeper than the explicit theme of remorse, displays a disturbing relationship of ambivalence with the representation of the female as the wielder of the billhook and, indirectly, of the guillotine blade. It is a vision in which the erotic is fused with a depiction of Nature and its colors in the language of art and architecture:

> . . . les caprices de la magnifique tapisserie que fait une forêt en automne. Les chênes formaient des masses de bronze florentin; les noyers, les châtaigniers offraient leurs tons de vert-de-gris; les arbres hâtifs brillaient par leur feuillage d'or, et toutes ces couleurs étaient nuancées par des places grises incultes. Les troncs des arbres entièrement dépouillés de feuilles montraient leurs colonnades blanchâtres. Ces couleurs rousses, fauves, grises, artistement fondues par les reflets pâles du soleil d'octobre, s'harmonisaient à cette plaine infertile, à cette immense jachère, verdâtre comme une eau stagnante. (757–58)

> (. . . the caprices of the magnificent tapestry that is a forest in autumn. The massive forms of the oaks were the color of Florentine bronze; the walnut trees and chestnuts displayed their varying shades of verdigris; the early flowering trees were resplendent in their golden foliage. Each of these colors was relieved by patches of gray where nothing grew. The trunks of trees bereft of leaves formed colonnades of a whitish hue. The russets, fawns, and grays blended artistically in the pale reflection of the October sunlight, and fused harmoniously with this infertile plain, a vast expanse of fallow land, a dullish green, the color of stagnant water.)

But, essentially, this is a softer version, appropriate to the presence of the Abbé Bonnet, of the way the forest is for Véronique a constant reminder not just of her crime but also of the sexual passion that led, in a fashion vaguely reminiscent of the Paolo and Francesca story, from the reading of *Paul et Virginie* to her adultery and the execution of her lover.

The sexual dimension of the story is thereafter evoked indirectly but unmistakably by the phallic suggestiveness of the trees in such details as "quelque pin solitaire d'une hauteur prodigieuse" ("the occasional solitary pine of prodigious height") (761) or "des châtaigniers centenaires aussi droits que des sapins des Alpes" ("hundred-year-old chestnut trees, as erect as Alpine firs") (762), and, more graphically still, in the comparison present in the description of certain shrubs, "nains partout ailleurs, mais qui, par des circonstances curieuses, atteignent à des développements gigantesques et sont quelquefois aussi vieux que le sol" ("dwarfs everywhere else, but which, by some curious set of circumstances, grow to gigantic heights and are sometimes as old as the ground itself") (761). The vocabulary employed in the effect on Véronique continues the sexually charged atmosphere: "l'esprit de cette nature austère la frappa, lui suggéra des observations neuves pour elle, et excitées par les significations de ces divers spectacles" ("the spirit of this austere nature impressed itself upon her, arousing in her new observations stimulated by the meanings present in these varied spectacles") (762), and may be considered to sound an echo in the highly specific formulation: "Elle se surprit à désirer d'entendre l'eau bruissant dans ces ravines ardentes" ("She found herself longing to hear the water murmuring in these torrid ravines") (763). Such indirect forms of expression may be found appropriate with regard to a woman who lives by proxy and through sublimation.

Within this same extensive description, which, despite its origins in Balzac's journey from Limoges to Clermont-Ferrand in late-August 1832, bears only the most superficial resemblance to the guidebook, there is also embodied the novel's underlying concern with [religious] certainty:

> Si l'on recherchait bien les causes de la sensation, à la fois grave, simple, douce, mystérieuse qui vous y saisit, peut-être la trouverait-on dans le spectacle sublime et ingénieux de toutes ces créatures obéissant à leurs destinées, et immuablement soumises. Tôt ou tard le sentiment écrasant de la permanence de la nature vous emplit le cœur, vous remue profondément, et vous finissez par y être inquiets de Dieu. Aussi Véronique recueillit-elle dans le silence de ces cimes, dans la senteur des bois, dans la sérénité de l'air, comme elle le dit le soir à M. Bonnet, la certitude d'une clémence auguste (pp. 762–63).

> (If one were to seek out the causes of the feeling which takes hold of you in this place, a feeling that is at once grave and simple, sweet and mysterious, one would perhaps encounter it in the sublime and ingenious spectacle of all these creatures obeying their destiny and remaining immutably in submission to it. Sooner or later, your heart is filled with an overwhelming sense of the permanence of nature which stirs you deeply, and you end up troubled by God. Thus, amid these silent peaks, the fragrance of the woods, and that air of serenity, Véronique experienced, as she said to Monsieur Bonnet that evening, the guarantee of an august clemency.)

What these various illustrations from a work of Balzac's maturity show is the novelist retaining the conventional associations of the forest of popular fiction but reworking them in a way that produces a novelistic composition which is fundamentally distinct from the linear adventure story narrative that is nonetheless present *en filigrane* and in a fragmented and decentered form. The result is a practice that is radically different from the use of a conventional story of crime and punishment as a framework for a philosophical, religious, or economic treatise. The forest is no mere backcloth nor is it depicted in a single specialized language. Instead, it becomes open to a host of different languages, those, for example, of art, science, technology, religion, poetry, and sex, and as such assumes a dominant textual presence that sidelines the gaps in the information provided at the level of characterization and plot by this most fragmented of personal histories. Accordingly, it has much to teach us concerning the unique identity of the mature Balzac composition.

Although *Les Paysans* bears scant resemblance to the monolithic adventure story with which Balzac toys in his *romans de jeunesse*, the representation of the forest that lies at its heart retains the conventional starting points that have been observed. As the prime location of crime, the forest is the scene not just of infractions of the forestry code but also of sexual violence (the near-rape of Geneviève) and killings (the murder of the keeper Michaud and the slitting of the throat of his favorite greyhound). The passing references to "le loup-cervier" (Rigou is "le loup-cervier de la vallée" ("the valley's lynx"), (166) and "le loup-garou" ("the werewolf") (208) confirm its status as a receptacle for superstitions.[13] Yet in contrast to Gothic practice, the evil associated with the forest is not fully established from the outset. If the forest ends up reasserting its atavistic role, the buildup to this explosion of violence is largely imperceptible. The peasants are not depicted as naturally murderous, a fact which may be taken as illustration of the point that Balzac makes explicitly with regard to the peasants' despoliation of the forest: "Ne croyez pas d'ailleurs que jamais Tonsard, sa femme, ses enfants et sa vieille mère se fussent dit de propos délibéré: «nous vivrons de vols et nous les commettrons avec habileté!» Ces habitudes avaient grandi lentement" ("Do not suppose that Tonsard, his wife, his children and his old mother ever said to themselves in so many words: 'we'll live by thieving and we'll be good at it!' These habits had developed slowly") (92).

The complexity of this novel in relation to the culminating act of violence only emerges, however, from a consideration of the deceptively innocent way in which the events and their setting are described. More specifically, it is a question of seeing the ways in which the story of Blondet and Mme de Montcornet, which, as in the case of Véronique's relationship with Tascheron in *Le Curé de village*, is almost entirely relegated to the silences that punctuate the text, is tightly interwoven[14] with the life of the forest and thereby the novel's documentary dimension. (In an important metatextual aside, the Balzacian narrator warns—or rather promises—the reader that this is not going to be the "drame de chambre à coucher" ("bedroom-drama") prevalent in so many "livres modernes" ("books nowadays") (65).) The novel's development is only to a limited extent one of characterization and plot and may instead be said to hinge on an opposition between the forest and the park, an opposition which, it will be argued, needs to be maintained for the benefit of the social order but which is constantly being disturbed by the actions and responses of the protagonists. What allows this topographical opposition to fuse with the conventional fictional dimension—the adulterous affair between the *châtelaine* and her houseguest—is precisely its definition in terms of masculine and feminine sexual characteristics.

Our starting point must be the knowingly excessive account of Les Aigues in the letter from Blondet to Nathan with which the novel opens. The letter is multifunctional, not just in terms of the various levels in which it operates as an exposition, but because Blondet may be regarded as Balzac's surrogate in more than one respect: as writer; as outsider (like Mme de Montcornet, he comes originally from Alençon, the opposition between Normandy and Burgundy forming another strand in the tapestry); and as Royalist. But our concern here is with the way Blondet's letter establishes the femininity of the park. Ostensibly, his description is a celebration of the natural beauty of Les Aigues, but this idyllic landscape is in fact coded. It is impregnated with his desire for the *châtelaine*. The strategies he adopts in his letter are predicated on the recipient's (and the reader's) ability to decipher the true referent.

Les Aigues was, he says, obviously "bâtis par une femme ou pour une femme" ("built by, or for, a woman")[15] and he later goes on to describe the opera singer Mlle Laguerre who was its owner both prior to and during the Revolution. (The punning relationship with the subtitle of the first part of the novel: "Qui terre a, guerre a" ["Own a piece of land and you will know no peace"] is doubtless intentional.) But it is in the actual descriptive details that the femininity is readable: the "ronces semblables à des cheveux follets" ("brambles reminiscent of straggly wisps of hair"); "de belles fleurs baignent leurs pieds" ("beautiful flowers bathe their feet"); the "odeurs forestières" ("forest smells"); "toutes ces vigoureuses fécondations" ("all these examples of vigorous fertilization"); "[c]e mystère enivre, il inspire de vagues désirs" ("this mystery is intoxicating and inspires vague desires"). That these are not merely the clichés of natural description is half confirmed by the confession "Je pensais alors à une robe rose" ("my thoughts at that moment were of a pink dress") and by the almost gratuitous reference to Nathan's mistress, Florine. The hints are further continued in the final phrase in Blondet's variation on the topos of trees as people:

> L'allée finit brusquement par un dernier bouquet où tremblent les bouleaux, les peupliers et tous les arbres frémissants, famille intelligente, à tiges gracieuses, d'un port élégant, les arbres *de l'amour libre*. (my emphasis)
>
> (The path comes to an abrupt end with one last group of trees, where the birches, poplars and all the other quivering trees tremble, an intelligent family, with their graceful stems, deporting themselves with elegance, the trees *of free love*!)

Following the evocation of water-lilies ("un étang couvert de nymphéas" ["a pond covered in water-lilies"]), the real referent makes her appearance as a flower, and not just any flower but the symbol of Bourbon legitimacy, tellingly referred to here as the "queen of flowers":

> Au sommet du perron, comme la reine des fleurs, vois enfin une femme en blanc et en cheveux, sous une ombrelle doublée de soie blanche, mais plus blanche que la soie, plus blanche que les lys qui sont à ses pieds, plus blanche que les jasmins étoilés qui se fourrent effrontément dans les balustrades.
>
> (At the top of the steps, resembling the queen of flowers, imagine finally a woman, dressed in white and wearing nothing on her head, standing beneath a parasol lined with white satin, but herself whiter than satin, whiter than the lilies at her feet, whiter than the star-shaped jasmine flowers which brazenly occupy the balustrades.)

(The châtelaine might thus be said to emerge as "le lys dans le parc.") Later, Blondet will reflect on the feminine gender of *lou-*

tre in a manner that does not suggest the preoccupation of a philologist. The "chasse à la loutre" ("otter-trapping") would appear to be identified by him with a rather different pursuit.

Paradoxically, the park is also linked to a network of allusions to virginity that involve others beyond Madame de Montcornet. It is defined by the "spirituel écrivain" ("witty writer") and "maître en ironie" ("master of irony"), in his letter, as a "une forêt redevenue vierge par un phénomène exclusivement réservé aux forêts" ("a forest returned to the state of maidenhood by a phenomenon exclusively reserved for forests"). Her Christian name is Virginie and the Montcornets' childless marriage ("il attendait encore un commencement de postérité" ["he was still awaiting a start to posterity"], 152) is the subject of a witty exchange between Fourchon and a member of the chateau staff:

> —[. . .] Voyons, mon gars, sais-tu si Monsieur et Madame ont chacun leur chambre? . . .
> —Parbleu, sans cela Monsieur n'aimerait pas tant madame! . . . dit Charles (108).
>
> (. . . Now then, my boy, do you know whether Monsieur and Madame each have their separate bedchamber?—By gad, if that were not so, Monsieur would love Madame a lot less, said Charles.)

(The reader is doubtless intended to note that Montcornet's status as cuckold is immortalized in his name.) Virginie's maternal instincts are obliged to find their outlet in her "adoption" of Geneviève. The painting that Blondet first thinks of as an illustration of "le beau" is Luini's "Mariage de la Vierge" (55). He himself later blushes "comme une vierge" (108). It is stressed that among other attributes Mme Rigou had lost her "yeux de vierge" ("virginal expression") in childbirth (240–41), while the fact of the attack on Geneviève causing her to jettison the pitcher of milk she was carrying (207) might be held to recall Greuze's famous painting "La Cruche cassée" ("The Broken Pitcher"), in which the object is manifestly a symbol of the girl's loss of virginity.

At the same time as being the object of male desire, the park is also the embodiment of that desire. It is the individuality of the trees surrounding the Henri IV chateau, their rivalry in size, that distinguishes this from other possible descriptions that would equally well have satisfied the general needs of the idyll:

> Il y là le pin d'Italie à écorce rouge avec son majestueux parasol; il y a un cèdre âgé de deux cents ans, des saules pleureurs, un sapin du Nord, un hêtre qui le dépasse. (54)
>
> (There is the Italian pine with its red bark and majestic umbrella, a two-hundred-year-old cedar, weeping willows, a Scandinavian pine, and an even taller beech tree.)

The result is a highly charged atmosphere that is strangely out of proportion to the banality of the referent, a reciprocal adulterous passion.

Both Les Aigues and its *châtelaine* are in fact the subject of writing that constantly stresses its own ambiguity and artificiality. A comparison with the description of the forest in *Le Curé de village* or with the description of Clochegourde by the no less lovestruck Félix de Vandenesse in *Le Lys dans la vallée* shows Blondet to be incapable of writing naively. The journalist remains at all times the witty phrasemaker. He takes delight in ironizing his own attempt to create the impression of a topographical setting of unrivaled perfection, referring to the content of his letter as "cette narration de Parisien stupéfait" ("this account by a dumbfounded Parisian") and contriving such concoctions as "c'est les Invalides des héros de l'horticulture, tour à tour à la mode et oubliés, comme tous les héros" ("it's the Invalides of the heroes of horticulture, successively fêted and forgotten, like all heroes"). He excuses his extravagant idiom as an example of what in modern-day usage would be termed "déformation professionnelle": "Vois, mon très cher, où vous conduit l'habitude de tartiner dans un journal" ("That, my dear chap, is where scribbling for a newspaper gets one"). He also has a keen sense of the way the letter is going to be received by his *destinataire*, whom he (or the Balzacian narrator on his behalf) is in fact creating, and both provokes and plays with Nathan's likely skepticism and mockery.

More generally, these extravagant pages exude a self-conscious concern with themselves as writing and therefore as hyperbole and cliché. Blondet's predicament as a professional writer consists in knowing that the gap between writing and its referent can never be closed. The perfection he professes to identify in Les Aigues and its *châtelaine* has an unfortunate habit of finding its expression in set discourses that are instantly identifiable as such. As he details the features and contents of the principal rooms of the chateau, he slips into the language of the estate-agent, but it might easily have been the equally stereotyped language of the architectural historian or the author of the tourist guide. As if in belated recognition of this, the Balzacian narrator ironizes the succinctness (questions of length are always relative in Balzac) of his own description of Rigou's house, comparing it, quite unjustifiably it should be added, with the style of "des affiches de vente" ("sale-posters") (240). The result is not just the introduction of a self-mocking character who will also on occasion be an inadvertent figure of fun, but a sense of the location as an artificial décor, the theatrical nature of which is an echo of the "fille d'opéra" who was its previous owner (and who, for ironic effect is sometimes referred to as the "ancien Premier Sujet du Chant" ["former Principal Singer"]). There follow later in the novel examples of a similar theatricalization in the form of Père Fourchon as comic actor and the likening of the square in Soulanges to a stage with wings (256). Only the smoke emerging from one of the chimneys indicates that the chateau is not "une décoration d'opéra."

The sense of ironic artifice is subsequently confirmed outside Blondet's letter, with the narrator in the following chapter likening him to Tasso's Rinaldo ensnared by the charms of Armida in her magic garden, and introducing mocking allusions to the pastoral poetry of Virgil and Theocritus.

What this ironic undermining of Arcadian perfection and this pervasion of a sense of self-conscious artifice point to is the unreality of this "oasis que nous avons si souvent rêvée d'après quelques romans" ("oasis of the kind we have so often dreamed of from reading of them in novels") and thus the failure to create a valid opposition between the park and the forest, a failure perhaps already hinted at in the ambiguous function of the gate to the park: the "deux petits pavillons en brique rouge" ("two tiny red-brick houses") can, it is said, be thought of as either "réunis" ("joined") or "séparés" ("separated") by the gate.

The distinction between the park and the forest is, in fact, blurred almost as soon as the separateness of the Arcadian walled park has been established. In addition to being an artistic creation, the park is a clearly defined social space, which although described as sharing with the forest a labyrinthine quality, is an artificially organized structure of paths for walks that lead nowhere. It is the symbol of a different kind of order, the countryhouse routine to which Blondet refers in his letter. But this routine is one that this particular houseguest immediately disturbs by being so late for lunch. What makes him late is the irresistible attraction of what lies beyond the park, which is a world in which the otherwise fly Parisian journalist is out of his depth. His transgression is treated indulgently, not least because this expedition born of boredom is a temptation to which Montcornet himself has succumbed; he too has enjoyed being the victim of Père Fourchon's wheeze. The occasion is one of careless mirth but the gravity of the transgression may be glimpsed when it is seen to lead to the introduction of the ragged and smelly Fourchon and grandson Mouche into the chateau dining room.

The forest in *Les Paysans* thus loses its sense of being a distinct location. It is true that in *Le Curé de village* the forest is eventually incorporated with the park, but this is the result of a carefully thought out scientific and economic strategy devised by the polytechnicien Gérard. In *Les Paysans*, Michaud's proposed solution of enclosing the forest by a wall is instantly ridiculed, albeit by the self-interested Sibilet. (In his role as spy for the bourgeoisie, the latter is obliged to dismiss a scheme prejudicial to their speculative interests, but a more fundamental negativity attaches itself to Michaud's proposal by virtue of its being, in contrast to the project at Montégnac, a desperate defensive measure.) At Les Aigues there is lacking a clear demarcation between forest and park and the responsibility for this is implicit in the text. The ambiguity or confusion is, for example, apparent in heightened form in the description of the land surrounding the Porte d'Avonne after the latter has been refurbished by Virginie de Montcornet for the Michauds following the "brutale insouciance" ("stark lack of care and attention") of the previous occupant (191).

The pavilion is an extension of the chateau ("[l]es abords désobstrués et sablés étaient soignés par l'homme chargé d'entretenir les allées du parc" ["the approaches having been cleared and sanded, were looked after by the man charged with tending the paths in the park"]) and is redolent with its smells ("[q]uelques prairies du parc, récemment fauchées à l'entour, répandaient l'odeur des foins coupés" ["some of the park's surrounding meadows, recently mown, spread the smell of newly cut hay"]). At the same time, it exists in a relationship of harmony with the forest: "[l]es parfums de quelques corbeilles de fleurs se mariaient à la sauvage senteur des bois" ("the scent of several baskets of flowers mingled with the smell of the woods"), while la basse-cour, les écuries, l'étable reportées dans les bâtiments de la Faisanderie et cachées par des massifs, au lieu d'attrister le regard par leurs inconvénients, mêlaient au continuel bruissement particulier aux forêts ces murmures, ces roucoulements, ces battements d'ailes, l'un des plus délicieux accompagnements de la continuelle mélodie que chante la nature.

(the farmyard, the stables, the cowshed, brought within the buildings of La Faisanderie but concealed behind clumps of trees, so as not to interfere with the pleasing outlook, added to the continual rustling peculiar to forests a murmuring, cooing and beating of wings which formed the most delightful accompaniment to the continuous melody of Nature's song.)

The artificiality of this reconciliation of the contrasting characteristics of park and forest is plain to behold: "Ce lieu tenait donc à la fois au genre inculte des forêts peu pratiquées et à l'élégance d'un parc anglais" ("the place combined the unkempt appearance of forests that have scarcely been opened up with the elegance of an English park"). The feminizing influence, the extension of the sphere of the genteel chateau, is again suspect, as the falsely benign behavior of Mlle Laguerre had been before. As if in order to emphasize the inappropriateness of Mme de Montcornet's intervention, Balzac has her introduce an architect from Paris who brings with him his own workforce.

This, then, is the context from which Madame de Montcornet's encounter with the act of violence in the forest derives its full significance. The episode of Michaud's murder is introduced by a departure from the norm: Virginie is being taken to the forest, by Blondet, for the first time. The extension of the feminine conception of the park in the description that follows represents a blindness to the harsh realities of the forest. The postharvest landscape is described in terms that evoke unmistakably Virginie's sexual and maternal yearnings:

Jamais le magnifique paysage et le parc des Aigues n'avait été plus voluptueusement beau qu'il l'était alors. Aux premiers jours de l'automne, au moment où la terre, après son accouchement [etc]

(Never had the magnificent landscape and park at Les Aigues been more voluptuously beautiful. In the first days of autumn, when the land, after giving birth [etc.])[16]

The description continues with an evocation of color in the language of art such as was seen in the case of Véronique Graslin's experience of the forest of Montégnac:

> les bois surtout sont délicieux, ils commencent à prendre ces teintes de vert bronzé, chaudes couleurs de terre de Sienne, qui composent les belles tapis-series sous lesquelles ils se cachent comme pour défier le froid de l'hiver.
>
> (the woods, above all, are delightful, they begin to assume those tints of bronzed green and those warm colors of Sienna earth, which make up the beautiful tapestries beneath which they conceal themselves as if in order to ward off the winter cold.)

But here it is soon part of an implicit demonstration of the heedlessness of the protagonists, their lack of engagement with the real. Nature is described as "pimpante et piquante comme une brune au printemps" ("as fresh and provocative as a brunette in spring") and "mélancolique et douce comme une blonde" ("as melancholy and gentle as a blond"), while the traces of the daylight are said to disappear "comme les robes traînantes des femmes qui disent adieu" ("like the trailing dresses of women bidding 'Farewell' "). Blondet's inadequacy is seen in the combination of his nonchalance and the banality of his observations: "Ce temps-là inspire tout le monde! [. . .] Ha çà! Joseph, tu connais les bois?" ("This weather inspires us all [. . .] Ah! ha! Joseph, you know these woods, then?"), to which the answer is a laconic "Oui Monsieur." The inappropriateness of their presence in the forest had already been conveyed through Virginie's reluctance to agree to the excursion, since she had assumed it would be necessary to go on foot ("J'ai la marche en horreur" ["I have a horror of walking"]). In the event, they go as far as they can "en tilbury."

Yet as they penetrate further into the forest, its sexual dimension becomes more evident. The femininity of the countryside gives way to a more highly charged female sexuality:

> La terre sous cette couverture était tiède comme une femme à son lever, elle exhalait ces odeurs, suaves et chaudes, mais sauvages; l'odeur des cultures était mêlée à l'odeur des forêts.
>
> (The earth beneath its covering was warm, like a woman rising from her bed; it exuded those warm, sweet, yet wild, smells; the smell of the cultivated land mingled with that of the forest.)

The autumnal scents remain predominant: "les senteurs du serpolet, du chèvrefeuille, et des feuilles qui tombent en rendant un soupir" ("the scent of mother-of-thyme, honeysuckle and the leaves that utter a sigh as they fall"). The forest nonetheless retains its conventional masculinity: the beech-tree clearings are "dominés par un arbre centenaire, l'hercule de la forêt" ("dominated by a one-hundred-year-old tree, the Hercules of the forest"), while "ces magnifiques assemblages de troncs noueux, moussus, blanchâtres, à sillons creux, qui dessinent des maculatures gigantesques" ("these magnificent patterns of gnarled, mossy, whitish trunks, with their hollow furrows, assuming the form of gigantic interleaves") are a source of wonder. A coupling is the inevitable next stage:

> Certes, il y a des voluptés inouïes à conduire une femme qui, dans les hauts et bas des allées glissantes, où la terre est grasse et tapissée de mousse, fait semblant d'avoir peur ou réellement a peur, et se colle à vous, et vous fait sentir une pression involontaire, la fraîcheur de son bras, le poids de son épaule élastique [. . .]
>
> (Assuredly there are untold delights in guiding a woman, who, up and down the slippery pathways, where the ground is slimy and covered in moss, either pretends to be afraid or really is so, and fastens on to you, causing you to feel an involuntary pressure, the coolness of her arm, the weight of her shoulder as it expands.)

Virginie's response to the novelty of the experience is to give herself up to the realm of sensuous pleasure:

> Ce spectacle nouveau pour la comtesse, cette nature si vigoureuse en ses effets, si peu connue et si grande, la plongea dans une rêverie molle, elle s'accota sur le tilbury et se laissa aller au plaisir, ses yeux étaient occupés, son cœur parlait, elle écoutait cette voix intérieure en harmonie avec la sienne, lorsqu'il la regardait à la dérobée, et il jouissait de cette méditation qui avait dénoué la capote, et qui livrait au vent du matin les boucles et la chevelure avec un abandon voluptueux.
>
> (This novel spectacle for the countess of Nature so vigorous in its effects, yet at once so little known and so immense, plunged her into a soft dream-like mood. She leaned against the tilbury and yielded to her pleasure. Her eyes were at work, her heart was speaking. She was listening to that inner voice in harmony with her own when he stole a glance in her direction, taking pleasure in this meditation which was unfastening her bonnet and delivering up her ringlets and the rest of her coiffure to the morning breeze with voluptuous abandon.)

In order to pass through the gate into the inner part of the forest ("un petit paysage intérieur" ["a tiny interior landscape"]), a key is necessary. A new intimacy is achieved, reflected in the components of this privileged scene, which combines the motifs of the secret garden and the earthly paradise: the wild flower beds that have sprung up on the ground cleared through the activity of the charcoal burners, the effect of a baldacchino created by the trees and, at its heart, "une mare toujours pleine, où l'eau est pure" ("a pool that is always full, and where the water is always pure.") It is an appropriate moment for the trees to present a highly phallic impression:

> Sur vos têtes les arbres pendent tous dans des attitudes diverses; c'est des troncs qui descendent en forme de boas constrictors; c'est des fûts de hêtres droits comme des colonnes grecques.

> (Above your head, the trees all lean at different angles; there are trunks that descend in the manner of boa constrictors, there are beech trunks as erect as Greek columns.")

The language used at the moment of communion—"cette poésie pénétrante les pénétrait" ("they were penetrated by this penetrating beauty")—reveals the extent to which the description of the landscape is a substitution for the consummation towards which the two protagonists are bound. The climax, however, is interrupted by the sound of the death of the greyhound, who, in keeping with the legitimist undertones of the novel, is named "Prince." It is a rehearsal for the death of the greyhound's owner. The threat of death has been hanging over the entire composition, in that Les Aigues, as the Balzacian narrator reveals, was originally known as Aigues-Vives. And if the novel begins with a celebration of the poetic charms of the landscape, the *vers* that are explicitly mentioned at the end are the worms eating away at the trees.

Ironically, *Les Paysans* ends with the periphery coming ever closer to the center, tightening its noose and expelling all life from it. Echoes of this latter figure recur throughout the composition: the traps set by the peasants; Fourchon's trade as ropemaker, together with Tonsard's "Attic" greeting to his father-in-law: "Il y a longtemps que vous auriez dû tortiller celle qui mettra fin à votre existence, car vous nous devenez beaucoup trop cher" ("It's high time you twisted the one that'll put an end to your existence, you are beginning to cost us way too much")

(94). It is Fourchon too who proclaims: "Ça vaut mieux que d'étrangler un homme!" ("That's better than strangling a man") (116). La Péchina at one point has her hands round Nicolas's Tonsard's throat, albeit in self-defense (214). Prince, as has been recalled, has his throat slit. The same figure appears in the some of the descriptive details. The likening of the trees in the forest to boa constrictors has been noted. But this is preceded by an evocation of the snake in a purely figurative forest: "les rameaux généalogiques par lesquels Gaubertin embrassait le pays comme un boa tourné sur un arbre gigantesque avec tant d'art, que le voyageur croit y voir un effet naturel de la végétation asiatique" ("the genealogical branches by which Gaubertin had the village in his clutches, in the manner of a boa that artfully wraps itself round an enormous tree, so that the traveler mistakes it for a natural effect of Asiatic vegetation") (180–81). Several variations may be combined in a single statement, as in this evocation of the despotic family connections: "Quand le despotique cousinage bourgeois fait une victime, elle est si bien entortillée ou bâillonnée, qu'elle n'ose se plaindre; elle est enveloppée de glu, de cire, comme un colimaçon introduit dans une ruche" ("When the despotic bourgeois cousinhood traps its victim, the latter is so completely entwined or muffled that it dares not to complain; it is totally ensnared by birdlime or wax, like a snail inside a hive") (186). It was doubtless only the interference of the need for verisimilitude that caused Michaud to be shot rather than strangled.

The contrast between the representation of the forest as the center of crime in the *romans de jeunesse* and its thematic counterpart in *Les Paysans* is, then, extreme. Replacing the adventure story scenario is a complex tapestry of interweaving patterns of behavior that unite private and public concerns. The antagonistic behavior of the peasants, the scheming of the local bourgeois officeholders are clear to behold. But woven into the fabric is the behavior of the landowning class. Here we need to see how the apparently incidental details of their lives and their private conduct are not in fact separate from the catastrophic nexus of forces that destroy both the forest and its hired defender. Both Mlle Laguerre and Montcornet are presented as illegitimate landowners. The "fils d'ébéniste" 's dubious progression from the Faubourg St Antoine to the Faubourg St Germain is paralleled by his inappropriate desire to go backwards from the article of completed furniture to the trees that constitute its raw material. It is, however, in the illegitimate encroachment by the park and its social norms on the forest that the demonstration finds its most telling expression. The fact that the full destructiveness of this transgression is unleashed at the moment when the forest receives its most highly charged erotic evocation is a dramatic revelation of the mature Balzac's ability to create a work in which the novelistic interest and the political demonstration are fused in a dynamic and mutually sustaining progression.

Although my concern has been with the specificity of the forest in Balzac's landscape, its complex function may also point us towards an understanding of the very originality of the Balzacian composition. Its shift from being a mere setting to constituting the point at which all the different levels in the production of meaning converge is Balzac's answer to the need for a new kind of unifying principle following his explosion of the traditional adventure story composition. The mature Balzac novel can be seen to expand to incorporate a host of embryonic novels of a more conventional kind, none of which is given either the central focus or the complete expression his early readers, at least, would have expected. In other words, its dominant characteristic is its lacunary nature. Its concern to be a representation of the plurality of dynamic forces that define the field within which the real has always to be located is dependent upon the short-circuiting of any attempt to identify the real with the fictional. At the same time, this fragmentation of the fictional machinery generates an impetus for an alternative order through form. Having lost their dominant position, the familiar elements of that machinery therefore fuse with the master didactic discourse to create compositions that are tightly unified at the level of textual poetics. In the final analysis, Balzac's multidimensional forest is to be seen as but one example of the way his novels seek to devise a new source of coherence, in an attempt to compensate for the loss of that specious but superficially alluring order exhibited by the uncritical fictional narratives that were his inherited models.

Notes

1. See Arlette Brosselin, *La Forêt bourguignonne (1660–1789)* (Dijon: Editions universitaires de Dijon, 1987).
2. Theodore Zeldin, *France 1848–1945* (Oxford: Clarendon Press, 1973–77), vol. 1, 477.

3. Ann Radcliffe, *The Romance of the Forest*, The World's Classics (Oxford and New York: Oxford University Press, 1986), 14.

4. Quoted in *Trésor de la langue française*, vol. 8 (Paris: CNRS, 1980), 1076; translations are by the author.

5. Radcliffe, *The Romance of the Forest*, 88.

6. Balzac, *Annette et le criminel* (Paris: Garnier-Flammarion, 1982), 355.

7. Ibid., 240.

8. Balzac, *Le Vicaire des Ardennes* (Paris: Les Bibliophiles de l'Originale, 1962), vol. 4, 89.

9. Ibid., vol. 2, 170.

10. Balzac, *Annette et le criminel*, 183.

11. Balzac, *Le Vicaire des Ardennes*, vol. 1, 73.

12. Balzac, *La Comédie humaine*, Bibliothèque de la Pléiade (Paris: Gallimard, 1976–80), vol. 9, 761. All subsequent parenthetical references to both *Le Curé de village* and *Les Paysans* will be to this volume.

13. A study of the function of the numerous references to wolves, both literal and figurative, within the poetics of *Les Paysans* may be regarded as having the potential to cast significant light on the generative principles at work in the Balzacian text.

14. The image of the tapestry is prominent in both novels.

15. The extracts quoted from Blondet's letter will be found between pages 50 and 64.

16. The episode from which this and subsequent quotations are taken will be found on 326ff. See Arlette Brosselin, *La Forêt bourguignonne (1660–1789)* (Dijon: Editions universitaires de Dijon, 1987).

Rewriting Reproduction: Balzac's Fantasy of Creation

DOROTHY KELLY

ONE OF BALZAC'S DEEP-SEATED FASCINATIONS, AND ONE WHICH HE repeatedly scripts in his texts, is the ability of the immaterial world to affect the material world in very real and physical ways. By linking three seemingly disconnected themes of his works and by viewing them side by side, we can see that together they illuminate the power of "immaterial" human culture—be it manifested in social, linguistic, or artistic activities—to change, even create, "material" reality. In abbreviated form, these three themes are: 1. Mesmerism and the power of thought, 2. the social construction of human identity, and 3. Balzac's revised myth of Pygmalion. What will emerge from an investigation of these three themes is a certain fantasy about man's power to change, even create, humans, specifically women.

Mesmerism and the Power of Thought

Mesmerism and Balzac's use and interpretation of the phenomenon give us important insights into his understanding of the power of the will and of thought. Although today we think of Mesmerism as some kind of charlatan medical practice, it seems pretty clear that magnetizers had discovered hypnosis. One can only imagine what effects the spectacle of hypnotism had on witnesses at the end of the eighteenth and the beginning of the nineteenth centuries. Here is a description by Mesmer himself of one of his early experiments:

> My social relations with Father Hehl, Jesuit and Professor of Astronomy at Vienna, then provided me with an opportunity of asking him to have made for me by his craftsmen a number of magnetized

> pieces, of convenient shape for application. He was kind enough to do this for me and let me have them. On 28th July 1774, after the patient had a renewal of her usual attacks [a convulsive malady . . . toothaches and earaches followed by delirium, rage, vomiting, and swooning] I applied three magnetized pieces on the stomach and both legs. Not long afterwards, this was followed by extraordinary sensations; she felt inside her some painful currents of a subtle material which, after different attempts at taking a direction, made their way towards the lower part and caused all the symptoms of the attack to cease for six hours.[1]

Mesmerism, here possibly hypnosis treating hysteria, seemed to have the power to affect real bodies.

We can see Balzac's fascination with Mesmerism in his representation of the power of the will in his fictional creations. Five important characters in *La Comédie humaine* embody a kind of superhuman power of the scientific or artistic mind that manifests itself in Mesmerist interests or abilities. The thinker, Louis Lambert, in his lost work, the *Traité de la Volonté,* although ignorant of Mesmer's works, managed to come to the same conclusions as Mesmer: "La découverte de Mesmer, si importante et si mal appréciée encore, se trouvait tout entière dans un seul développement de ce Traité, quoique Louis ne connût pas les œuvres d'ailleurs assez laconiques, du célèbre docteur suisse" ("Mesmer's discovery, so important, though as yet so little appreciated, was also embodied in a single section of this treatise, though Louis did not know the Swiss doctor's writings, which were few and brief").[2] Balthazar Claës, a cross between a chemist and an alchemist, has the magnetic fluid of the Mesmerist in his gaze: "Séduisant comme le serpent, sa parole, ses regards épanchaient un fluide magnétique, et il prodigua cette puissance de génie, ce doux esprit qui fascinait Joséphine, et il mit pour ainsi dire ses filles dans son cœur" ("There was something magnetic in his looks and tones, a fascination like that of the serpent; the genius and kindly wit that had attracted Josephine were called into play; he seemed, as it were, to take his daughters to his heart").[3]

Sarrasine, an artist, manifests several of the telltale signs of the magnetic personality, specifically in his influence over Zambinella: "Son regard flamboyant eut une sorte d'influence magnétique sur Zambinella, car le musico finit par détourner subitement la vue vers Sarrasine, et alors sa voix céleste s'altéra" ("His burning gaze had a kind of magnetic influence on La

Zambinella, for the *musicien* ended by turning his eyes towards Sarrasine, and then his celestial voice faltered").[4] Frenhofer, the artist of *Le Chef d'œuvre inconnu*, has eyes "ternisen apparence par l'âge, mais qui, par le contraste du blanc nacré dans lequel flottait la prunelle, devaient parfois jeter des regards magnétiques au fort de la colère ou de l'enthousiasme" ("eyes that age might seem to have dimmed were it not for the contrast between the iris and the surrounding mother-of-pear tints, so that it seemed as if under the stress of anger or enthusiasm there would be a magnetic power to quell or kindle in their glances").[5] And finally Raphaël de Valentin in *La Peau de chagrin*, who also writes on the human will (his *Théorie de la volonté*), completes Mesmer's work (104) and has a kind of telepathic power that Balzac equates with certain skilled observers of society (such as himself and Louis Lambert). Raphaël describes his first attempt at gambling as a manifestation of this power of observation

> . . . à laquelle j'ai dû cette espèce de pénétration qui m'a permis de saisir quelques mystères de notre double nature. Je tournais le dos à la table où se disputait mon futur bonheur . . . entre les deux joueurs et moi, il se trouvait une haie d'hommes, épaisse de quatre ou cinq rangées de causeurs; le bourdonnement des voix empêchait de distinguer le son de l'or qui se mêlait au bruit de l'orchestre; malgré tous ces obstacles, par un privilège acccordé aux passions qui leur donne le pouvoir d'anéantir l'espace et le temps, j'entendais distinctement les paroles des deux joueurs.

> (. . . to it I owe a kind of insight into certain mysteries of our double nature that I have since been enabled to penetrate. I had my back turned on the table where my future felicity lay at stake. . . . Between me and the players stood a wall of onlookers some five deep, who were chatting; the murmur of voices drowned the clinking of gold, which mingled in the sounds sent up by this orchestra; yet despite all the obstacles, I distinctly heard the words of the two players by a gift accorded to the passions, which enables them to annihilate time and space.)[6]

Furthermore, Raphaël claims to be able to use his magnetic powers to fascinate women: "Je vainquis alors la comtesse par la puissance d'une fascination magnétique" ("The countess was subdued and fascinated by my magnetic influence") (214, 1:141). These Mesmerist characters are special people who know how to send forth their thoughts as a kind of magnetic force in order to impose their will on others. Although this attempt to understand the will in terms of magnetic fluids flowing from one person to another seems quaintly archaic to us now, it is easy to understand why someone witnessing a version of hypnosis as Mesmerism in Balzac's time would naturally find a material explanation much more plausible than what we imperfectly understand today as hypnotic suggestion (the real power of words in another sense).

Now this power of the will is not merely symbolic of, say, an influential person's ability to manipulate others, but, as I emphasize, the power is quite literal and physical according to Balzac, and stems from the very magnetic fluid described by Mesmer. Balzac, and this is substantially the influence of Mesmerism, writes through Louis Lambert that thought is a physical, material substance: "Louis avait été conduit invinciblement à reconnaître la matérialité de la pensée" ("Louis, at first purely Spiritualist, had been irresistibly led to recognize the Material conditions of Mind") (304, 2:51). The Mesmerist's power to impose his will on another person means for Balzac that thought can be materially transported from one person to another, as other invisible but real things such as electricity or magnetic charges can. As Gauld describes in his massive *A History of Hypnosis,*

> The magnetic fluid of the operator and that of the patient [mingles] to establish a conjoint circulation directed by the operator's will. The operator can then move the patient's body pretty well as he can move his own, simply by willing the result he desires. The patient is now in the somnambulic state, and in extreme cases may almost become an automaton controlled by the magnetizer.[7]

In this way, the material world and the thought world are not so different for Balzac, and the influence of thought on the material world does not seem so far-fetched. Both thought and matter come from the same source as Louis Lambert claims "les principes constituants de la Matière et ceux de la Pensée . . . procèdent de la même source" ("the constituent elements of matter and those of mind, which proceed from the same source") (301; 2:43).

Since the will and thought can be transmitted physically outside the body, it is clear that in Balzac's imagination, the power of thought takes precedence over the material world. We can see this in the ability of thought to impose itself on material things:

"Une logique et simple déduction de ses principes lui avait fait reconnaître que la Volonté pouvait, par un mouvement tout contractile de l'être intérieur, s'amasser; puis, par un autre mouvement, être projetée au dehors, et même être confiée à des objets matériels" ("A simple and logical inference from these principles led him to perceive that the will might be accumulated by a contractile effort of the inner man, and the, by another effort, projected, or even imparted, to material objects") (*Louis Lambert,* 302; 2:44–45). If one knew how, one could control material reality in very literal ways. Raphaël claims that a man can "tout modifier relativement à l'humanité, même les lois de la nature" ("modify all things relatively to man, even the peremptory laws of nature") (159; 1:99). Balthazar Claës aims to use science to create reality, and succeeds however without really understanding how he does so. In this way his thoughts not only alter the real world but create the real world: "Je fais les métaux, je fais les diamants, je répète la nature! s'écria-t-il" ("I make metals, I make diamonds; all that nature does I will do") (118 1:73).[8]

It is the *peau de chagrin* that best illustrates this power of the will as it symbolizes the accomplishments of a man's wishes. When Raphaël makes his performative pact with the *peau,* all he has to do is say "I wish" and his will becomes reality. He wishes aloud for a dinner, he gets one; he expresses the wish that the *antiquaire* will fall in love with a dancer, he does. The *peau* also illustrates the intimate tie between the will and language, because it is by stating a wish, not just by wishing, that the *peau* controls the real. In fact, language changes, determines, in a sense, creates the real in a very literal way.[9] (Significantly, the type of ass from which this talisman was made has, as Balzac notes, a kind of Mesmeric eye: ". . . son œil est muni d'une espèce de tapis réflecteur auquel les Orientaux attribuent le pouvoir de la fascination" ["Its eyes are provided with a sort of burnished covering, to which the Orientals attribute the powers of fascination"] [293; 1:201].) Thus even though thc *peau de chagrin* is a fantastic object, it materially represents the material power of human thought and will. Thought can change the world through articulation, as Mesmerists seemed to show that the will could change bodies.

The Social Construction of Human Identity

Balzac's representation of the influence of the environment on humans is well-known. Madame Vauquer and her pension have long stood for this mutual influence. Yet once again, this has not been thought about literally enough, and certain of Balzac's texts show quite clearly that even though humans have a real, physical being, that being takes second place to society's definition of that being.

A closer reading of Balzac's works with this understanding of social and cultural construction in mind reveals that the issue of the construction of human identity is very far-reaching indeed. Balzac will often open the questioning of identity at the very start of his novels by refraining from giving the name of the main character for pages at a time. *La Peau de chagrin* begins with "l'inconnu" and we don't learn Raphaël's name for many more pages. *Splendeurs et misères des courtisanes* begins, significantly, with masked characters. And *Le Colonel Chabert*, perhaps the Balzac text most clearly centered on problems of human identity, begins with a description of poor Chabert as a "vieux carrick" ("old Box-coat").[10]

However, what is most interesting for our purposes here is the importance of language in determining the identity of the individual. In a humorous vein, Rastignac in *La Peau de chagrin* describes a publisher by saying "Ce n'est pas un homme, c'est un nom, une étiquette familière au public" ("He is not a man so much as a name, a label that the public is familiar with") (182; 1:116). More seriously, Raphaël later, when imagining his future humiliation at being in debt and having his name circulated, says "Notre nom, c'est nous-mêmes" ("One's name is oneself") (232; 1:155). In these two contexts, one's name focuses social identity and makes it visible to all. It is one's name that determines just who one is.

Perhaps the best example of the power of social definitions and constructions of identity, and the concomitant power of language to define us, is the Colonel Chabert. Although he is a living, breathing being, Chabert has officially been declared dead, so he goes to the lawyer, Derville, to attempt to reinstate his life. In this text, it is not just his identity that is at stake, it is his very existence: is he alive, in existence, or dead? Words are the things that keep him "dead" as he says, his death has been inscribed in official documents: "Malheureusement pour moi, ma mort est un fait historique consigné dans les *Victoires et Conquêtes*, où elle est rapportée en détail" ("Unhappily for me, my death is a historical fact, recorded in *Victoires et Conquêtes*, where it is related in full detail") (40; 13:13). Once again, language shows its power to determine human identity. And it is clear here that the social proclamation of one's existence or nonexistence is stronger than the very existence of the body. As Chabert says, first he was buried under dead people, now he is buried under words, under social documents: "J'ai été enterré sous des morts, mais maintenant je suis enterré sous des vivants, sous des actes, sous des faits, sous la société tout entière, qui veut me faire rentrer sous terre!" ("I have been buried under the dead; but now I am buried under the living, under papers, under facts, under the whole of society, which wants to shove me underground again") (48; 13:19). If human corpses weighed him down in the past, now social documents do: "Le monde social et judiciaire lui pesait sur la poitrine comme un cauchemar" ("The social and legal world weighed on his breast like a nightmare") (72; 13:34). Chabert rightly realizes that only words, documents, can restore him to "life": "Depuis le jour où je fus chassé de cette ville par les événements de la guerre, j'ai constamment erré comme un vagabond, mendiant mon pain, traité de fou lorsque je racontais mon aventure, et sans avoir ni trouvé, ni gagné un sou pour me procurer les actes qui pouvaient prouver mes dires, et me rendre à la vie sociale" ("From the day when I was turned out of that town by the events of war, I have wandered about like a vagabond, begging my bread, treated as a madman when I have told my story, without ever having found or earned a sou to enable me to recover the deeds which would prove my statements, and restore me to society") (46; 13:17–18). It is remarkable that when this text confronts the literal meaning of life and death with the social definition of life and death, the social definition prevails and Chabert, in the end, becomes a mere number, a body without an identity because social language has obliterated him: ". . . dès qu'un homme tombe entre les mains de la justice, il n'est plus qu'un être moral, une question de Droit ou de Fait, comme aux yeux des statisticiens il devient un chiffre" ("as soon as a man has fallen into the hands of justice, he is no more than a moral entity, a matter of law or of fact, just as to statisticians he has become a zero") (113; 13:62). "Je ne suis plus un homme, je suis le numéro 164" ("I am no longer a man, I am No. 164"), claims Chabert (118; 13:65).

In his dealings with Derville, Chabert has a very difficult time understanding why he should have to come to any agreement about his existence. As he says, is he alive or is he dead? He is there in body, but this literal presence cannot outweigh society's proclamations. Balzac's text shows in this case that the literal world comes second after our linguistic definition of it;

language supersedes reality. This is symbolized, in fact, in the birth and death of Chabert; an orphan raised by the state, he ends his life as a "madman" looked after by the state. Derville, one of those Balzac characters who understands society, recognizes this fact: Quelle destinée! . . . Sorti de l'hospice des Enfants trouvés, il revient mourir à l'hospice de la Vieillesse" ("What a destiny! . . . Taken out of the Foundling Hospital to die in the Infirmary for the Aged") (119; 13:66). Significantly, Chabert thinks of Napoleon as his father, he is a child of the state: "Je me trompe! j'avais un père: l'Empereur!" ("Nay, I am wrong! I had a father—the Emperor!") (53; 13:22). Symbolically, then, one's identity stems less from one's biological parents than from the social constructions that define one's place. Balzac seems to be saying that we are the children of language and society more than we are children of our parents. This is a first step on the path to imagining that the control of human identity is not a given, it is constructed by social rules and conventions, by language.

That small group of powerful Mesmerists (Raphaël, Claës, Sarrasine, Lambert, and Frenhofer) share not only a special force of the will but also a troubling ambiguity created by this very ability of language to cross over into the material world. If language creates the world, where does this process stop? What is the limit between linguistic pronouncements and the alteration of the real? Is there a limit? These five characters, who through their Mesmeric powers put into question our normal views of thought, language, and the real, who show that language is not always a secondary label placed onto the real but can sometimes be a force that determines just what reality is, manifest two kinds of ambiguity.

The first is the possibility that these characters are insane. When Sarrasine first sees Zambinella, he has an attack of madness: "Il n'applaudit pas, il ne dit rien, il éprouvait un mouvement de folie, espèce de frénésie qui ne nous agit qu'à cet âge où le désir a je ne sais quoi de terrible et d'infernal" ("He did not applaud, he spoke not at all; he gave way to a frantic movement of desire, a frenzy that at this time I can only term terrible and infernal") (40; 17:20). Frenhofer, when he learns that he has painted a massive confusion of colors on his canvas, appears to be mad and then burns his paintings and kills himself (68–69; 1:28–29). Louis Lambert's gifts put him in a dangerous place on the fringes of insanity: "Déjà ses sensations intuitives avaient cette acuité qui doit appartenir aux perceptions intellectuelles des grands poètes, et les faire souvent approcher de la folie" (296) and he becomes "mad" at the end of his life. Balthazar Claës's wife fears that he is going mad (45; 1:43) and he becomes one of Balzac's monomaniacs (198; 1:196). And there always remains the possibility that Raphaël de Valentin merely imagines that he gains powers from the *peau*. The blurring of borders between language and reality is linked in Balzac's imagination with the blurring of the borders between madness and sanity.[11]

The second ambiguity shared by several of these characters concerns their gender identity. Two of these men are described in various ways as having particularly feminine qualities. Lambert becomes "pâle et blanc comme une femme" ("as pale and white as a woman") (292; 2:17); he has a "teint de femme" ("his girlish complexion") (294; 2:23); he has a nervous system "vaporeux autant qu'une femme" ("as sensitive as a woman") (295; 2:25), and he has to be prevented from castrating himself (319). Raphaël, too, is feminine and is also associated with castration: ". . . il s'était fait chaste à la manière d'Origène, en châtrant son imagination" ("he had followed Origen's example, and had maimed and chastened his imagination") (259; 1:176). Sarrasine, of course, is associated with castration.[12] Thus the power of these men to use thought and language to control reality is associated with gender ambiguities and problems, possibly as a manifestation of anxiety about the extent to which, more specifically than general identity alone, gender identity is constructed, and what such a nonphysical identity might involve. Indeed, one remarkable sentence in Louis Lambert describes the manner in which a social construct can work to feminize a man (court etiquette feminizes the king's body): ". . . les lois de l'étiquette et des cours influent sur la moelle épinière au point de féminiser le bassin des rois, d'amollir leurs fibres cérébrales et d'abâtardir ainsi la race" ("the laws of etiquette and Court manners can act on the spinal marrow to such an extent as to affect the pelvis of kings, to soften their cerebral tissue and to degenerate the race") (293; 2:21).

Balzac's Revised Myth of Pygmalion

It is my contention that these anxieties about identity and gender, the realization of the importance of social convention and language in the construction of identity and gender, and the fantasy of controlling that construction combine in Balzac's text to give rise to a specific fantasy of the artist in his texts: a new version of Pygmalion. Through art, the male would create a perfect woman, one that would be more than just a woman, she would be his creation: "C'était plus qu'une femme, c'était un chef-d'œuvre!" ("This was more than a woman, it was a *chef-d'œuvre*!") (Sarrasine, 40; 17:20). If language can construct identity, then why should a writer not create a woman?

The general idea of Pygmalion, the ability of the artist to create the real and to create more specifically a real woman, is widespread in Balzac's works. It can take the form of the power of a painting to become real, or of the way in which the real seems to be a secondary product derived from paintings. Chabert is "un portrait de Rembrandt, sans cadre" ("a portrait by Rembrandt, without a frame") (38; 13:12) as is Frenhofer—"une toile de Rembrandt marchant silencieusement et sans cadre" ("One of Rembrandt's portraits might have stepped down from its frame to walk in an appropriate atmosphere of gloom") (39; 1:3). The old man in *La Peau de chagrin* could make Raphaël believe that "le Peseur d'or de Gérard Dow était sorti de son cadre" ("Gerard Dow's 'Money Changer' had come down from his frame") (52; 1:23). Sometimes the most remarkable women seem to be works of art that have come alive. Aquilina in *La Peau de chagrin* is "une statue colossale tombée du haut de quelque temple grec, sublime à distance, mais grossière à voir de près" ("some colossal statue fallen from the height of a Greek temple, so grand when seen afar, to roughly hewn to be seen anear") (101; 1:58).

The literal myth of Pygmalion appears sporadically throughout Balzac's narratives such as in *Sarrasine*, where the artist "dévorait des yeux la statue de Pygmalion, pour lui descendue de son piédestal" ("Sarrasine's eyes devoured this statue of Pygmalion, which had descended from its pedestal") (40; 17:20). It also appears in *Le Chef d'œuvre inconnu*, where it receives its clearest expression: "Nous ignorons le temps qu'employa le seigneur Pygmalion pour faire la seule statue qui ait marché!" ("Do we know how long Sir Pygmalion wrought at the one statue that came to life?") (52; 1:15). In this text, Frenhofer shares Pygmalion's goal of creating a living woman through his art, and he criticizes his colleague, Porbus, whose paintings do not succeed in doing this: "malgré de si louables efforts, je ne saurais croire que ce beau corps soit animé par le tiède souffle de la vie. . . . ici c'est une femme, là une statue, plus loin un cadavre" ("in spite of these praiseworthy efforts, I could never bring myself to believe that the warm breath of life comes and goes in that beautiful body. . . . here you see a woman, there a statue, and there again only a corpse") (41–42; 1:5). Indeed, Frenhofer believes that he himself has created a living, breathing woman in his painting: "ce n'est pas une toile, c'est une femme! une femme avec laquelle je pleure, je ris, je cause et pense" ("It is not a canvas, it is a woman—a woman with whom I talk. I share her thoughts, her tears, her laughter") (60; 1:21). When the two other artists look at his painting and cannot see anything, Frenhofer says: "Vous êtes devant une femme et vous cherchez un tableau" ("You are looking for a picture, and you see a woman before you") (65; 1:26). Frenhofer, the artist with the magnetic eyes, represents the fantasy of the artist who would through his own creative powers make a woman. His failure puts into question the possibility of realizing this fantasy, but it does not destroy its existence. The theme of Pygmalion finds its most complete expression in *La Peau de chagrin*. Raphaël admits that he prefers his own fantasies to the very real Pauline: "En présence de mes romanesques fantaisies, qu'était Pauline?" ("What place had Pauline among these far-fetched imaginings?") (149:1:91). He desires to create two perfect women by revising and perfecting existing women. In fact, Raphaël calls himself a "Pygmalion nouveau" ("another Pygmalion") because he wants to make "d'une vierge vivante et colorée, sensible et parlante, un marbre" ("the maiden with the hues of life and the living voice . . . a form of inanimate marble") (147; 1:90). He wants to transform, rewrite the real woman into his imaginary, artistic creation, his masterpiece.

Like Shaw's Pygmalion, Raphaël attempts to do this through education. He thinks of Pauline as his Galatea, his painting, his statue, his child: "[J]'admirais cette charmante fille comme un tableau, comme le portrait d'une maîtresse morte. Enfin, c'était mon enfant, ma statue" ("I admired the lovely girl as if she had been a picture, or as the portrait of a dead mistress; she was at once my child and my statue") (147; 1:90). The addition of the father-daughter role is interesting because it places Raphaël in the place of the parent, perhaps as a kind of rewriting of the role of the mother.

The second woman to be perfected by Raphaël is Fœdora. Before he meets her, he imagines her, creates her in his mind: "Je me créai une femme, je la dessinai dans ma pensée, je la rêvai" ("I fashioned her for myself, drew her in fancy, and dreamed of her") (154; 1:95). What he cannot bear not to have is not the real

Fœdora, but rather his imaginary construction of her: "Il ne s'agit plus de la Fœdora vivante, de la Fœdora du faubourg Saint-Honoré, mais de ma Fœdora, de celle qui est là! dis-je en me frappant le front" (" 'I am not thinking of the living Fœdora in the Faubourg Saint Honoré, but of my Fœdora here,' and I tapped my forehead") (221; 1:146).

The character, Fœdora, brings together many of the various threads important in this Balzacian fantasy, and she shares many of these with another artificially created woman (and this is an artificial creation in a very literal way through an operation), Zambinella. First, they both symbolize the combination of art and reality. Fœdora is "plus qu'une femme, c'était un roman" ("She was not merely a woman, but a romance") (161; 1:100); she is a novel here rhetorically just as she is originally Raphaël's creation. Zambinella, too, is frequently linked with the idea of art become real: "C'était plus qu'une femme, c'était un chef-d'œuvre!" ("This was more than a woman, it was a *chef-d'œuvre*!") (40; 17:20).

Furthermore, both seem to be related in some way to sculpture and to gender change (Fœdora and Zambinella both have ambiguous gender identities). Zambinella was the model for a statue of a woman which was then itself a model for a painting. As for Fœdora, Raphaël believes he understands her when he remembers the recent publication of a work of literature that had its origin in a statue: "Je pensai tout à coup au livre récemment publié par un poète, une vraie conception d'artiste taillée dans la statue de Polyclès" ("I thought all at once of a book just published by a poet, a conception of the artist, in the shape of the statue of Polycletus") (202; 1:131). The fantasy of a man's creation of a woman brings with it, understandably, anxieties about and problems of gender identity since, at the least, this act represents a change in the creative function from woman who gives birth to man who creates.

What makes Raphaël's fantasies more than just another embodiment of the myth of Pygmalion are the other two themes of the power of the will as language and the parallel theme of the power of society to construct individuals through language. And it is the fact that Raphaël does, through the *peau*, have the to power to create. The text tells of Raphaël's desire to revise Pauline, to turn her into the perfect woman, it gives him the power to do that—and finally, Pauline does become that perfect woman after he makes the pact with the *peau* (although I must make it clear here that Pauline's transformation is not attributed to the *peau* in the text. Her father merely returns rich): "Il marchait, voyant, non plus la Pauline de l'hôtel de Saint-Quentin, mais la Pauline de la veille, cette maîtresse accomplie, si souvent rêvée" ("As he walked he beheld Pauline—not the Pauline of the Hôtel Saint-Quentin, but the Pauline of last evening. Here was the accomplished mistress he had so often dreamed of") (271; 1:187).

In conclusion, let us look at the combination of our three themes and where they lead us. The power of language, the power of the will to create a new reality, and the power of an artist to create a perfect woman unite into the symbolic fantasy of man' s power to create a perfect woman through language and the will. If identity is socially and linguistically constructed, if language changes the world, if the will changes the world; man's will and language can be harnessed to fabricate perfect creatures, preferably women.

But what does this mean? It is possibly a symptom of the realization that human identity is constructed by social conventions more than one would wish. It perhaps represents the desire to take charge of the power of identity construction so as to shape human beings by the will rather than merely submitting to random or anonymous convention. It is perhaps also a fantasy of male procreation that would be superior to natural procreation. The wild ass's skin, a product of nature like a real woman, can be perfected by man. It becomes powerful after man's magic intervention, after man writes on it and changes it. Similarly, real women can be rewritten and perfected by man's artistry. Man can make a better woman than can nature, i.e., women. This is, perhaps, a power fantasy of the bourgeois male who hopes to compose for himself a perfect bourgeoise companion. As we know now about the ways in which female possibilities became more and more relegated to the private sphere in the nineteenth century, this fantasy did indeed realize itself. The open-ended question that remains concerns the extent to which our fascination with social constructionism today itself manifests this very fantasy of control which was just discernible at the beginning of the nineteenth century.

Notes

1. Maurice M. Tinterow, *Foundations of Hypnosis: From Mesmer to Freud* (Springfield, IL: Charles C. Thomas, 1970), 36–37.

2. Honoré de Balzac, *Louis Lambert* (Paris: Seuil, 1966), vol. 7; Honoré de Balzac, *Balzac's Works*, George Saintsbury, trans., (Freeport, NY: Books for Libraries Press, 1901), 2:44. Further references to Balzac's works will be included in the text after the first mention; the first reference will be to the French text, the second to the Saintsbury translation.

3. Balzac, *La Recherche de l'absolu* (Paris: Livre de Poche, 1967), 997; Saintsbury, *Balzac's Works,* 1:150.

4. Balzac, *Sarrasine* (Paris: Garnier Flammarion, 1989), 60–61; Saintsbury, *Balzac's Works,* 17:34.

5. Balzac, *Le Chef d'œuvre inconnu* (Paris: Folio, 1994), 39; Saintsbury, *Balzac's Works,* 1:3.

6. Balzac, *La Peau de chagrin* (Paris: Folio, 1974), 120; Saintsbury, *Balzac's Works,* 1:70–71.

7. Gauld, Alan, *A History of Hypnotism* (New York: Cambridge University Press, 1992), 47.

8. Don Juan and his father in "L'Elixir de longue vie" similarly use alchemy or magic, but in that case, to create life from death.

9. Louis Lambert describes the power of words and actually theorizes about it. Words, according to Lambert, do things, have power: "Tous [les verbes] sont empreints d'un vivant pouvoir qu'ils tiennent de l'âme, et qu'ils y restituent par les mystères d'une action et d'une réaction merveilleuse entre la parole et la pensée" (287).

10. Honoré de Balzac, *Le Colonel Chabert* (Paris: Folio, 1974), 91; Saintsbury, *Balzac's Works,* 13:1.

11. For Chabert, who shows the socially constructed nature of identities, Charenton always lurks in the distance as a possibility for him and, indeed, he becomes "mad" in the end.

12. I explore gender identity in *Sarrasine* and in *La Peau de chagrin* in two previous books, *Fictional Genders* (Lincoln: University of Nebraska Press, 1989), and *Telling Glance* (New Brunswick, NJ: Rutgers University Press, 1992).

Playing with the *Coup de foudre*: The Subversion of Drag in *Sarrasine* and *The Crying Game*

OWEN HEATHCOTE

"[Le] sujet profond de *Sarrasine* est le contraste entre deux formes de sexualité."

—Pierre Citron

"Despite its play with sexual ambivalence, the tale of *The Crying Game* finally endorses a classic and familiar hetero-gendered script."

—Rosemary Hennessy

I

ALTHOUGH MORE THAN ONE HUNDRED AND FIFTY YEARS SEPARATE Honoré de Balzac's novella Sarrasine (1830) and Neil Jordan's film *The Crying Game* (1992), there are a number of structural and thematic parallels between them. In both works an ostensibly heterosexual male has a *coup de foudre* attraction for what he believes to be a young woman singer. In *Sarrasine*, this singer is discovered to be a boy *castrato*, and, in *The Crying Game*, she is revealed to be to be a male transvestite. In each case the *coup de foudre* is provoked by an ostensible woman, seen at a distance. In *The Crying Game*, the IRA volunteer Fergus first sees Dil in a photograph taken from the wallet of his prisoner, Jody. The separation is accentuated by their being in hiding in Ireland while she is at liberty in London. In *Sarrasine*, the eponymous Sarrasine first sees La Zambinella singing on stage at the Rome opera house: although Sarrasine is close to her, he, too, is separated from her in his confined seat, while she has "cette voix agile, fraîche et de timbre argenté, souple comme un fil auquel le moindre souffle d'air donne une forme"[1] ("this agile voice, fresh and silvery in timbre, supple as a thread shaped by the slightest breath of air") (239). Since shortly after the first time Fergus sees Dil in the flesh, Dil is also onstage in a London club, both "women" are first seen by their eventual prospective lovers when *in performance*. Both La Zambinella and Dil are first seen and heard not only when they are cross-dressed but also when they are performing as cross-dressed artistes. Rather than describing Dil for what she might be, Colin the barman tells the still ignorant Fergus: "She's . . . on."[2] From the outset, then, the *coup de foudre* is associated not only with transvestism but also with transvestism as an act performed before an appreciative, and, apart from Sarrasine and Fergus themselves, initiated, audience.

A further parallel between the two works is that the *coup de foudre* is accompanied by, or associated with, violence. There is, first of all, the violence of confinement: when Fergus first sees Dil's photograph, Jody is bound, head covered, on his seat, and Fergus is repeatedly ordered to confine himself to being his guard. When Sarrasine first hears La Zambinella, he, too, is confined to his seat, "pressé par deux *abbati* notablement gros" ("squeezed between two notably fat abbots") (1060, 237). Although close to La Zambinella, Sarrasine is also paralyzed as "l'amoureux transi" ("a lover transfixed"). Violence further characterizes Sarrasine's reactions to her singing: "Quand la Zambinella chanta, ce fut un délire . . . [Sarrasine] éprouvait un mouvement de folie, espèce de frénésie qui ne nous agite qu'à cet âge où le désir a je ne sais quoi de terrible et d'infernal" ("When La Zambinella sang, the effect was delirium. . . . [Sarrasine] experienced an impulse of madness, a kind of frenzy which overcomes us only when we are at the age when desire has something frightening and infernal about it") (1061, 238). Her later performances provoke even more violent reactions: "cette voix attaquait si vivement son âme qu'il laissa plus d'une fois échapper de ces cris involontaires arrachés par les délices convulsives trop rarement donnés par les passions humaines" ("this voice attacked his soul so vividly that several times he gave vent to involuntary cries torn from him by convulsive feelings of pleasure which are all too rarely vouchsafed by human passions") (1061, 239). Such is the violence of Sarrasine's reaction that he is obliged to leave the theater. Such, moreover, is the violence of his attraction to La Zambinella that he contrives her abduction and, arousing the jealousy of her protector, the Cardinal Cicognara, is murdered at his command. In the case of *The Crying Game*, the violence of abduction is even greater, with the British soldier, Jody, a prisoner of the IRA. Although Fergus, his guard, allows him to escape being executed, Jody is run over by a British Saracen and the IRA hideaway is burnt down. Fergus, moreover, is obliged to leave not just a theater (as is Sarrasine), but his "job" and his country. Reneging on the IRA, he departs for London, where he becomes involved in multiple acts of violence—the violence of Dil's boyfriend, Dave, and renewed terrorism from the IRA leading to the murder of his former lover, Jude. In the case of both *Sarrasine* and *The Crying Game*, the *coup de foudre* is, therefore, associated with both personal and interpersonal violence, with the violence of imprisonment or abduction and with the violence of multiple murder and death.

The aim of this essay will be to examine this relationship between cross-dressing as gender in performance and the violence of the *coup de foudre*, its context and its aftermath. Do these various acts of violence expose the constructedness of sexual identities, whether male or female, or do they rather result from an inevitable binary distinction between men and women which both book and film, despite their apparent gender-bending, simply reinforce and confirm? Or—and this may be a very different question—does this violence suggest that heterosexual desire is grounded in an unavowed homosociality or even homosexuality? In other words, is drag subversive, suggesting that sexual identities are indeterminate and indeterminable? Or is drag itself being subverted to expose a homosexuality *within* heterosexuality? In either scenario, the violence of the *coup de foudre* may be seen to flout convention, whether that of biological sexual identity or that of heterosexuality.

A final section of the essay will assess and compare the radical potential of the cross-dressing in the two works. It will be interesting to see, for example, whether the *novella* of 1830 is more or less sexually radical than the film of 1992. For however seemingly subversive of gender identities and of compulsory heterosexuality, the most vicious violence is, as has been repeatedly noted, associated with the female (Jude the IRA terrorist in *The Crying Game*) and with the sexually ambivalent (the jealous, vengeful cardinal in *Sarrasine*). As critics have noted repeatedly, in these and other respects, therefore, both book and film may reinforce the very stereotypes they elsewhere demolish. The danger therefore is that they may only *play* with the violence of the *coup de foudre* and with the subversion of drag.

II Drag as Subversion

With the proliferation of research in the area of gender, sexuality, and the body, cross-dressing, transvestism, and drag have been the object of increasing critical attention. One of the productive confusions surrounding drag, transvestism, and cross-dressing is the very existence of these different terms and their different connotations for different users and audiences. Whereas drag is often associated with camp, queens, and gay female impersonation which for some demonstrate "a virulent misogyny and a cruel travesty of the feminine,"[3] cross-dressing, gender-b(l)ending, and "gender-fuck" emphasize, according to Bullough and Bullough, "a confusion of costume whereby the illusion of assuming the opposite sex is not intended to convince the viewer of authenticity but to suggest ambiguity" (Bullough and Bullough, 246). The overlaying of the more corrosive edge of other terms such as "gender-bending," "male femaling," and "transgendering" on the erstwhile more conventional "drag" has enabled drag to come out of the closet, both in practice and in theory. By this I mean that the "drag" phenomenon is today the source of a radical reappraisal. As Carole-Anne Tyler remarks in her careful conclusion to "Boys Will Be Girls: The Politics of Gay Drag," "[t]he play of identification and disidentification in drag could be the very condition of autocritique."[4]

Whatever the term used, critics are agreed about two aspects of drag, cross-dressing, or transvestism. The first, as Bullough and Bullough state, is that "cross-dressing and gender-blending have been ubiquitous throughout human history" (Bullough and Bullough, 360). Moreover, as Richard Ekins writes in *Male Femaling*, "[p]eople often think that male femaling is a rather minority and unimportant matter. In fact, it is both widespread and fundamental to each of our lives."[5] The second, as Marjorie Garber has eloquently shown, is that the transvestite is habitually "that which is looked *through*, rather than *at*, in contemporary criticism and culture."[6] In her *Vested Interests: Cross-Dressing and Cultural Anxiety,* Garber argues that "the phantom appearance of the transvestite (. . .) marks a category crisis *elsewhere*" (Garber, 233). As she explains, "the borderline between gender and sexuality so important to much recent feminist and gender theory is one of the many boundaries tested and queried by the transvestite. The cultural effect of transvestism is to destabilize all such binaries: not only 'male' and 'female,' but also 'gay' and 'straight,' and 'sex' and 'gender.' This is the sense—the radical sense—in which transvestism is a 'third' " (Garber, 133). In her earlier, celebrated *Gender Trouble*, Judith Butler had also pointed to the radical character of drag, although without Garber's wealth of documented examples. Butler asserts that "*[i]n imitating gender, drag implicitly reveals the imitative structure of gender itself—as well as its contingency.*"[7] Although in her later *Bodies That Matter*, Butler says, "there is no necessary relation between drag and subversion" she still argues that "drag is subversive to the extent that it reflects on the imitative structure by which hegemonic gender is itself produced and disputes heterosexuality's claim on naturalness and originality" (125). While regretting that Jennie Livingston's film of the gay street gangs of Harlem and their drag balls, *Paris is Burning* (1990), does not thematize Livingston's cinematic desire within the film itself,[8] Butler nevertheless contends that it may well open up a distance "*between* that hegemonic call to normativizing gender and its critical appropriation" (137). Thus even if Butler feels that Livingston's camera "trades on the masculine privilege of the disembodied gaze" and encourages the fetishization of the body in drag, she also argues that "[t]he film attests to the painful pleasures of eroticizing and miming the very norms that wield their power by foreclosing the very reverse-occupations that the children nevertheless perform" (137). According to Butler, then, for drag to be read as self-conscious and constructed "gender trouble," it does not have to be foregrounded by a similar self-reflexivity in the medium of its representation. Drag can be sexually radical even if it is filmed and framed "straight."

What Butler does not, however, emphasize about the elaborately prepared drag competitions shown in *Paris is Burning* is that the cross-dressers are consciously constructing their outfits and their performances for enthusiastic aficionados. However short-lived, derivative, and dangerous each performer's self-creation as an indisputably glamorous star is, so warmly endorsed by the audience that the performers become their own construction: they are, momentarily, their own performance. Their reward is that they not only *pass* as, but also *are*, what they have created. It is for this reason that Livingston's camera work cannot and should not be self-reflexive. Any distancing by the filmmaker's lens would distract from the performers' self-reconstruction and make it less convincing. The role of the spectators is to confirm rather than to question the realization of a dream, a fantasy. For while cross-dressing in *Paris is Burning* epitomizes the ultimate in theatrical performance, the emphasis is on cross-dressing to achieve the reality of a performance rather than on performance to stage the ambiguities of cross-dressing. In a way that neither Butler nor Garber fully acknowledge, cross-dressing here is a means to an end, and on such occasions it is legitimate to look *through* as well as, and possibly more than, at transvestism.

Despite the cultural ubiquity of drag, transvestism, and cross-dressing, what is striking about reactions to *Sarrasine* and even to *The Crying Game* is that they have rarely been analyzed for their presentation of the complexities of transvestism, whether looked through or at. Although in *Sarrasine* it is the sight of La Zambinella no longer embellished by "les prestiges d'une toilette qui, à cette époque, était assez engageante" ("the glamour of a style of dress which in those days was quite attractive") (1060, 237) but "habillée en homme" ("dressed like a man") (1072, 250) that makes Sarrasine ask questions which reveal "par quelles créatures les rôles de femme sont remplis dans les États du pape" ("the creatures who sing female roles in the Papal States") (1072, 250), the role of cross-dressing in the novella has barely figured in *Sarrasine* criticism. Whereas before Barthes' *S/Z*, the work was relatively ignored, thereafter critics reacted as much to Barthes as to Balzac.[9] They thus followed Barthes in reviewing *Sarrasine* as a protocol for reading rather than a source of meanings whose potency Barthes in any case blocked by foregrounding a *Sarrasine* inscribed by castration.[10] Although Michel Serres has sought to provide an alternative to Barthes's emphasis on castration, circularity and closure by exploring the artistic spaciousness and sexual comprehensiveness of the work—symbolized for Serres by the panharmonicon and the hermaphrodite—neither panharmonicon nor hermaphrodite are any more present in Balzac's actual text than Barthes's castration and the word "castrato." Similarly, in analysis of *The Crying Game*, cross-dressing has been less an issue than might be expected. While there have been rich and suggestive critiques of Jordan's apparent endorsement of essentialism—whether racial, sexual, national, or even animal (prompted by the twice-told parable of the scorpion and the frog)[11]—and, as will be seen in the next section, of the heterosexism or hetero-genderism of the relations between Dil and Fergus, there has been relatively little interrogation of Dil as a cross-dressing performer.[12] No doubt because they thought it would be politically incorrect to wonder why Dil should cross-dress, critics have followed Fergus's lead in not asking. No doubt because, once Roman customs were understood, it was assumed castrati had to cross-dress for at least some of their roles, again critics have not asked the question. That La Zambinella and Dil cross-dress has, therefore, with surprisingly few exceptions, been taken *as read*. It is, however, now necessary to ask what is being elided by these omissions.

As a number of critics have pointed out, the original version of *Sarrasine* was divided into two named chapters: *Les Deux portraits* and *Une passion d'artiste*. Although it is not entirely clear which two portraits of the first chapter are being referred to—there is also one of Mme de Lanty—it is plausible that they are the two "versions" or two "ages" of La Zambinella. The first portrait would therefore be that of the ancient, emaciated "créature sans nom" ("this creature for which the human language had no name") (1051, 229) whose "multitude de rides" ("multitude of circular wrinkles") contrasts with his "coquetterie féminine" ("feminine coquetry") making him "une espèce d'idole japonaise" ("a sort of Japanese idol") (1051, 230). The second portrait is, literally, a picture, of "Adonis étendu sur une peau de lion" ("Adonis lying on a lion's skin"), "trop beau," according to Mme de Rochefide, "pour être un homme" ("too beautiful for a man") and indeed painted from "une statue de femme" ("a statue of a woman")—the statue of La Zambinella sculpted by the amorous Sarrasine (1054, 232). What is interesting about this description is not just the sexual ambivalence of the old man and of the picture but the fact that no one in this highly inquisitive, gossipy society and not even the especially curious Mme de Rochefide, has drawn parallels between the sexual ambivalence of the portrait and the sexual ambivalence of the elderly relative of the Lanty. Why has no one, apparently, made the connection? One reason is undoubtedly that the sexual ambivalence, though common to both old man and portrait, is *different* in the two cases. With the old man, sexual ambivalence is epitomized in *dress* whereas in the portrait sexual ambivalence is in *anatomy*. With his extravagant lace *jabot*, enormous but tasteless diamond, elaborate watch-chain, rings, and earrings, this "être bizarre" ("strange creature") (1052, 229) is, according to Per Nykrog, "a withered and glassy-eyed old transvestite dolled up and painted in a disgustingly grotesque way."[13] In the portrait, sexual ambivalence is conveyed, as we know from Girodet's *Endymion*, by a mixture of beauty, subdued lighting, and a pose which disguise the genital area. By juxtaposing the possible transvestite and the possible androgyne or even hermaphrodite, Balzac confuses the Lanty society about the link between old man and portrait and makes the narration of *Sarrasine* necessary. At the same time, and more importantly here, sexual ambiguity is shown to be *both* a matter of biology *and* performance. In the way he dresses, the old man *becomes what he performs*. At the same time, because he is also not only androgynous but a castrato, he can be said to *perform what he is*. The issue is, however, complicated by the fact that the sexual ambiguity of the body is in *representation*—in a picture—whereas the sexual ambiguity of dress is "in life"—the actual old man. If anatomy is only perceived through the chiaroscuro of art and the transvestite's clothes are real to the point of embarrassment, then *Sarrasine* makes both dress and body sexually undecidable and Balzac anticipates Butler in showing the unresolvable reciprocal contamination of sexuality and gender. As if these complexities were not enough, this undecidability is also read in different ways by different people in different places and different times. As Nykrog observes, the story tells about how a "central object, which barely exists *en soi* is seen by and reacted to by a number of observers" (441). If the very problematization of categories and categorization is itself relative, then, as Sandy Petrey has argued: "the castrato makes meaning impossible and leaves realism indistinguishable from postmodernism."[14] Paris is indeed burning and not least the Paris of 1830.

The issue is thus indeed complicated by the fact that the transvestite is also a castrato and the castrato is also a transvestite. Per Nykrog reminded us that the trail of *Sarrasine*'s plot leads "to a boy being maimed" (440), to a body which has indeed been constructed, or perhaps more accurately, deconstructed, a fact that has eluded most critics. That neither 1830 Parisians nor the young French Sarrasine in Rome can *see* the anatomy of La Zambinella and his youthful portrait—he would, after all, still have a penis, a factor which is recognized by Serres if not Barthes[15]—again means that anatomy is not self-evident but dependent on performance and, moreover, on where and when that performance takes place. As if the construction of biology were not enough, that construction itself varies according to a given audience's knowledge and preparedness to accept the conventions of the performance. As with the drag artistes of *Paris is Burning*, collusion between performers and viewers can change the perception of what perhaps we should perhaps no longer call transvestism. For the irony is that while La Zambinella's cross-dressing becomes devastating for Sarrasine who was unaware of it, it is a matter of little importance to those who were. While La Zambinella's Roman audience can, in a sense, see *through* his transvestism and enjoy his music, Sarrasine, once he knows, can see *only* his transvestism and, faced with Sarrasine's hostile stare, La Zambinella's singing collapses. Ironically, then, whereas those in the know allow the illusion to become a reality, the one for whom it was real succumbs when faced with the illusion. In *Sarrasine*, then, drag is both subversive *and subverted*. La Zambinella's drag certainly subverts Sarrasine since his whole worldview collapses once he knows the truth. At the same time drag is also subverted, since the Romans, like the audiences of *Paris is Burning*, take it and want it as real. Indeed perhaps the ultimate subversion of drag is not only to subvert the norm but to normalize the already subverted.

Given that one of Neil Jordan's most celebrated films is *Interview with the Vampire* (1994), it is interesting that one of the analogies Balzac uses to try to describe the old Zambinella is, precisely, that of the vampire: "Sans être précisément un vampire, une goule, un homme artificiel (. . .) il participait (. . .) de toutes ces natures anthropomorphiques" ("Although not a vampire, a ghoul, or an artificial man . . . he had something of all these anthropomorphic natures about him") (1047, 225). For Jordan, what characterizes the vampires is that they are *made* what they are—Louis (Brad Pitt) and Celia (Kirsten Dunst) are not born as vampires, but take on the vampire's nature when they swallow another's blood—and once *made* they cannot be *unmade*. As Lestat (Tom Cruise) cries: "You are what you are" and, later: "Do what it is in your nature to do." Lestat, Louis, and Celia thus spend their time searching out "their own kind" and, with increasing desperation, fulfilling the instincts of their own reconstructed but indestructible bodies. Like the scorpion of the parable in *The Crying Game*, the vampires cannot help killing because it is in their nature. At the same time, they know that their cultivated nature is both unnatural and countercultural. For the vampire's nature and its reception also seem to depend on place, period, and circumstances—common in certain times and virtually nonexistent in the Paris of the film. Of Jordan's vampires, too, then, one may soon be able to say: "On n'y fait plus de ces malheureuses créatures" ("They no longer create these unfortunate creatures") (1075, 254). The paradox of identity is that it derives from a mixture of anatomy and culture the proportions and the reception of which depend as much on the viewer as on their creator, whether Lestat in *Interview with the Vampire* or le prince Chigi in *Sarrasine* (1072).

At first, or perhaps rather at second glance, it seems that identity in *The Crying Game* is attributable to nature rather than to culture. Once Dil is known to be a male transvestite, then "she" is seen to be a male dressed up and disguised as a female. The woman is really a man. This, the US distributors claimed, was the film's great secret. As Jane Giles has noted, the film's unexpected box office success was at least partly due to its US distributors billing it (preemptively) as "the movie that everyone's talking about, but no-one is giving away its secrets."[16] That the "secret" of the film was the presence or absence of a penis seems to be confirmed by the foregrounding of the penis of her boyfriend, Jody. Hands tied behind his back, Jody must enlist the help of his guard Fergus to take out and hold his "piece of meat" when he needs to urinate. The fact that identity depends on the presence or absence of a penis—on the ability to urinate standing up—also seems to be confirmed by the twice-told parable of the scorpion and the frog, which suggests there is an essential nature underlying cultural or local circumstances: although the frog is helping the scorpion cross a river, the latter cannot help stinging and killing its bearer because it's "in [its] nature." This parable seems to confirm the notion of an innate, biological identity: if Fergus is "naturally kind" his political involvement is a mask he can later, naturally, discard. If Dil is a biological male, his transvestism is also a (mere) mask which is ultimately immaterial to him as a *person*. Given that the parable is recounted at both the beginning and end of the film, the framing of *The Crying Game*, like that of *Sarrasine* (framed by a pensive narrator and listener), can be seen as circular and closed. As Sharon Willis points out, the *reprise* of the parable "suggests that the story's meaning remains unchanged by the film's progress":[17] human nature, like animal (and vampire) nature, is immutable. The IRA, represented by Jude and Peter, is "naturally" sadistic. In the case of Dil, layers of masquerade can be peeled away to reveal first her maleness and then her humanity. Indeed, as the situations of both Fergus and Dil attest, transvestism and gender-bending dissolve before man's humanity to man. To quote again from Sharon Willis, this has enabled many critics to "follow the film by presenting the love story as its overarching meaning" (108). By this token, the drag of *The*

Crying Game subverts little or nothing but is, rather, coopted to convey a conventional, hegemonic message.

On the other hand, a number of factors unsettle this recuperative reading. Firstly, the sexuality of Dil is less univocal than the above comments would suggest in that, paradoxically, the revelation of her hidden penis throws her cultivated femininity into dramatic relief; it accentuates her visibility as female. Moreover, as Willis has shown, "[b]ecause we never see the whole body here—Dil's head and penis are never in frame together—we may retain a picture of Dil as a woman" (103). Secondly, the femaleness of Dil is all the easier to accept since that is how she is as a hairdresser and, more important, how she is for the audience at the Metro club. As in *Sarrasine* and *Paris is Burning*, perceptions depend on time, place, and circumstances and in all three works the complicity between performer and audience can create and sustain a gender identity in performance which can coexist with, and even supplant, a seemingly contradictory biology. In this way, cross-dressing can overlay and subvert anatomy. It may now be clearer why no one, including Fergus, actually *asks* why Dil should cross-dress: the question seems unnecessary because she cannot be imagined as other than she is. It is not her male genitalia which define her. That is not her momentous secret. If Dil has a secret it is that not that he is a man who dresses as a woman but that she is a woman with male genitalia. As Rosemary Hennessy writes: "Both before and after we know Dil is not female, she nonetheless remains a real woman" (10). Perhaps this is what Fergus eventually senses or knows—unlike Sarrasine who, once he realizes La Zambinella has a penis, recoils in horror and stupefaction. By being—and performing—a woman-man rather than a man-woman, Dil releases the full subversive power of drag while again, in a sense, making it irrelevant. Since it is not only her norm, but that of the society of the Metro, and, eventually, also that of Fergus, she shows that she has *crossed*. As Amy Zilliax writes: "As the material site of convergence for identities coerced from without and asserted from within, Dil's body becomes a site of contradiction in the world of the film, a sign, which while it may not overturn the binary terms that govern it, recombines those terms in ways the system cannot fully describe" (48). Indeed, for drag to be both subversive and subverted, those binaries need to be acknowledged, but only as fleetingly and as confusingly as the revelation of that so-called secret.

III Homosexuality in Drag?

It would seem from the above comments on sexuality in *Sarrasine* and *The Crying Game* that both works unsettle and redistribute conventional distinctions between sex (as essence) and gender (as construct). Both *Sarrasine* and *The Crying Game* show that anatomy itself is an unreliable guide to sex. La Zambinella's body has itself been sexually reconstructed by le prince Chigi and a portrait of "her" suggests he/she is an androgyne.[18] Thus although she still has a penis, and although Sarrasine recoils from her when he no longer sees her as a woman, he does not know in what category to place him/her: "Tu n'es rien. Homme ou femme je te tuerais!" ("You are nothing. If you were a man or a woman, I would kill you") (1074, 252). For Sarrasine, La Zambinella's biological ambiguity will, moreover, affect his perception of all women: "Monstre! Toi qui ne peux donner la vie à rien, tu m'as dépeuplé la terre de toutes ses femmes" ("Monster! You who can give life to nothing. For me, you have wiped women from the earth") (1074, 252). So corrosive has La Zambinella's effect been on the biological separation of men and women that, for Sarrasine, women as a "real" category no longer exist: "Sans cesse je penserai à cette femme imaginaire en voyant une femme réelle" ("I shall forever think of this imaginary woman when I see a real woman") (1074, 252). As has been seen, biology and identity are similarly unhooked in *The Crying Game*. If Dil remains a woman even after she has been shown to have a penis, then what is the value of the biological distinction between men and women? Although Fergus sees the situation in rather less dramatic terms than Sarrasine, it is no longer clear whether he is in a relationship with a man or a woman. As in *Paris is Burning*, the effective deployment of drag has evacuated anatomy of its traditional taxonomical and identificatory power.

Given the ineffectiveness of biological binaries to categorize La Zambinella and Dil, it is tempting to resort to notions of "otherness" and even "thirdness" to explain both characters and the attraction Sarrasine and Fergus feel for them. What better here than the notion of the "third sex," of hidden or latent homosexuality to explain the *coups de foudre* which overwhelm Sarrasine and Fergus? Thus for Pierre Citron "[l]e destin de Sarrasine est celui d'un être dont les tendances sont inconsciemment homosexuelles"[19] ("Sarrasine's destiny is to be one whose inclinations are unconsciously homosexual"). If Sarrasine reacts so violently to the "monster" that is La Zambinella, it because his attraction to La Zambinella is a revelation of himself: "tout amour devient impossible pour Sarrasine, il est assimilé au "monstre" que son aberration l'a conduit à aimer"[20] ("all love becomes impossible for Sarrasine: he becomes one with the monster his aberration has led him to love"). The same observation applies to Fergus. When he reacts almost as violently as Sarrasine to the revelation that his would-be lover is a transvestite, Fergus' "nauseous fear emanates," according to Mark Simpson, "from his own repressed homosexuality" (173). Both La Zambinella and Dil are already in homosexual relationships—La Zambinella with her "protector," the Cardinal Cicognara, and Dil with both Jody and the violent Dave—and Sarrasine and Fergus simply replace them. Simpson argues that "Fergus and Jody fall very much in love with one another" (171), and, as a number of critics have pointed out, Fergus is haunted throughout his developing relationship with Dil by "the dreamy icon of Jody in his white flannels."[21] Just as Fergus replaces Jody and expels Dave, so will Sarrasine threaten the Cardinal. For why else would the Cardinal have Sarrasine killed if it is not out of jealousy? La Zambinella may well have played along with Sarrasine "pour plaire à [s]es camarades, qui voulaient rire" ("to please [her] friends, who wanted to laugh") (1073, 251) but the Cardinal "qui avait épié du coin de l'œil la direction que prit le regard de son protégé" ("who had glanced out of the corner of his eye to see what had attracted his protégé's attention") (1072, 250) and sees that it is Sarrasine who has such a devastating effect on the singer, is in no doubt: here is a rival to be eliminated. What Jane Giles writes of *The Crying Game*, for example, that "homosexuality is [. . .] the plot line that dare not speak its name" (64), could therefore apply equally well to *Sarrasine*. This homosexual appeal is, moreover, not restricted to the couples already mentioned but, in both works, characterizes a whole community, even a whole society. *The Crying Game's* Dil is, for Crewe, "posited as the universal object of desire,"[22] surrounded by admiring or desiring men. In *Sarrasine*, likewise, La Zambinella is the star: "Quand la Zambinella chanta, ce fut un délire" ("When La Zambinella sang, the effect was delirium") (1061, 238).

It is interesting that those critics who see *Sarrasine* and *The Crying Game* as works about repressed homosexuality also pronounce on the appropriateness of this repression. For Pierre Citron, *Sarrasine* marks the collision of "deux univers, celui d'un passé coupable et celui d'un présent rassurant et ouvert"[23] ("two universes, one of a guilt-ridden past and the other of an open and reassuring present"), showing a Balzac emerging from youthful homosexual (or, as Citron would have it, "ambisexual") tendencies into "[une] période de fixation sexuelle, d'insertion dans la société, de distance prise par rapport à la jeunesse, mais aussi de lucidité et d'interrogation créatrice"[24] ("a period of settled sexuality, social integration, and growing away from his youth, but at the same time one of self-awareness and creative questioning"). For Citron, then, *Sarrasine* represents a watershed between "le noir et le froid qui règnent autour de l'hôtel de Lanty") ("the gloom and cold pervading the hôtel de Lanty") and "la figure de la chaleur et de la vie" of "l'amour licite" (1977, 1041) ("the figure of warmth and light" of "legitimate love"), between the sexual confusion and rebelliousness of the early Balzac and the solidity of his heterosexual maturity. Critics of *The Crying Game* have taken the opposite stance, deploring the pusillanimity of the representation of homosexual desire, activity, and fulfillment. What has been particularly regretted has been Jordan's recycling of certain stereotypes such as the gay hairdresser[25] and the gay transvestite[26] and his failure to "interrogate a reactionary equation between sexual and racial difference."[27] Not only does Jordan "use black actors to play characters whose sex is ambiguous," as he did in *Mona Lisa* (1986), but he also fails to exploit the imperialist implications of this portrayal by turning a gay black male into "the dreamy icon of Jody in his white flannels," thus displacing "a potential countercolonial affiliation onto the homoerotics of sport."[28] Also regretted is the emphasis on the (unseen) penis of Jody and the (flaccid) penis of Dil, and the failure to mention that of Fergus "as if there were nothing to be learned from Fergus's organ and everything to be learned from Dil's."[29] This critique of homosexuality without homosex culminates in analyses of the final scene of Dil visiting Fergus in prison, when "the two can speak only through the security glass that literalizes the safe separation and sexual deferral"[30] and when, for Simpson, "Dil's virtue and Fergus' heterosexuality are preserved like butterflies under glass."[31] It seems from all this, then, that whereas for Citron, sexual ambiguity can be rich and provocative, sexual ambiguity in *The Crying Game* is seen as an unwelcome deferral. Difference is no longer "différance" but good old difference with an "e" once more. While there should be no partition between Dil and Fergus, there is certainly a partition, and not a glass one, between heterosexuality and homosexuality.

It is at this point that it will be useful to return to Marjorie Garber's insistence that transvestism represents a category crisis whose "cultural effect is," as we have seen, "to destabilize all such binaries: not only 'male' and 'female,' but also 'gay' and 'straight,' and 'sex' and 'gender.' This is the sense—the radical sense—in which transvestism is a 'third.' " If the previous section has shown that "sex" and "gender" and "male" and "female" are indeed unsettled and redistributed in both *Sarrasine* and *The Crying Game* why should that other binary, homosexuality and heterosexuality, have to be preserved so untouched and intact, with heterosexuals embracing on one side of the partition and homosexuals on the other? If transvestites subvert definition by anatomy, what does Simpson mean by finding in *The Crying Game* "a *male heterosexual* variety of homosexuality: desiring 'women' who have penises" (171)? If transvestites transgender gender, how can Hennessy argue that the film's "sexual ambivalence nonetheless turns out to be a strictly hetergendered affair"?[32] And why should Citron claim that "[L]e sujet profond de *Sarrasine* est le contraste entre deux formes de sexualité"[33] ("the profound subject of *Sarrasine* is the contrast between two forms of sexuality"), when these two forms are manifestly confused and combined in the youthful androgyny and the aged transvestism of dressed and cross-dressed (but which is which?) [La] Zambinella? In each case critics seem to wish to superimpose heterosexuality or homosexuality on a sex and a gender which are too mobile and too chameleon-like to offer an appropriate foundation. What, then, are the implications of transvestism's destabilization of sex and gender for homosexuality/heterosexuality in *Sarrasine* and *The Crying Game*?

One way to begin to answer this question is to look once again at the violence of Sarrasine's *coup de foudre* for La Zambinella. Her effect on him is twofold. First of all he admires "la beauté idéale de laquelle il avait jusqu'alors cherché ça et là les perfections dans la nature, en demandant à un modèle, souvent ignoble, les rondeurs d'une jambe accomplie; à tel autre, les contours du sein; à celui-là les blanches épaules (. . .) sans rencontrer jamais sous le ciel froid de Paris les riches et suaves créations de la Grèce antique" ("the ideal beauty he had hitherto sought in life, seeking in one often unworthy model the roundness of a perfect leg; in another, the curve of a breast; in another, white shoulders; . . . without ever having encountered under the cold Parisian sky the rich, sweet creations of ancient

Greece") (1060, 238). Secondly, her voice magnetizes him: "Une puissance presque diabolique lui permetttait de sentir le vent de cette voix, de respirer la poudre embaumée dont ces cheveux étaient embaumés, de voir les méplats de ce visage, d'y compter les veines bleues qui en nuançaient la peau satinée" ("An almost diabolical power enabled him to feel the breath of this voice, to smell the scented powder covering her hair, to see the planes of her face, to count the blue veins shadowing her satin skin") (1061, 239). What is striking about these descriptions, as other critics have noted,[34] is that La Zambinella presents Sarrasine with the work of art he craved: "C'était plus qu'une femme, c'était un chef-d'œuvre!" ("This was more than a woman, this was a masterpiece!") (1061, 238). What has, however, been less noticed is the fact that La Zambinella is a work of art whose elements and ingredients Sarrasine *recognizes and remembers*. In making the *coup de foudre* an act whose violence derives from repetition, Sarrasine himself reactivates a familiar Balzacian topos whereby love is seen as a reenergizing of memory. As Claudine du Bruel writes in *Un prince de la bohème*, "L'espoir est une mémoire qui désire"[35] ("Hope is a memory which desires") and, famously, as we read in *La Femme de trente ans*: "En se rendant chez la marquise, Charles obéissait à l'un de ces textes préexistants dont notre expérience et les conquêtes de notre esprit ne sont, plus tard, que les développements sensibles"[36] ("When going to see the marquise, Charles was prompted by one of those texts already in existence, for which our experience and the triumphs of our mind are but the later, material development"). Since the *coup de foudre* has no unique essence but is a combination of fixation and process, it lends itself to repeated reconstruction in further combinations of art, desire, and memory. In the privacy of his own studio, Sarrasine can assemble or, perhaps more accurately since he had already imagined their combination, *reassemble* La Zambinella: "il voulut tromper son impatience et son délire en dessinant La Zambinella de mémoire" ("he tried to appease his impatience and his delirium by drawing La Zambinella from memory") (1062, 239). In thus reworking La Zambinella, Sarrasine shows two crucial things. First of all he shows that the object of sexual desire is consciously constructed and reconstructed. Secondly, he shows that he as sculptor is not, as has been argued elsewhere, Narcissus.[37] He is not reconstructing himself but his anticipatory vision of La Zambinella to which can now be added his memory of her presence before him. La Zambinella is thus a replica of his dreams and yet he can still work on her to make further, even more perfect, replicas of that replica. She offers sameness with difference both as an essence (Sarrasine's ideal) and yet also as a construct (her body has been made both by le prince Chigi and now again by Sarrasine) and can thus be remade. Since she both corresponds to his desire and yet remains other than that desire, La Zambinella does not simply reflect pure, narcissistic self but a replica of the self-in-the-other for which the model is not Narcissus but what may be seen as a *homosexualization of desire*. La Zambinella figures a homosexualization of desire by prompting a *coup de foudre* which crystallizes both past and present sameness and difference while also triggering *reprises* of even closer crystallizations of sameness and difference. By figuring the *coup de foudre* as reiterated desire for the same in the other, *Sarrasine* moves beyond both the confines of male-to-male eroticism and the above-mentioned binary opposition between heterosex and homosex and offers a homosexualization of desire that structures the whole narrative. This homology between homosexual desire and the narrative that is *Sarrasine* would, however, have been impossible without La Zambinella as a castrato in drag, for it is because she can be both made, unmade, and remade that she can figure the infinite permutations of self and other that ground the homosexualization of desire.

It is possible to argue that a similar structure can be found in *The Crying Game*. When Fergus falls for Dil he is also repeating the attraction he felt for Jody as a number of critics have shown. At each of the stages in his growing intimacy with Dil, there are flashes of memory of the cricketer and, at one stage, Fergus even dresses Dil in the famous white sweater which she keeps alongside photographs of her former boyfriend. It can be seen that the *coup de foudre* instigated by the photograph of Dil and repeated when Fergus sees her in performance, is paralleled with other repetitions whereby Fergus falls in love with another (Dil as woman) who is also the same (Dil as male like Jody and like Fergus). By showing that identity is other and that other is identity—as Zilliax points out: "Fergus is more interested in *being* Jody than in recalling him" (48)—homosexuality in the sense of reiterated love of the same/other is woven into the *structure* of *The Crying Game* in the same way that it is woven into the structure of *Sarrasine*. For if *Sarrasine* shows how the *same* character (Sarrasine) falls in love with the *same* person (La Zambinella) in *different* ways, *The Crying Game* shows how the *same* person (Fergus) can fall in love with *different* people in the *same* way (Jody, Dil).

It is clear that the persistence of what can be seen as a homosexual structuring of both works gives them a power very different from that of those works that merely foreground explicit male-to-male sex. For these works show, after Sedgwick's *Epistemology of the Closet*, Edelman's *Homographesis*, and Dollimore's *Sexual Dissidence*, that homosexuality is not just represented in same-sex relationships but as a fundamental if unacknowledged structure in culture, here in the form of the urge to repeat the same-in-the-other during the *coup de foudre* and after it. At the same time, in *The Crying Game* too, it is the provocative presence of the drag artiste that alerts the reader to the availability of such play with the *coup de foudre* and to the structure of repetition of self and other in what is not simply homosexuality but the homosexualization of both desire and of the whole filmic narrative. However "homosexualized" the structures of *Sarrasine* and *The Crying Game*, and although it can be argued that both La Zambinella and Dil are " 'women' who have penises,"[38] the fact remains that both Dil and La Zambinella are still biological men and that Fergus and Sarrasine fall for them while also being biological men. Whatever the destabilizing effect of drag on binaries such as male/female and homosex/heterosex, it must be acknowledged that both works present characters who believe they may have been drawn unwittingly into a homosexual relationship. At least initially, both recoil in horror: Fergus vomits and Sarrasine explodes. For however destabilized, homosexuality is itself portrayed as destabilizing, and part of that destabilization results from the way it catches ostensibly heterosexual men unaware. Fergus had been having an affair with Jude and, despite being antisocial, unprepossessing, and absorbed by art, Sarrasine had had an affair with the actress Clotilde. How is it that such seemingly "normal" men go so badly astray?

One reason may be that both are uprooted from their familiar environments. With Fergus leaving Northern Ireland for London and Sarrasine leaving Paris for Rome, neither can read the new cultures in which they find themselves. Fergus cannot read the Metro as a gay/TV club and Sarrasine is ignorant of Roman operatic convention. This does not, however, mean that sexual variety—whether in the form of transvestism, castrati, or homosexuality—depends on individual crosscultural awareness. It is not the blindness of Sarrasine that *makes* La Zambinella a castrato and the *mignon* of her Cardinal any more than it is the Irishness of Fergus that *makes* Dil a gay transvestite. What the blindness of Fergus and Sarrasine shows is that, *wherever they are*, they remain ignorant of the prevalence of sexual variety, and, notably, of homosexuality. Fergus was just as blind in relation to Jody when he met him "at home" as are the Parisians of the Lanty society of La Zambinella when they are all together in central Paris. What both works show is not that sexual variety depends on cultures or that it resides, somehow, in the eye of the beholder, but that it is ubiquitous yet ignored. Like the purloined letter it is obvious yet unseen. Thus when Mme de Rochefide interrupts the narrator's story with "je ne vois encore ni Marianina ni son petit vieillard" ("I still don't see anything about either Marianina or her little old man"), he retorts: "-Vous ne voyez que lui" ("You are seeing nothing but him!") (1063, 240–41). Sexual variety is everywhere but still—even in the sophisticated Paris of 1830—everywhere unacknowledged. The Lanty family may speak multiple languages but Paris cannot understand any of them. Jody may be seen as a black English soldier but perhaps that is difference enough for Fergus to absorb in one day: he cannot also be gay. And yet what *The Crying Game* shows is that even black, working-class soldiers—even *real men*—can be gay, in the same way that *Sarrasine* shows the very hub of *real* Parisian society to be founded on the sexually unmentionable. Thus at the very same time that both works subvert such seeming sine qua non as male and female bodies, they also show their readers like Mme de Rochefide that the taboo is not just in remote Rome or the marginal Metro, but at the core of the supposedly familiar and reassuring. It is, therefore, a little unfair to chastise *The Crying Game* for taking the sex out of homosexuality (Zilliax, 34) or to claim that "the taboo desire remains taboo" (174), when the power of both works is to keep taboo as taboo while showing taboo to be an invisible norm. It is, moreover, only by keeping this tension between taboo and norm that the binary line between homosex and heterosex may be destabilized at the same time as homosex is made both central and ubiquitous for all with eyes to see.

IV Women and Drag

However sexually subversive the drag of *Sarrasine* and *The Crying Game* may be, other characters in the works have been thought to receive less subtle treatment. In *Sarrasine*, Marianina may be a beauty noted for her "voix enchanteresse" ("enchanting voice") (1047, 225) but she is also "[une] jeune folle" ("mad young girl") who exchanges a priceless diamond for "une roulade bien exécutée" ("a marvelously well-executed trill") (1055, 233) and whose attentions towards her elderly relative may, therefore, be seen as tinged with self-interest. The power of Mme de Lanty's voice, of "les mélodieuses richesses des tons les plus coquettement doux et tendres" ("the melodious wealth of the most coquettishly soft and tender notes"), makes her similarly charming but also redoubtable: "Aimer ces puissantes sirènes, n'est-ce pas jouer sa vie?" ("In loving these powerful sirens, one gambles with one's life") (1045, 223–24). This beguiling power of the woman is also, notoriously, one of the characteristics of the even more redoubtable Jude in *The Crying Game*, who, according to Simpson, begins as a "Venus Man-Trap" to seduce Jody and then becomes a "White Witch" (166–68), seeking to kill Dil and, if necessary, Fergus. It seems, then, that in *Sarrasine* the women have inherited the charms of La Zambinella without his capacity for sexual variety and that *The Crying Game*, to borrow M. Kathryn Ayers' felicitous formula, "celebrates femininity but not women." The price of drag seems to be, as Ayers puts it, that "anyone can be feminine" and that "the best women are men."[39] It is at this point that further parallels between *Sarrasine* and *The Crying Game* become apparent. In *Sarrasine* the narration of the story can be assumed to be contemporaneous with its writing by Balzac in 1830 whereas the events between Sarrasine and La Zambinella began after Sarrasine went to Rome in 1758. This time difference, epitomized by the two ages of La Zambinella, means that by 1830 La Zambinella has moved to Paris and has thus, as Yvonne Noble points out, "successfully escaped from 'protectors' in the Papal States, reconnected with his blood family, and lifted at least some of his relatives to secure footing in international society. He has outlived his tormentors" (33). At the same time, as Noble also notes, "Zambinella's voice sings on in Marianina" (36). This means that the castrato lives long enough to forget the murder of Sarrasine, to reintegrate into society and, in a sense, to be reborn in and through the voices and charisma of two women: Mme de Lanty and her daughter Marianina. Thus, however different from the Paris society of 1830, Zambinella is still a key figure in one of its main households and lives on through his female family among whom, again according to Noble, "he is still cared for and loved" (33). Although his identity and his history are taboo knowledge, he lives harmoniously with women—not least because M de Lanty is a nonentity—"petit, laid et grêlé; sombre comme un Espagnol, ennuyeux comme un banquier" ("small, ugly, and pock-marked; dark as a Spaniard, dull as a banker") (1046, 224)—and because Marianina's brother, Filippo, who "tenait, comme sa sœur, de la beauté merveilleuse de la comtesse" ("shared with his sister in the Countess's marvelous beauty") (1046, 224), is also feminized. However unorthodox, Zambinella's unorthodoxy thus also merges with his home environment. In harmony with his ambisexual past and appearance, he even has male and female guardian spirits—"un grand homme sec, espèce de génie familier" ("a tall, stern man, a kind of family genie") (1055, 232) and the attentive Marianina. Contrary to expectations, the castrato finds a family, including substitute daughter, substitute granddaughter, and even substitute wife.[40]

Since, in *The Crying Game*, Dil has neither history nor progeny, she cannot develop in the same fashion. However, she, too, escapes her much shorter past (in the form of the violent David) and also outlives her other tormentor: Jude. She does so, however, by killing her. Unlike Zambinella who, in a sense, moves over to the feminine, Dil does the opposite: she executes her female rival and settles into a male-to-male *ménage*. Like Zambinella who can forget the murdered Sarrasine, Dil can forget the dead Jude for whom Fergus is paying vicarious penitence. As in *Sarrasine* some of the subversions and perversions of the past seem to recede before the sight of Dil visiting Fergus in prison to the accompaniment of the song "The Crying Game." She may, in a sense, still be performing in drag, but she no longer appears in her own show or on her own terms. The poignancy and point of song and singer have mutated into acquiescence: "Don't want no more of *The Crying Game*" indeed. Since she will, in the words of another of the film's songs, "stand by her man," Hennessy is not altogether wrong in claiming that *The Crying Game* "turns out to be a strictly heterogendered affair" (11). As again in *Sarrasine*, the transvestite moves away from murder and marginality and reintegrates into the conventions and the routines of family or substitute marriage.

It would seem then that both *Sarrasine* and *The Crying Game* chart not only the subversiveness of drag but the fading of that subversive force. The sexual rebel, La Zambinella, like the criminal, Vautrin, is finally if a little uneasily, coopted into the Parisian establishment. Even corrosive diabolic power, as in *Melmoth réconcilié*, eventually wanes and dies. *La* Zambinella becomes (male) Zambinella; his former charisma before packed houses becomes a mere *frisson* for the bored, curious, and flirtatious Mme de Rochefide. As Abigail Solomon-Godeau has shown in her survey of the male body in French neoclassical art, the period between the Restoration and the July Monarchy marks an end to the sexual and artistic ambiguity embodied by "the legions of feminized youths that populate the art of Neoclassicism" (222). In the art of the 1820s and 1830s, the androgynous ephebe gives way to new representations of men and women whose sexual difference from each other is marked by dress, physique, and posture and where it is the women, not the scantily clad youths, who are the object of the erotically charged, æsthetic gaze. By being associated with the Italy of the eighteenth century, La Zambinella harks back to the feminized decadence of the ancien régime. As an aging dandy and former *Endymion*, Zambinella is about to retreat before the new models of the 1830s, with an emphasis on the unitary, individual (male) subject, family values, and the new bourgeois realism.[41] He has become an anachronism: as a latter-day dandy and former *Endymion*, he now offers in the Lanty salon an outdated embodiment of "classical drag."[42]

And yet. . . . And yet the reader of *Sarrasine*, like Mme de Rochefide, knows that gender ambiguity will not die with Zambinella,—witness the reference to Filippo, "image vivante de l'Antinoüs, avec des formes plus grêles" ("a living image of Antinous, even more slender") (1046, 224), whose charm, like that of his sister, "venaient uniquement de leur mère" ("came solely from their mother") (1046, 224). Who, then, is the father of this new generation of troublingly similar sexual twins? Is it really the insignificant M. de Lanty or could it possibly be La Zambinella him/herself, whose voice lives on in Marianina and whose ephebic beauty is repeated in Filippo? Is Marianina *really* neither Zambinella's granddaughter nor wife or could she, just possibly, be both? How should, how *can*, the relationship of Dil and Fergus be described? What is (their) *statut civil* as individuals and in relation to one another? Does their developing relationship with which the film ends represent new marriage or the end of marriage? Does Dil's last prison visit to Fergus simply repeat or parody the conventional heterosexual *ménage*? It can be seen from this variety of questions that it is not just to Sarrasine and Jude that violence is done in *Sarrasine* and *The Crying*

Game, nor even just to the binaries of sexuality/gender and heterosexuality/homosexuality. For by exposing the vulnerability of the distinctions between sexuality and gender as between homosexuality and heterosexuality, both works expose the frailty of all individual and social identities and of the marital, family, and social groupings which shore up such identities and on which such identities depend. In their different ways and for very different periods, both works problematize the whole notion of *état civil* as an embodiment and intersection of individual and social meaning. What new regime will be ushered in by a family whose "patriarch" is La Zambinella? And what new models of gendering and engendering will be offered by Fergus and Dil? Whatever the meaning of the silence of Mme de Rochefide and of the song that is "The Crying Game," both song and silence bear witness to a sea change in the world as its characters—and its readers—know it. For the subversive play of drag has the power to prise open what "is," and replace it with a layering and a scattering of multiple perceptions across both space and time. Indeed, without the changes in perceptions mobilized by drag in *Sarrasine* and *The Crying Game*, there would be little sense of different times and different spaces, and the meaning of different meanings would itself have little meaning.

Notes

Epigraphs: Pierre Citron, "Interprétation de *Sarrasine*," *L'Année balzacienne*, 1972: 90–91. "The profound subject of *Sarrasine* is the contrast between two forms of sexuality." Rosemary Hennessy, "Ambivalence as Alibi: On the Historical Materiality of Late Capitalist Myth in *The Crying Game* and Cultural Theory," *Genders* 24 (1996): 11.

1. Honoré de Balzac, *La Comédie humaine*, ed. Pierre-Georges Castex et al., 12 vols. (Paris: Gallimard [Bibliothèque de la Pléiade], 1976–81), 6:1061. Subsequent references to the text of *Sarrasine* will be given in the text. English translations of *Sarrasine* are taken from Richard Miller, trans., *S/Z*, by Honoré de Balzac; all other translations are by the author.

2. After noting this remark, Zilliax writes: "The sequence implies not only that Col cannot specify Dil's identity, but also that only the sight of her can. It is only her performance—literally her body—that can say what she is, for the binary labels offered by the film cannot specify." Amy Zilliax, "The Scorpion and the Frog: Agency and Identity in Neil Jordan's *The Crying Game*," *Camera Obscura* 35 (1995):, 48.

3. Vern L. Bullough and Bonnie Bullough, *Cross Dressing, Sex, and Gender* (Philadelphia: University of Pennsylvania Press, 1993), 239.

4. Carole-Anne Tyler, "Boys Will Be Girls: The Politics of Gay Drag," in

Inside/Out: Lesbian Theories, Gay Theories, ed. Diana Fuss (London: Routledge, 1991), 62.

5. Richard Ekins, *Male Femaling: A Grounded Theory Approach to Cross-Dressing and Sex-Changing* (London: Routledge, 1997), 163.

6. Marjorie Garber, *Vested Interests: Cross-Dressing and Cultural Anxiety* (London: Routledge, 1992), 268.

7. Judith Butler, *Gender Trouble: Feminism and the Subversion of Identity*. London: Routledge, 1990, 137 (Butler's emphasis).

8. Ibid., 136.

9. *S/Z* has provoked innumerable reviews and commentaries—and still does. See for example Pierre Barbéris, "A propos du *S/Z* de Roland Barthes: Deux pas en avant, un pas en arrière?" *L'Année balzacienne* 1971: 109–23; Owen Heathcote, "*Sarrasine* and Balzac Criticism," *Paragraph* 1 (March 1993): 18–28, Barbara Johnson, "The Critical Difference: BartheS/BalZac," in *The Critical Difference: Essays in the Contemporary Rhetoric of Reading* (Baltimore: Johns Hopkins University Press, 1980), 3–12, "Parcours de Barthes," *Communications* 63 (1996), Yvonne Noble, "Castrati, Balzac, and BartheS/Z," *Comparative Drama* 31 (spring 1997), 28–41.

10. Various critics have, in very different ways, sought to disengage Sarrasine from the theme of castration: see for example Bremond, Johnson, Knight, Rice, and Schofer, and Serres. See also below n. 26.

11. For a number of critics the film's insistence on the scorpion and frog parable emphasizes the mutability of identity—whether sexual, racial, or individual personality (Fergus's kindness). See Zilliax, 26.

12. Crewe highlights the cross-dressing but not the performance.

13. Per Nykrog, "On Seeing and Nothingness: Balzac's *Sarrasine*," *Romanic Review* 83 (1992): 442.

14. Sandy Petrey, "Castration, Speech Acts, and the Realist Difference: *S/Z* versus *Sarrasine*," *PMLA* 102 (1987): 153–65.

15. See n. 10 and, for the nature and implications of the castration operation, Agnus Heriot, *The Castrati in Opera* (London: Secker and Warburg, 1956), 44, and Michel Serres, *L'Hermaphrodite*, in *Sarrasine*, by Honoré de Balzac (Paris: Garnier-Flammarion, 1989), 155. According to Pierre Barbier, *The World of the Castrati*, trans. Margaret Crosland (London: Souvenir Press, 1996), 13, "most castrati could experience virtually normal sexual relations: castration did not prevent either erection or the emission of sperm and prostatic fluid, although of course it contained no spermatozoa." Referring to such sources as Heriot and the film *Farinelli* (dir. Gérard Corbia, 1994), Yvonne Noble seems to agree that the castrati could be either homosexually or heterosexually active, according to their orientation and preferences (38 n. 39).

16. Jane Giles, *The Crying Game* (London: British Film Institute, 1997), 9. According to Mark Simpson, *Male Impersonators: Men Performing Masculinity* (London: Cassell, 1994), this secret is no secret since Dil, "it must be said, is an obvious transvestite to anyone who has not lived a sheltered life" (172).

17. Sharon Willis, "Telling Differences: Race, Gender, and Sexuality in *The Crying Game*," in *Boys: Masculinities in Contemporary Culture*, ed. Paul Smith (Boulder: Colorado Westview, 1996), 108.

18. On the androgyny of the ephebe with particular reference to Girodet's *Endymion* see James Smalls, "Making Trouble for Art History: The Queer Case of Girodet," *Art Journal* 55: 4 (winter 1996): 20–27, and Abigail Solomon-Godeau, *Male Trouble: A Crisis in Representation* (London: Thames and Hudson, 1997), 65–68.

19. Citron, "Interprétation," 92.
20. Pierre Citron, introduction to *Sarrasine*, in *La Comédie humaine*, by Honoré de Balzac (Paris: Gallimard [Bibliothèque de la Pléiade], 1977), 6:1041.
21. Hennessy, "Ambivalence as Alibi," 20.
22. Jonathan Crewe, "In the Field of Dreams: Transvestism in *Twelfth Night* and *The Crying Game*," *Representations* 50 (spring 1995): 113.
23. Citron, "Interprétation," 94.
24. Ibid., 95; Citron, introduction, 1–41.
25. Giles, *The Crying Game*, 53.
26. Ibid., 53; Willis, "Telling Differences," 107.
27. Giles, *The Crying Game*, 67.
28. Hennessy, "Ambivalence as Alibi," 20.
29. Willis, "Telling Differences," 105.
30. Crewe, "In the Field of Dreams," 114–15.
31. Simpson, *Male Impersonators*, 174.
32. Hennessy, "Ambivalence as Alibi," 11.
33. Citron, "Interprétation," 90–91.
34. See Ross Chambers, "*Sarrasine* and the Impact of Art," *French Forum* 5 (1980): 218–38.
35. Balzac, 7:821.
36. Balzac, 2:1128. See also *Honorine* (2:596). As Graham Falconer pointed out in reaction to this essay, this point and a number of those that follow, have parallels in both Stendhal and Proust.
37. Notably by Helen O. Borowitz, "Balzac's *Sarrasine*: The Sculptor as Narcissus," *Nineteenth-Century French Studies* 5, nos. 3 & 4 (spring–summer 1997): 171–85.
38. Simpson, *Male Impersonators*, 171.
39. M. Kathryn Ayers, "The Only Good Woman Isn't a Woman At All: *The Crying Game* and the Politics of Misogyny," *Women's Studies International Forum* 20 (1997): 334. This critique was also articulated in a private communication by Carrie Tarr.
40. For the impression that Marianina may be the wife of La Zambinella, see *Sarrasine*, 1052, 1055.
41. For the way in which such a marginalization of the artist/sculptor can be contextualized in Balzac's work, see Alexandra K. Wettlaufer, "Painters on the Periphery: Balzac's Nascent Realism and the Marginalization of the Artist, 1829–1832" (paper presented at the 23rd annual Nineteenth-Century French Studies Colloquium, Athens, GA, 1997).
42. Simpson, *Male Impersonators*, 172.

Part IV
Epilogue

Aurélia, or The Twilight of the Gods

FRANÇOISE GAILLARD

"EURYDICE! EURYDICE!" THE CALL COMES OUT OF THE NIGHT LIKE a cry of pain, for the poet fears the night brings no hope. "Qu'est-ce donc que la mort? Si c'était le néant . . ." ("What then is death? Suppose it is mere oblivion?").[1] Yes, what if death is oblivion? Gérard de Nerval immediately sets this terrifying hypothesis aside with an almost superstitious spell: "Plût à Dieu!" ("Would to God it were!") (53/61). When this does not suffice, he tries to reassure himself with a reasoning where logic and theology are combined: "Mais Dieu lui-même ne peut faire que la mort soit le néant!" ("But God himself cannot make death be nothing but oblivion") (53/61). After the occult/esoteric disorder of *Aurélia*'s first visions, the poem's second part thus opens clearly onto preoccupations of an explicitly religious order where the veil of unbelief that the period had woven seems suddenly to tear. And Gérard de Nerval is the first to be surprised: "Pourquoi donc est-ce la première fois," he asks, "que je songe à *lui*? Le système fatal qui s'était créé dans mon esprit n'admettait pas cette royauté solitaire . . ." ("Now why was this the first time I had thought of Him in such a long while? In the fatal cosmic system which had taken shape in my mind there was no place for that solitary Majesty") (53/61). We know however that scarcely had his mind accepted the consoling revelation of God's existence, the pledge of a promise of immortality, than the certainty of his damnation fell also into place. And we know the rest of the story: "Désespéré, je me dirigeai en pleurant vers Notre Dame de Lorette, où j'allai me jeter au pied de l'autel de la Vierge, demandant pardon pour mes fautes" ("Desperate and weeping, I headed for Notre-Dame de Lorette, where I prostrated myself at the foot of the altar of the Virgin, asking forgiveness for my transgressions") (65/76). It was here, on leaving this church where, despite his spiritual yearning, he had failed to participate in the mass celebrated by the community of believers, that Gérard de Nerval fell prey to a strange hallucination, one that contradicted the spiritual certainties he had just acquired. This is what I would recall to the reader:

> Arrivé sur la place de la Concorde ma pensée était de me détruire. À plusieurs reprises, je me dirigeai vers la Seine, mais quelque chose m'empêchait d'accomplir mon dessein. Les étoiles brillaient dans le firmament. Tout à coup il me sembla qu'elles venaient de s'éteindre à la fois comme des bougies que j'avais vues à l'église. Je crus que les temps étaient accomplis, et que nous touchions à la fin du monde annoncée dans l'Apocalypse de Saint Jean. Je croyais voir un soleil noir dans le ciel désert et un globe rouge de sang au-dessus des Tuileries. Je me dis: 'La nuit éternelle commence, et elle va être terrible. Que va-t-il arriver quand les hommes s'apercevront qu'il n'y a plus de soleil?'
>
> (By the time I reached the Place de la Concorde, I was thinking of destroying myself. Several times I started toward the Seine, but something prevented me from carrying out my intention. The stars were shining brilliantly in the firmament. Suddenly I had the impression that all of them had just gone out, all at once, like the candles I had seen in the church. I thought our time had come—that we were to witness the end of the world as predicted in the Apocalypse of Saint John. I thought I saw a black sun hanging in the empty sky and a blood-red globe over the Tuileries. I said to myself: "The eternal night is beginning, and it is going to be frightful. What will happen when men realize that there is no sun anymore?") (66/76–77)

My citation closes with the question that the nineteenth century bequeathed to us. But when he asks it, doesn't the poet know that this eternal night, belittling the proud torch of the Enlightenment, opens onto the nocturnal concept of modernity? The question however is as vain as it is impertinent. Who cares what Gérard de Nerval knew or didn't know? The speaker's voice has only come to us because the epoch's thought is accomplished in it. And the question can be asked differently. As he opens himself—almost like a medium—to the "epoch," the dreamer concentrates on himself and in himself all the anxieties of a century, the water of whose baptismal fonts was used to wash the sky—to wash it so well that Nietzsche was, many years later, to say: "Who gave us the sponge to wipe away the entire horizon?"[2]

But let us return to the text.

While the philanthropic poet concerns himself with the fate of humans who, still unconscious of the cosmic upheaval taking place before their eyes, go about their worldly business, the prophetic poet for his part worries about the fate of humanity who will arrive only to find heaven empty. For, despite its references to Saint John, this vision has nothing to do with the Apocalypse—where, for example, is the Christian promise of the resurrection of the body? Texts must not be taken literally, even if they are testaments. The great cataclysm (on the very spot, let me note in passing, where the king was beheaded), whose only witness was the poet, does not announce the last judgment, but rather the death of God. Indeed, it would be better to say the "second death of God," the better to differentiate the philosophical moment of the murder from the existential moment of consciousness's awakening to its consequences. In a certain way this really is the end of the world, the end of the religious world, the end of what with Nietzsche I call *the twilight of the idols.* If need be the serene response from his uncle to a question—one the narrator has asked, heavy with metaphysical anxiety, one the narrator has asked—comes to support this interpretation: "Dieu c'est le soleil" ("God is the sun") (62/72).

And the "soleil noir dans le ciel désert" ("black sun in the empty sky") (66/77) is thus the negative trace of a God who once was and no longer is. It is the imprint on the sky of a dead God, of a murdered God; something like a chalk outline on the ground remains, tracing the contours of a murdered body that is no longer there. The murderers, in this case, are the men of the Enlightenment who, the murder once committed, forgot to perform the long and tragic work of mourning. Everything went so fast. There were kings to be killed too. And in the Nervalian vision, the sovereign's sliced neck comes, symbolically, to halo the Tuileries Palace with its bloody orb. A black hole in the sky where the divinity was once enthroned . . . Gérard de Nerval, born "dans des jours de révolution et d'orages, où toutes les croyances ont été brisées" (". . . in a time of revolution and upheaval, in which all faiths and beliefs have been shattered . . .") (53–54/62), is the son of these deicides—is the son of regicides all-too-confident in philosophical rationalism. He carries their sin: the parents kill; the children have nightmares. For one cannot rid oneself either of God or of the king by throwing them into the common grave of ideas whose time has passed. Nietzsche, for his part, would recall this through the voice of the madman "who lit a lantern in the bright morning, ran to the marketplace, and cried . . .": "God is dead! God remains dead!"

Yes, God, dead, remains. He remains as a corpse. And one thinks of Ionesco's play, *Amédée ou comment s'en débarasser.*

Amédée has died, no one knows what from. So what? What is important is that on the stage Amédee's corpse never stops swelling, ever taking up the space of the living who, at last, are affected with an indisposition as physical as it is psychological. They literally can no longer breathe. This feeling of respiratory distress has a name—*anxiety*—and we all know that it is one of the manifestations of metaphysical concern. For Nietzsche too the unmourned death of God provokes asphyxia, but the image chosen by the philosopher is not the same. God's corpse does not swell, it decomposes, and it is the miasma of this decomposition that invades the air of the living. Each epoch has its phantasms, and the nineteenth century as it finishes is rather hygienic. This does not change its meaning at all, for in both cases, the meaning of the allegory is the same. Rarefied or infected, what counts is that man's air has become unbreatheable. And the madman is astonished that the atheists who crowd, laughing, around him are not offended by the smell: "Do we smell as yet of the divine putrefaction?" he asks them. No, they smell nothing; they pretend to be strong-minded; they joke, for in their presumptuous carelessness these enlightened men thought they could get rid of God by getting rid of the question of God. They believed that it sufficed to imagine his nonexistence to remove him from human preoccupations, to live as before, just relieved of the weighty thought of God, that is, of the worry of God—in order to live better than before, in order to live as autonomous, self-sovereign individuals.

It is because they thought that, once God was dead, the central place that had been His would remain. And that, henceforth, it would be unoccupied, empty, and thus, still to be filled. They thought that the time had come for man to install himself there, either by keeping for himself His transcendental character, or by bringing it down from heaven to earth without allowing its centrality to diminish. In the first case, a transcendental humanism would result, the spiritualist version of atheism; as for the other case, which is the materialist version of this adventure, it gave birth to philosophies of history.

The luminous part of modernity for the entire length of the nineteenth and twentieth centuries has been confronted with these two philosophical options. But the point essential for understanding Gérard de Nerval's text is not the see-saw between materialism or transcendental humanism, no more so than the dialogue of these terms or their confrontation. It is the fact that the death of God has brought man to think of himself as the autonomous source of all meaning.

For everything depends on an illusion on which the poet, in his madness, has just lifted the veil, just as the madman to whom Nietzsche tried to give voice, would do. These men (whom, to simplify, we shall call the Enlightenment), did not foresee that this central place, this eminent place which for so long had been acknowledged as God's, would be taken away by God on His death. For that matter, they still have not understood it.

On the Place de la Concorde as in the rue Saint Honoré life goes on. Peasants deliver their goods as though nothing has happened, and Gérard de Nerval is the only witness to the chaos and cosmic confusion that result from this death. The spectacle, however, is terrifying:

> Arrivé vers le Louvre, je marchais jusqu'à la place et là un spectacle étrange m'attendait. A travers les nuages rapidement chassés par le vent, je vis plusieurs lunes qui passaient avec une grande rapidité. Je pensais que la terre était sortie de son orbite et qu'elle errait dans le firmament comme un vaisseau démâté, se rapprochant ou s'éloignant des étoiles qui grandissaient ou diminuaient tour à tour. Pendant deux ou trois heures, je comtemplai ce désordre et je finis par me diriger du côté des Halles.
>
> (I walked on as far as the Place du Louvre, and there a strange spectacle awaited me. Through clouds being rapidly driven before the wind I saw several moons passing overhead at great speed. I thought that the earth had left its orbit and was wandering about the firmament like a dismasted ship, coming closer to the stars or veering away from them, making them appear larger or smaller by turns. For two or three hours I sat contemplating all this confusion, and finally I started off in the direction of the city market.) (66/77)

The allegory is almost too clear. God dead, our poor world has no mooring-point, no center of gravity, no directional axis. Having left its circle, it wanders, possessed of a frenzied and disorderly movement. And Gérard de Nerval suffers because he is the only one to see what the others, in their proud blindness, cannot. This clairvoyant isolation has a name given to it by human society: *madness*. Nietzsche's spokesman is mad, too, for what Nietzsche sees in his madness strongly resembles the spectacle described by Gérard de Nerval:

> What did we do when we unchained the earth from its sun? Whither is it moving now? Whither are we moving? Away from all suns? Are we not plunging continually? Backward, sideway, forward, in all directions? Is there still any up or down? Do we not feel the breath of empty space? Has it not become colder? Is not night continually closing in on us? Do we not need to light lanterns in the morning?

In a certain way, but not as he understood it, Nerval's uncle was right: *God is the sun*. Let me translate in the light of the two fragments of *Aurélia* and *The Gay Science* that I have no doubt cited at too-great length: God is, for Western thought, the equivalent of the sun in the solar system. He is a pole of attraction, a magnetic power working against disorder, chaos, and centrifugal impulses, in brief, a mooring-point for meaning, from whence paradoxically reason has drawn the certainty of its preeminence. All that remains of God's place now, this sun from whose fire our reason and our modern concept of subjectivity were born, is a sort of black hole charged with a negative gravitational force.

There is thus nothing surprising in that, around this hole (this black sun), the entire intellectual cosmogony erected by reason comes undone, disintegrates, and decomposes. This is the decomposition which, according to Nietzsche's madman, poisons the atmosphere! The great blast produced by the center's explosion as it is swallowed up in nothingness, destroying with it any idea of centrality, has made the illusion of autonomy, as well as the idea of reason's preeminence, fall to pieces. What indeed remains for man who has experienced the terrible trauma of decentering, if he does not wish to sink into melancholy, his gaze fixed on the black sun? Nothing other than to say good-bye to the fiction of his autonomy and to try, as Gérard de Nerval did, to reconstitute subjectivity in a medium-like relation to the hidden harmony that exists among all of the things of the world. What is left for him if not to put an end to his dream of becoming a subject, in the sense that modern philosophy gives to this term, or to become God, in the sense understood by transcendental humanism? What is left for him but to reconstitute subjectivity by reexploring the archaic relations that the modern process of individuation has disrupted, cut, and broken? And we know how painful and frequent the theme or the image of cutting, disrupting, discontinuity, and untying is in *Aurélia*. Over the course of his dreams, we discover that Gérard de Nerval seeks meaning less than a bond, I was going to say a "binder." A bond with the work, a bond with life, a bond with the living current in which other beings, dead or alive, participate. "Je me sentais emporté sans souffrance par un courant de métal fondu . . . Tous coulaient, circulaient et vibraient ainsi, et j'eus le sentiment que ces courants étaient composés d'âmes vivantes, à l'état moléculaire, que la rapidité de ce voyage m'empêchait seule de distinguer" ("I felt myself being carried off without pain by a current of molten metal. . . . These streams were all flowing, circulating, and pulsating in that fashion, and I had the feeling that they were consisted of living souls, in a molecular state which only my speed of movement kept me from discerning") (31–32/35). This dream of harmony that takes the form of an erotic return to the bosom of the earth and of the collectivity, is part of the postreligious exploration of subjectivity that the century was about to pursue. And this, after having lost one's way on many esoteric, occult, parapsychological, etc. shortcuts, would lead to the discovery of the archaisms that make up the ego, and which have the *unconscious* as their name. Is it unimportant that it was the surrealists who made us reread Gérard de Nerval? Is it unimportant that one of their preferred texts was, in point of fact, *Aurélia*? One can of course argue from the fact that all the ingredients were present to make this story a dish to suit their taste: dreams, madness, objective hazard, obsessive phantasms . . . but would their interest have been the same if they hadn't recognized a work close to theirs in this neocosmological jumble where the idioms of myths, religions, superstitions, and occult beliefs are mixed? A postreligious work deepening the enigma of subjectivity, such is the obscure bequest given to modernity by the philosophy of the Enlightenment.

What do I mean by that? It is a work rediscovering the most primitive links that unite the individual to a sort of great whole. This latter is done in dreams or in poetry. It opens, in the case of Gérard de Nerval, onto an aspiration to take his place in the living and continuous tissue of the world, an aspiration which has nothing to do with the Judeo-Christian concept of immortality. One could speak here of "orphic materialism." The admission comes at the end: ". . . la certitude de l'immortalité et de la coexistence de toutes les personnes que j'avais aimées m'était arrivée matériellement pour ainsi dire" (". . . the certitude of my own immortality and of the coexistence of all the persons I had loved had come to me, as it were, in a material, tangible way. . . .") (84/99). The word "matériellement" is essential here, for it makes the feeling of immortality an effect of the impulse characteristic of all living beings to merge, and not a relic of thought or of religious conscience.

These are statements that will seem bizarre to any reader who knows that the story is built on the initiatory model and that it ends (in appearance, at least) with a return to faith: ". . . et je bénissais l'âme fraternelle qui, du sein du désespoir m'avait fait rentrer dans les voies lumineuses de la religion" (". . . and I blessed the brotherly soul who had rescued me from the depths of despair had brought me back to the luminous pathways of religion") (84/9). But is anyone really taken in by this theatrical "happy ending"? The rediscovery of religion is just like a reaction that consists in turning away from an insufferable truth seen in a moment of mad lucidity, only to take refuge in a consoling illusion. The curtain falls and we pretend that we have seen nothing. It remains that the truth is there, as cruel as it can be, and *Aurélia* speaks only of that. "La nuit éternelle commence et elle va être terrible" ("The eternal night is beginning, and it will be frightful") (66/77).

Like Nietzsche later, Gérard de Nerval is not a prophet announcing the death of God. The murder has already taken place. This action whose greatness exceeds even that of the men who accomplished it, *has indeed taken place*. And this is why the great cosmic upheaval that the poet and the philosopher describe in almost identical terms does not correspond to the moment when God sinks into nothingness, but to the moment immediately afterwards, to the time of consequences. What they paint in dark colors is not a terrible shock after which calm will return, but the definitive state of a world which has entered into its *postreligious*, or, philosophically speaking, its *postmetaphysical* phase. Gérard de Nerval, just like the madman, has come in fact to raise the curtain on the unbearable truth of the philosophical and existential consequences of God's death. For the murderers have not yet reached the moment of consciousness. They committed the murder in a state of lightness, and thought that by no longer believing in Him, they had succeeded in pretending that there had never been any God. They never envisaged the profound disturbances produced by atheism, and they are not yet ready to face them. In other words, they are still unable to assume their action in all of its implications. And, in a certain way, the truth of what they did has not yet reached them; they indulge in their daily occupations. Gérard de Nerval worries about this: "Les paysans apportaient leurs denrées, et je me disais: 'quel sera leur étonnement en voyant que la nuit se prolonge . . .' " ("The peasants were bringing in their produce, and I thought: 'How amazed they will be when they see that the dark of the night is being prolonged . . .' ") (66/77). For they see nothing, see nothing yet—nothing of the changing times whose metaphor is the astronomical catastrophe revealed to the hallucinating poet. It is still too early. As Nietzsche said: "Lightning and thunder require time, the light of the stars requires time; deeds, though done, require time to be seen and heard. This deed is still more distant from them than the most distant stars,—*and yet they have done it themselves*!" But will that time ever come? Will men be able to see it? Will men ever want to see this cruel truth? Will they ever be strong enough? Will they have the courage to live not with the feeling of emptiness (which would condemn them to be melancholics in a disenchanted world), but with the euphoria born of the full realization of the fact that there is nothing, where metaphysics once located the seat of meaning. In order to assume this knowledge in joy, you must be mad, mad like the madman, or like Gérard de Nerval whose return to wisdom would consist precisely in refusing this knowledge and in going "back to the luminous pathways of religion." The curtain is drawn. There is nothing to see . . . truth has withdrawn into the wings. . . . But for how long? Nerval's biography brings a personal response to this question. The history of nocturnal modernity which, in the case of modern (thus autonomous) individuals produced affects of merging within rationality and thus broke through into dreams, brings us another. The man of the twilight of the Gods is also the one who discovered depth psychology.

It is not by accident that the *Aurélia*'s story begins with the opening of doors "d'ivoire et de corne" ("of ivory or horn") (23/25) where the abstract and rational subjectivity of enlightened modernity's subject is undone, to the benefit of a diffuse subjectivity, in direct contact with a subject-less cosmic reality, whose every dream illustrates it. Like an Orpheus sacrificing Eurydice to us, the poet takes advantage of the doors opening to look back and find, after night's reason, reasons that come to enlighten the mystery that, since the death of God, man has become to himself. It is to this mystery that the human sciences will be harnessed, especially the one that explores the psyche. Orpheus's sacrifice is accomplished not on God's altar, but on that of the science that advanced by tearing the occult from the stench of the sacred.

Notes

This essay was translated by Timothy Raser.

1. Gérard de Nerval, *Aurélia*, ed. Pierre-Georges Castex (Paris: SEDES-CDU, 1971), 53; Gérard de Nerval, *Aurelia followed by Sylvie*, trans. Kendall Lappin (Santa Maria, CA: Asylum Arts, 1993), 31. Subsequent page references to Nerval's *Aurélia* will be included in the text; the first reference will be to the French edition, the second to the English translation.

2. Friedrich Nietzsche, *The Gay Science*, trans. Walter Kaufmann (Princeton: Princeton University Press, 1964), 181–82. All subsequent references to *The Gay Science* come from this fragment, #125, found on pp. 181–82 of the edition cited above.

Notes on Contributors

JOHN ANZALONE is Professor of French at Skidmore College in Saratoga Springs, NY. His research interests lie in late-nineteenth-century French fiction (Zola, Villiers de l'Isle-Adam), and French cinema. He has translated many books for Salmagundi, notably those of Tsvetan Todorov.

SARAH DAVIES CORDOVA is Associate Professor of French at Marquette University, where her area of specialization is nineteenth-century French literature and culture. The author of *Paris Dances: Textual Choreographies in the Nineteenth-Century French Novel*, she has also published in *Paroles gelées*, *Excavatio*, and *Littérature*.

MARY JANE COWLES teaches at Kenyon College in Gambier, Ohio, where she is Associate Professor of French. Her research centers on the topics of the French Revolution and the Terror; she has published in *L'Esprit créateur* and has given papers at many colloquia.

GRANT CRICHFIELD teaches in the Department of Romance Languages of the University of Vermont, where he is Associate Professor of French. The author of *Three novels of Madame de Duras: Ourika, Edouard, Olivier*, his research centers on the subject of the African diaspora, and on relations between literature and the visual arts.

JENNIFER FORREST is Associate Professor of French at Southwest Texas State University. She has published on Huysmans and Villiers de l'Isle-Adam, in *Nineteenth-Century French Studies*, the *South Central Review*, and the *South Atlantic Review*.

FRANÇOISE GAILLARD teaches at l'Université de Paris 7—Denis Diderot. She has written extensively on French literature and modern European philosophy, and is on the editorial boards of *Romantisme* and the *Revue d'histoire littéraire de la France*.

Most recently, she has edited the proceedings of the 1993 colloquium at Cérisy-la-salle: *La Modernité en questions: de Richard Rorty à Jürgen Habermas*.

M. MARTIN GUINEY is Associate Professor of French at Kenyon College. His research focuses on the latter half of the French nineteenth century, and continues into the twentieth. In addition to his work on the subject of national education, he has written on André Gide and Rainer Maria Rilke.

MELANIE HAWTHORNE teaches at Texas A&M University, where she is Associate Professor of French. The author of *Rachilde* and the editor of the *Proceedings of the Fourteenth Annual Nineteenth Century French Studies Colloquium*, Professor Hawthorne's research interests focus on late-ninteenth- and early-twentieth-century French fiction.

OWEN HEATHCOTE teaches French at the University of Bradford. The author of many articles on nineteenth-century French topics in such journals as *Nineteenth-Century French Studies*, he is the editor of *Gay Signatures: Gay and Lesbian Theory, Fiction, and Film in France, 1945–1995*.

FREDRIC JAMESON teaches at Duke University, where he is currently Chair of the Literature Program. He has taught at Yale University, at the University of California, Irvine, and at UC San Diego. He is the author of many books, including *The Prison-House of Language*, *The Political Unconscious*, and *Signatures of the Visible*.

DOROTHY KELLY is Professor of French and Chair of the Department of Modern Foreign Languages and Literatures at Boston University. She is the author of *Telling Glances: Voyeurism in the French Novel* and *Fictional Genders: Role and Representation in the Nineteenth-Century French Novel*.

MARIE-PIERRE LE HIR teaches French at Case Western Reserve University, where she is Associate Professor and Chair of the Department of Modern Languages and Literatures. She is the author of *Le romantisme aux enchères: Ducange, Pixerécout, Hugo*.

ROSEMARY LLOYD is Rudy Professor of French in the Department of French and Italian at Indiana University. Among the most recent of her many books are *The Lost Content of Childhood: Representations of Children and Childhood in Nineteenth-Century France, George Sand: The Master Piper, Closer and Closer Apart: Jealousy in Literature,* and *Revolutions in Writing: Nineteenth-Century French Prose.*

TIMOTHY RASER is Associate Professor of French at the University of Georgia in Athens, where, with Doris Kadish, he organized the 23rd Annual Nineteenth-Century French Studies Colloquium at which these essays were first read. He is the author of *A Poetics of Art Criticism: The Case of Baudelaire.*

MICHAEL TILBY is College Teaching Fellow at Selwyn College, Cambridge University. The author and editor of books on Balzac, Pascal Lainé, and Gide, his most recent book is entitled *Beyond the Nouveau Roman: Essays on the Contemporary French Novel.*

BRUNO VIARD teaches at the Université de Provence (Aix-Marseille I). He is the editor of two books of writings by Pierre Leroux: *A la source perdue du socialisme français: Pierre Leroux* and *De l'égalité précédé de De l'individualisme et du socialisme.*

ILLINCA ZARIFOPOL-JOHNSTON is Assistant Professor of French in the Department of Comparative Literature of Indiana University. Professor Zarifopol-Johnston is author of *To Kill a Text: The Dialogic Fiction of Hugo, Dickens, and Zola.* She has also written on several occasions on the subject of *Notre-Dame de Paris.*

Bibliography

Adam's Rib. Directed by George Cukor. Performers: Katherine Hepburn and Spencer Tracy. 101 mins. The Voyage Co., 1949.

Adrien Dauzats et "Les voyages pittoresques et romantiques dans l'Ancienne France" du Baron Taylor. Ouvrage réalisé sous la direction de Bruno Foucart. Paris: Fondation Taylor, 1990.

Allen, Robert C. *Horrible Prettiness: Burlesque and American Culture*. Chapel Hill: University of North Carolina Press, 1991.

Althusser, Louis. "Ideology and Ideological State Apparatuses (notes towards an investigation)." In *"Lenin and Philosophy" and Other Essays*. Translated by Ben Brewster, 127–86. New York: 1971.

Anderson, Benedict. *Imagined Communities: Reflection on the Origin and Spread of Nationalism*. London: Verso, 1983.

Andrew, Dudley. *Mists of Regret: Culture and Sensibility in Classic French Film*. Princeton: Princeton University Press, 1995.

Angenot, Marc. *1889: un état du discours social*. Montréal: Le Préambule, 1989.

Arendt, Hannah. *Eichmann in Jerusalem: A Report on the Banality of Evil*. London: Faber and Faber, 1963.

Au Balcon, 1871–1914. 1.6 (June 1995).

Auslander, Leora. "The Gendering of Consumer Practices in Nineteenth-Century France." In *Sex of Things*, edited by Victoria de Grazia with Ellen Furlough, 79–112. Berkeley: University of California Press, 1996.

Ayers, M. Kathryn. "The Only Good Woman, Isn't a Woman At All: *The Crying Game* and The Politics of Mysogyny." *Women's Studies International Forum* 20 (1997): 329–35.

Aynesworth, Donald. "The Making and Un-making of History in *Les Chouans*." *Romantic Review* 76, no. 1 (January 1985): 36–54.

Baguley, David. *Naturalist Fiction: The Entropic Vision*. Cambridge: Cambridge University Press, 1990.

Balzac, Honoré de. *Balzac's Works*. Translated by George Saintsbury. 18 vols. Freeport, NY: Books for Libraries Press, 1901.

———. *Le Vicaire des Ardennes*. Vol. 4 of *La Comédie humaine*. Paris: Les Bibliophiles de l'Originale, 1962.

———. Balzac. *La Recherche de l'absolu*. Paris: Livre de Poche, 1967.

———. *Le Colonel Chabert*. Paris: Folio. 1974.

———. *La Peau de chagrin*. Paris: Folio, 1974.

———. *Sarrasine*. In vol. 6 of *La Comédie humaine*, edited by Pierre-Georges Castex et al. 12 vols. Paris: Gallimard [Bibliothèque de la Pléiade], 1976–81.

———. *Les Chouans, ou la Bretagne en 1799*. Paris: Gallimard, 1977.

———. *Louis Lambert*. Paris: Seuil, 1966.Vol. 7, 285–324.

———. *Béatrix*. Paris: Garnier-Flammarion, 1979.

———. *Annette et le criminel*. Paris: Garnier-Flammarion, 1982.

———. *Sarrasine*. Paris: Garnier-Flammarion, 1989.

———. *Le Chef d'œuvre inconnu*. Paris: Folio. 1994.

Barbéris, Pierre. "A propos du *S/Z* de Roland Barthes. Deux pas en avant, un pas en arrière?" In *L'Année balzacienne 1971*, 109–23. Paris: Garnier, 1971.

———. *Lectures du réel*. Paris: Editions sociales, 1973.

Barbier, Pierre. *The World of the Castrati: The History of an Extraordinary Operatic Phenomenon*. Translated by Margaret Crosland. London: Souvenir Press, 1996.

Barrière, Didier. *Nodier l'homme du livre. Le rôle de la bibliophilie dans la littérature*. Bassac: Plein Chant, 1989.

Barthes, Roland. *S/Z*. Paris: Seuil, 1970.

———. *Barthes par lui-même*, in *Œuvres complètes*. Paris: Seuil, 1993.

———. *S/Z*. Translated by Richard Miller. Oxford: Blackwell, 1996.

Batman. Directed by Tim Burton. Performers: Kim Basinger, Michael Keaton, and Jack Nicholson. Warner Brothers, 1989.

Baudelaire, Charles. *Œuvres complètes*. Edited by Claude Pichois. 2 vols. Paris: Gallimard (Bibliothèque de la Pléiade), 1975.

Bazin, André. *Jean Renoir*. Edited by F. Truffaut. Paris: Champ Libre, 1971.

Beizer, Janet. *Ventriloquized Bodies: Narratives of Hysteria in Nineteenth-Century France*. Ithaca: Cornell University Press, 1994.

Bell, David. "The Play of Fashion: *Au bonheur des dames*." In *Models of Power: Politics and Economics in Zola's "Rougon-Macquart."* Lincoln: University of Nebraska Press, 1988.

Benjamin, Walter. "Allegory and Trauerspiel." In *The Origin of German Tragic Drama*. Translated by John Osborne, 159–235. London: New Left Books, 1977.

———. *Gesammelte Schriften*, vol. 1, edited by Rolf Tiedemann and Hermann Schweppenhaüser. Frankfurt: 1972–74.

Benjamin, Walter. *Gesammelte Schriften*, vol. 5. Frankfurt: Suhrkamp, 1982.

Ben Jelloun, Tahar. "Prologue." *Delacroix: Le Voyage au Maroc*. Paris: Institut du monde arabe—Flammarion, 1994. N. p.

Bernard, Claudie. *Le Chouan romanesque: Balzac, Barbey d'Aurevilly, Hugo*. Paris: Presses Universitaires de France, 1989.

Bertho, Catherine. "L'Invention de la Bretagne: Génèse sociale d'un stéréotype." *Actes de la Recherche en Sciences Sociales* 35 (1980): 45–62.

Bertin, Celia. Jean Renoir: A Life in Pictures. Baltimore: Johns Hopkins University Press, 1991.

Biès, Jean. *Littérature française et pensée hindoue des origines à 1950*. Paris: Klincksieck, 1974.

Bigot, Charles. *Le Petit Français*. Paris: Weill et Maurice, 1883.

Birnbaum, Pierre. *"La France aux Français" Histoire des haines nationalistes*. Paris: Seuil, 1993.

Boichel, Bill. "Batman: Commodity as Myth." In *The Many Lives of Batman: Critical Approaches to a Superhero and His Media*, edited by Roberta E. Pearson and William Uricchio, 5–17. New York: Routledge, 1991.

Bollella, James. "The Aberrations of Good and Evil: A Vesperal Perspective on Societal Decay in Tim Burton's *Batman*." In *Film and Society: Proceedings of the Eighth Annual Kent State University International Film Conference*. April 17–18, 1990.

Borowitz, Helen O. "Balzac's *Sarrasine*: The Sculptor as Narcissus." *Nineteenth-Century French Studies* 5, nos. 3–4 (spring–summer 1977): 171–85.

Bowlby, Rachel. *Just Looking: Consumer Culture in Dreiser, Gissing, and Zola*. New York: Methuen, 1985.

Braudy, Leo. "Zola on Film: Ambiguities of Naturalism." *Yale French Studies* 42 (1969): 68–88.

Bremond, Claude. "Variations sur un thème de Balzac." *Communications* 63 (1996): 133–58.

Brooks, Peter. *Body Work: Objects of Desire in Modern Narrative*. Cambridge: Harvard University Press, 1993.

Brosselin, Arlette. *La Forêt bourguignonne (1660–1789)*. Dijon: Editions universitaires de Dijon, 1987.

Bruno, G. (Augustine Fouillée). *Le Tour de la France par deux enfants*. Paris: Hachette, 1877.

Bryson, Norman. *Looking at the Overlooked*. Cambridge: Harvard University Press, 1990.

Bullough, Vern L., and Bonnie Bullough. *Cross Dressing, Sex, and Gender*. Philadelphia: University of Pennsylvania Press, 1993.

Burns, Michael. *Dreyfus: A Family Affair, 1789–1945*. New York: HarperCollins, 1991.

Butler, Judith. *Gender Trouble: Feminism and the Subversion of Identity*. London and New York: Routledge, 1990.

———. *Bodies That Matter: On the Discursive Limits of "Sex."* London: Routledge, 1993.

Byrnes, Robert F. "Morès, 'The First National Socialist.' " *The Review of Politics* 12 (July 1950): 341–62.

Chakravorty Spivak, Gayatri. *In Other Worlds: Essays in Cultural Politics*. London: Routledge, 1988.

Chambers, Ross. "*Sarrasine* and the Impact of Art." *French Forum* 5 (1980): 218–38.

Chanson de Roland, La. Edited by T. Atkinson Jenkins. Boston: D. C. Heath, 1924.

La Chienne. Directed by Jean Renoir. Performers: Flamant Béruchet, Jane Marèze, Michel Simon. 93 mins. Braunberger-Richébé, 1931.

" '*La Chienne*': découpage intégral." Avant-Scène, cinéma 162 (October 1975).

Citron, Pierre. "Interprétation de *Sarrasine*." In *L'Année balzacienne 1972*, 81–95. Paris: Garnier, 1972.

———. Introduction to *Sarrasine*. Vol. 6 of *La Comédie humaine*, pp.1035–41. Paris: Gallimard [Bibliothèque de la Pléiade], 1977.

Clayson, Hollis. *Painted Love: Prostitution in French Art of the Impressionist Era*. New Haven: Yale University Press, 1991.

Collins, Jim. "Batman: The Movie, Narrative: The Hyperconscious." In *The Many Lives of Batman: Critical Approaches to a Superhero and His Media*, edited by Roberta E. Pearson and William Uricchio, 164–81. New York: Routledge, 1991.

Communications 63 (1996): "Parcours de Barthes."

Compagnon, Antoine. *La Troisième République des lettres: de Flaubert à Proust*. Paris: Seuil, 1983.

Cooper, Clarissa Burnham. *Women Poets of the Twentieth Century in France: A Critical Bibliography*. New York: King's Crown Press, 1943.

Courteix, René-Alexandre. *Balzac et la Révolution française: aspects idéologiques et politiques*. Paris: Presses Universitaires de France, 1997.

Cousin, Victor. *Cours de l'histoire de la philosophie*, Paris: Pichon et Didier, 1829.

Crewe, Jonathan. "In the Field of Dreams: Tranvestism in *Twelfth Night* and *The Crying Game*." *Representations* 50 (spring 1995): 101–21.

Crichfield, Grant. "Decamps, Orientalist Intertext, and Counter-Discourse in Gautier's Constantinople." *Nineteenth Century French Studies* 21: 3–4 (spring–summer 1993): 305–21.

Croutier, Alev Lytle. *Harem: The World behind the Veil*. New York: Abbeville, 1989.

The Crying Game. Directed by Neil Jordan. Performers: Jaye Davidson, Stephen Rea, Miranda Richardson, Forest Whitaker. 112 mins. Palace Pictures, 1992.

Daguerre de Hureaux, Alain and Stéphane Guégan. *L'ABCdaire de Delacroix et de l'Orient*. Paris: Institut du monde arabe—Flammarion: 1994.

Darragon, Eric. "Pégase à Fernando: A propos de *Cirque* et du réalisme de Seurat en 1891." *Revue de l'Art* 86 (1989): 44–57.

Dauzats, Adrien, and Alexandre Dumas. *Nouvelles impressions de voyage. Quinze jours au Sinaï*. 2 vols. Paris: Dumont, 1839.

Deslandes, Jacques, and Jacques Richard. *Du cinématographe au cinéma, 1896–1906*. Vol. 2 of *Histoire comparée du cinéma*. 3 vols. Paris: Casterman, 1968.

Djebar, Assia. *Femmes d'Alger dans leur appartement*. 3ème éd. Paris: Des femmes, 1983.

———. *Women of Algiers in Their Apartment*. Translated by Marjolijn de Jager. Charlottesville: University Press of Virginia, 1992.

Dollimore, Jonathan. *Sexual Dissidence: Augustine to Wilde, Freud to Foucault*. Oxford: Clarendon Press, 1991.

Donnard, Jean-Hervé. "Les intuitions révolutionnaires de Balzac." *L'Année Balzacienne* 11 (1990): 421–35.

Dorian, Tola. *Stixhotvorenia* (poems). Geneva: n.p., 1879; rpt. Paris: n.p., 1913.

———, trans. *Les Cenci*, by P. B. Shelley. Paris: A. Lemerre, 1883.

———, trans. *Hellas*, by P. B. Shelley. Paris: n.p., 1884.

———. *Poèmes lyriques*. Paris: C. Marpon et E. Flammarion, 1888; rpt. Paris: A. Lemerre 1891.

———. *Ames slaves*. Paris: A. Lemerre, 1890; rpt. Paris: Beaudelot, 1908.

———, directeur-gérant. *La Revue d'Aujourd'hui*, 1890.

———. *Vespérales*. Paris: Mercure de France, 1894.

———. *Mineur et soldat, drame en un tableau*. Paris: Stock, 1896.

———. *Roses remontantes*. Paris: P. Ollendorff, 1897.

———. *L'Invincible race*. Paris: E. Pelletan, 1899.

———. *Théâtre*, vol. 1: *Domitien, Le Précurseur, Georges Carel*. Paris: E. Pelletan, 1902.

———. *La Revanche de l'aigle, drame historique en 5 actes*. Paris: Collection Tola Dorian, 1905.

———. *Cendres des anciens jours*. N.p.: L'Œuvre internationale, 1905.

———. *Poésies complètes*. Paris: Beaudelot, 1908.

———. *Le Semeur de la mort*, drame en 10 tableaux. Paris: Beaudelot, 1910.

———, trans. *Prométhée délivré*. By P. B. Shelley. Paris: A. Lemerre, 1910.

Droit, Roger-Pol. *L'Oubli de l'Inde. Une amnésie philosophique*. Paris: Presses Universitaires de France, 1989.

———. *Le culte du néant. Les philosophes et le Bouddha*. N.p., 1997.

Durgnat, Raymond. *Jean Renoir*. Berkeley: University of California Press, 1974.

Edelman, Lee. *Homographesis: Essays in Gay Literary and Cultural History*. London and New York: Routledge, 1994.

Ekins, Richard. *Male Femaling: A Grounded Theory Approach to Cross-Dressing and Sex-Changing*. London: Routledge, 1997.

Ekins, Richard, and Dave King, eds. *Blending Genders: Social Aspects of Cross-dressing and Sex-changing*. London: Routledge, 1996.

Ferry, Luc, and Alain Renaut. *La pensée 68. Essai sur l'anti-humanisme théorique*. Paris: Gallimard, 1985.

Fischer, Lucy. "The Lady Vanishes: Women, Magic, and the Movies." In *Film Before Griffith*, edited by John L. Fell, 339–54. Berkeley: University of California Press, 1983.

Flynn, M. "Pious Pathologies: Medical and Religious Discourse in the Female-Centered Narratives of Emile Zola." (Ph.D. dissertation, Indiana University, 1997).

Foucault, Michel. *Discipline and Punish: The Birth of the Prison*. Translated by Alan Sheridan. New York: Vintage Books, 1979.

Fouillée, Alfred. *L'Enseignement au point de vue national*. Paris: Librairie Hachette, 1909.

Frappier-Mazur, Lucienne. *L'Expression métaphorique dans la "Comédie humaine": domaine social et physiologique*. Paris: Klincksieck, 1976.

Frary, Raoul. *La Question du latin*. Paris: Léopold Cerf, 1885.

Frazer, John. *Artificially Arranged Scenes: The Films of Georges Méliès*. Boston: G. K. Hall, 1979.

Fromentin, Eugène. *Journal*. Edited by André Joubin. Paris: Plon, 1931–32.

Garber, Marjorie. *Vested Interests: Cross-Dressing and Cultural Anxiety*. London: Routledge, 1992.

Gascar, Pierre. Preface to *Les Chouans, ou la Bretagne en 1799*, by Honoré de Balzac. Paris: Gallimard, 1977 (7–15).

Gauld, Alan. *A History of Hypnotism*. New York: Cambridge University Press, 1992.

Gautier, Théophile. *Constantinople et autres textes sur la Turquie*. Edited by Sarga Moussa. Paris: La Boîte à Documents, 1990.

Giles, Jane. *The Crying Game*. London: British Film Institute, 1997.

Gilman, Sander L. "Black Bodies, White Bodies: Toward an Iconography of Female Sexuality in Late Nineteenth-Century Art, Medicine, Literature." In *"Race," Writing, and Difference*, edited by Henry Louis Gates, Jr., 223–61. Chicago: University of Chicago Press: 1986.

Girard, René. *L'Orient et la pensée romantique allemande*. Paris: n. p., 1963.

Goncourt, Edmond de. *Les Frères Zemganno*. Paris: Flammarion and Fasquelle, n.d.

Goncourt, Edmond et Jules de. *Mémoires de la vie littéraire, 1851–1865*. Vol. 1 of *Journal*. Edited by Robert Ricatte. 3 vols. Paris: Robert Laffont, 1989.

Gozlan, Martine. *L'Evènement du Jeudi*. 11–17 sept. 1997: 42–45.

Grand Larousse encyclopédique. 10 tomes. Paris: 1962.

Grazia, Victoria de. "Changing Consumption Regimes." In *The Sex of Things*, edited by Victoria de Grazia with Ellen Furlough, 11–24. Berkeley: University of California Press, 1996.

Guerrin, Michel. "Une Madone en enfer." *Le Monde*. 26 sept. 1997: 12.

Guichardet, Jeannine. *Balzac, "Archéologue" de Paris*. Paris: SEDES, 1986.

Guillen, Claudio. *Literature as System*. Princeton: Princeton University Press, 1971.

Hamilton, James. "The Novelist as Historian: A Contrast between Balzac's *Les Chouans* and Hugo's *Quatre-vingt-treize*. *French Review* 49 (1976): 661–68.

Heathcote, Owen. "*Sarrasine* and Balzac Criticism." *Paragraph* 1 (March 1993): 18–28.

Hegel, Georg W. F. *Leçons sur la philosophie de l'histoire*. N.p., n.d.

Hennessy, Rosemary. "Ambivalence as Alibi: On the Historical Materiality of Late Capitalist Myth in *The Crying Game* and Cultural Theory." *Genders* 24 (1996): 1–34.

Heriot, Angus. *The Castrati in Opera*. London: Secker & Warburg, 1956.

Hobsbawm, E. J. *Nations and Nationalism since 1780: Programme, Myth, Reality*. Cambridge: Cambridge University Press, 1990.

Hotier, Hugues. "La transgression au cirque." *Kodikas Code Ars semeiotica* 7:1–2 (1984): 9–16.

Hugo, Victor. "Les Orientales." *Œuvres poétiques* I. Paris: Pléiade—Gallimard, 1964.

———. *Notre-Dame de Paris*. Paris: Garnier-Flammarion, 1967.

Huysmans, J. K. *A rebours*. Edited by Marc Fumaroli. Paris: Gallimard, 1977.

Interview with the Vampire. Directed by Neil Jordan. Performers: Tom Cruise, Brad Pitt. Geffen Pictures, 1994.

Johnson, Barbara. "The Critical Difference: BartheS/BalZac." In *The Critical*

Difference: Essays in the Contemporary Rhetoric of Reading, 3–12. Baltimore: The Johns Hopkins University Press, 1980.

Jullian, Philippe. *Les Orientalistes. La Vision de l'Orient par les peintres européens au XIXe siècle*. Fribourg: Office du Livre, 1977.

Kadish, Doris. *The Literature of Images: Narrative Landscape from Julie to Jane Eyre*. New Brunswick, NJ: Rutgers University Press, 1986.

Kane, Bob. *Batman and Me: An Autobiography*. Forestville, CA: Eclipse Books, 1989.

Kaplan, Alice Yaeger. *Reproductions of Banality: Fascism, Literature, and French Intellectual Life*. Minneapolis: University of Minnesota Press, 1986.

Keller, Evelyn Fox. *Reflections on Gender and Science*. New Haven: Yale University Press, 1985.

Kelly, Dorothy. *Fictional Genders*. Lincoln: University of Nebraska Press, 1989.

———. *Telling Glances: Voyeurism in the French Novel*. New Brunswick, NJ: Rutgers University Press, 1992.

Knight, Diana. "*S/Z*, Realism, and Compulsory Heterosexuality." In *Spectacles of Realism: Gender, Body, Genre*, edited by Margaret Cohen and Christopher Prendergast. Minneapolis: University of Minnesota Press, 1995.

Kolm, Serge-Cristophe. *Le Bonheur-liberté. Bouddhisme profond et modernité*. Paris: Presses Universitaires de France, 1982.

La Fouchardière, Georges de. *La Chienne*. Paris: Albin Michel, 1930.

Lambert, Elie. *Delacroix et les Femmes d'Alger*. Paris: H. Laurens, 1937.

Laqueur, Thomas. *Making Sex: Body and Gender from the Greeks to Freud*. Cambridge: Harvard University Press, 1990.

Larue, Anne. "Delacroix and His Critics: Stakes and Strategies." In *Art Criticism and Its Institutions in Nineteenth-Century France*, edited by Michael R. Orwicz, 63–87. Manchester University Press, 1994.

Le Hir, Marie-Pierre. "Génèse des stéréotypes sur la Bretagne: la contribution du théâtre." Paper presented at the Nineteenth-Century French Studies Colloquium, Toronto, 1996.

———. "Landscapes of Brittany in Chateaubriand, Balzac, and Flaubert. *West Virginia Philological Papers* 37 (1991): 20–31.

Le Roux, Hugues. *Les Jeux du cirque et de la vie foraine*. Paris: Librairie Plon, 1899.

Leroux, Pierre. "Brahmanisme et Bouddhisme." In *L'Encyclopédie nouvelle*. Paris: n.p., 1836.

Lethbridge, Robert. " 'Le Delacroix de la musique': Zola's Critical Conflations." In *Le Champ littéraire: Etudes offertes à Michael Pakenham*, edited by K. Cameron and J. Kearns. Amsterdam: Rodopi, 1996.

Leutrat, Jean-Louis. La Chienne. Belgique: Editions Yellow Now, 1994.

Lewis, Reina. *Gendering Orientalism: Race, Femininity, and Representation*. London: Routledge, 1996.

Liard, Louis. *Lectures morales et littéraires*. Paris: Belin, 1882.

Lorrain, Jean. "L'acrobate." In *Une Femme par jour*, edited by Michel Desbruères, 202–3. Saint-Cyr-sur-Loire: Christian Pirot, 1983.

Lowe, Lisa. "Nationalism and Exoticism: Nineteenth-Century Others in Flaubert's *Salammbô* and *L'Education sentimentale*." In *Macropolitics of Nineteenth-Century Literature: Nationalism, Exoticism, Imperialism*, edited by Jonathan Arac and Harriet Ritvo, 213–42. Philadelphia: University of Pennsylvania Press, 1991.

Lowe-Dupas, Hélène. *Poétique de la coupure chez Charles Nodier*. Amsterdam/Atlanta: Rodopi, 1995.

Lukás, Gyorgy. *The Historical Novel*. Translated by Hannah and Stanley Mitchell. Lincoln: University of Nebraska Press, 1983.

MacKenzie, John M. *Orientalism: History, Theory, and the Arts*. Manchester: Manchester University Press, 1995.

Mainardi, Patricia. *Art and Politics of the Second Empire: The Universal Expositions of 1855 and 1867*. New Haven: Yale University Press, 1987.

Maupassant, Guy de. *Contes et Nouvelles*, 1886. Paris: Albin Michel, 1959–60.

Maxwell, Richard. *The Mysteries of Paris and London*. Charlottesville and London: University of Virginia Press, 1992.

Mayne, Judith. "Uncovering the Female Body." In *Before Hollywood: Turn-of-the-Century American Film*, edited by Jay Leyda and Charles Musser, 63–67. New York: Hudson Hills, 1987.

Melman, Billie. *Women's Orients: English Women and the Middle East, 1718–1918; Sexuality, Religion, and Work*. Ann Arbor: University of Michigan Press, 1992.

Mirbeau, Octave. *Gens de théâtre*. Paris: Flammarion, 1924.

Mosby, Dewey F. *Alexandre-Gabriel Decamps*. 2 vols. New York: Garland, 1977.

Moyal, Gabriel. "Making the Revolution Private: Balzac's *Les Chouans* and *Un Episode sous la Terreur*." *Studies in Romanticism* 28, no. 4 (winter 1989): 601–22.

Nelson, Brian. Introduction to *The Ladies' Paradise* by Emile Zola. Oxford: Oxford University Press, 1995.

Nerval, Gérard de. *Aurélia*. Edited by Pierre-Georges Castex. Paris: SEDES-CDU, 1971.

———. *Aurelia followed by Sylvie*. Translated by Kendall Lappin. Santa Maria, CA: Asylum Arts, 1993.

Nietzsche, Friedrich. *The Gay Science*. Translated by Walter Kaufmann. Princeton: Princeton University Press, 1964.

Noble, Yvonne. "Castrati, Balzac, and BartheS/Z." *Comparative Drama* 31 (spring 1997): 28–41.

Nodier, Charles. *Journal de l'Expédition des Portes de Fer*. Paris: Imprimerie Royale, 1844.

———. *Promenade de Dieppe aux montagnes d'Ecosse*. Paris: Barba, 1821.

———, J. Taylor, and Alphonse de Cailleux. *Voyages pittoresques et romantiques dans l'ancienne France*. 17 vols. Paris: Didot, Gide, 1820–46.

Norvins, Jacques Marquet de Montbreton de. *Histoire de Napoléon*. Paris: Furne, 1839.

Nykrog, Per. "On Seeing and Nothingness: Balzac's *Sarrasine*." *Romanic Review* 83 (1992): 437–41.

Olender, Maurice. *Aryens et sémites au XIXe siècle*. Paris: Editions du Seuil-Editions Gallimard, 1989.

Orléans, Duc d' [Ferdinand-Philippe-Louis-Charles-Henri]. *Récits de campagne 1833–1841*, publiés par ses fils Le Comte de Paris et le Duc de Chartres. Paris: Calmann Lévy, 1890.

Orléans, Robert d'. Introduction in Orléans, duc d', to *Récits de campagne 1833–1841*, by Le duc d'Orléans, i–xiii. Paris: Calmann Lévy, 1890.

Owens, Craig. "The Medusa Effect, or, the Specular Ruse." In *Beyond Recognition: Representation, Power, and Culture*, edited by Norman Bryson et al., 191–200. Berkeley: University of California Press, 1992.

Paris is Burning. Directed by Jennie Livingston. Performers: Peppier Labeija, Dorian Lorey, Octavia St. Laurent. 76 mins. Dangerous to Know, 1990.

Le Petit Robert. Paris: Dictionnaires Le Robert, 1989.

Petrey, Sandy. "Castration, Speech Acts, and the Realist Difference: *S/Z* versus *Sarrasine*." *PMLA* 102 (1987): 153–65.

Philibert-Soupé, A. *Analyse des ouvrages français indiqués aux programmes du baccalauréat ès lettres (première partie) des baccalauréats ès sciences complet et restreint, de l'enseignement secondaire spécial, de l'enseignement secondaire des jeunes filles et de l'enseignement primaire supérieur*. Paris: Foucart, 1888.

Pierrot, Roger. "Notice," in *Les Chouans, ou la Bretagne en 1799*. Paris: Gallimard, 1977 (481–84).

Pisani, Edgard. Preface to *Delacroix: Le voyage au Maroc*. Paris: Institut du monde arabe—Flammarion, 1994.

Plessier, Ghislaine. *Adrien Dauzats ou la tentation de l'Orient. Catalogue raisonné de l'œuvre peint*. Bordeaux: Musée des Beaux-Arts de Bordeaux/William Blake and Co. Edit., 1990.

Pound, Ezra. *Kulchur*. New York: New Directions, n.d.

Quinet, Edgar. *Le Génie des religions*. In *Philosophie, France, XIX siècle*. Paris: Le livre de poche, 1994.

Radcliffe, Ann. *The Romance of the Forest*. Oxford: Oxford University Press (The World's Classics), 1986.

Rafferty, Terrence. "The Essence of the Landscape." *New Yorker*, 25 June 1990, 80–92.

Renoir, Jean. *Renoir, My Father*. Boston: Little, Brown, 1962.

———. *Entretiens et Propos*. Paris: Cahiers du cinéma. 1979.

La Revue d'Aujourd'hui. Geneva: Slatkine Reprints, 1971 [1890].

Rice, Donald, and Peter Schofer. "*S/Z*: Rhetoric and Open Reading." *Esprit Créateur* 22, no. 1 (1982): 20–34.

Rinn, Wilhelm. *Littérature, composition et style*. Paris: Delalain, 1880 (3e édition, 1891).

Ritter, Naomi. "Art and Androgyny: The Aerialist." *Studies in Twentieth-Century Literature* 13:2 (1989): 173–93.

Robichez, Jacques. *Le Symbolisme au théâtre: Lugné-Poe et les débuts de l'Œuvre*. Paris: L'Arche, 1957.

Roehrich, Edouard. *La Chanson de Roland: traduction nouvelle à l'usage des écoles précédée d'une introduction sur l'importance de la Chanson de Roland pour l'éducation de la jeunesse*. Paris: Fischbacher, 1885.

Ross, Kristin. Introduction to *The Ladies' Paradise* by Emile Zola. Berkeley, CA; University of California Press, 1992.

Ruskin, John. *The Works of John Ruskin*. Edited by T. Cook and Alexander Wedderburn. 39 vols. London: George Allen, 1908.

Said, Edward. *Culture and Imperialism*. New York: Vintage Books, 1993.

Schor, Naomi. *Zola 's Crowds*. Baltimore: Johns Hopkins University Press, 1978.

———. "Devant le château: femmes, marchandises, et modernité dans *Au bonheur des dames*." In *Mimésis et sémiosis. lttérature et représentation*, edited by Philippe Hamon and Jean-Pierre Leduc-Adine, 179–86. Paris: Nathan, 1993.

Schwab, Léon. *La Renaissance orientale*. Paris: Payot, 1953.

Schwarzschild, Steven S. "The Marquis de Morès: The Story of a Failure (1858–1896)." *Jewish Social Studies* 22:1 (January 1960): 3–26.

Sedgwick, Eve Kosofsky. *Epistemology of the Closet*. New York: Harvester Wheatsheaf, 1990.

Serres, Michel. "L'Hermaphrodite." In *Sarrasine* by Honoré de Balzac. Paris: Garnier-Flammarion, 1989.

Sesonske, Alexander. *Jean Renoir: The French Films, 1924–1939*. Cambridge, MA: Harvard University Press, 1978.

Sharrett, Christopher. "Batman and the Twilight of the Idols: An Interview with Frank Miller." In *The Many Lives of Batman: Critical Approaches to a Superhero and His Media*. Edited by Roberta E. Pearson and William Uricchio, 33–46. New York: Routledge, 1991.

Simpson, Mark. *Male Impersonators: Men Performing Masculinity*. London: Cassell, 1994.

Smalls, James. "Making Trouble for Art History: The Queer Case of Girodet." *Art Journal* 55, no. 4 (winter 1996): 20–27.

Smyth, Gerry. "*The Crying Game*: Postcolonial or Postmodern?" *Paragraph* 20 (1997): 154–73.

Solomon-Godeau, Abigail. *Male Trouble: A Crisis in Representation*. London: Thames and Hudson, 1997.

Spacks, Patricia Meyer. *Gossip*. New York: Knopf, 1985.

Starobinski, Jean. *Portrait de l'artiste en saltimbanque*. Genève: Albert Skira, 1940.

Sternhell, Zeev. *La Droite révolutionnaire, 1885–1914: Les origines françaises du fascisme*. Paris: Seuil, 1978.

Stoler, Ann Laura. *Race and the Education of Desire: Foucault's History of Sexuality and the Colonial Order of Things*. Durham, NC: Duke University Press, 1995.

Tait, Peta. "Danger Delights: Texts of Gender and Race in Aerial Performance." *New Theatre Quarterly* 12:5 (1996): 43–49.

———. "Feminine Free Fall: A Fantasy of Freedom." *Theatre Journal* 48 (1996): 27–34.

Taylor, J. [Isidore Justin Séverin], Baron. *La Syrie, l'Egypte, la Palestine et la Judée*. Paris: Imprimerie de Bourgogne et Marinet, 1839.

Télérama Hors série: *Delacroix*. Paris: Institut du Monde Arabe, September 1994.

Thétard, Henry. *La Merveilleuse Histoire du cirque*. 2 vols. Paris: Prisma, 1947.

Thiers, Adolphe. *Histoire de la révolution française*. Nouvelle édition. Paris: Jouvet, 1837.

Thornton, Lynne. *The Orientalists: Painter-Travelers, 1828–1908*. Preface by William R. Johnston. Paris: ACR, 1983.

Tinterow, Maurice M. *Foundations of Hypnosis: From Mesmer to Freud*. Springfield, IL: Charles C. Thomas, 1970.

"Tout Renoir." *Cahiers du cinéma* 482 (July–August, 1994).

Trésor de la langue française. Vol. 8. Paris: CNRS, 1980.

Tyler, Carole-Anne. "Boys Will Be Girls: The Politics of Gay Drag." In *Inside/Out: Lesbian Theories, Gay Theories*, edited by Diana Fuss, 32–70. London: Routledge, 1991.

Uricchio, William, and Roberta E. Pearson. "I'm Not Fooled by That Cheap Disguise." In *The Many Lives of Batman: Critical Approaches to a Superhero and his Media*, edited by Roberta E. Pearson and William Uricchio, 182–213. New York: Routledge, 1991.

Viard, Bruno, ed. *De l'égalité précédé de De l'individualisme et du socialisme*, by Pierre Leroux. Geneva: Slatkine (Collection Fleuron), 1996).

———, ed. *A la source perdue du socialisme français*, by Pierre Leroux. Paris: Desclée de Brouwer, 1997.

Villiers de l'Isle-Adam. *Œuvres complètes*. Edited by Alan Raitt and Pierre-Georges Castex, in collaboration with Jean-Marie Bellefroid. 2 vols. Paris: Gallimard, 1986.

Wettlaufer, Alexandra K. "Painters on the Periphery: Balzac's Nascent Realism and the Marginalization of the Artist, 1829–1832." Paper read at the Twenty-Third Annual Nineteenth-Century French Studies Colloquium, Athens, GA, October 1997.

Willis, Sharon. "Telling Differences: Race, Gender, and Sexuality in *The Crying Game*." *Boys: Masculinities in Contemporary Culture*, edited by Paul Smith, 97–112. Boulder, CO: Westview, 1996.

Wilson, Edmund. *Axel's Castle: A Study in the Imaginative Literature of 1870–1930*. New York: Charles Scribner's Sons, 1969 [1931].

Wright, Gordon. "Marquis de Morès, Adventurer in Four Worlds." In *Notable or Notorious? A Gallery of Parisians*, 73–84. Cambridge: Harvard University Press, 1991.

Zeldin, Theodore. Vol. 1 of *France 1848–1945*. Oxford: Clarendon Press, 1973.

Zilliax, Amy. "The Scorpion and the Frog: Agency and Identity in Neil Jordan's *The Crying Game*." *Camera Obscura* 35 (1995): 24–51.

Zola, Emile. *Au bonheur des dames*. Paris: Flammarion, 1971.

———. *The Ladies' Paradise*. Translated by Brian Nelson. Oxford: Oxford University Press, 1995.

Index